VD

The Australian Army's Experience Of Sexually Transmitted Diseases During The Twentieth Century

Ian Howie-Willis

16pt

Copyright Page from the Original Book

Copyright © Ian Howie-Willis

First published 2020

This book is copyright. Apart from any fair dealing for the purposes of private study, research, criticism or review as permitted under the Copyright Act, no part may be reproduced, stored in a retrieval system or transmitted in any form or by any means, electronic, mechanical, photocopying, recording or otherwise, without written permission.

All inquiries should be made to the publishers.

Big Sky Publishing Pty Ltd
PO Box 303, Newport, NSW 2106, Australia
Phone: 1300 364 611
Fax: (61 2) 9918 2396
Email: info@bigskypublishing.com.au
Web: www.bigskypublishing.com.au

Cover design and typesetting: Think Productions
Printed in China by Jilin GIGO International

A catalogue record for this book is available from the National Library of Australia

TABLE OF CONTENTS

Preface	i
Acknowledgements	v
Introduction	viii
CHAPTER 1: Sexually Transmitted Diseases: An overview	1
CHAPTER 2: Venereal disease in the Australian Army during World War I: August 1914-March 1916	49
CHAPTER 3: Venereal Disease in the Australian Army, 1916-1919: Egypt and the United Kingdom	120
CHAPTER 4: Venereal Disease in the Australian Army, 1916-1919: Australia and the Western Front	178
CHAPTER 5: Venereal Disease in Australia between the two World Wars, 1919-1939	227
CHAPTER 6: The Army and Venereal Diseases during World War II, 1939-1941	289
CHAPTER 7: The Army and Venereal Diseases during World War II, 1942-1945	343
CHAPTER 8: The British Commonwealth Occupation Force in Japan, 1946-1952	400
CHAPTER 9: Korea and Malaya, 1950-1963	471
CHAPTER 10: Vietnam, 1962-1975	510
CHAPTER 11: Post-Vietnam deployments, 1976-2000, and some conclusions	559
Abbreviations	591
Glossary	595
Bibliography	603
Endnotes	643
Back Cover Material	744
Index	745

Preface

Sexually transmitted diseases (STDs) have always infected soldiers in armies everywhere. The Australian Army, like those of its allies and those it opposed, has suffered epidemics of STDs. During the 20th century more than 125,000 Australian soldiers contracted venereal disease (VD), often while serving overseas.

Modern antibiotics have greatly alleviated the burden imposed by the STDs, but until the advent of penicillin in the mid-1940s, two of the most common and most wasteful of diseases afflicting the Army were gonorrhoea and syphilis. They are different diseases caused by wholly dissimilar bacterial organisms but were collectively known as 'venereal disease' or simply 'VD'.

Despite antibiotics, both gonorrhoea and syphilis remain serious diseases. They are a major cause of infertility, but may nevertheless be acquired congenitally, in which case they are a cruel legacy from the parent to the child. Both are debilitating, disfiguring, embarrassing and potentially lethal diseases.

These two diseases caused major wastage among the troops of the Australian Army during the wars of the 20th century, especially World Wars I and II. World War I was fought before the advent of penicillin. The new drug became available during World War II, but because it remained scarce, it was not widely used in the Army's VD hospitals. Without penicillin, gonorrhoea and syphilis were difficult to treat and to cure. Six-or-seven weeks' hospitalisation was commonly required before a patient could be discharged as 'VD-free'.

In most overseas deployments of the Australian Army during the 20th century, gonorrhoea and syphilis infections weakened the Army greatly, removing tens of thousands of its troops from service and thus reducing its operational capability.

VD was also an economic burden for the citizens of Australia. Their taxes paid for the troops replacing those hospitalised by VD and effectively lost to the Army for months on end. VD also placed great pressure on the Army's healthcare services, because scarce resources had to be diverted into treating needlessly occurring VD cases.

VD was a disciplinary as well as a medical problem for the Army. Like the notorious 'self-inflicted wound', VD did not have to occur. Simple precautions in most cases could have prevented it. High VD infection rates greatly angered Army commanders because they knew VD was essentially self-inflicted and that it needlessly used overstretched medical resources that would otherwise have been available for treating and rehabilitating battle casualties and victims of other diseases.

This book tells the Australian Army's VD story in detail. It is a courageous book because it deals sympathetically but objectively with a subject that remains taboo for most people other than the medical professionals who must manage the STDs.

The author's scholarship is evident on every page. Dr Howie-Willis has tackled his difficult, confronting topic with characteristic thoroughness. His achievement in producing this book is remarkable because he has demonstrated how the STDs have impacted on Australian society. They have not only been medically and militarily important, but have had widespread psychological, sociological and political consequences as well.

By publishing this volume, Dr Howie-Willis has given the Australian public a book which is not only highly readable and informative but will remain an important reference work for decades to come. Sexually transmitted infections (by whatever term they will be designated in the future) will challenge commanders and policymakers in the future, as they have done in the past. New infections will emerge, as has *Mycoplasma genitalium*, or 'MG', in the first decades of the 21st century. That infection has already developed resistance to its first-line antibiotic treatment, azithromycin, and even with the current bestpractice 'two-drug' regimen (doxycycline and azithromycin), some 10 percent of patients remain infected and infectious.

I trust that the book's audience is a wide one. It deserves that because it deals sensitively and fairly with a challenging topic with widespread societal ramifications, not least in Australia.

Emeritus Professor John Pearn
Emeritus, School of Medicine, University of
 Queensland
Senior Paediatrician
Queensland Children's Hospital
South Brisbane
Queensland
Australia

Acknowledgements

This book has been a collaborative effort, with input from many individuals. Heading the list of people I must accordingly thank are Dr Andrew Richardson of the Australian War Memorial (previously of the Australian Army History Unit), Professor Dennis Shanks of the Australian Defence Force Malaria & Infectious Diseases Institute and Professor John Pearn of the Queensland Children's Hospital in Brisbane. These three friends and advisers made possible the Army History Research Grant enabling me to research and write this book.

I thank the Australian Army History Unit, and especially its Director, Mr Tim Gellel, for making the research grant available. Particular thanks to Mr Nick Anderson for providing the backup support which helped me undertake and complete the research and writing phases of my project. The unit does a magnificent job of supporting grantees and stimulating general interest in Army history.

I owe a great debt to the members of my panel of critics who patiently read and commented on my chapter drafts as I produced them. They walked along journey with me. They were: Professor Gavan Daws, Dr Brian

Fotheringham, Dr Gavin Hart, Mr Ross Kennedy, Professor John Pearn, Dr Tom Roberts Professor Dennis Shanks, Dr John Taylor, Mr David Willis, and the late Mr Stan Walden, who made a heroic effort to ensure that the book accurately reflected a serving soldier's view of the subject. I also thank Professor Pearn for contributing the Preface to this book.

My thanks go to Gavin and Astrid Hart for their hospitality. I am particularly grateful to Gavin for granting me access to his autobiography, MD thesis and journal publications on sexually transmitted diseases.

I gratefully acknowledge the assistance of the staff of the Australian War Memorial, the National Archives of Australia and the National Library of Australia, three great national repositories of historical records.

My editor, Dr Evelyn Graham, has ensured that the original manuscript was efficiently translated into a published book, and a much better book than it would otherwise have been. Behind every good book is an excellent editor, and with gratitude I can say that this book and its author have been especially fortunate that Evelyn was the editor.

With the greatest pleasure I acknowledge the efforts of Denny Neave, my publisher at Big Sky Publishing, and his team of specialists. These include Pat Kan (graphic designer), Chris Nesci (designer-typesetter), Phillipa (indexer) and Sharon Evans (marketing and sales). As previously, being able to work with this obliging, talented team has been a special pleasure.

Finally I thank my family for their support. My wife, Margaret Willis, my children and children-in-law, Rosemary Willis and Jon Garde, Anthony Willis and Kym-Marie Turnbull, Catherine Willis and Bruce Hoogendoorn, and my grandchildren, Grace Garde, Heidi and James Willis and Hamish, Owen and Thomas Hoogendoorn. They know I spend most of my waking hours working on my research and writing projects. Perhaps they might also appreciate that they, rather than those endeavours, are what matter most to me.

Ian Howie-Willis
Canberra
January 2020

Introduction

The first question an author producing a book like this must answer is 'Why?' Why write a book about the history of sexually transmitted infections, particularly gonorrhoea and syphilis, when there are other, 'nicer' subjects to be written about?

I will start answering these questions by explaining what first sparked my interest. It was my sense of surprise when I found a snippet of information about an Australian 'Digger' while checking his Army service record file in the National Archives of Australia. I had known him well and admired him greatly because he was a kindly, wise, accomplished chap, someone who had risen to the top of his profession, was widely respected in the community and dearly loved by his friends and large extended family. I discovered from his file that he had spent five weeks in a military hospital being treated for gonorrhoea.

This came as a shock because the notion of my friend picking up 'VD' from a prostitute while serving overseas did not square with my perceptions of the honourable, respectable man I had known. Uncovering his secret got me thinking about how that episode might have impacted on his life. The more I thought about it, the more I realised how a gonorrhoea infection when he was 25 years old helped shape the rest of his long life.

Having decided that I needed to know more about the way gonorrhoea and other sexually transmitted diseases had affected the Army, as well as individual soldiers like my friend, I got the idea of writing a book about it. At that point, the questions began accumulating. My answers as they arose are indicated in the following paragraphs.

The topic had been much written about previously, mainly by the official medical-military historians of Australia's involvement in World War I, World War II and the conflicts in South-East Asia between 1950 and 1972. No one, however, had attempted to cover it across the entire 20th century, bringing together what the official histories revealed and linking that to other published and unpublished materials.

The Australian Army History Unit had encouraged me when I first inquired about the suitability of a study such as this. The unit also provided funding through the Army History Research Grant scheme, and I was grateful for that support.

The research project that resulted in this book grew from my last book, *An Unending War: The Australian Army's struggle against malaria*

1885-2015, which taught me that, serious though malaria is, the sexually transmitted diseases (STDs) have afflicted the Army more frequently and on a greater scale than malaria has ever done. That fact needed explaining.

Militarily, STDs are an important topic because they are well known for having caused major troop wastage in the wars of the 20th century. For that reason they needed further investigation.

A historian should not shy away from a subject because others regard it as 'unpleasant'. Many excellent histories would never have been written if their authors had self-censored because they feared their subject matter was distasteful. Nor should historians be deterred from tackling a topic because they fear what others might think of them for doing so.

The topic is a difficult one, demanding balance. The danger in writing about it is twofold. On the one hand, because it is both controversial and confronting, the temptation is to discuss it 'clinically', from a safely neutral medical standpoint as a medical textbook might. That, however, might result in a tedious tome that no one but sexual health specialists would wish to read. On the other hand, there is a countervailing danger that the subject could be sensationalised by dwelling on its scandalous and salacious aspects.

A tabloid journalist tackling the subject might do that, without probing the reasons why STDs were such a problem for the Army during the 20th century. I believed I had the professional historiographical skills and perspective to deal with it comprehensively while maintaining a judicious balance between its medical, military and psychosociological aspects.

The topic also calls for sympathy and sensitivity. For many decades it was taboo—not one to be discussed in polite society. Yet for the people who suffered STDs and transmitted their diseases to others, gonorrhoea, syphilis and the other STDs were often humiliating, disfiguring, uncomfortable and dangerous to treat.

Early in my research various pessimists warned me that I would never be allowed to see the critical records. The Australian Defence Force (ADF) was so protective of its reputation, they averred, I would not be allowed to see the key documents I must consult. I was told apocryphal tales of how the ADF had blocked access to all the relevant records in archival collections such as those maintained by the Australian War Memorial and the National Archives of Australia. That soon proved to be a calumny against the ADF because I was permitted to see whatever files I wanted as soon as I requested them. There was no prohibition on

STD research in any of the national archival repositories.

A continuing difficulty as I researched and wrote the book was the thought that it might bring Australian soldiers into disrepute. Although I have never been a soldier, I admire the Army for the integrative function it has always served in Australian society. Through grants and subsidies, the Army had sponsored the research and publication of my previous three books, as it was doing with this present book, and I did not wish to be seen as ungrateful.

The Army tackled its STD problems diligently and earnestly through successive military campaigns. Its commanders tried everything possible to control and reduce the incidence of STDs among their troops. Time and again, the Army had demonstrated itself to be a responsible corporate citizen by doing everything in its power to manage its soldiers' STDs and minimise the damage these were causing.

Late in my writing of the book, I came across a counter-historical argument presented by an American journalist, David Rieff, who had reported on many wars of the late 20th century. Rieff's experience prompted him to write about the uses of history in his book *In Praise of Forgetting: Historical Memory and Its Ironies* (Yale University Press, 2016). There are virtues in forgetting the past, Rieff argues, and dangers in continually retrieving it, as military history habitually does. Many books of military history serve to dredge up toxic memories' that fuel 'atavistic hatreds', thus generating further bloodshed. Moreover, 'national remembrances are almost always political, sometimes imposed by victorious armies, at other times drummed up by manipulative politicians seeking to fabricate an epic past to legitimize their present-day intentions'[1]

Rieff's line of argument caused me to wonder whether any good could come from writing in detail about a century of the Army's experience with STDs. The story is not an edifying one and it has no heroes. Does anyone need to know about it? Why persist with it instead of allowing it to fade from memory?

I decided I disagreed with Rieff because people will continue discussing this book's subject matter. Historians will keep on alluding to it. Some writers will distort it by seeking to sensationalise it. Moreover, the Australian people have a right to know what their Army's health

---

[1] Gary J. Bass, 'In Praise of Forgetting', review of David Rieff, In Praise of Forgetting: Historical Memory and Its Ironies, in New York Times 10 June 2016.

problems have been and how they have been managed. Amid this discourse, I decided that a book like this could serve useful purposes.

CHAPTER 1

Sexually Transmitted Diseases: An overview

Sexually transmitted diseases (STDs) marched in lock step with the Australian Army in most, if not all, its overseas campaigns during the 20th century. Two particular STDs—gonorrhoea and syphilis—caused enormous loss of personnel, especially during overseas deployments. These bacterial infections, spread most commonly through sexual intercourse, were the Army's unwelcome companions in all the wars in which it participated after its formation in 1901. Enteric diseases and malaria have also plagued the Army periodically, but gonorrhoea and syphilis caused vastly more troop wastage than either of these.

1. Semantics of 'sexually transmitted disease'

'Sexually transmitted disease' (STD) is a term that came into popularity among medical professionals during the mid-1970s. It replaced a previous expression, the much older collective term 'venereal disease' (VD), used by many previous generations. 'VD' was part of common parlance in all English-speaking societies until the wish for a less values-laden phrase led to the adoption of 'sexually transmitted disease', which was itself replaced by 'sexually transmitted infection' (STI) in the early 21st century.[1]

Both STI and STD are euphemisms for what are often distressing, debilitating and embarrassing diseases that can be passed on to the innocent partners and children of sufferers. Such diseases may leave psychological as well as physical scarring. The adoption of STD and then STI in preference to VD represented a wish among medical professionals to use a more neutral, less morally and emotionally loaded expression. Also, historically 'VD' referred predominantly to syphilis and gonorrhoea, whereas 'STI' includes conditions such chlamydia and HIV-AIDS. This book will use all such terms and their acronyms, endeavouring where possible to match the terminology to the period under discussion.

Similar semantic changes have occurred in the terms used for medical practitioners specialising in STIs. Until the mid-1970s such specialists were known as 'venereologists' and their specialisation as 'venereology'. After that, they became known as 'sexual health physicians' and their field of expertise as 'sexual health'.[2]

2. What are sexually transmitted diseases?

STDs are many and varied. The organisms causing them include bacteria (as in chlamydia, gonorrhoea and syphilis), viruses (genital herpes, genital warts and HIV-AIDS), protozoa (such as the vaginal infection trichomoniasis), yeasts (genital candidiasis), insects (genital lice) and mites (scabies). Common to all is their mode of transmission, which is mostly through sexual intercourse.

Many STDs are better known by their colloquial rather than scientific names. Thus gonorrhoea, caused by the bacterium *Neisseria gonorrhoeae*, has been called 'the clap' in English since the 16th century. The slang term is from Old French *clapoir*, a venereal sore, often acquired in a *clapier* or brothel. Syphilis is universally known as 'the pox', the plural of Old English *poc*, a pustule characteristically appearing after infection by the spirochaete bacterium *Treponema pallidum*. Genital pediculosis, an infestation of pubic lice, *Phthirus pubis*, is known as 'the crabs' although the culprit is an insect.[3] Colloquial terms are similarly used for most of the other STDs.

3. Gonorrhoea

Gonorrhoea is caused by the gonococcus (plural 'gonococci'), a motile diplococcal (coffee-bean shaped) bacterium of the species *Neisseria gonorrhoeae* (Figure 1.1). Gonococci are most commonly transmitted from one partner to another during coitus. Infection sites are typically the areas of sexual contact—the soft, moist membranes of the penis, vagina, anus, rectum, throat and eyes. The gonococci move through bodily fluids by twitching their pili (hair-like appendages) and attach themselves to tissue which they then infect.[4]

Babies born to infected mothers may also contract gonorrhoea, often around the eyes, after becoming infected during vaginal childbirth. If untreated, they may suffer gonococcal conjunctivitis, an infection of the conjunctiva or mucous membrane covering the front of the eye and lining the inside of the eyelids. Adults may also contract gonococcal conjunctivitis, usually after being touched around the eyes by an infected partner.[5]

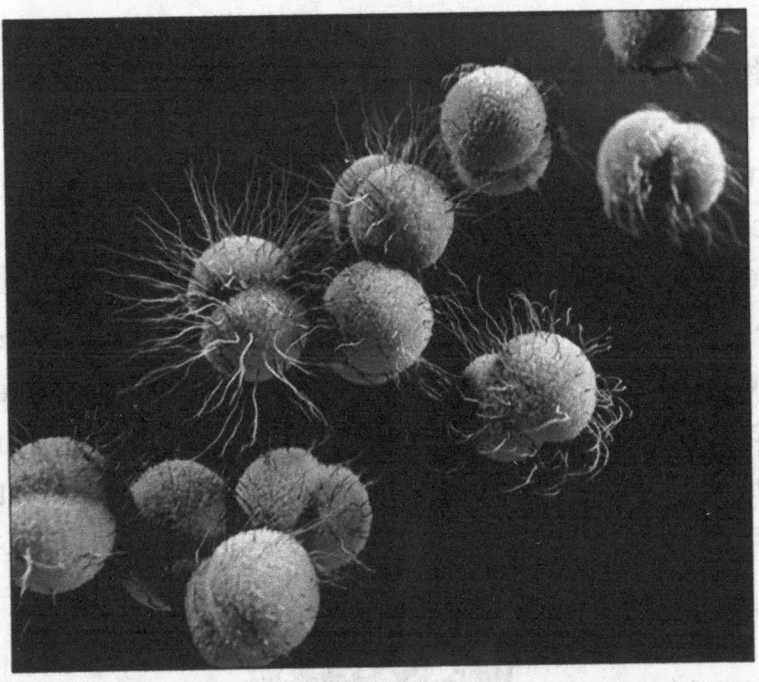

Figure 1.1: A medical illustration of drug-resistant Neisseria gonorrhoeae, the gonococcus causing gonorrhoea. It occurs as a diplococcus, a round bacterium comprising two joined cells. The gonococcus has pili or hair-like appendages enabling it to attach itself to proteins in bodily fluids, which help move it to sites it will infect (Medical illustrator: Alissa Eckert, CDC/Antibiotic Resistance Coordination and Strategy Unit, Public Health Image Library 23244).

In both men and women gonorrhoeal infection commonly spreads along the genital and urinary tracts. In men, the gonococci cause acute urethritis (infection and inflammation of the urethra), usually producing a discharge of pus from the urethra and a scalding sensation when urinating. A common sign of gonorrhoeal infection is the presence of many pus cells and gonococci when the urine is examined microscopically. Such symptoms occur two to ten days after infection. The infection may, however, be asymptomatic, occurring without such symptoms. In that case the presence of the gonococci must be determined by culturing a specimen taken from the urethra. In men the infection may spread along the genital tract, to the prostate gland, epididymides (tubes storing sperm made in the testicles) and the testicles as well (Figure 1.2).[6]

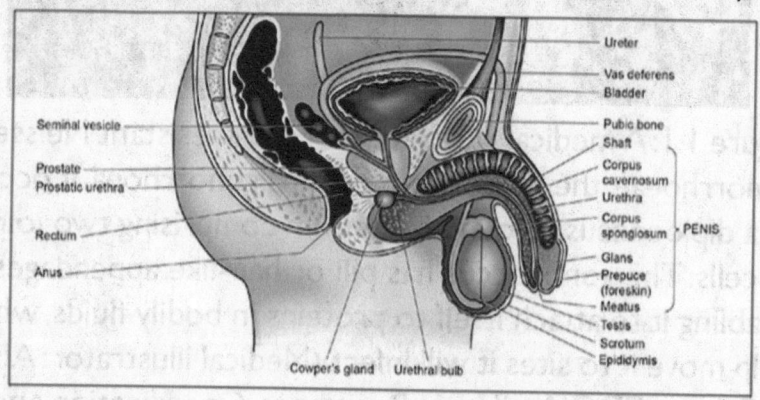

Figure 1.2: Male genitalia. (Gavin Hart, Sexually Transmitted Diseases, 1984, p.4. Copyright 1984 by Carolina Biological Supply Company. Reprinted with permission.)

In women the infection often occurs around the cervix, the neck of the uterus opening into the vagina (Figure 1.3). It may spread into the fallopian tubes connecting the ovaries to the uterus. Infection and inflammation of the fallopian tubes is known as salpingitis, which may lead to partial or complete blockage of the tubes. That in turn can cause infertility. Blocked fallopian tubes can also result in ectopic or tubal pregnancy, in which the foetus develops in the tube rather than the uterus. Such a pregnancy is potentially fatal for the mother. Gonococcal infection of the fallopian tubes usually becomes apparent after the first menstrual period following the initial infection. The victim often experiences abdominal pain, which a medical practitioner may misdiagnose unless gonorrhoea is suspected. If untreated, gonorrhoea may become a chronic condition, resulting in chronic pelvic inflammatory disease.[7]

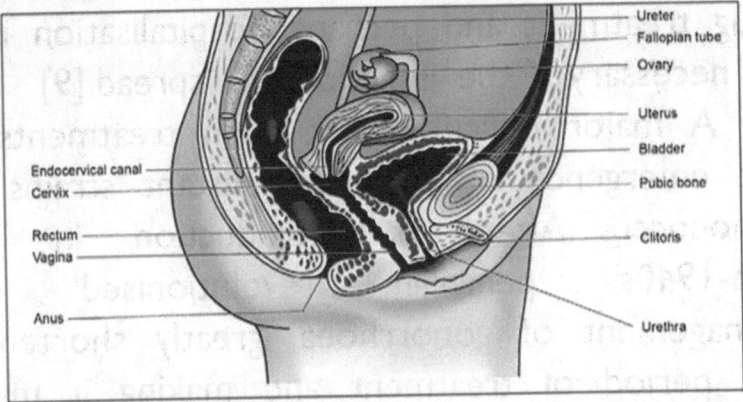

Figure 1.3: Female genitalia. (Gavin Hart, Sexually Transmitted Diseases, 1984, p.4. Copyright 1984 by Carolina Biological Supply Company. Reprinted with permission.)

In a small proportion of victims the gonococci may enter the bloodstream, spreading throughout the body, initially producing fevers and chills. Later the infection becomes localised, producing small pustules on the skin and arthritic inflammation of the joints. The fingers and hands are the most commonly affected regions (Figure 1.4).[8]

In the present era, uncomplicated gonorrhoea has often been treated effectively with a single large-dose injection of penicillin or its derivatives such as amoxycillin or ampicillin. An alternative is a single course of the same antibiotics taken orally, in which case the drug probenecid® is often also administered to increase the blood concentration of penicillin. A longer regimen of drug treatment and perhaps hospitalisation may be necessary if the infection has spread.[9]

A major difficulty with such treatments is the emergence of penicillin-resistant strains of gonococci. After its introduction in the mid-1940s, penicillin revolutionised the management of gonorrhoea, greatly shortening the period of treatment and making it much more comfortable for the patient and medical practitioner alike. Within 20 years, however, medical researchers were reporting cases where *Neisseria gonorrhoeae* had proved penicillin resistant. For example, in 1968 the *Medical Journal of Australia (MJA)* noted that in Vietnam an 'incurable' form of gonorrhoea had seemingly emerged among Australian troops.[10]

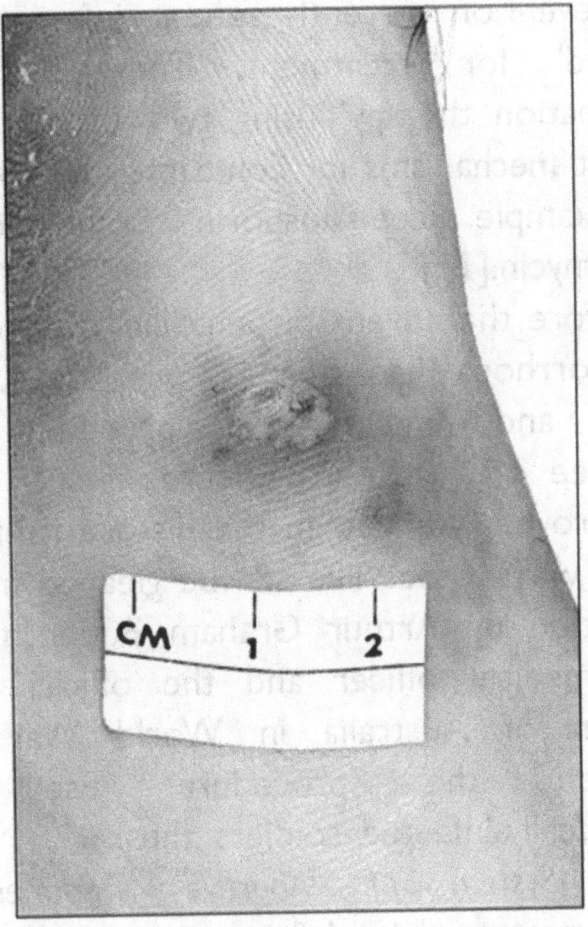

Figure 1.4: A cutaneous gonococcal lesion due to a disseminated Neisseria gonorrhoeae bacterial infection (Public Health Image Library, CDC/Dr Wiesner).

Experience has meanwhile proved that such strains develop and spread rapidly. Consequently, and as with other infectious diseases, drug resistance among gonococci obliges pharmacologists to continually develop new antibiotics targeting Neisseria gonorrhoeae. The Atlanta-based US Centers for Disease Control and Prevention currently sets an informal 'world standard' for treatment. They recommend 'combination therapy' using two antibiotics with different mechanisms for combating the gonococci, for example cephalosporin combined with azithromycin.[11]

Before the advent of penicillin, the treatment of gonorrhoea had been a protracted, messy, painful and embarrassing process without guarantee of a cure. The 'cure', if such it was, often proved worse than the disease itself. Some idea of what it was like can be gleaned from the description by Arthur Graham Butler, a senior Army medical officer and the official medical historian of Australia in World War I. He described the procedure used with gonococcally-infected soldiers thus:

> *System of 'Abortive' Treatment, i.e. treatment when definite signs of disease are present, for Gonorrhoea*
>
> Three methods are in use: (a) Sealing up. (b) Massage, (c) Plugging.
>
> For all three a silver salt (the best being Argyrol), and a Glycerine of B. Naphthol (Benetol) are used as anterior injections, whilst Pot. Permang. is used as a posterior irrigation. The guiding principle is to use as

much weak strengths as possible, and as few applications as possible consistent with efficiency. Each case is judged alone according to the degree of tenderness present and the irritation produced. The strengths used are: silver salt, about 5 per cent, Benetol about 1/60 to 1/150, and Pot. Permang. 1/8,000. The microscope controls diagnosis and cure.[12]

Butler did not elaborate on what the procedure for 'abortive' treatment entailed, but it was roughly as described in a 1919 urological textbook by a contemporary American urologist, Victor Cox Pedersen (1867-1958).[13] The routine was as follows:

1. After the patient had emptied his bladder, the urethra was 'irrigated'. That is, 'Argyrol' (an antiseptic derived from silver nitrate) was injected by a syringe along a catheter inserted into the anterior urethra, the section of the urinary tract passing through the penis. Argyrol was widely used to control infection in organs lined with mucous membrane. [Figure 1.5 shows an image of a contemporary syringe and catheter kit.]

2. In addition, a mixture of glycerol and b (beta)-napthol, commercially available as 'Benetol', was also injected into the

anterior urethra. Glycerol is a viscous liquid used pharmaceutically to improve the smoothness and lubricating quality of fluids, b-napthol, also called hydroxynaphthalene, is a moderately toxic compound and a homologue (chemically similar) of phenol or carbolic acid, a corrosive antiseptic.

3. These injections of powerful antiseptics were given twice daily for the first four days of treatment and then daily for the following six days.

4. To retain the antiseptic fluids within the urinary tract, collodion was applied to seal off the urethra. Collodion is a flammable, syrupy solution mainly used in wet-plate photography and in the manufacture of plastics, but when applied to the skin it dries quickly to form a flexible, sealant film.

5. While the antiseptic fluids were being held within the urethra, the penis would be massaged, that is, manually manipulated to ensure that the fluids were being forced along the urethra and distributed along its entire lining.

6. The antiseptic fluids were retained in the urethra for six hours before the collodion

seal was dissolved with acetone, allowing the fluids to be drained into a basin.

7. The patient assisted the medical practitioner, nurse or medical orderly conducting the irrigation process by holding the basin, which caught spillage and received the drained fluids.

8. If the patient's urethra became irritated by the antiseptics, weaker solutions of the fluids were used.

9. A similar procedure was followed if the infection was deemed to be in the posterior urethra—the section of the tract passing through the prostate gland into the bladder. For posterior urethral irrigation, a solution of potassium permanganate was used. This compound is an antiseptic commonly (and almost always ineffectually) used as both a disinfectant in handwashes and to clear away fungal skin infections.

10. Swabs were periodically taken from the urethra and then examined under a microscope. That would indicate whether gonococci were still present. If they were, the treatment would continue until there were no further signs of gonococcal infection. A general indicator

of the absence of gonococci was clear urine without traces of pus.

11. Should the symptoms of infection recur after the treatment had ended, for example if a discharge of pus from the penis reappeared or if pus could be detected in the urine, the patient was readmitted to hospital and the procedure began again. Repeated hospitalisation might be necessary in some cases.[14]

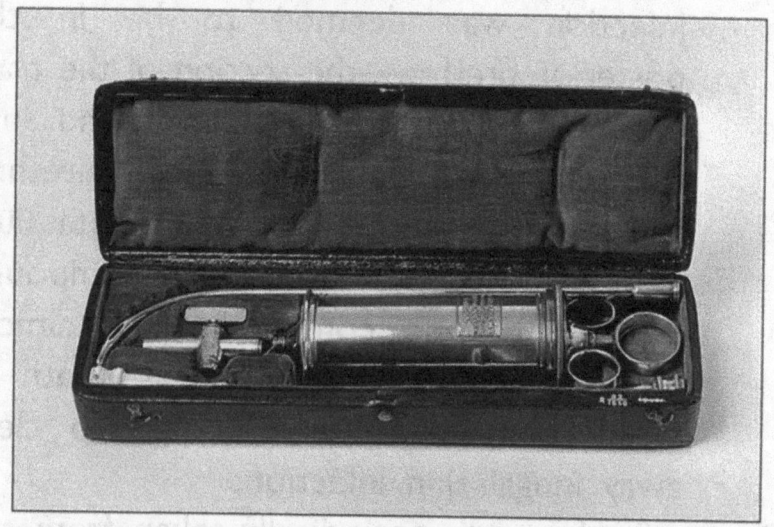

Figure 1.5: Metal syringe, with curved metal urethral catheter, used for irrigating the urethra with antiseptic compounds (Wellcome Collection, L0008780, CC BY).

The foregoing treatment regimen was so unpleasant that many soldiers (and civilians) tried to conceal their infection. Of the estimated 38,790 Australian soldiers treated for gonorrhoea on the Western Front 1916-1919, we can be confident that many tried to hide their symptoms from their comrades, superiors and medical officers. As the Army's best-known venereologist, Lieutenant Colonel George Raffan, pointed out, the result was that 'when the infection was ultimately discovered or confessed, the golden opportunity of effecting a speedy cure has been lost, and the disease has become chronic'.[15]

The complications of chronic gonorrhoea in males include urethral stricture. Treatment requires the serial insertion up the penis of progressively larger urethral sounds or expanders. Many a regimental medical officer (RMO) used his obligatory lecture on the avoidance of STDs to dramatic effect. At the end of his lecture to the troops of his battalion the RMO would produce the largest of his expanders with a flourish. It consisted of a long, curved metal probe with a blunt rounded point and a diameter of one centimetre. A long silence inevitably followed its display as each of the seated soldiers contemplated the torture of penile dilation.[16]

Concealment of symptoms was one reason why governments and military authorities introduced regulations making gonorrhoea and syphilis notifiable diseases, obliging medical practitioners to report them to government authorities. Most Australian states had enacted legislation to control these two major venereal diseases by the end of World War I.

The first Australian book on VD, *Venereal Disease in Australia*, published in 1919, summarised the three principles on which such legislation was based.[17] The author, Dr J.H.L. Cumpston, the Director of the Australian Quarantine Service, enumerated these as follows:

1. That the treatment of venereal disease shall be carried out by qualified medical practitioners only, and that treatment by chemists, quacks, herbalists, or other unqualified persons shall be an offence.
2. That every person who is suffering from venereal disease shall be obliged to obtain immediate treatment, and shall also continue under treatment until he [Cumpston's language suggested that only males suffered VD] has received a certificate of cure.
3. That each person suffering from venereal disease shall upon his [sic] first consulting a doctor receive a warning notice in the prescribed form, setting out the dangers associated with these diseases.[18]

These three principles ensured that the management of VD would be scientifically based. They were also coercive but would help educate patients.

4. Syphilis

Whereas gonococci cause gonorrhoea, syphilis results from infection by *Treponema pallidum*, a very small organism, a spirochaete, commonly transmitted during sexual intercourse. Like gonorrhoea, it can be passed from a mother to an unborn baby, in which case it is called congenital syphilis.[19]

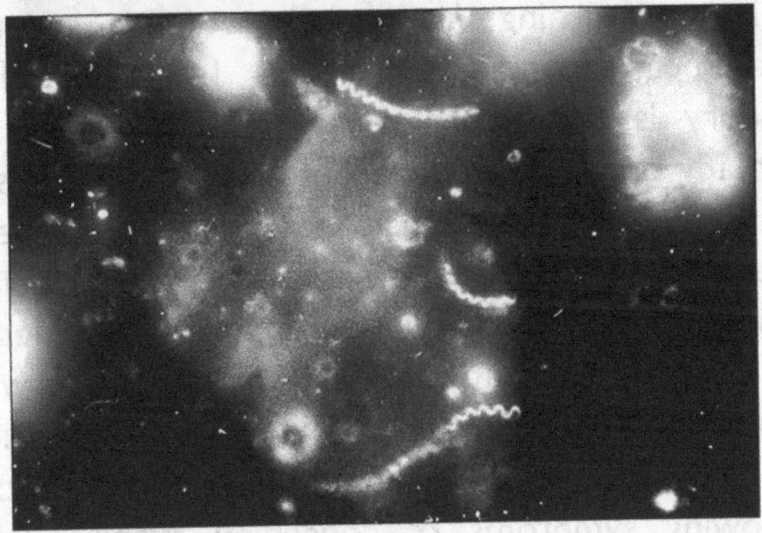

Figure 1.6: This digitially colourised photomicrograph depicts a blood sample extracted from a syphilis patient. Note the corkscrew-shaped Treponema pallidum bacterial spirochaete (CDC/Susan Lindsley, Public Health Image Library 1248).

Syphilis has claimed many famous victims. Those thought to have died from the disease include the composer Franz Schubert (1797-1828), the US gangster Al Capone (1899-1947) and

Vladimir Lenin (1870-1924), founder of the Soviet empire. Others thought to have suffered from syphilis include the writer Leo Tolstoy (1828-1910), the artist Paul Gaugin (1848-1903), the US president Abraham Lincoln (1809-1865) and the dictator Adolf Hitler (1889-1945).[20]

The origins of syphilis have been much debated. One hypothesis is that the disease was brought to Europe by Christopher Columbus's sailors returning from their voyages to the Caribbean islands during the 1490s. Another theory is that syphilis was 'pre-Columbian' — already active in Europe but not yet recognised as such. Tertiary syphilis is said to have been described by the ancient Greek physician, Hippocrates. Skeletal remains showing evidence of the degenerative change associated with tertiary syphilis have been found among the ruins of Pompeii; similarly, 14th century skeletons showing symptoms of congenital syphilis were discovered in Austria in 2015. The first known outbreak of syphilis in Europe occurred among French troops besieging Naples in 1495.[21]

Syphilis and gonorrhoea together have been much written about in Australia. The *MJA* has published many hundreds of editorials, original articles, case reports, book reviews and letters about the two diseases since its first edition in 1914. Few of the *MJA's* twice-monthly editions are published without some reference to syphilis, gonorrhoea or the various other STDs.[22] Syphilis in particular seems to have fascinated the Australian medical profession. One military medical officer, John Frith, expressed a view probably common among many colleagues when he observed:

> From the beginning, syphilis was greatly feared by society—because of the repulsiveness of its symptoms, the pain and disfigurement that was endured, the severe after effects of the mercury treatment [once used to control it], but most of all because it was transmitted and spread by an inescapable facet of human behaviour, sexual intercourse.[23]

Syphilis acquired through coition passes through a series of phases that may extend across decades. The first of these is an incubation period lasting an average of about three weeks, during which no symptoms are apparent. The second phase, known as primary stage syphilis, is when the first symptom appears—often a chancre or hard, usually painless ulcer at the infection site. If untreated the chancre disappears within about four weeks. Symptoms of secondary stage syphilis subsequently appear, from two to four months after infection. The most common symptom is a rash of red, flat lesions covering the whole body, often including the palms of the hands and soles of the feet, as the spirochaetes multiply and spread via the blood to the skin, liver, joints, lymph nodes, muscles, the brain, bones, and mucous membranes of the mouth and throat. The rash heals within several weeks and the disease will enter a dormant phase that may last for many years. During the latent phase, the spirochaetes remain inactive in the lymph nodes and spleen.[24]

Tertiary stage syphilis may appear in 30 to 40 per cent of untreated individuals, in whom the spirochaetes reactivate, multiply and spread throughout the body. As they do, they irreversibly damage the parts of the body they attack, including the heart, eyes, brain, nervous system, bones and joints. Tumours may develop on skin, bone, testicles and other tissues; cardiovascular symptoms such as aortic aneurysm and aortic valve insufficiency may develop; degenerative central nervous system disease can produce dementia, tremors, loss of muscle coordination, paralysis, and blindness.[25] The end result is a condition known as 'general paralysis of the insane'. Damage to the brain and spinal cord is called neurosyphilis, while the damage to the heart and blood vessels is known as cardiovascular syphilis. Deaths from syphilis typically occur during the tertiary stage because of the heavy impact of the disease on the central nervous and cardiovascular systems.[26]

The extended period over which tertiary syphilis may develop is evident in an anecdote of Dr M. Geoffrey Miller, a physician and naval historian in Mosman, Sydney. 'I recall treating an aged lady in 1986 who had developed a manifestation of tertiary syphilis,' he wrote. 'Her primary infection in 1919, of which she was unaware, was from her husband who had returned to Australia from the Western Front [after military service].'[27]

The treatment of primary, secondary, congenital and early latent syphilis is through a single intramuscular injection of a long-lasting penicillin that remains active in the bloodstream for up to three weeks. Some sexual health physicians prefer to administer daily injections of penicillin throughout this period. People allergic to penicillin are given other antibiotics. Tertiary syphilis requires longer-term treatment, with regular blood tests for at least a year to determine if the spirochaetes have been eliminated. Although such treatment will eradicate the spirochaetes, it cannot restore damaged tissue.[28]

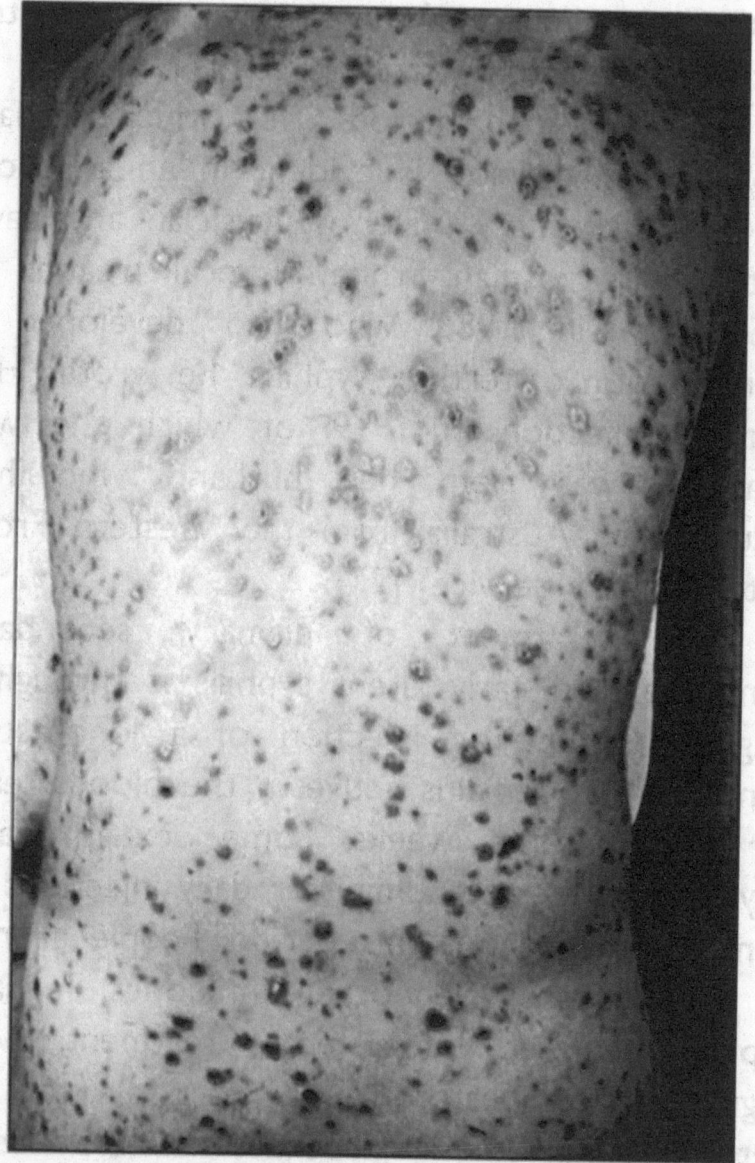

Figure 1.7: Viewed from behind, this patient's torso and upper extremities exhibited a widespread papulosquamous rash, which proved to be a case of secondary syphilis caused by the bacterial spirochaete Treponema pallidum (CDC/Dr Gavin Hart, Public Health Image Library 17838).

The pre-antibiotic treatment of syphilis was a long, unpleasant ordeal for the patient, without certainty of a cure. It was explained by Captain Robert J. Silverton, an Australian Army Medical Corps (AAMC) officer serving with the 2nd Australian Stationary Hospital (2 ASH), a unit specialising in treating VD cases among Australian and New Zealand troops in Egypt and Palestine 1915-1918.[29] Silverton described the 10 steps of the treatment regimen as follows:

1. During the **primary stage,** if syphilis was suspected the Wassermann blood test was administered. This was a blood test aimed at detecting diagnostic antibodies. A difficulty with the test was that it could yield 'false negatives', that is, the spirochaetes might still be present without the test indicating this. Further, the test could give positive results for diseases other than syphilis including malaria and tuberculosis, which confused the situation in relation to syphilis.

2. Chancres were treated with antiseptics in the field. In hospitals, saline dressings — gauze soaked in a saline solution—were applied.

3. Swabs of the chancres were taken for microscopic examination for proof of the presence of *Treponema pallidum.*

4. Once the spirochaetes were shown to be present, a course of treatment began, using an arsenic-based drug administered by intramuscular injection. A number of arsenic-compound preparations were used, including salvarsan (also known as arsphenamine and 'Compound 606'), neosalvarsan, galyl, arsenobenzol and kharsivan, in doses of between 0.2 and 0.5 grams twice weekly for two weeks. Salvarsan had first been synthesised in 1907 and by 1909 was known to kill *Treponema pallidum*. An organoarsenic compound, it was the first modern chemotherapeutic agent. Salvarsan was difficult to prepare and tended to cause liver damage, so by 1912 a less toxic and more readily managed derivative, neosalvarsan, was also being used. Captain Silverton wrote that he preferred using galyl, which was generally less toxic.

5. After an interval of three weeks, two more doses were given in the next week, making a total of six injections over a six-week course of treatment. All these drugs were toxic and so dosages were calculated to take account of the patient's weight and physical condition, and the record of patient tolerance of the drugs.

6. During the six weeks when the arsenic compound injections were being administered, the patient also received a weekly injection of between 0.3 and 0.6 cubic centimetres of 'grey oil'—an oil-based mixture containing calomel (mercuric chloride). Mercury had been used in treating syphilis for centuries and the risks of mercury poisoning were well known. Side effects included severe mouth ulcers, the loss of teeth and kidney failure. In previous centuries the mercury treatment often continued for years, giving rise to the wry quip, 'A day with Bacchus, a night with Venus and a lifetime with Mercury'.[30]

7. At the end of the six-week course of treatment, a further Wassermann test was administered. If it returned a negative result and no symptoms of syphilis were present, the patient was discharged.

8. The treatment for **secondary stage** syphilis was essentially the same as for the six-week treatment of primary stage syphilis. If, however, the case was deemed to be late secondary stage syphilis, iodides were administered as well. After each meal the patient drank a concoction of potassium iodide, aromatic spirits of

ammonia (a solution of ammonium hydroxide, mixed with water, alcohol and the essential oils of lemon, nutmeg and lavender) and chloroform water (a solution of the anaesthetic chloroform, a colourless sweet-smelling liquid), all mixed with half a pint (0.284 litre) of water. The amount of iodide was gradually increased from five to 30 or more grains three times a day, that is, from 0.3 gram to 2.0 grams. The risk of treatment with iodides was the development of iodism—iodine poisoning, inducing a series of adverse reactions including diarrhoea, vomiting and convulsions.

9. At the end of the treatment period the Wasserman test was administered, and if this still returned a positive result the patient was detained for a further fortnight to receive one salvarsan and two grey-oil injections.

10. In treating **tertiary stage** syphilis, a similar regimen was followed as for the two earlier stages, but for eight weeks rather than six. The only difference was that the treatment with iodides continued from the outset, with the strength of the dose increased

progressively. If iodism appeared, the strength of the dose was reduced.[31]

The procedure outlined above was fraught with serious risk for the patient. Unless carefully managed, the drugs injected into and ingested by the patient could poison him, causing permanent disability. Militarily, the cost in lost manpower was huge. With six to eight weeks required for each course of treatment the 10,674 Australian soldiers treated for syphilis on the Western Front 1916-1919 spent a total of at least 64,000 weeks or some 1230 'man-years' in hospital.

5. Trends in gonorrhoea and syphilis infections in Australia

Until the widespread introduction of penicillin near the end of World War II, the incidence of both gonorrhoea and syphilis in Australia was relatively high. After that, the rates of infection of both diseases declined steadily. Australia-wide infection statistics are unavailable before 1961, however the contemporary medical literature indicates high rates of infection.[32]

The impact of penicillin can be seen in the mortality rate for syphilis, always the more lethal disease. The number of deaths from syphilis fell dramatically from 522 in 1940 (a rate of 73.7 deaths per million of population) to 76 (7.3 per million) in 1960. This was a sevenfold reduction in number of deaths and a tenfold decline in the rate. By 1973 there were 18 deaths and a negligible mortality rate of 1.3 per million.[33] The decline is shown by the graph in Figure 1.8. From the early 1960s, however, the incidence of both syphilis and gonorrhoea in the Australian population rose steadily.

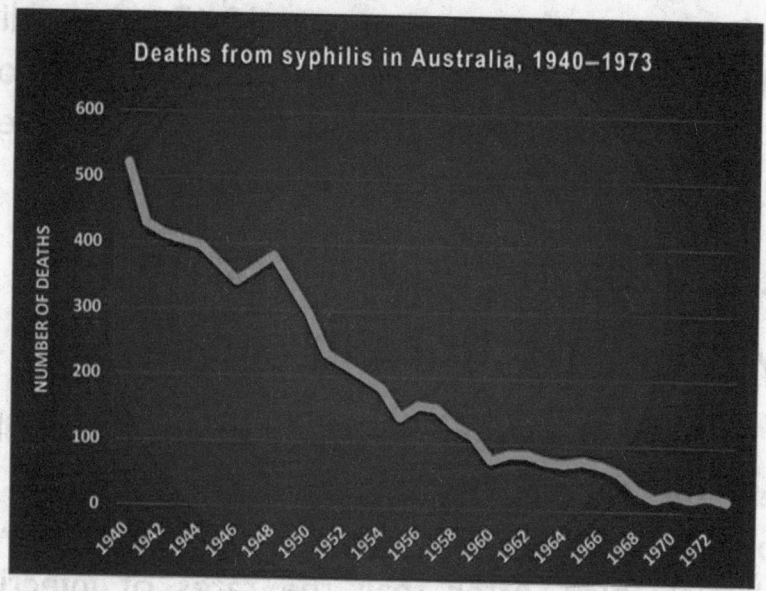

Figure 1.8: Reduction of deaths from syphilis in Australia 1940-1973 ('Causes of death', Year Book Australia, Australian Bureau of Statistics, Canberra, 1974).

The number of cases of gonorrhoea Australia-wide peaked at 12,352 in 1978 while the number of syphilis cases peaked at 3594 in 1986. The incidence of both diseases fell away after that but then began climbing again from 1990. Gonorrhoea cases rose from 1919 in 1990 to 9971 in 2010. Syphilis cases, not as volatile, tended to plateau but rose from a 'new' low of 1125 in 2001 to a new high of 3245 in 2008.[34] The graph in Figure 1.9 indicates the changing epidemiology of both diseases.

Epidemiologists and sexual health physicians debated the reasons for these trends. The emergence of antibiotic-resistant strains of the bacteria responsible for gonorrhoea and syphilis was one factor. Changing societal mores was another. Generations grown blasé about the risks of casual sex and less heeding of social and religious sanctions against promiscuity were probably uninterested in knowing what stigma had blighted the lives of gonorrhoea and syphilis sufferers in earlier generations.[35] It is also possible that the later generations were unaware of the earlier incidence of STIs and the stigma they caused. Most likely the stigma continues, with the result that people feel uncomfortable talking about STIs. If so, one effect of that could be wide misperceptions and misinformation about STIs among the population.

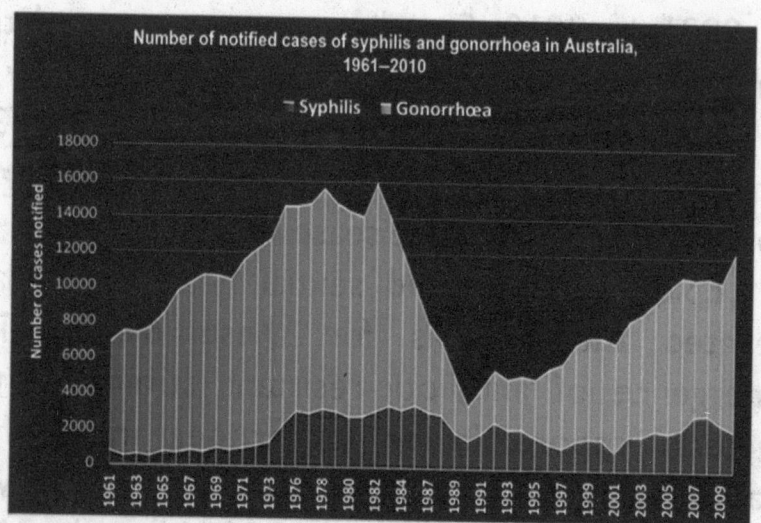

Figure 1.9: Australian trends in the incidence of gonorrhoea and syphilis, 1961—2010 ('Notifiable diseases', Year Book Australia, Australian Bureau of Statistics, Canberra, 2011).

6. Chancroid

Chancroid is an STD producing painful ulcerated genital lesions, often accompanied by enlargement of the lymph nodes. Also called 'soft chancre', it was thought to be a symptom of syphilis until the mid-19th century. In 1899 its cause was shown to be *Haemophilus ducreyi*, a bacterium of the coccobacillus group. If untreated, the lesions become chronic ulcers on the penis and in the groin, or on either the penis or in the groin area.[36]

Uncommon in developed nations, chancroid is a disease usually afflicting the poor. At one time it was most common in East Asian nations, however many Westerners subsequently diagnosed with chancroid visited regions in which the disease is common. Outbreaks in developed nations have occurred in association with crack cocaine use and prostitution in poor urban areas. Chancroid is also a risk factor in contracting HIV because regions of the world in which chancroid is most prevalent are also those with the highest HIV infection rates. Young promiscuous men are the most at risk; women at most comprise 10 percent of the sufferers.[37]

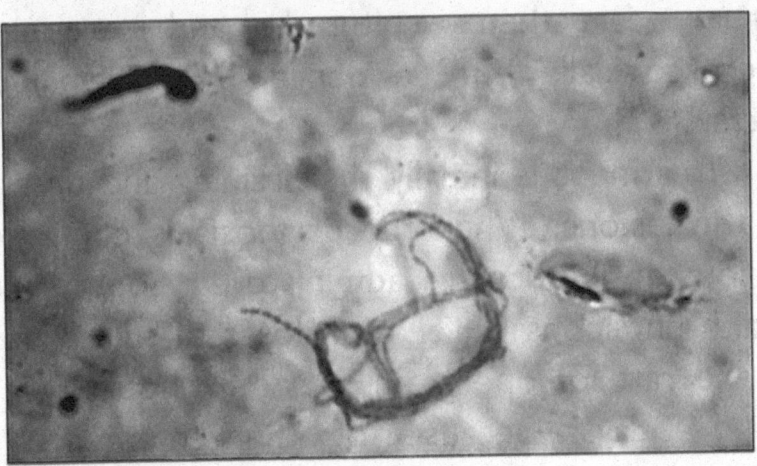

Figure 1.10: This photomicrograph revealed the presence of Haemophilus ducreyi bacteria which had formed observable strands of streptobacilli. H. ducreyi causes chancroid, a highly contagious sexually transmitted disease that begins with the formation of painful open sores on the genitals (CDC, Public Health Image Library 15211).

The incubation period for chancroid is short, averaging four to five days after infection. The first symptom is usually a papule or pimple-like eruption surrounded by a rash, usually occurring on the penis in men and the vulva in women. The papule soon transforms into a ragged-edged ulcer, several of which may develop. The ulcers bleed readily. In about half the cases, chancroidal buboes (swollen lymph nodes) develop in the groin.[38]

Diagnosis is confirmed by culturing serum taken from the chancroid or the buboes. The serum is then cultured and examined microscopically for evidence of *Haemophilus ducreyi*.[39]

Treatment is initially the draining and dressing of the lesions. When the diagnosis is confirmed, various antibiotics are administered. Some sexual health physicians prefer oral doses of sulfisoxazole at the rate of one gram every six hours for 10 to 14 days. Because of the emergence of drug-resistant strains of the bacillus, a combination of other antibiotics is commonly used.[40]

Before the adoption of penicillin-based therapies the treatment for chancroid (like that for gonorrhoea and syphilis) was prolonged, messy, embarrassing and painful, but it was usually effective. Captain Ronald J. Silverton described the method at 2 ASH as proceeding through these steps:

1. The chancroid ulcer was initially washed with a saline solution and dressed with sterile gauze.
2. The ulcer was subsequently rubbed with 'Black Wash' (an escharotic—a caustic substance, comprising a mixture of calomel and limewater used to remove dead tissue). The Black Wash was applied with a tuft of wool mounted on a thin metal rod.
3. The patient then exposed his penis to direct sunlight for half an hour, after which iodoform powder (an antiseptic organoiodine compound) was rubbed into the ulcer and then another sterile gauze dressing was applied.
4. Depending on the extent to which granulation (healing of the ulcerated tissue) was occurring, the ulcer might be cauterised with copper sulphate, carbolic acid or a 50 per cent zinc chloride solution a couple of times weekly until it showed 'a healthy granulating surface'.
5. After the healing stage had been reached, 'Red Ointment' was applied to hasten the healing process. (Silverton did not describe this ointment but it was probably

'unguentum rubrum', a cream used to dry out scabs.)

6. Where there was evidence of swelling in the lymph glands, the patient was confined to bed and treated with an injection of calomel (mercuric chloride), as in the treatment for syphilis. The skin over the buboes was inuncted, that is, rubbed with an ointment, for 20 minutes twice a day. The ointment was Scott's Dressing, a preparation containing camphorated mercury. An ice pack was applied during the whole of the day and bandaged in place at night. In addition, 30 minims (1.85 millilitres) of 'Fibro Lysin' (a substance causing bacterial cell membrane to disintegrate) were injected near the swelling every three days.

7. Most buboes disappeared after this treatment. If the swelling continued, the buboes were curetted—incised under general anaesthesia and the infected tissue scraped out with a surgical spoon. The resulting cavity was then packed with iodoform gauze (thin strips of gauze impregnated with iodoform), which was left in place for between one and two days. After that, the wound was cleaned with Eusol (an antiseptic solution of

chlorinated lime and boric acid) and packed again with iodoform gauze. (During the 1980s, Eusol was found to impair blood flow through the capillaries, and so its use was discontinued. While it probably killed the *Haemophilus ducreyi* bacteria, it would have impeded the healing process.)

8. After three to four days of such treatment the wound was electrically cauterised through a procedure called 'Zinc Ionisation'. This was carried out after a local anaesthetic using cocaine. The anaesthetic involved applying a four per cent cocaine hydrochloride solution to every part of the cavity with a swab of wool. An aluminium or platinum electrode was then fitted into the cavity and connected to a battery delivering three milliamperes of current per square centimetre of the cavity. The current was allowed to flow for 10 minutes. If necessary, for example if pus continued oozing from the wound, the cauterisation procedure was repeated once or twice.

9. After that, the cauterised wound was dressed in a 'soothing starch poultice' three times daily for two days. The treatment with Eusol and iodoform gauze then resumed. To hasten healing, dressings

with a substance that Captain Silverton called 'Loteic rubra' were also applied and subsequently 'unguentum rubrum' as well.[41]

Few of the steps outlined by Captain Silverton could be described as 'soothingly therapeutic'. Like the contemporary treatments for gonorrhoea and syphilis, there was an inference that the pain and indignity of treatment were the just desserts of soldiers who had contracted VD.

The reader might be curious about how many patients might have been frightened away from sexual intercourse for the rest of their lives through the pre-penicillin therapies for VD. What proportion of patients might have fallen into that category is unknown. Such treatments, however, seem likely to have left emotional and mental as well as physical scars.

7. Non-specific urethritis and chlamydia

Urethritis, inflammation of the urethra, has many causes. Among them are the STDs chlamydia and gonorrhoea. Various other organisms may also cause the condition, however, and need not necessarily be transmitted sexually. In the pre-penicillin era, such infections were collectively known as 'non-specific urethritis' (NSU), 'non-specific' meaning that the agent causing the inflammation was unknown.[42] The mysterious nature of NSU gave rise to a wry adage among Army medical officers. Wary of embarrassing superiors, they used to say that: 'Junior officers and other ranks get venereal diseases; senior officers contract non-specific urethritis'.[43]

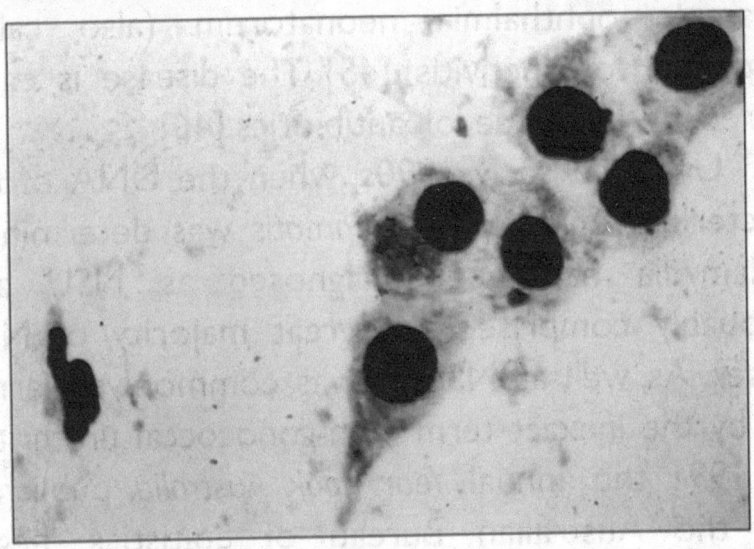

Figure 1.11: A photomicrograph of Chlamydia trachomatis taken from a urethral scrape. Note the presence of a cluster of spore-like C. trachomatis elementary bodies located intracellularly inside one of the larger epithelial cells (CDC/Dr Wiesner, Dr Kaufman, Public Health Image Library 2295).

Sexual health physicians regard NSU as 'a fairly mild disease'. Seeing it as a 'urinary tract infection', they usually prescribe a course of antibiotics, often the same drugs used to manage chlamydia.[44]

Chlamydia is caused by the *Chlamydia trachomatis* bacterium. In men, the bacterium produces urethritis similar to that resulting from gonorrhoea. In women the infection often does not produce symptoms but will commonly infect the cervix and fallopian tubes. Babies born to infected women often suffer eye infections, for example ophthalmia neonatorum (also called neonatal conjunctivitis).[45] The disease is easily cured by a course of antibiotics.[46]

Until the early 1990s, when the DNA of the bacterium *Chlamydia trachomatis* was determined, chlamydia had been diagnosed as NSU and probably comprised the great majority of NSU cases. As well as NSU, it was commonly referred to by the inexact term 'non-gonococcal urethritis'. In 1991 the annual *Year Book Australia*, published by the Australian Bureau of Statistics, began reporting chlamydia. The figures for chlamydia rose from 4044 in 1991 to 74,305 in 2010.[47]

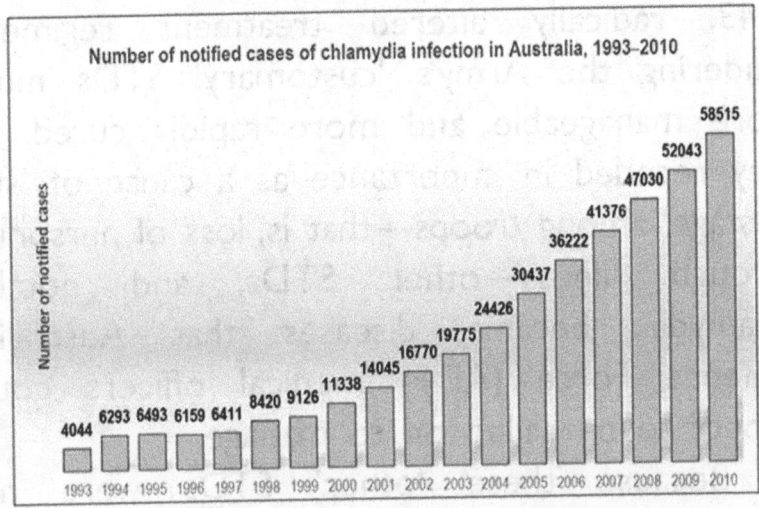

Figure 1.12: The rise of chlamydia infection in Australia from the early 1990s ('Notifiable diseases, 1907-2011', Year Book Australia, Australian Bureau of Statistics, 2012).

The logarithmic increase in the chlamydia infection rate is seen in the chart in Figure 1.12. The huge increase in reported chlamydia infections might not have been as alarming as the chart suggests, reflecting instead improved diagnostic testing rather than a new disease spreading plague-like through the population.

8. Other sexually transmitted infections

The STDs summarised above were those 'traditionally' suffered in the Australian Army during much of the 20th century. The advent of antibiotics, available to the military forces from

1943, radically altered treatment regimens, rendering the Army's 'customary' STDs much more manageable and more rapidly cured. As they receded in importance as a cause of 'sick wastage' among troops—that is, loss of personnel through illness—other STDs, and notably chlamydia, became diseases that Australian Defence Force (ADF) medical officers could expect to be called on to manage.

Because these 'other' STDs were not historically significant during the Army's overseas deployments throughout most of the 20th century, only a brief summary is given here. Readers wanting an amplified narration are directed to the many internet websites providing authoritative comment, for example, that of the Centers for Disease Control and Prevention. *Wikipedia*, the online encyclopaedia, also contains easily accessible articles on all the other STDs. The following summary deals with STDs alphabetically.

Acquired immune deficiency syndrome (AIDS) and human immunodeficiency virus (HIV)

The cause of AIDS was identified in 1983 as a retrovirus named 'human immunodeficiency virus', soon known commonly as 'HIV'. A retrovirus has the ability to insert a DNA copy of its genome into a host cell in order to replicate itself. HIV attacks T-lymphocytes which have a key role in giving individuals immunity to disease. About 30 per cent of HIV infections progress to AIDS.[48]

The beneficial impact of the research on HIV-AIDS and publicity given to the disease eventually became apparent in the statistics published by the Australian Bureau of Statistics. After peaking at 953 cases of AIDS in 1994, the number of cases notified fell dramatically to 99 in 2008—almost a tenfold reduction. Over the same period, mortality from AIDS declined from 753 deaths to 24, a decrease by a factor of 31. HIV infections fell from 1703 new cases in 1988 to a low of 714 in 1999, however, after that the number of new cases rose steadily to 1082 ten years later.[49] Figure 1.13 shows the trends in the period 1983-2010 in notified cases of HIV and AIDS.[50]

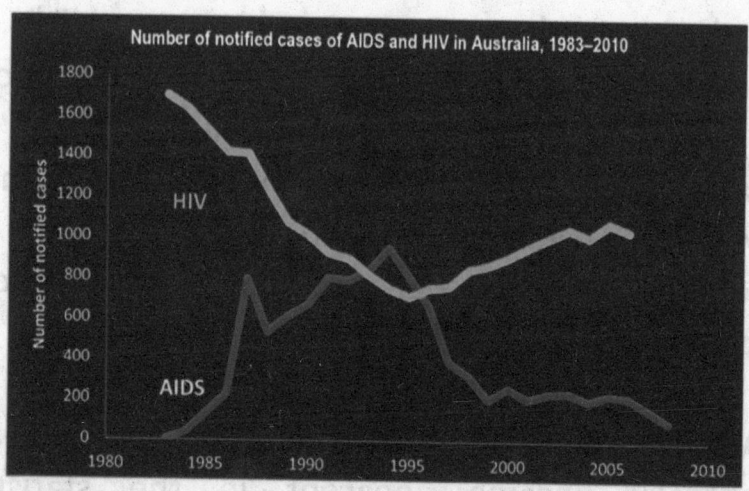

Figure 1.13: Trends in HIV and AIDS in Australia, 1983-2010 ('Notifiable diseases, 1983-2011, Year Book of Australia, Australian Bureau of Statistics, 2012).

Despite the post-1995 increase in HIV cases, Australia remains a nation with a relatively low rate of HIV infection when compared with other developed nations. Australia was in the group of nations in which the prevalence of HIV infection was below one per cent of the adult population between the ages of 15 and 49.[51]

Candidiasis

Commonly called 'thrush', Candidiasis is a soft-tissue infection caused by *Candida albicans*, a yeast occurring in the mouths, vaginas and intestines of most healthy people. It causes inflammation of the vagina in women, known as Candida vaginitis, and inflammation of the glans of the penis in uncircumcised men, in whom it might cause balanitis or tightness in the foreskin.[52]

Condylomata acuminata

Commonly known as genital warts, this condition is caused by the human papilloma virus (HPV), of which more than 100 strains are known to exist. The warts produced by HPV resemble those appearing on other parts of the body.[53]

Donovanosis

Also called granuloma inguinale, this disease is caused by a bacterium called *Klebsiella granulomatis* (formerly known as *Calymmatobacterium granulomatis*). The bacteria invade and multiply within histiocytic cells. The cells eventually rupture, releasing the organisms to invade other cells.[54] Symptoms of infection include multiple subcutaneous nodules in the skin of the genitalia and anus, which then erode through the skin to produce lesions on the skin surface. The lesions enlarge and bleed readily and are then liable to secondary infections. They can also spread to the mouth, lips, throat and face.[55]

Corynebacterium vaginalis infection

Known also as *Gardnerella vaginalis*, this disease is caused by a bacterium which produces mild vaginitis (inflammation of the vagina) in women.[56]

Genital herpes

Herpes of the genital regions is caused by the herpes simplex virus, which frequently affects the skin around the mouth as well. It typically produces a blister, and sometimes many blisters, which soon burst leaving small, shallow and often painful ulcers. These often heal themselves in 10 to 14 days but may recur spontaneously.[57] Chronic herpes infection is one cause of cancer of the cervix in women. The infection is often passed on to the babies of infected women during vaginal childbirth.[58]

Hepatitis B

Hepatitis B is a viral liver disease caused by 'HBV', a virus of the genus *Orthohepadnavirus*. It can be acquired sexually, especially through anal intercourse and contact with people having low levels of personal hygiene. It is less common in nations with advanced economies and more common in 'Third World' nations.[59] HBV-infected people usually suffer no initial illness, unless they develop an acute form of the disease and display symptoms such as jaundice, darkened urine and loss of energy. A vaccine is given to individuals in high-risk groups and to children who have acquired hepatitis B during birth by infected women.[60]

Lymphogranuloma venereum

Commonly abbreviated as 'LGV', this STD is also known variously as 'Climactic bubo', 'Durand-Nicholas-Favre disease', 'Frei's disease', 'Poradenitis inguinale' and 'Strumous bubo'. LGV occurs most commonly in Southeast Asia but occasionally occurs in developed Western nations as well.[61] It is caused by the bacterium *Chlamydia trachomatis*, responsible for the STD chlamydia discussed above. If the disease is not halted it may progress to chronic buboes, elephantiasis (gross swelling of tissue, often into pendulous lobes), fistulae (permanent abnormal passageways between two organs in the body or between an organ and the exterior of the body) and strictures (narrowing or stenosis of the body's tubal passageways).[62] The first symptom is usually a lesion on the genitalia or anus. Painful enlargement of the lymph nodes follows within about 30 days and may then proceed to the formation of abscesses, which rupture to produce chronic draining sinuses (cavities) or fistulae.[63]

Molluscum Contagiosum

This is a contagious viral skin infection producing round, domed, pearl-coloured lumps with central depressions. They can occur on the genitalia or anywhere on the skin. It is a relatively harmless condition and can be transmitted non-sexually to children, in whom the lesions will occur on other parts of the body.[64]

Pediculosis—lice

Pediculosis is an infestation by lice. Genital or pubic lice are of the species *Phthirus pubis*, commonly known as crab lice and in slang 'crabs'. The crab louse is a parasitic insect that feeds on the blood of its host. Crab lice are almost always passed on from an infested individual to a sexual partner during intercourse. The lice, which usually hide among the pubic hair, can be seen with the naked eye. Causing pubic itching, they can be treated with insecticide in the form of a cream or soap.[65]

Scabies

This condition is caused by a blood-sucking arthropod, a mite called *Sarcoptes scabiei*. The female of the species burrows into the skin of humans to lay its eggs. While there, it also deposits its faeces. The attack by the mite becomes evident through an allergic reaction in the host as itchy, red, raised, rash-like lumps appear on the skin. Scratching the rash often introduces secondary infections. The disease is common among children living in poor, deprived communities, to whom it is transmitted non-sexually in the squalor of their homes. In developed Western nations, scabies is usually acquired through sexual contact. Scabies is readily treated with the lotions 'Lindane' ® or 'Scabanca ® applied to the infected skin.[66]

Trichomoniasis

Trichomoniasis is most commonly a vaginal infection. It is caused by a motile single-celled protozoan parasite, *Trichomonas vaginalis*, with flagella that propel it along the genital tract. The infection characteristically results in vaginitis (inflammation of the vagina) and often produces a thin discharge that stains the underwear and exudes an offensive 'fishy' odour. The symptoms are aggravated by sexual intercourse. Men can acquire the parasite, often without symptoms or being aware of their infection. The infection can be readily controlled by a single oral dose of metronidazole or tinidazole.[67]

CHAPTER 2

Venereal disease in the Australian Army during World War I: August 1914–March 1916

1. Before World War I—STDs during the overseas military excursions of the Australian colonies

The incidence of STDs in the overseas conflicts to which the pre-federation Australian colonies sent troops is unknown. These were the New Zealand land wars of 1845-46 and 1860-72, the Sudan campaign in 1885, the South African War of 1899-1902 and the Boxer Rebellion in China during 1900-1901. Given the high rates of STD infection among Australia troops in later overseas deployments, it would be surprising if STDs had not occurred among the Australian contingents in these earlier conflicts.

The best-documented of the late colonial-era conflicts was the South African War. Various histories of the war, both British and Australian, deal at length with the organisational arrangements made for the various field ambulances and stationary hospitals set up to treat injured and sick soldiers. The only infectious diseases discussed in any detail are two other historical scourges of armies—dysentery and malaria. VD never rates a mention.

For some reason, perhaps because of the prudery of the era, VD is ignored in the official accounts. Neither the 300-page report of the 1903 British commission of inquiry into the War[1] nor the 395-page 1904 official British government report on the medical arrangements for the war by the Army's surgeon general[2] include any reference to STDs. Nor does the six-volume quasi-official British history of the war published by *The Times* newspaper of London.[3]

Despite the official silence, we might surmise that some of the troops arriving in South Africa either brought STDs with them or acquired STDs in Africa and took the diseases back home to Australia, because that was certainly the situation during the next war 12 years later—World War I. The possibility that some Australians might have contracted STDs during their South African service is hinted at by the most recent Australian historian of that war, Craig Wilcox. He describes the Australian colonial contingents arriving at the port of Beira in Mozambique, from where they caught trains into South Africa. The Australians generally thought the town 'immoral' but many, appreciating the 'free-flowing liquor', went on 'drunken sprees'.[4] Did that lead to STDs? Wilcox does not say, but as we shall see time and again in this book, the nexus between inebriated soldiers, accessible prostitutes and high rates of STDs is a common theme in the Australian Army's experience of disease.

Eventually the British Army did publish the VD figures for the South African War, but not until 1931 in the statistical volume of the official medical history of World War I. The VD cases comprised 8538 of gonorrhoea, 8620 of syphilis and 1969 of chancroid.[5] The 19,127 VD cases treated during the war amounted to 4.7 per cent of all 404,126 hospitalisations for disease and were the equivalent of 5.5 per cent of the 347,000 British troops who served in the war.[6] If the 16,000 Australian soldiers who served in South Africa had contracted VD at a similar rate, about 880 of them would have been infected.[7] If so, VD must have been a problem for the medical officers serving with the Australian contingents.

2. Medical politics and STDs on the eve of World War I

By the outbreak of World War I, the Australian medical profession knew much about STDs and their treatment. Professional periodicals such as the *Australasian Medical Gazette* kept doctors well-informed about gonorrhoea and syphilis in particular.[8]

At the time, 1914, STDs were known collectively as 'venereal disease (s)', which most often signified gonorrhoea or syphilis and less frequently chancroid—diseases very different from each other and caused by dissimilar bacteria.

By 1914, too, the Australian states had begun legislating to control VD. As early as the 1860s, several of the colonial parliaments had conducted inquiries into contagious diseases, which included VD, and had enacted legislation to give government medical officers and health authorities coercive powers over the VD-infected. Under such legislation, syphilis became a notifiable disease and those suffering from it had to be reported to the health authorities. The powers given to officials were far-reaching. For example, the New South Wales *Prisoners' Detention Act*

1908 provided for the continued incarceration of VD-infected inmates after their prison sentences had expired so that their treatment could continue. For prisoners suffering tertiary syphilis, that could effectively have meant imprisonment for life.[9]

The medical profession had been the instigator of such legislation. The biennial Australasian Medical Congresses discussed VD at length at several pre-war conferences. A general session of the 1908 Congress in Melbourne, for example, agreed to the resolution khat syphilis is responsible for an enormous amount of damage to mankind, and that preventive or remedial measures directed against it are worthy of the utmost consideration'.[10]

The 1914 Congress, in Auckland, more insistent on discussing VD than those preceding it, considered VD at length and then called on governments to adopt a series of measures aimed at curbing VD. Briefly, these included:
- public education on the 'causes, consequences and mode of prevention' of VD
- laboratory facilities to help diagnose VD swiftly
- free treatment as both in-and outpatients of VD sufferers

- legislation to control VD coercively, including severe punishments for (1) sufferers knowingly passing VD to other people; and (2) for the treatment of VD by anyone but medical practitioners.[11]

As if to persuade cost-conscious governments, the Congress concluded its argument with an appeal to economy. 'The expenditure,' the resolution argued, 'would be very small by comparison with the expenditure resulting from the present wholesale infection of the population.'[12] The benefits would include 'diminution of mortality; diminution of insanity; diminution of the expenditure in hospitals and asylums; increased human efficiency; and better and healthier enjoyment of life'.[13]

After such prodding, in January 1916 the Commonwealth Parliament established a four-member 'Committee Concerning Causes of Death and Invalidity in the Commonwealth'. Chaired by a parliamentarian, James Mathews, its other three members were eminent medical practitioners. On 24 May 1916 the committee published a *Report on Venereal Diseases*, which recommended more or less what the Australasian Medical Congresses had been advocating during the preceding decade.[14]

Meanwhile, in Britain the UK government had established a Royal Commission on the

Prevention and Treatment of Venereal Diseases, which began reporting its findings in February 1916.[15] By this time, the high incidence of VD among Australian troops at home and overseas had become a concern for the Australian government as well. The report of the UK royal commission, which dealt inter alia with VD among Australian, British, Canadian and New Zealand troops in the UK, added urgency to the task of the Mathews committee.[16]

In the meantime, too, the exigencies of the war distracted the Australian medical profession from its advocacy of legislation to control VD in the states. As hundreds of doctors enlisted in the AAMC, the focus shifted to the immediate problem of 'the occurrence of large numbers of venereal cases among troops in training for military service abroad, with the consequent loss of efficiency in the military forces'.[17]

During the 1920s the state governments did eventually adopt the measures proposed by the Mathews committee. In this they were prompted by the high wartime VD infection rates as well as continued pressure from the medical profession. Commonwealth subsidies for implementing programs to control VD were an additional inducement.[18]

3. An initiation—the Army's experience of STDs in Australia 1914-1915

The Australian Army began confronting its first cases of STDs almost as soon as recruiting began after Britain declared war against Germany on 4 August 1914.[2] Volunteers flooded into the Army's enlistment depots to sign up when these opened on 8 August. Service with the Australian Imperial Force (AIF), the formation hastily established to enable soldiers to serve outside Australia, required the recruit to be declared physically fit and healthy even before he signed his enlistment form. 'The first experience of the volunteer for active service, preceding even his "attestation",[3] was his medical examination,' as Colonel A.G. Butler, the official medical historian of the war, later wrote.[19]

---

[2] Britain declared war at 11.00pm on 3 August, however, because Eastern Australian Time was 10 hours ahead of British time, the declaration in Australia came at 9.00 am on 4 August.

[3] The recruitment form signed by all aspiring AIF members was called the 'Attestation Form'.

The medical officers of the AAMC, who usually conducted the examinations, in all probability swiftly rejected those displaying VD symptoms. Many AAMC medical officers shared the prevailing moralistic community views about VD and prejudice against the VD-infected, however, they had to remain clinically objective in managing VD cases. One leader of the profession in Melbourne, Dr (later Sir) James Barrett, stated the situation nicely in 'Venereal Diseases', an article he published in the *MJA* in March 1914:

> The extent of the evil [of VD] is obvious to everyone who inquires about it; and the question arises—What can we do? ... As men of trained intelligence, our sympathies lie entirely with the moralists, and that as citizens we should always be glad to take our part in any moral campaign. As physicians, however, I think we have one duty, and one duty alone, and that is the prevention and treatment of disease.[20]

VD-infected recruits who might have escaped detection at the pre-attestation examination faced a second screening soon afterwards, when they had gone into the training camps established on the outskirts of the state capital cities. Soon after the enlistees began moving into the camps, they were medically examined again because on 20

August 1914 the Surgeon General, William Daniel Campbell Williams, ordered that 'all recruits arriving in camp should be re-examined'.[21] Anyone found to be suffering from VD, was discharged from the AIF.[22]

How many would-be AIF members were rejected or soon discharged because of VD infection is uncertain, because the statistics have not survived. Butler published figures hinting at the scale of the problem. In his volume of clinical studies and statistics, *Special Problems and Services*, he included a table indicating that of a total of 416,809 men who enlisted,[4] 33,906 were discharged as medically unfit.[23]

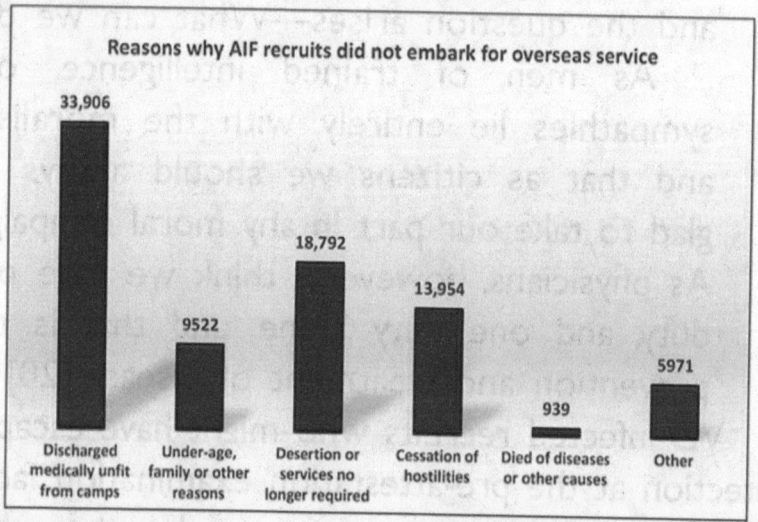

Figure 2.1. Reasons why AIF recruits did not embark for overseas service (A.G. Butler, The Australian Army Medical

---

[4] In addition, 2861 women also enlisted in the Australian Army Nursing Service.

Services in the War of 1914-1918, Vol.3, Special Problems and Services, p.882).

The 33,906 was the largest group among the 83,064 recruits who did not depart for service abroad.[24] Figure 2.1 shows the number of recruits in each of the main categories precluding AIF service. The proportion of VD-infected recruits is unknown because Butler's figures did not give such fine-grained detail. The 33,906 'discharged medically unfit from camps', however, probably included many who were VD-infected.

The other group likely to have included VD sufferers was the second largest, the 18,792 soldiers in the 'Desertion or services no longer required' group. 'Services no longer required' is a phrase needing some qualification. According to Butler, it was 'a very valuable power ... for removing officers or men from the [Army] without stating a reason'.[25] How many of those 'no longer required' were VD sufferers is unknown, but given the prevailing moralistic attitude of the Army towards VD, one might infer that some recruits were discharged because they were VD-infected and accordingly regarded as unsuitable.

Rejection or discharge because of VD did not necessarily mean that an aspiring recruit could never enlist in the AIF. Enlistment under another name and when the recruit was no longer displaying physical symptoms of VD infection was an alternative route into the AIF. In such cases, the VD-infected recruit would be hospitalised and treated, either in Australia or after he had been shipped overseas. The Army was probably aware of this likelihood, because according to Butler 'multiple enlistments were common among certain classes of men who were unfit or for other reasons resorted to impersonation or misstatements at enrolments'.[26]

Eliminating and discharging the VD-infected in the early weeks of recruitment for the AIF was but the beginning of the Army's experience of VD in World War I, however. This was merely the first skirmish in a long-running battle.

One immediate difficulty was that the recruit who had been accepted as VD-free at the time of his initial medical examinations could become infected when he took leave. A pattern of behaviour leading to infection soon emerged. It was that of the off-duty soldier with money in his pocket, time on his hands, unconstrained by the usual home environment, enjoying a few drinks with friends in a bar, and an act of bravado in showing his mates he was a 'real man' by finding a prostitute. Most often, the consequence was VD infection.

This stereotypical pattern became familiar to the AAMC medical officers who had to manage the VD cases.

Figure 2.2: The Isolation Hospital at the Broadmeadows Army Camp, World War I, possibly 1914-15 (AWM H18401). Little is known about this hospital, which was probably short-lived because it is not mentioned in A.G. Butler's three-volume medical history of the war. It was probably a secure section of a larger camp hospital at Broadmeadows, established to manage contagious diseases such as measles, influenza, tuberculosis, meningitis and VD until specialised infectious diseases hospitals could be established elsewhere. In the case of VD, the patients were sent to the Langwarrin Camp Hospital, near Frankston, south of Melbourne, which opened in March 1915.

That the Army would have to treat its VD-infected recruits rather than expel them soon became clear. If treatment for VD was not given, as it was for other infectious diseases, the Army might never have reached its initial AIF recruitment and retention target of 20,000 soldiers. During 1915 the Army seems to have accepted the reality that a proportion of its recruits would always be VD sufferers and that if it wished to retain the AIF at full strength, it must treat those afflicted with VD.

Tacit acknowledgement of the need to treat VD-infected recruits was the establishment of specialised VD hospitals in each of the mainland states during 1915-1916 (Table 2.1).[27]

Table 2.1 -**Army hospitals established in Australia to treat VD-infected soldiers**

State	Hospital	Date opened
Victoria	Langwarrin Camp Hospital	13 March 1915
New South Wales	Milson Island	14 October 1915
South Australia	Torrens Island	15 October 1915
Western Australia	VD Compound, Blackboy Hill Camp	uncertain (closed 19 December 1916)
Western Australia	Rockingham Camp Hospital	19 December 1916
Queensland	Lytton Camp Compound	14 July 1916

Source: A.G. Butler, The Australian Army Medical Services, Vol.3, Special Problems and Services, Table 12, p.882.

Most of these hospitals were situated at what were then remote locations outside the capital cities and well away from suburbia and nearby towns. The isolation, presumably, was thought appropriate for such a shameful condition as VD. It also minimised the chances of the patients passing on their infections to the civilian population.[28]

How serious, then, was the situation in relation to VD infection? Was there really an epidemic, as influential medical opinion suggested?

If the *MJA* was to be believed, there certainly was. Editorials, correspondence and articles in the journal continued alluding to the apparently high incidence of VD in the Army camps in Australia and especially in Egypt.

In May 1916, for example, the journal ran a leading article by Dr Richard Arthur MD, a recent Minister for Health in New South Wales with an interest in venereology.[29] The article was based on a lecture Arthur had delivered to AIF officers in Sydney. Looking back on recruitment for the AIF during 1914 and 1915, he told the officers they were 'confronted with a tremendous problem in military efficiency by the prevalence of venereal diseases among the recruits'.[30] He went on to say that 'it [was] difficult to over-estimate the injury that is being done to the Australian Imperial Force, both in Australia and in Egypt from this cause' because 'numbers of men have been either temporarily or permanently disabled by syphilis and gonorrhoea'.[31] There were, he pointed out, both immediate economic and longterm socio-medical dimensions to the problem. Thus, on the one hand 'the cost to the Commonwealth ... amount[ed] to a huge sum', and on the other hand, a 'further lamentable aspect' was that 'men from the backblocks of Australia, who, had there been no war, would never have become infected, [would] now return home and carry infection far and wide, with disastrous results to the next generation'.[32]

Similar sentiments had already been expressed in the *MJA* editorials. In February 1915, for example, the journal editorialised on 'The Spread of Syphilis'. Lambasting the VD-infected soldiers sent home from the training camps in Egypt, the editorial claimed that 'our men who volunteered to fight for their country are now returning, not wounded but invalided by syphilis'.[33] With a sense of imperial outrage, it continued:

> These men, instead of serving their country in a useful manner, and instead of making sacrifices which, when made, lend splendour to the Empire on which the sun never sets, have wasted their country's money, have sullied their country's name, and are, or might be but for the foresight of those in power, a disgraceful danger to the welfare of the population at home.[34]

As things turned out, the situation might not have been quite as dire as the *MJA* would have its readers believe. The reason for thinking so is that the VD infection rates in Army camps in Australia remained at much the same level—at between three and four per cent of those in camp. Table 2.2 indicates the number of VD cases and their proportion of Army camp strength in Australia for the two years 1915-16 and 1916-17.[35]

Table 2.2 - Hospital admissions of VD cases in Army camps in Australia, 1915-16 and 1916-17

	Camp strength	Number of VD cases	Proportion of total camp strength
1915–16	208,870	6796	3.3%
1916–17	118,440	4434	3.7%

Source: A.G. Butler, The Australian Army Medical Services, Vol.3, Special Problems and Services, Table 12, pp.886-7.

Butler did not provide figures for 1914 because they were unavailable to him, but he believed that the proportions for the years 1915 to 1917 'may be held fairly to reflect that for the whole period of the war'.[36] We may consequently extrapolate, estimating the number of VD cases in the camps in Australia in 1914. According to Butler, the average strength in the camps August to December 1914 was 14,094.[37] If the VD hospitalisations were somewhere between 3.3 and 3.7 per cent of camp strength, the number of soldiers hospitalised for VD in Australia during August to December 1914 would have been a minimum of about 460 and a maximum of about 530, with a median figure of 495.

Although at any one time the hospitalised VD-infected soldiers were a relatively small percentage of the Army camp residents, VD was the second most common cause of hospitalisation in the Army camps in Australia in 1915-16 after influenza. In that 12-month period, influenza accounted for 13,999 out of a total of 52,657 hospitalisations or almost 27 percent of all hospital admissions; VD was responsible for almost 13 per cent of admissions. The other four most common hospitalisations were for measles (5246 cases, 10 per cent), accidental injuries (5 per cent), tonsillitis (3 per cent) and diseases of the respiratory system (2.7 per cent).[38] Despite such statistics the health of recruits in the training camps remained 'in general good'.[39]

The problem with the VD infection rates was not so much the sheer volume of VD cases but rather the cost in terms of 'military efficiency', as argued by Arthur in the *MJA*. This point may be appreciated through reference to the number of VD hospitalisations in Table 2.2 plus the extrapolated number for 1914—a total of 11,725 cases. How many lost 'man-years' did that many hospitalisations represent? A notional figure is possible, given later average hospitalisation duration rates at the AIF's VD treatment centres in Egypt. During the 16-month period December 1914 to March 1916, the average duration of hospitalisation for VD was 35 days.[40]

Extrapolating again, and assuming the 11,725 hospitalisations in the Australian camps, we may calculate that the lost 'man-years' would have been:

11,725 cases x 35 days each = 410,375 days = 1152 years. That many 'man-years' would represent a sizeable diminution in the operational capability of any army.

4. Discipline in the AIF in Egypt, 1914-15

The first contingent of the AIF despatched for overseas service comprised the 1st Australian Division. Totalling some 18,000 troops and accompanied by two New Zealand divisions, the 1st Division departed Albany, Western Australia, in a great fleet early on the morning of 1 November 1914. The fleet sailed in convoy, 42 ships in all, bound for Alexandria where the troops would disembark for training in Egypt because accommodation was unavailable in Britain, the original destination.[41] The troops of the convoy began arriving in Alexandria on 3 December. That same morning the first of them, the 5th Battalion, moved by rail to Cairo, which they reached that evening. They were then marched to a large, hastily established camp at Mena, 16 kilometres from Cairo, west of the Nile River and alongside the Giza pyramids. There 'the 5th Battalion rolled itself in its grey blankets under the moon and slept'.[42] The AIF would spend the next four-and-a-half months training at the Mena Camp. Though they did not know it yet, they would fight in the Gallipoli campaign, which began on 25 April 1915.

In the months the AIF spent training at Mena, the Australian soldiers gained a reputation for being boisterous and unruly. They were variously accused of being 'indifferent to military authority', 'lacking in respect for military rank', 'likely to refuse to salute officers', 'sloppy in dress', and 'prone to misbehaviour and public drunkenness during leave'. To this, 'sexually adventurous' could be added. British officers in particular regarded the Australians as ill-disciplined colonial riffraff.[43]

The official war historian, Charles Edwin Woodrow Bean, strove to excuse the Australians' various peccadilloes in Egypt. He began his exculpation by emphasising the point that the AIF comprised mostly citizen soldiers.[44] Bean pointed out that the troops 'had been cooped up for nearly two months in transports [troopships] without leave at any port', after which 'straight from that voyage there were poured on to the desert round Cairo twenty thousand Australians'.[45] He argued, pragmatically if not quite correctly, that their misbehaviour in Cairo was little more than the larrikin exuberance of young men away from home on an overseas adventure. 'They had money,' he wrote, 'the youngsters among them were bursting with high spirits, ready for any adventure, reckless of the cost.'[46]

Further, few recreational amenities were available in Cairo and none out in the desert at Mena Camp. The Australians had little to do off-duty. The bustle, bars and bazaars of Cairo beckoned. 'To many a young Australian this city seemed a place for unlimited holiday,' Bean observed.[47] Shifting the blame to unscrupulous local inhabitants, he argued that:

> ...proprietors of the lower cafés ... pressed upon the newcomers drinks amounting to poison, and natives along the roads sold them stuff of unheard-of vileness. Touts led them to 'amusements' descending to any degree of filth ... Many a youngster plunged into excitement which seemed only too sordid when the blood cooled ... Much of this behaviour was little more than high spirits. The trams constantly went into Cairo

[from Mena Camp] crowded on footboard and roof with many more soldiers than had leave to go.[48]

Not even a Charles Bean could excuse the criminal element within the AIF, however. By the end of 1914, Bean wrote, worrying signs of insubordination and criminality had emerged within the AIF in Egypt—'heavy drinking, desertion, attacks upon natives, in some instances robbery'.[49]

In early January 1915 General Sir William Birdwood,[5] the British commander of the ANZAC forces, wrote to the AIF through its Australian commander, Major General Sir William Throsby Bridges, appealing to the troops not to let their country's reputation suffer at the hands of a small minority. The letter, printed and distributed to the troops, advised them that 'Cairo is full of temptations' and that 'the worst of it is that Cairo is full of some of the most unscrupulous people in the world, who are only too anxious

---

[5] General Sir William Birdwood (later Field Marshal and Baron Birdwood of Anzac and Totnes, 1865—1951) was the British Army officer who commanded the Australian and New Zealand Army Corps—the Anzacs—in Egypt, during the Gallipoli campaign and later at the Western Front in Europe.

to do all they can to entice our boys into the worst of places'. It then argued:

> There is no possibility of our doing ourselves full justice unless every one of us is absolutely physically fit, and this no man can possibly do if he allows himself to become sodden with drink or rotten from women—and unless he is doing his best to keep himself efficient he is swindling the Government which has sent him to represent it and fight for it.[50]

At this time some 300 Australians were absent without leave in Egypt and were technically 'deserters'. Matters had come 'to a point when discipline in the AIF must either be upheld or abandoned' and so Bridges took drastic action. He sent the worst offenders back to Australia for discharge from the Army. Following this judicious weeding-out of offenders, repatriation and subsequent discharge remained 'the most dreaded instrument of discipline among Australian soldiers'.[51]

5. VD within the AIF in Egypt before the Gallipoli campaign

Bean, who had prudish views on sex, was one historian who was unlikely to allude to the sexual adventures of the Anzacs in Egypt in any detail, nor to the inevitable consequence of time lost and resources expended by the VD-infected having to be treated. On the other hand, as official medical historian, Butler wrote a whole chapter on the consequences of VD infections for the AIF. His emphasis, however, was always the epidemiology of VD and the Army's efforts to contain it.

Almost inevitably, after arriving at the Mena Camp large numbers of AIF gravitated to the bars and brothels of Cairo at the first opportunity. Many of these were situated in a seedy 'red-light' area in a series of streets and alleyways in the city's Haret-el-Wasser precinct. The AIF called it the 'Wozzer', alternatively spelt 'Wazzir'.

Within a fortnight of the AIF's arrival at the Mena Camp, 'a startling outburst of venereal disease occurred'.[52] According to Butler, the outbreak was the one 'disquieting' aspect of the AIF's general health, which otherwise remained good during the first weeks at the camp. Butler later wrote that during the AIF's first four months in Egypt, December 1914 to April 1915, the VD outbreak 'incapacitated over 2,000 men and sent 3 per cent of the force "constantly sick"'.[53]

At first the VD-infected troops were treated at No.2 Australian General Hospital (2 AGH) within the camp. This hospital comprised 35 marquees for general cases and another seven for 'isolation' cases. 2 AGH filled quickly, mainly with cases of influenza, measles and gastric conditions but also with VD patients. By the end of December 1914 the hospital was overflowing with 612 patients under treatment. After that, the additional sick were 'dammed back' in the 'field units'—the field ambulances attached to the various AIF brigades—where they continued accumulating. The VD cases had begun clogging the treatment centres, placing unwanted strain on the AIF's medical facilities.[54]

Some relief came with the arrival of 2 ASH at the Mena Camp on 22 January 1915. It opened for business four days later on 26 January, when the first 151 patients were admitted. Situated adjacent to 2 AGH, 2 ASH became the Mena Camp's VD hospital. By 30 January 2 ASH was full, with 300 patients under treatment and another 150 in the field ambulances awaiting admission.[55]

Figure 2.3: No.2 Australian General Hospital, Mena Camp, Egypt, in January 1915, about a month after it opened. It could not handle the influx of cases of infectious disease and so that month a separate VD hospital, No.2 Australian Stationary Hospital, was established adjacent to it (AWM H12179).

2 ASH, in contemporary parlance, was a 'lock-hospital'; its patients were compulsorily detained within a compound surrounded by high fencing and locked gates, with an armed guard posted to patrol the perimeter and prevent escape. Even though they were not criminals, the 2 ASH inmates were made to feel as if they were. They were forced to wear a white armband on the right sleeve of their uniforms to indicate who and what they were. The guards watching over them were instructed not to speak to them, not to allow them visitors and not to let them receive food or articles from outside. According to Butler, this was 'fierce' and 'deplorable' discipline.[56]

These measures both shocked and shamed the patients, who had previously experienced a relaxed treatment regimen in 2 AGH and the field ambulances.[57] Butler, who doubted the efficacy of the lock-hospital principle, described the shift to the harsher regimen in these terms:

> The free and easy conditions under which treatment in the lines had been carried out were replaced by a relentless quarantine quite unrelated to any actual risk of transmission. The change was, indeed, a terribly drastic one, and, while the earlier laxity may have failed to inculcate a salutary fear, the new stringency (which accorded with that in all such hospitals at this period of the war) did not conduce to the restoration of self-respect.[58]

Despite that, Butler believed 'the professional treatment of this most difficult class of case ... was carried out with sympathy and skill'.[59]

Butler might not have appreciated all the reasons why many VD patients were obstreperous. The treatment regimen was horrendous by present-day standards. The painful and toxic treatments for VD, long confinement in lock-hospitals and the loss of pay while being treated prompted many soldiers to conceal their infections.

Various contemporary observers wrote accounts of the nexus between alcohol consumption, prostitution and VD infection among the AIF troops in Egypt, and especially in Cairo. Among the first to do so was Major Bernhard Zwar, a 38-year-old AAMC officer from South Australia serving with 2 ASH. Zwar was in charge of one of its two sections. He wrote an account of the hospital's work from the time it arrived in Egypt in mid-January 1915 until it embarked for the Gallipoli campaign three months later.[60] After the war he published this material as an article in the *MJA* under the title 'The Army Medical Service and the prevention of venereal disease'.[61]

Major Zwar's report on the work of 2 ASH provides a window into the problems that VD infections posed for the AIF. He started his account by pointing out that 2 ASH arrived in Egypt not knowing that it would become the VD hospital for the Mena Camp. The Army Medical Service (AMS), he said, had 'failed in regard to venereal disease' through lack of foresight.[62] The AMS had not apparently realised that the VD infection rate during the AIF's first weeks in Egypt would be 'unduly high'. He then showed how the rate had increased. The hospital had been opened for 200 patients but by the time it was closed nine weeks later on 1 April, prior to deployment to Mudros on the island of Lemnos for the Gallipoli campaign, patient numbers had trebled. New marquees had to be added to accommodate the increasing numbers. Figure 2.4 illustrates the growth in patient numbers 26 January to 1 April 1915.[63]

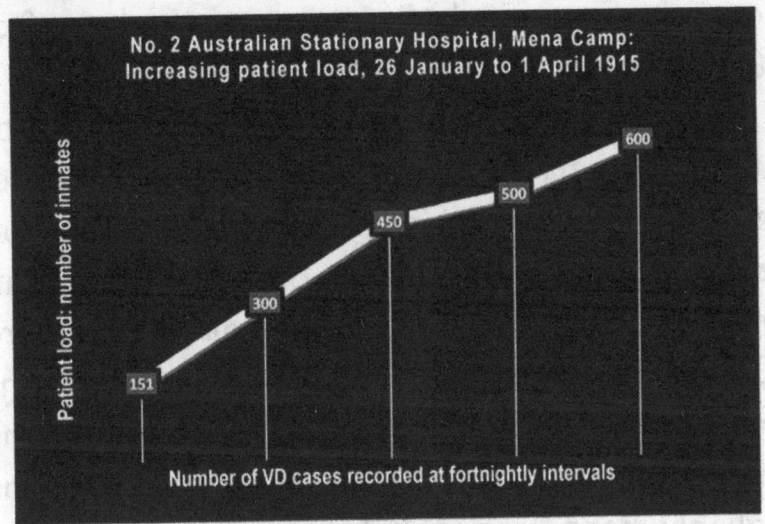

Figure 2.4: VD cases at 2 ASH, 26 January to 1 April 1915 (Zwar, 'The Army Medical Service and the prevention of venereal disease', Medical Journal of Australia, 5 July 1919, pp.1-7).

The patients who were inmates of 2 ASH were not the only VD sufferers being treated. More were being tended to elsewhere in other hospitals and regimental medical units, while those convalescing and on 'light duties' after finishing their courses of treatment were additional to those being treated. Zwar estimated that in the Mena Camp 'between 600 and 800 were constantly off from duty on account of venereal infection' during the months before the Gallipoli campaign. Other camps in Egypt also 'had their venereal diseases hospitals', for which Zwar had no statistics but wrote that 'it was estimated that the invalidity or "constantly sick" rate on account of venereal disease amounted to from 4% to 5%' of AIF strength'.[64]

Zwar also provided information about the patients he had treated in 2 ASH. 'The great majority of these patients were youths,' he wrote, 'some still in their teens, others in the early twenties.' Most, 83 per cent, had not suffered VD before. They told him 'that they had not previously incurred the risk of infection, nor had they known of the risk'.[65] That is, they had probably been virgins before being infected and had been unaware that their sexual adventure might result in VD. Most, but not all, were 'innocents abroad'! Those who were not, the 17 per cent, knew what risks they were running because they had all previously contracted VD. Of those fifty, 42 admitted one previous infection, four admitted two, one admitted five, two admitted 10 and one owned up to no fewer than 12 earlier infections.[66] More than half of the VD patients in 2 ASH told Zwar 'they had been under the influence of alcohol at the time infection was incurred'. A surprising 88 per cent

(265) claimed they had 'employed preventive measures'.[67]

What the 'preventive measures' might have been is uncertain, but they were obviously ineffective. Some medical officers recommended washing the genitalia with medicinal soap post-intercourse, but that was not of much use in preventing VD, especially if not done immediately after intercourse.[68] Probably just as effective was the 'old soldier's trick' of urinating into the cupped hands post-coitus then washing the penis with that. Australians in Vietnam were still using that method more than 50 years later.[69]

Unlike Butler, Zwar regarded the 'lock-hospital' conditions at 2 ASH as beneficial for the inmates. Confinement in the hospital during treatment enabled them to enjoy 'an enforced rest'. He thought this assisted in the treatment of gonorrhoea and helped prevent gonorrhoeal complications'.[70]

As a result of his experience in treating VD cases, Major Zwar thought through the socio-medical issues involved in preventing infection. By its very nature the AIF, he believed, had been partly responsible for the VD situation that had developed in Egypt because it had been 'a rapidly organised force of mainly untrained men and officers'. Now that VD had become a problem, he believed the AIF should adopt a program of action against VD incorporating three aims: first, avoidance of risk of infection; second, the use of prophylactic measures; and third, efficient treatment. For such a program to be effective, every AIF officer should 'recognise the tremendous importance of the prevention of venereal disease in the Army, and should be trained to help in the achievement of that object'.[71]

Such a program would require the AMS to be more proactive in helping the troops avoid becoming VD-infected. Zwar accordingly proposed a seven-point plan of measures he thought the AMS should implement. This entailed a commitment to:

1. preventing VD among AIF troops
2. educating all officers and men about the risks and consequences of VD
3. instructing both officers and men in sex hygiene
4. promoting the need for personal hygiene
5. providing healthy amusements and recreations for the troops
6. controlling the quality and sale of alcoholic liquor to the troops
7. suppressing 'vice' (the sex trade).[72]

A plan of this kind was subsequently adopted and became the basis for managing VD during the rest of the war.

Among Zwar's other beliefs was that abstention from sexual intercourse was the best safeguard against VD infection. 'It is a fact that continence is not harmful to health,' he wrote, 'that it is not unmanly, but that, on the contrary, the quality of self-restraint that is necessary to carry it out, is the quality that distinguishes the manly from the unmanly'. If the AIF troops resisted the temptations of places like the 'Wozzer' and could eschew the sexual adventures available there, 'venereal disease [would be] more certainly preventable than any other preventable disease'.[73] This, too, was an idea strongly promoted in subsequent AMS-AIF campaigns against VD. It was, however, a vain and naïve hope because many AIF soldiers would or could not commit themselves to 'continence'.

6. Stern measures: forfeiture of pay and repatriation to Australia

In the meantime, the AIF and AMS adopted other, sterner means for managing the outbreak of VD in Egypt. The first was to stop the pay of VD-infected soldiers. At the end of January 1915 Bridges ordered that the pay of men with

VD be halted for the period they were absent from duty undergoing treatment. It was a decision supported by the Australian Government.[74] It was also in line with the sentiments that General Birdwood had expressed in his circular letter to the Anzacs earlier that month. Troops who contracted VD, Birdwood argued, were 'swindling [their] Government'.

This was a harsh punitive measure!

First, the financial penalty was severe, because a soldier receiving the average 35-day course of treatment remained unpaid for five weeks, and he could never recover the wages foregone. Second, the stopping of pay encouraged the VD-afflicted to try to conceal their infection to avoid being hospitalised. Third, and probably not immediately obvious, was the effect on the VD sufferers' families, who often depended on regular remittances from the soldiers' pay. Where that was the case, the family as well as the VD sufferer was punished. Fourth, it embarrassed and shamed the VD-infected, who had to try explaining to friends and relatives why they were no longer being paid.

Fifth, if the soldier's family suddenly stopped receiving payments, that was effectively an open declaration by the Army that he was VD-infected. Discovery of infection and subsequent treatment therefore incurred prohibitive social as well as monetary costs.

The other drastic measure was one instigated by the AIF's Director of Medical Services (DMS), Colonel Neville Reginald Howse VC,[6] and subsequently approved by the Minister for Defence, Senator George Pearce. This was to return to Australia 'all cases of venereal disease' to relieve pressure on the Army hospitals in Egypt, mainly 2 ASH at the Mena Camp and No.1 Australian General Hospital (1 AGH) at Heliopolis, a north-eastern suburb of Cairo, each of which were filled beyond capacity.[75] The first 16 VD patients were repatriated aboard the *Ulysses* on 20 March 1915. They were most likely 'trouble-makers' of whom the AIF commanders wished to rid themselves.[76] On 26 March another 450, a mixed group of Australian and New Zealand VD patients, were sent to Malta where there was apparently spare hospital space.[77] A further 261 went back to Australia aboard the *Ceramic* on 4 May, by which time

---

6 Colonel Howse (1863-1930) was later promoted to Major General. He was knighted at the end of the war and subsequently headed the AMS as Director General of Medical Services (DGMS). His VC was awarded for bravery under fire at Vredefort during the Boer (South African) War in 1900.

seriously wounded troops from the Gallipoli campaign were being returned to Egypt for hospitalisation, adding yet more pressure on the hospitals.[78]

Other reasons for sending the VD-infected home were enumerated by Sir James Barrett in a book he published at the end of the war, *The Australian Army Medical Corps in Egypt*. According to Barrett:

> In Egypt they were useless as soldiers, whether suffering from gonorrhoea or syphilis. They required a large number of medical men and attendants to take care of them. They knew they had disgraced themselves and were a source of trouble to everyone concerned. On shipboard they could not get into trouble. They were more likely to be cured [in Australia], and could then be returned to Egypt, and if not cured could be treated in Australia at leisure ... Furthermore the business of those conducting the campaign [in the Middle East] was to wage a successful war, and to keep the base as free from encumbrance as possible.[79]

The repatriated VD sufferers were sent to the Langwarrin isolation and detention camp 56 kilometres south of Melbourne, a secure facility established in March 1915 for the express purpose of treating VD-infected soldiers.[80] During 1915 a total of 1474 VD-infected troops were returned to Australia.[81] Unless they somehow managed to escape, they went to Langwarrin.

Figure 2.5: Entrance to the Langwarrin Venereal Diseases Hospital, 1917 (Museums Victoria photograph MM 140028, reproduced with permission).

Those within the AIF arguing against repatriation feared that the returning VD sufferers would spread their diseases, especially if they absconded from Langwarrin.[82] In Australia, opposition to repatriation was led by 'morals crusaders', who were often leading members of the major Protestant denominations. They usually had links with organisations that sprang up to defend traditional community values. The latter included groups such as the Australasian Temperance Society, the Council for Civic and Moral Advancement, and the 'Strength of Empire' movement.[83] Opposed to such groups were various patriotic associations, the leading one being the Returned Soldiers' and Sailors' Imperial League of Australia (RSL). From its inception in 1916, the RSL regarded the defence of the AIF's reputation as a sacred trust. Any imputation that the AIF might be riddled with VD would accordingly be resisted strenuously.[84]

Despite the controversy, the repatriation of VD sufferers would continue as needs and circumstances required. Eventually the AMS and AIF realised that repatriation was prejudicial to discipline. For example, it was feared that malingerers might deliberately contract VD to ensure that they were sent home.

7. The case of one individual returnee

The pathos of individual cases among the repatriated troops is revealed in the case of Private 'ABC', a 29-year old tradesman from Rockdale, Sydney. ABC had enlisted in the AIF on 10 December 1914. Three months later, on 11 February 1915, he embarked for overseas service with reinforcements for the 1st Battalion.

On 19 April, suffering from gonorrhoea after only four or five weeks in Egypt, he was admitted to the VD detention and isolation hospital at Abbassia near Cairo. Following 16 days in hospital, ABC was shipped back to Australia aboard the troopship *Ceramic*.[85]

On arrival in Melbourne on 25 May, ABC was sent to the Langwarrin VD Hospital. Discharged from there on 2 June, he was posted to the Broadmeadows camp.[86] Eventually he was returned to Sydney, where he was medically examined by an Army doctor. During the examination he complained of neuritis in his right arm. He was then ordered to appear before a medical board on 24 September.[87] The board recommended that he be discharged as medically unfit. The board determined that most likely the neuritis was caused by gonorrhoea and that the condition was 'probably' being aggravated by ABC's 'intemperance' and 'misconduct'.[88]

ABC was formally discharged from the AIF on 18 October 1915.[89] He died by drowning less than three weeks later, on 6 November.[90] His place of death was The Gap at Watson's Bay—a notorious suicide site. The location and manner of ABC's death leave little doubt that he took his own life. He was as much a victim of the war as any of his erstwhile comrades killed in action.

What made ABC's experience of VD even more sorrowful was the way in which his wife learned of it. After he had been returned to Australia, she heard that he had been sent home with pneumonia. She then caught the train to Melbourne with her two small sons, which, she later claimed, cost her £110, a sum she could 'ill afford'.[91] When she arrived at Broadmeadows a few days after her husband had been sent there, she was not allowed to see him. The staff officer who interviewed her showed her a paper on which 'Venereal Disease' was written. He asked her if she knew what that meant. When she replied that she did not, he told her that it was not for him to explain the meaning to her.

After ABC's wife returned to Sydney, she wrote to the military authorities seeking further information about her husband. She requested that the reasons for his continued detention at Broadmeadows be given to her in writing. She wanted that because 'his father and mother will not believe me when I tell the truth about it and what [is] more he will dyney [deny] that anything like that was the matter with him'.[92]

Whether or not Mrs ABC received the letter she requested is unknown. The only surviving official note in relation to her case is a request of the Adjutant General by the captain in charge of personnel records, asking 'whether in this and other similar applications the nature of the disease is to be communicated to the wife'.[93]

The reader might imagine what a homecoming awaited ABC in Sydney. Perhaps the shame of facing his wife, sons and parents, and of trying to explain to them why he had fallen short of their expectations was a burden too great for him to bear. They must have forgiven him, however, for a year to the day after his death they published loving 'In Memoriam' notices in *The Sydney Morning Herald*.[94]

For many of those sent home, the humiliation probably lasted a lifetime. They knew that many among their former comrades regarded them as pariahs. Whatever counselling they received, usually from chaplains and medical officers, was moralistic in tone. They were reminded that they were a disappointment to the AIF and that they risked passing on their diseases to their wives and unborn children. They had difficulty in explaining to their families and friends why they had come home early and were being held in close confinement. And perhaps they felt guilty that so many of their comrades were dying in a war they, too, should have been helping to fight.[95]

8. The 'Battle of the Wazzir'

Most historians of the AIF make obligatory reference to a notorious riot by Anzacs in Cairo—the so-called 'Battle of Wazzir'. The 'battle' actually consisted of two separate riots four months apart. Both involved Australian and New Zealand troops. The first erupted on Good Friday 2 April 1915 and the second on 31 July.

That Bean was not greatly perturbed by the 'battle' can be seen in the way he dealt with it, consigning it to a footnote—albeit half a page long—in his official history. He conceded that the two riots were 'not heroic' but downplayed them as being little more serious than a university 'rag'.[96] They certainly did more damage than that.

What essentially happened was that a crowd of up to 400 soldiers caused disturbances in the Wazzir after some of them had tried to extort money from the brothel-keepers and prostitutes, whom they blamed for the VD they had contracted there. In accordance with Army practice, their pay had been stopped while they had undergone treatment, and so they wanted compensation. On each occasion large crowds of other soldiers gathered, but mainly as onlookers. Property damage occurred and further destruction followed when fires were lit. On both occasions the disturbances ended when troops with fixed bayonets were brought in to disperse the crowds. Several dozen troops received minor injuries. Damages payments were subsequently paid by the Australian and New Zealand governments after the first riot, and by the Australian Government alone after the second.[97]

For critics of Australian soldiers, the Wazzir riots confirmed their every prejudice against the AIF, demonstrating its lack of discipline. For morals crusaders, it probably convinced them that debauchery was inevitable when liquor and vice went hand in hand. For the crowds of onlookers, it possibly provided an entertaining diversion from the tedium of military training in the desert. For the Wazzir shopkeepers and residents, it demonstrated that AIF troops were temperamental, violent, destructive louts. And for the perpetrators, it could well have been their last excitement before being thrown into real battles at Gallipoli, against foes who could not be so easily intimidated.

Figure 2.6: Aftermath of the 'Battle of Wazzir' in Cairo's red-light area on 2 April 1915 (AWM PS 1373).

9. Abbassia Detention Barracks

2 ASH was withdrawn from the VD hospital at the Mena Camp on 7 March 1915. This was to enable 2 ASH to be deployed to Lemnos in readiness for the Gallipoli campaign and there revert to its intended role. The Mena VD hospital was then conducted by a British unit, the 3/1st East Lancashire Field Ambulance, until the facility was closed about four weeks later, on 1 April.[98]

After the closure of the Mena Camp VD facility, the 'dregs' remaining in it—Butler's description—were sent to the Abbassia Detention

Barracks within the Army's Abbassia compound on the north-eastern outskirts of Cairo. A tented VD treatment facility was established within the barracks. This remained the AIF's VD 'hospital' in Egypt for the next 10 months, until No.1 Australian Dermatological Hospital (1 ADH) arrived in Cairo in January 1916.[99]

Figure 2.7: Venereal Diseases Hospital, Abbassia Detention Centre, Cairo, c. January 1916 (J.W. Barrett and P.E. Deane, The Australian Army Medical Corps in Egypt).

A casual observer might have expected that the period April 1915 to January 1916 would be relatively quiet in the hospital compound of Abbassia Detention Barracks. After all, the bulk of the AIF had been deployed to Gallipoli and was fighting a desperate, bloody campaign there, and those evacuated from Gallipoli on 18-20

December arrived back in Egypt in dribs and drabs during late December and early January.

This 10-month interlude afforded little respite, however. Reinforcements continued arriving from Australia and they had to be trained at Mena and other camps before being sent to Gallipoli. Like those who had passed through the camps before them, the newcomers fell prey to the temptations of Cairo's fleshpots. Butler wrote that 'of all diseases occurring in camps ... venereal infections were again the most difficult to prevent, the most troublesome to treat, and the most productive of absence from duty'.[100]

Because of staff shortages, the VD sufferers received little treatment. Most AMS personnel were preoccupied with the Gallipoli campaign and its heavy toll of wounded, and so only a 'scratch staff' was available to tend patients in the hospital compound. For the six months April to October 1915, the VD patients were expected to treat themselves under staff supervision.[101] In October 1915 their chances of more effective treatment improved because an 'improvised' VD unit replaced the 'scratch staff' arrangement. This unit provided treatment for the three months or so before being replaced by 1 ADH in late January 1916.[102]

In the meantime, the numbers of soldiers under treatment for VD multiplied alarmingly.

The number rose from 183 in October 1915 to 607 in January 1916, 1187 in February then 1493 in March—an eightfold increase. Figure 2.8 emonstrates the surge in VD cases.[103]

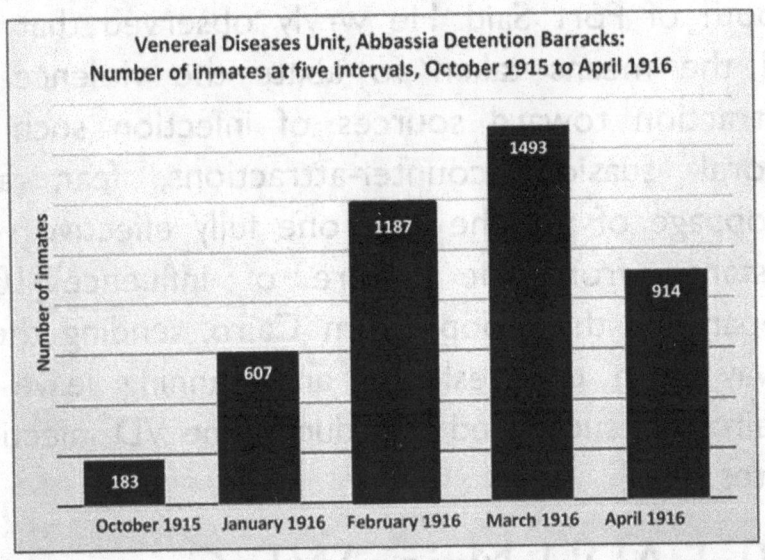

Figure 2.8: VD cases at the Venereal Diseases Unit, Abbassia Detention Barracks, October 1915 to April 1916 (A.G. Butler, The Australian Army Medical Services in the War of 1914-1918, Vol.1, The Gallipoli Campaign).

The great increases January to March 1916 may be explained by the return to Egypt of the Gallipoli veterans plus the arrival of new reinforcements to form additional AIF divisions. The official historian, Butler, regarded the latter as by far the more important factor. But why was there a 39 per cent fall, from 1493 to 914 cases, from March to April?

According to Butler, the answer lay in the removal of the main training camp for AIF reinforcements from Cairo to Tel El Kebir, 110 kilometres to the north-east and 75 kilometres south of Port Said. He wryly observed that 'of all the means taken to abate the violence of attraction toward sources of infection such as moral suasion, counter-attractions, fear, and stoppage of pay, the only one fully effective was distance from the sphere of influence'.[104] Separating the troops from Cairo, sending them away from the fleshpots and banning leave in Cairo had succeeded in reducing the VD infection rates.[105]

10. 1 ADH, Major W.E. Grigor and Colonel N.R. Howse

The relocation of the reinforcements' training camp to Tel El Kebir followed correspondence from the AIF's DMS, Colonel Howse, to General Birdwood. As the AIF's chief medical officer, Howse was continually briefed about VD infection rates by the venereologists of the AMS. In early February 1916 he received a report from the commanding officer (CO) of the recently arrived 1 ADH, Major William Ernest Grigor, on conditions in the VD unit of the Abbassia Detention Barracks. Within a week of his arrival at Abbassia, Grigor wrote to draw Howse's attention to the 'extremely overcrowded state' of the VD unit.[106] 'Patients are simply packed together,' he wrote.[107] He said the unit had been considered overcrowded when it held 800 patients, but he now had 1156 patients as well as 140 staff members to accommodate.[108]

Grigor pointed out to Howse that the new admissions to 1 ADH greatly exceeded the number of discharges and exacerbated the overcrowding, which posed a threat to all the inmates because of the paucity of the ablution facilities. There were only four showers for well over a thousand patients; the patients were infested with lice because they were unable to bathe frequently; the 'disgusting' latrines were wholly insufficient; and the inadequate cookhouse was located too far away from the hospital.[109] Under these conditions, 'if any infection should break out, it [would] spread like wildfire'.[110]

Another problem was that the VD cases were not being identified early enough because 'short-arm' parades were being conducted too infrequently. The short-arm parade—Army slang for the medical inspection of soldiers' penises for tell-tale signs of VD infection (lesions, gleet [a discharge of pus-filled fluid] and swollen glands in the groin)—by this time had become an AMS routine. It was also the subject of much drollery.

Grigor pointed out that because such inspections were carried out so infrequently, by the time the VD sufferers were identified they had reached the stage of chronic infection. That in turn meant they took longer to treat and contributed to the rising excess of hospital admissions over discharges. Further, if the men thought they might not be detected they were more inclined to run the risk of VD infection by not practising 'safe sex'. Grigor suggested that more frequent and regular short-arm parades would deter soldiers from taking such risks, which would consequently help reduce VD infection rates.[111]

Ten days after that letter, on 13 February 1916, Major Grigor sent Colonel Howse a 'Special Report on Venereal Disease Cases' summarising the VD situation in Egypt. The report provided these instructive statistics:

- VD patients returned to Australia since the beginning of the military operations in Egypt in December 1914 totalled 1344.
- A total of 8898 VD cases had been treated by the various Australian hospitals in Egypt since the commencement of military operations.
- Of the total 8898 cases, 5924 were Australians, 1979 were British and 995 were New Zealanders.

- At the present time 1493 VD cases were being treated at 1 ADH, and none were being treated elsewhere.
- To care for these patients, 1 ADH had a staff of 132 attendants.
- The average stay in hospital for each case treated was 35 days.
- The total number of Australians admitted to the hospital for treatment during December 1915 had been 556, and in January 1916 the figure had been 827.[112]

Grigor's report did not go on to estimate the loss to the AIF of the 'man-days' spent in detention in the VD hospitals, nor the financial cost to the Australian taxpayer. His figures nevertheless invite speculation. Thus, if we apply the same formula used in Section 2 of this chapter, this calculation is possible:

5924 Australian cases × average of 35 days each = 207,340 days = 568 years.

By any measure, that was a huge waste of manpower. It helps explain why the AMS's senior doctors were so anxious to prevent VD and to encourage the troops either to abstain from sex or, if they could not, to use effective prophylaxis.

Putting a figure on the financial cost is not so easy. Such a calculation would necessitate factoring in the price of medications, equipment, the number of doctors, nurses, medical attendants and camp guards plus their wages, as well as transport costs. A century later, it is doubtful that such data could be retrieved in its entirety.

Despite that, it is possible to estimate the loss to the VD patients themselves in wages foregone. Australian troops were considered well paid by comparison with their British comrades because in 1914 the Australian private soldier was paid six shillings a day, about three times what British troops received.[113] The 207,340 'man-days' lost to VD in Egypt may therefore be estimated to have cost the VD sufferers a total of £62,202 in pay forfeited. The calculation is as follows:

> Cost of 207,340 days lost @ 6 shillings per day = 1,244,040 shillings = £62,202 in wages forfeited.

If an inflation factor is applied to that amount across the 105 years 1914 to 2020, assuming that six shillings in 1916 had the same value as $35.40 did in 2018, the amount of wages forfeited by the VD sufferers was $7,339,000 in the values of 2020. In terms of an individual soldier's loss, if he was detained for 35 days' treatment, he lost a total of 210 shillings or £10/10/0, the equivalent of $1240 in 2020 values.[114] Apart from the embarrassment caused if a large proportion of that amount was being withheld from the soldiers' dependants in Australia, it was enough to cause the aggravation and resentment that prompted the Wazzir riots.

Several days after Major Grigor submitted his 'Special Report' to the DMS, he compiled 1 ADH's weekly return of new admissions for the week ended 14 February 1916, which showed that the hospital had received 238 new patients that week.[115] Such statistical summaries provided useful information which, elicited by the 1 ADH staff, gave information about where the incoming patients had contracted VD and who they thought might have been responsible for transmitting the infection to them. The weekly return for 14 February, that of the 238 patients, showed that 133 had been infected in Cairo, 43 in Australia, 27 in Ismailia, 13 in Alexandria and the rest in either Port Said, England or New Zealand.[116] Almost a quarter admitted that they had been VD-infected before arriving in Egypt.[117] How many of those who brought VD with them had then passed it on to prostitutes in Egypt is unknown, however, there was a strong possibility that some of them had.

The return also provided addresses of where the patients thought they had contracted VD and the names of those who had infected them. These included women such as 'Minnie', 'Madame

Tena' and 'Madame Cabie', all of the Wazzir.[118] If not in Egypt, then certainly later in Britain and France, such information would be used to trace the women who were thought to be transmitting VD to soldiers. The military and police authorities would then endeavour to coerce such women into being treated. Whether such use was made of the information in the 1 ADH weekly returns is uncertain.

The information that Major Grigor was providing to Colonel Howse prompted the DMS to make further representations to General Birdwood. On 19 January, before he received the first of Grigor's formal reports, he wrote to Birdwood and in characteristically direct terms, he described the AIF's VD problem in five numbered sentences.[119] His memorandum ran as follows:

I have the honour to bring under [your] notice:

1. The large number of your Corps who are suffering from Venereal Disease.
2. The prevalence of Venereal Disease in the big towns of Egypt, and the many temptations which beset young men on their first introduction to Eastern life.
3. The majority of the reinforcements now arriving are drawn from country districts in Australia and New Zealand,

consequently they have not been exposed to the temptations of city life.

4. Australians and New Zealanders have very little acquired or racial immunity, consequently Venereal Disease is a very serious thing, and not only reduces your Corps as a fighting force but causes in a number of cases irreparable damage which renders them permanently unfit for service and entails a heavy charge against the finances of Australia and New Zealand...

5. I respectfully submit that each of these factors requires the gravest consideration, and I consider it my duty as your Director of Medical Services to earnestly request, if the exigencies of the Service will permit, the selection of a training camp which will minimise in every way possible the dangers referred to in this communication.[120]

The memorandum appealed to Birdwood on two sensitive issues—one military, the other economic. Militarily, the DMS was advising the ANZAC commander that VD was rendering the corps inefficient. Economically, VD was an increasingly heavy burden for the nations supplying the ANZAC troops.

Howse wrote again to Birdwood about these matters seven weeks later, on 7 March 1916.

His letter began by saying he had given the 'gravest consideration' to 'the appalling condition of Cairo', in view of which he believed that the ANZAC troops under Birdwood's command should be 'trained and kept out of' the city because of the VD infections occurring there.[121] Alluding to admissions into I ADH, he pointed out that 'the alarming number of 1246' new patients had been admitted during February, with 80 or more patients being admitted on some days. In Alexandria another '70 or 80' were under treatment 'and I have reason to believe that a very big number of men are being treated privately'.[122] He concluded by saying that if the military situation prevented ANZAC reinforcements being kept away from Cairo, he would have to apply to the Australian government for the VD treatment centres to be expanded to 'provide further accommodation for two thousand more Venereal cases'.[123]

By the time Howse wrote this letter, AIF reinforcements from Australia were already being sent to Tel El Kebir for training. Moreover, a decision had already been made to send the ANZAC infantry divisions to Britain for the war on the Western Front. They began departing that month, March 1916. The mounted divisions, the light horse, remained in Egypt because they were being used to help form the Egyptian

Expeditionary Force (EEF), a new multinational British-led formation being deployed to the Sinai region to meet the Ottoman (Turkish) threat to the Suez Canal. With the departure of the infantry divisions to Europe a large part of the problem of VD went with them. Henceforth the focus of the AMS's major anti-VD effort would be in Britain.

11. Keeping the Prime Minister of Australia informed

The problem posed by VD infection in Egypt had probably become well known in Australia within a few weeks of the AIF's arrival at the Mena Camp in December 1914. Letters home to Australia from the AIF doctors, chaplains, ordinary soldiers and perhaps even the VD-infected themselves, would have told relatives and friends what mischief some soldiers were getting into.

Before long, the newspapers were running articles about the scandalous adventures of many Australians in Cairo. An important article appeared in *The Sydney Morning Herald* under the prominent headline

Australia's Fair Fame.
Wasters in the Force.
Some not fit to be soldiers.[124]

It was by 'Captain Bean, Australian Press Representative with the Troops'—none other than C.E.W. Bean, the later official war historian, who had accompanied the AIF to Egypt as an official Army war correspondent. The Bean article criticised the behaviour of 'a handful of rowdies', who were drinking 'too much liquor'.[125] It trod warily around the matter of the soldiers' sexual adventures, managing to mention neither VD nor prostitution and referring to these subjects only obliquely. It did so by predicting that soon a 'weeding out of wasters' would occur.[126] Those sent home had been proved unsuitable for active service:

> ...because they have contracted certain diseases by which, after all the trouble and months of training and of the sea voyage, they have unfitted themselves to do the work for which they enlisted. They have damaged their country's reputation, and [will be] got rid of as the best means of preserving it.[127]

Although Bean had been a reporter with *The Sydney Morning Herald* for the past six years, his writing remained circumspect.[128] His newspaper article of 22 January hinted at the sex trade without mentioning it.[129] Reading between the lines, many of his readers would have understood exactly what he meant by his circumlocution.

The Australian government, too, knew about the reputation for larrikinism soon acquired by the AIF after leaving Australia in November 1914. William Morris ('Billy') Hughes was one politician who took particular interest in the AIF. He kept himself well informed about the activities of the AIF troops in Egypt through his correspondence with Colonel Robert Murray McCheyne Anderson, a senior AIF officer. Anderson, a Sydney businessman, Australian patriot and Army administrator, sent Hughes a series of long, frank letters from AIF headquarters in Cairo graphically describing the milieu in which the troops spent their leisure time. He also forwarded to Hughes copies of various reports and other people's correspondence, including that of Major Grigor, the CO of 1 ADH, to Colonel Howse and of Colonel Howse to General Birdwood. Whether or not Anderson was a prime ministerial 'mole' within AIF headquarters is unclear, but the material he passed on to Hughes would have fully informed the prime minister about the AIF soldiers' sexual exploits.[130]

Just one of Anderson's letters to Hughes exemplifies their tone and the kind of information he was sending. Dated 23 February 1916, it included these observations:

> The streets [of Cairo] are narrow and wide, ancient and modern and the

prostitutes ranging from black to white are housed to suit the tastes of all comers. We saw women, not only soliciting, but openly and shamelessly exposing themselves to soldiers in a more or less undressed condition. We saw queues of our soldiers waiting to go into the brothels and the military have a large police patrol on duty to keep order there so that the trade may be plied without any hindrance. There are special places set apart where officers only are allowed to go, where sodomy, in its filthiest forms, is practised for the benefit of those who pay the price to see it.

Chemists' shops are specially fitted up to deal with this trade and display such notices as 'GONORRHOEA PREVENTATIVES—INJECTIONS 3 PIASTRES' (seven-pence halfpenny), 'FRENCH LETTERS FOR SALE' etc. I am assured that so little care is taken to sterilise the instruments that their use spreads the disease the owners claim to prevent.[131]

Anderson even put a cost on the VD treatment program. He estimated that 1 ADH was costing the Army at least £2067 a month, or about $242,000 in the value of Australian currency a century later. Whatever the real cost was, Anderson's point was that it was money the Australian government need not have spent if VD had not been a problem.

Figure 2.9: Members of the New Zealand Volunteer Sisterhood, October 1915. Their leader and founder, Ettie Rout, is in the centre, hatless. This group was the first the Sisterhood sent overseas. Their original purpose was to work voluntarily as ancillaries in military hospitals. Ettie Rout, however, soon emerged as a safe sex and anti-VD campaigner (Alexander Turnbull Library, Wellington, New Zealand, image reference 1/1-014727-G, reproduced with permission).

Another report on the Wazzir that Anderson sent to the prime minister was by Ettie Annie Rout, a Tasmanian-born New Zealander. Rout became a prominent campaigner for sex education, the promoter of safe sex kits being distributed among the AIF and an advocate of enlightened means for controlling the spread of VD among soldiers. She had arrived in Cairo as the head of an organisation calling itself the New Zealand Volunteer Sisterhood, the self-appointed tasks of which included inspecting brothels to see if they were establishments in which New Zealand soldiers might have sex safely. One excerpt from Routs report on the Wazzir suffices to convey the tenor of her reportage:

> Outside notorious brothels long queues of soldiers waited their turn. One open door revealed a stairway with a line of soldiers going up and down, in and out. Soliciting and enticing was quite openly carried on. Bedizened and lustful women thronged the streets and doorways, many of them being embraced by soldiers. Doors were open and soldiers could be seen inside the rooms sitting on women's laps or vice versa. Other open street doors revealed beds ready made, or a partition with the doorway inside curtained to hide the inmates temporarily. Our soldiers were in these places. Outside the larger places there were crowds of soldiers, and several women soliciting at the doorways ... Streams of men in Khaki went in, to see the dancing, and to drink etc. I saw a considerable number of soldiers in the street, more or less

drunken ... On some of the wider streets the women were on the balconies, with soldiers in some cases, and one could see soldiers and women walking about in the bedrooms off these balconies—the French windows were open and fully lighted...[132]

What the prime minister made of such information is unclear, and whether he acted upon it is uncertain. If he read everything that Colonel Anderson sent him, he may have known more about the Wazzir than anyone who had never been there.

12. A VD epidemic more apparent than real?

Was the situation in Cairo as serious as claimed by observers such as Colonel Anderson and Ettie Rout? Did Army doctors like Colonel Howse, Colonel Butler, Lieutenant Colonel Barrett, Major Zwar and Major Grigor overstate the situation, perhaps to secure the facilities they believed the AMS needed? On the other hand, did the war correspondent, Charles Bean, *understate* the problem or not write about it compellingly enough?

Most contemporaries who wrote about prostitution and VD in Cairo emphasised the squalor of the brothels and the likelihood that drunken soldiers would contract VD by consorting with the prostitutes. Anderson, Ettie Rout and the AMS doctors were all agreed that the Cairo sex trade was impacting adversely on the AIF; yet there is also a possibility that the soldiers introduced VD to the brothels of the Wazzir. Peter Stanley, a present-day Australian military historian, argued in his 2010 book *Bad Characters: Sex, Crime, Mutiny, Murder and the Australian Imperial Force* that British colonial officials in Egypt were angry about the local prostitutes being blamed for the VD epidemic among the AIF. Their belief was that AIF soldiers had brought VD with them, having contracted it in Australia or perhaps in Colombo in time ashore during the voyage to Egypt.[133]

Stanley has also pointed out that the so-called VD epidemic in Egypt was a more complicated phenomenon than the AMS doctors, AIF administrators, war correspondents, guardians of public morality and safe sex campaigners might have realised. 'VD presented a complex medical, moral, disciplinary and operational problem,' he wrote in *Bad Characters*.[134] He then went on to argue:

> The military authorities could not control the behaviour of their men much less outlaw or control prostitution. The powers of evangelical Christianity—at home

more than in Egypt—prevented a rational medical solution. Padres refused to 'make vice safe' by condoning prevention in any form. (This argument was nothing new: it had been played out between medical pragmatists and religious moralists in garrison towns across Britain and in military cantonments throughout India over the previous century.) [135]

A *so-called* epidemic? Was there an epidemic at all? The AMS medical officers certainly thought so. Army doctors, especially those working in the VD treatment centres, were aghast at the floods of patients they had to admit. More senior medical officers were perturbed by the strain the VD patients placed on the Army hospitals, the medical system and the chain of evacuations.

Perhaps, however, the epidemic was more apparent than real. The reason for thinking so is the statistics of VD infection provided by Butler in the first volume of his official medical history of the war. Referring to the first four months of the AIF's sojourn in Egypt, December 1914 to April 1915, he wrote that 'the outbreak of the venereal contagions ... incapacitated over 2000 men and sent 3 per cent of the force "constantly sick"'.[136] The figure 'three per cent' is significant here, because it is a proportion comparable to the figures in the Army camps in

Australia at the same time. As already seen, the 1915-16 percentage in Australia was 3.3 per cent, slightly higher than the three per cent for Egypt, and as Butler himself observed, those levels reflected the percentages 'for the whole period of the war'.[137]

Butler also produced a graph (Figure 2.10) in his first volume to demonstrate the incidence of various groups of infectious diseases in the AIF in the Middle East during 1915.[138] As the graph shows, by far the most common causes of hospitalisation were 'Gastro-intestinal infections' causing 95.0 hospitalisations per thousand of troop strength during the month of peak infections, followed by 'Inspiratory and Naso-Pharyngial 'infections' causing 44 hospitalisations per thousand of troop strength. 'Venereal infections' coupled with 'Septic infections' were the third leading cause of hospitalisation with a rate of 7.4 per thousand of troop strength, but because this category combined two separate types of infection, the VD rate would have been less than that.

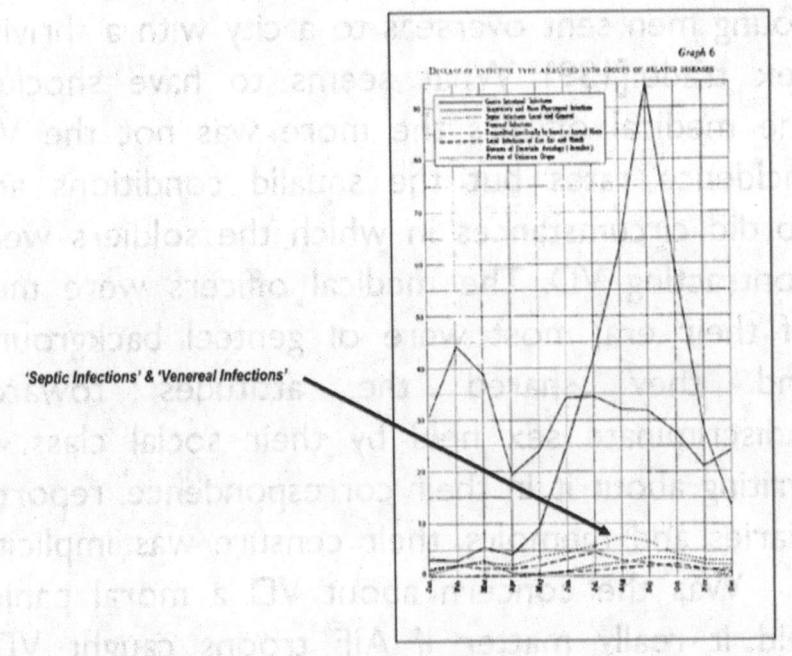

Figure 2.10: Disease of infective type analysed into groups of related diseases (Butler, The Australian Army Medical Services in the War of 1914-1918, Vol.1, The Gallipoli Campaign, Graph 6).

Seen in context with the other infection categories, the VD hospitalisation rates were not as disgracefully high as many contemporary observers believed. Each VD case was nevertheless a tragedy of its own because of its long-term medical and psycho-social effects on the individual soldier.

Butler wrote that although the AIF commanders were surprised by the VD infection rates, the AMS doctors were not. That was what they expected in a large army formation of virile young men sent overseas to a city with a thriving sex trade.[139] What seems to have shocked the medical officers the more was not the VD incidence rates but the squalid conditions and sordid circumstances in which the soldiers were contracting VD. The medical officers were men of their era; most were of genteel background and they shared the attitudes towards indiscriminate sex held by their social class. In writing about it in their correspondence, reports, diaries and memoirs, their censure was implicit.

Was the concern about VD a moral panic? Did it really matter if AIF troops caught VD? Were the medical officers over-reacting to VD infection rates that were not unmanageably high?

The answer to all three questions is that the AIF and ANZAC commanders as well as the AMS doctors were obliged to be concerned. They were also duty bound to take whatever action was appropriate to prevent soldiers contracting VD, to treat them if they did and eventually to send them home to their families VD-free.

Reasons for the AIF to take effective action against VD included medical, sociological, logistical, financial, political, diplomatic and moral imperatives. Briefly, the Army had at least nine reasons for taking action to halt the spread of VD. These were as follows:

1. VD-infected troops were not only soldiers but the sons, brothers, husbands, fiancés and fathers of Australian women. The Army could not allow the women's VD-infected menfolk to return home unless and until the VD-infected had been cured.
2. Soldiers debilitated by disease are less efficient, less durable and less reliable than those who are in full health. Important tasks of the AMS were therefore to prevent disease among the troops, to cure the soldiers who succumbed to disease and to return them to active duty as soon as practicable.
3. Healing the VD-infected soldier in the pre-penicillin era was a protracted process. The time taken to effect a cure was essentially wasted because it was unnecessary and could have been avoided if the soldier had made adequate effort to protect his health.
4. Syphilis in particular was a disease that could be treated but not cured. No 'cure' could ever be assumed to be complete and permanent. At the time, about 10 per cent of Australian mental asylum inmates were there because of dementia induced by tertiary stage syphilis. Syphilis patients

were deemed 'tainted for life' and so the presence of large numbers of them in the AIF reflected badly on the Army.

5. VD reduced the AIF's efficiency as a fighting force. If three per cent of any Army division's strength was away in hospital being treated for VD at any one time, the division could not be at full strength or peak combat efficiency. Assuming that the 1st Australian Division maintained its strength of 20,000, the soldiers in hospital with VD would have numbered about 600—about the size of an infantry battalion, a 'battalion' effectively lost to the AIF.

6. The VD-infected troops consumed a large amount of material, monetary and staff resources. Because VD was preventable, and need never have been contracted, those resources were a needless financial drain on the Australian government and ultimately the taxpayers of Australia.

7. Given contemporary moral values in Australia in 1915 and 1916, the Army had to be seen to be taking effective action to uphold societal standards. It could not accordingly ignore outbreaks of VD but must strive to quell them to prevent VD infection spreading back to Australia.

8. VD among the soldiers was a source of friction between them and the local Egyptian population, as seen in the Wazzir riots. This was a potential impediment to the ANZAC commanders in fulfilling their mission in Egypt.
9. Australia's international reputation as a reliable defender of Empire would be imperilled if VD were rife among its soldiers sent overseas.

And so it was that the AIF could not ignore the troops' VD infections.

CHAPTER 3

Venereal Disease in the Australian Army, 1916-1919: Egypt and the United Kingdom

1. Casualty rates in the AIF's post-Gallipoli deployments to the UK and the Western Front

After the AIF returned to Egypt from the Gallipoli campaign during December 1915 and January 1916, reinforcements from Australia enabled depleted battalions to regain full strength. Recruiting in Australia succeeded in providing the troops to replace the losses on Gallipoli. An ANZAC reorganisation enabled a second corps to be established and four more Australian divisions to be formed.[7] By the end of February

---

[7] Under the reorganisation, in February 1916 the original Australian and New Zealand Army Corps was replaced by two new corps, I Anzac Corps

1916, the strength of the AIF in Egypt had increased to 100,000.[1]

Eventually 330,714 soldiers would serve with the AIF in overseas theatres 1914 to 1919.[2] Of these, 65,350 or almost 20 per cent would be hospitalised for VD.[3]

What was to be done with this vast force, which was 16 times the size of the formation that had arrived in Egypt in December 1914? The short answer was that the infantry brigades were sent to England and France for further training before soon being thrown into the war against Germany on the Western Front in Belgium and France. They departed Egypt in the second half of March 1916.

Meanwhile, the mounted or light horse brigades were retained in Egypt as part of the EEF. Established on 10 March 1916, the EEF had the task of defending the Suez Canal against the Ottoman (Turkish) army[8] which had invaded Egypt east of the Canal early in the war.

The AIF troops who fought on the Western Front did so as a component of a wider Allied formation known as the British Expeditionary

---

and II Anzac Corps. Further reorganisations followed after these two formations arrived in France.

8   As well as its own troops, the Ottoman army included many German military advisers.

Force (BEF) to which Canada, India, New Zealand, the UK and Portugal contributed troops. During the period in which the AIF fought with the BEF, 1916 to 1918, the overall BEF Commander was Field Marshal Douglas Haig.

The official histories of the war distinguish between the AIF troops serving in the UK and those deployed with the BEF in France and Belgium. Those in the UK comprised units undergoing training for service with the BEF, troops on leave, troops who were patients in hospitals and convalescent homes, and soldiers attached to AIF headquarters and various depots and units based in Britain. Those serving with the BEF consisted of the combat units fighting on the Western Front and the service units supporting them. Altogether, an estimated total of 295,000 AIF soldiers served in the UK and with the BEF.[4]

AIF strength in the UK and with the BEF varied considerably from week to week, month to month and year to year as combat casualties and illness took their toll and reinforcements arrived from Australia. The statistical measure of strength used in the official histories was 'average daily strength per annum', namely the average number of troops in the AIF on any day in a particular year.[5] Table 3.1 indicates how the average daily strength fluctuated.

The large size of the AIF in Egypt in 1915 and 1916 is explained by the build-up for the Gallipoli campaign in 1915 and the arrival of reinforcements preceding the deployments to the UK and the Western Front. After that, during 1917 and 1918, the proportion of the AIF in Egypt, Sinai and Palestine dropped back to about 11 per cent of total AIF strength while the proportion in the UK and on the Western Front grew to about 89 per cent.

Table 3.1-**Average AIF daily strength in three theatres, 1915-1918**

Year	Egypt, Sinai & Palestine	United Kingdom	BEF in France & Belgium
1915	30,327	—	—
1916	42,424	41,199	59,978
1917	16,469	66,792	118,454
1918	18,050	35,912	110,031

Source: Derived from A.G. Butler, The Australian Army Medical Services, Vol.3, Special Problems and Services, p.187.

The strength of the AIF on the Western Front fluctuated between about 110,000 and 118,500 men during the two peak years of the Australian involvement in that theatre, 1917 and 1918. AIF combat casualties exceeded 181,000 men, over 46,000 of whom died. Battlefield casualties therefore amounted to 61 per cent of those who served with the AIF, and deaths in battle or as a result of battlefield injuries comprised 15.6 per cent—the highest rate among all British Commonwealth armies.[6]

Unfortunately, VD moved with the AIF from Egypt to Britain and France, and so the AIF's major venereological effort also moved to these nations with the infantry units. As well as the high rate of battlefield casualties, the AIF experienced in both the UK and the BEF high rates of illness unrelated to combat. In the three years from April 1916 to March 1919, the Army hospitals admitted a total of 582,248 sick AIF patients. In other words, on average each AIF soldier had almost two (1.97) hospitalisations each. Of the 582,848 hospitalisations, 40,880 were VD cases — seven per cent of non-combat-related hospital admissions.[7]

Placing the 40,880 VD cases alongside the 295,000 soldiers who served with the AIF in the UK and with the BEF, the reader will appreciate that they amounted to the equivalent of almost 14 per cent or a seventh of total AIF strength. That is a relatively large proportion and it explains why VD remained a major concern for both the AIF commanders and the AMS. After all, allowing an average of 35 days' treatment per case, the 40,880 VD hospitalisations represented about 1.4 million days when the VD-infected were in hospital and unavailable for duty. That many days was the equivalent of 3920 lost years—enormous and needless wastage in AIF strength and operational capability.

2. The AIF s participation in the Egyptian Expeditionary Force, 1916-1919

Except for the troops fighting on Gallipoli April to December 1915, from December 1914 to March 1916 the overseas component of the AIF was based in Egypt. As seen, the infantry brigades departed for the UK and the Western Front in March 1916. That left the light horse divisions to join the EEF in what turned out to be a long desert war across Sinai, then through Palestine and into Syria.[8]

The EEF was originally established to protect the Suez Canal. The British government feared that, post-Gallipoli, the Ottoman Empire would send its troops from the Gallipoli theatre to Palestine and Egypt to capture the Canal. With at least 130,000 Turkish troops from Gallipoli, the Ottoman forces east and north of the Canal, estimated at about 250,000, would be greatly bolstered.[9]

To meet this likely threat, the EEF was a large formation initially. By May 1916, two months after its establishment, it numbered almost 357,170 troops, made up of 14,186 officers and about 343,000 other ranks. It was a multinational grouping, including troops from Egypt, India, France and Italy as well as from the UK, Australia and New Zealand. Within a couple of months, however, the EEF had been reduced to 143,000, when the majority of the troops, but not the Australians and New Zealanders, were withdrawn for deployment on the Western Front in Europe.[10]

Through a series of battles in the north Sinai region during 1916 and 1917, the reduced EEF succeeded in pushing the Ottoman forces across the northern Sinai region, out of Egypt and back into Palestine. During 1917 and 1918 the desert war continued as the Turks were driven north through Palestine and Syria.

An estimated total of 35,000 Australians served with the EEF during these 'desert' campaigns.[11] As indicated in Table 3.1, once the desert campaigns began the AIF's average daily strength within the EEF was between 16,000 and 18,000. Australians accordingly comprised about 12 per cent of the EEF's initial strength.

The impact of the AIF on the EEF's campaigns was greater than that proportion might suggest because the Australian light horse spearheaded many EEF victories. These included the capture of Romani and other Sinai towns in 1916, the charge on Beersheba in 1917 and the capture of Damascus in 1918.

Although much of the EEF's fighting took place in and around small, remote desert towns, VD infection remained a problem in the EEF, and especially for its AIF component. The chart in Figure 3.1 summarises the situation. As it indicates, before the infantry brigades departed for the UK and the Western Front in March 1916, the AIF's VD annual hospitalisation rate was between about 133 and 138 cases admitted to hospital for every thousand soldiers—over 13 per cent of troop strength. Predictably, the rate dropped dramatically in 1917 to 53 cases per thousand troops, or 5.3 per cent of strength, because the troops were fighting out in the deserts of Sinai and southern Palestine with little chance of succumbing to the temptations of Cairo. By contrast, in 1918 the rate rose above 109 because the war in the Middle East ended in October that year and soldiers had access to prostitutes, especially in Jerusalem. Overall, one in ten Australians were hospitalised for VD—a great loss in fighting manpower.

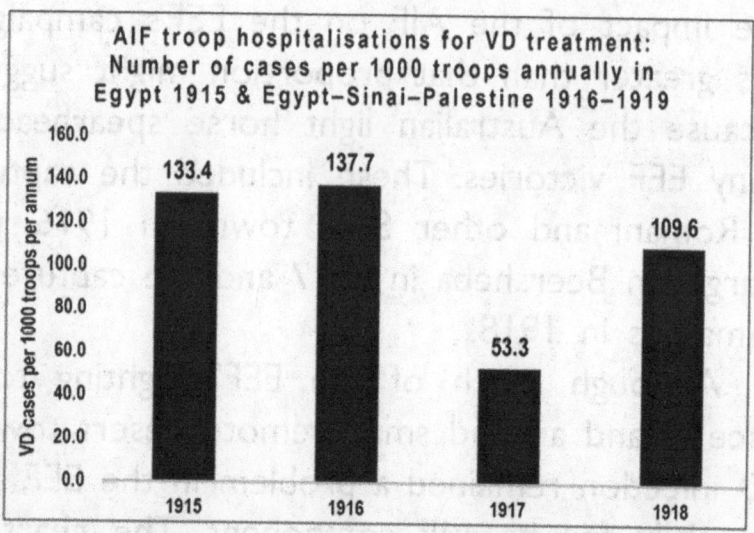

Figure 3.1: VD rates among the AIF in the Egypt-Sinai-Palestine theatre 1915-1919 (derived from A.G. Butler, The Australian Army Medical Services, Vol.3, Special Problems and Services, p.187).

The way in which VD infections fluctuated with the fortunes of war may be seen in the chart in Figure 3.2, which shows the number of *weekly* hospital admissions for VD in Egypt during 1918 and 1919. As the chart shows, during periods of combat the number of admissions would drop below 20, but after the end of the war the number of weekly hospital admissions rose above 70.[12]

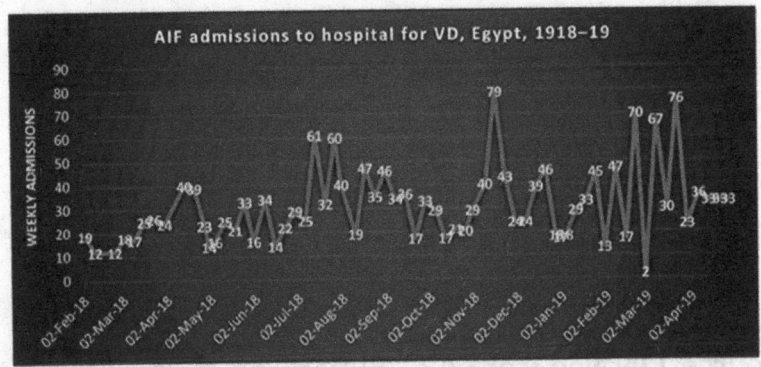

Figure 3.2: Weekly hospital admissions for VD within the AIF in Egypt, 1918-1919 (AWM27 376/164).

Altogether, a total of 12,475 AIF soldiers were admitted to hospital suffering from VD in Egypt in 1915 and then in Egypt, Sinai and Palestine in the three years 1916 to 1918. Table 3.2 shows the number of hospitalisations and their proportion of average daily strength.[13]

Table 3.2-**AIF soldier hospitalisations for VD: Egypt in 1915 and Egypt, Sinai and Palestine during 1916-1918**

Year	AIF average daily strength	Admissions to hospital for VD	Proportion (%) of average daily strength
1915	30,327	4046	13.3%
1916	42,424	5842	13.8%
1917	16,469	878	5.3%
1918	18,050	1979	11.0%
Total 1915–1918:		12,745	

Source: Derived from A.G. Butler, The Australian Army Medical Services, Vol.3, Special Problems and Services, p.187.

The main centre for treating Australian and New Zealand VD cases during the EEF desert campaigns was 2 ASH, which had operated as a specialist VD hospital in the months before the Gallipoli campaign. During the Gallipoli campaign it was relocated to Mudros on Lemnos Island, Greece, where it became a general rather than a VD hospital. After the Gallipoli evacuation, 2 ASH was brought back to Egypt and was subsequently relocated several times during the Sinai and Palestine campaigns. It continued as a general 800-bed hospital but also took in most (though not all) Australian and New Zealand VD cases from the desert campaigns of 1916 to 1918. The field ambulances attached to the light horse brigades also treated VD patients as the need arose.[14]

2 ASH tended to move with the AIF to the bases of operations where it was most needed. It returned to Egypt from Lemnos on 20 January 1916 and opened again with 400 beds at Tel El Kebir on 29 January. It subsequently moved to Mahemdia (also known as Mahamdiyah), on the coast north of Romani (present-day Bi'r ar rummanah). At Mahemdia, 30 kilometres east of Port Said in the north Sinai region, 2 ASH had 800 beds. After the Battle of Romani, it was relocated to Port Said at the northern entrance to the Suez Canal, where it remained for four months. In March 1917 it moved east to El Arish (el Arīsh), 45 kilometres from the Palestine border, where it became the main hospital for the battles to capture Gaza. In October that year, it was relocated for the final time to Moascar, an army training camp five kilometres west of Ismailia on the Suez Canal west bank. At Moascar 2 ASH once again became the principal VD treatment centre for Anzac troops.[15]

Figure 3.3: No.2 Australian Stationary Hospital at Mahemdia (Mahamdiyah) near Romani, North Sinai desert, 1916. The hospital's tents were situated between the railway siding and the Mediterranean Sea, with the desert behind (AWM J03007).

The author of the long, 13-chapter account of the Sinai—Palestine campaigns in Butler's official medical history of the war was Colonel Rupert M. Downes, who had been the most senior AIF medical officer within the EEF. During 1916 and 1917, with the rank of lieutenant colonel, he served simultaneously as the Assistant Director of Medical Services (ADMS) for the AIF in Egypt and as ADMS of the EEF's Anzac Mounted Division in the Sinai campaign. In 1917 he was promoted to colonel and elevated within the AMS hierarchy to be Deputy Director of Medical Services (DDMS) of both the AIF in

Egypt and Lieutenant General Sir Harry Chauvel's Desert Mounted Corps. As such, he was responsible for all AIF medical units in the Egypt-Palestine-Syria theatre and the medical support of the Desert Mounted Corps during 1917 and 1918.[16]

Figure 3.4: Soldiers (almost certainly staff) standing on the verandah of the X-ray and operating rooms of No.2 Australian Stationary Hospital at Moascar near Ismailia, Egypt, 1918. By this time, the hospital had reverted to its original function as a VD treatment centre (AWM B02450).

Downes's contribution to the official medical history has the simple title 'The Campaign in Sinai and Palestine'. It gives a book-length account of the support that the Australian AMS provided to the EEF's desert war.[17]

Colonel Downes's account of the AMS's action against VD during the desert campaigns is brief, extending across only three pages. After noting that 2 ASH had the major responsibility for treating the VD-infected, his account sets out three tables showing the statistics of infection rates. It then goes on to indicate what measures the AMS took to minimise the risk of infection. Unlike some of his AMS colleagues earlier in Egypt, he was not greatly perturbed by the infection rates. His calculation of the overall infection rate from September 1916 to June 1919 was 11.1 per cent of AIF strength in Egypt-Sinai-Palestine—one in nine of the Australians in the theatre of operations. This rate was higher than Butler's statistics for 1917 and 1918 (see Table 3.2), but Downes believed it was 'considerably lower than that frequently estimated for [VD] among the civil populations in large cities'.[18]

Downes also produced figures comparing Australian VD infection rates in the EEF to those for the British soldiers. Table 3.3 shows the comparative statistics for 1917, 1918 and 1919.[19]

Table 3.3-EEF hospitalisation rates for VD in 1917, 1918 and 1919—overall EEF, British, and Australian rates compared

Year	General EEF rate	British rate	Australian rate
1917	27	23	56
1918	44	44	82
1919	65	79	116

(Rate = number of admissions per thousand troops annually)

Source: R.M. Downes, 'The Campaign in Sinai and Palestine', Part 2 in A.G. Butler, The Australian Army Medical Services, Vol. I, p.772.

As the table suggests, the Australian rate was appreciably higher than both the British and general EEF rates (which included the Egyptian, Indian and New Zealand figures as well as the Australian and British). How might this disparity be explained? Was it the Australians' indiscipline, carelessness about personal hygiene, higher levels of libido, proclivity for drunkenness, fecklessness, immorality or a combination of these factors?

Downes believed that 'the only factor of importance' in differentiating the Australians from among the EEF's other nationalities was 'their higher rate of pay'.[20] He did not elaborate, leaving it to his readers to infer that with more money to spend on leave in places like Cairo, Port Said, Ismailia, Gaza, Jaffa and Jerusalem, they spent it on booze and prostitutes. By the same token, inferentially, if the British, Egyptians, Indians and New Zealanders had been as well paid as their Australian comrades, they, too, would have produced VD rates similar to the Australians' figures.

More than half (about 58 per cent) of the Australian EEF soldiers hospitalised for VD contracted the disease in Egypt. Another 32 per cent were infected in Palestine and the remaining 10 per cent contracted the disease elsewhere. Jerusalem was where many of the Palestine infections were contracted, Downes observing that 'as the result of the extreme poverty of the inhabitants, prostitution was' very common.[21]

Downes also provided details of the time taken to treat the three main STDs suffered in the AIF—gonorrhoea, syphilis and chancroid. This was as shown in Table 3.4, which covers the 34-month period September 1916 to June 1919.[22]

Table 3.4 -**Types of VD suffered by Australians in the EEF and time hospitalised because of VD**

Type of VD	Proportion (%) of cases	Estimated number of cases	Average number of days spent in hospital	Total days of hospitalisation	Years hospitalised
Gonorrhoea	58%	1781	53	94,402	258.6
Chancroid	27%	829	23	19,071	52.2
Syphilis	15%	461	47	21,650	59.3
Total	100%	3071	44	135,124	370.2

Source: R.M. Downes, 'The Campaign in Sinai and Palestine', Part 2 in A.G. Butler, The Australian Army Medical Services, Vol.1, p.773 and A.G. Butler, The Australian Army Medical Services, Vol.3, Special Problems and Services, p.187.

As Table 3.4 indicates, gonorrhoea was by far the most common VD contracted, accounting for 58 per cent of all hospitalisations for VD, with chancroid and syphilis responsible for 27 and 15 per cent respectively.

The average time required for treatment of each VD type varied appreciably. About three weeks' hospitalisation was necessary in the case of chancroid, over six-and-a-half weeks for syphilis, and seven-and-a-half weeks for gonorrhoea, resulting in an average of six weeks across all VD cases.

Expressed in terms of soldiers' pay, those lost 'man-years' amounted to over £40,500, equivalent to about $3,745,000 in Australian monetary values a century later. A private soldier treated for 53 days for gonorrhoea lost almost

£16 in pay foregone.[23] By contracting VD, an Australian soldier serving in the EEF suffered a heavy financial penalty.

The penalty was not for the soldier alone, however. VD treatment imposed a severe drain on AIF manpower. To maintain the operational strength of the units serving with the EEF in Egypt and Palestine, the Army in Australia was obliged to keep sending reinforcements. That in turn was an additional cost to the Australian taxpayers, who ultimately bore the cost.

Apart from withholding pay from the infected, the AIF's main means of trying to curb the infection rates was education. Cards were issued to the troops telling them how to avoid VD and what to do if they thought they were infected. AIF headquarters in Cairo also ordered troops to listen to lectures by the chaplains 'on the ethical side' of infection and by the Army doctors 'on the medical' aspects. Downes concluded his discussion of VD by wryly observing that 'this action was not followed by any appreciable decrease in the venereal rate'.[24]

3. The AIF in the United Kingdom, 1916-1919

As in Australia and Egypt, the Australian AMS in England was obliged to make provision for the

AIF's VD victims in the UK and across the Channel on the Western Front. In the UK, a more enlightened approach to VD management did not evolve as at Langwarrin, the VD hospital in Victoria (described in the next chapter). In the UK, management of the AIF's VD sufferers 1916 to 1918 is best described as 'fierce' and 'penitential'. Ironically, although fewer Australian soldiers were based in the UK at any one time than in France and Belgium with the BEF, England was the source of the great majority of the AIF's VD caseload after 1915. This situation is summarised in Table 3.5.[25]

Table 3.5—**Comparison of VD hospital admission rates for the AIF in the UK and in the BEF, 1916-1918**

Theatre	Year	Average daily strength	VD hospital admissions	VD hospital admissions as proportion (%) of average strength	Strength as a proportion (%) of total AIF strength in the UK & BEF
UK	1916	41,199	4146	10.1%	40.7%
UK	1917	66,792	9932	14.9%	36.1%
UK	1918	35,912	*8187	22.8%	24.6%
BEF	1916	59,978	3521	5.9%	59.3%
BEF	1917	118,454	8595	7.3%	63.9%
BEF	1918	110,031	6499	5.9%	75.4%
Total hospital admissions for VD:			40,880		

Source: A.G. Butler, The Australian Army Medical Services, Vol.3, Special Problems and Services, p.187.

What Table 3.5 demonstrates may be reduced to these two points:

1. Although the Australian soldiers in the UK never comprised more than two-fifths of total AIF strength in Europe, they yielded 54.5 per cent of all hospitalisations for VD.
2. On the other hand, the AIF in the BEF never constituted less than three-fifths of total AIF strength, but its VD hospitalisation rate never exceeded eight per cent of its strength and was about half the rate of AIF VD hospitalisations in the UK.

Why were these disparities so great? In answering this question, the AIF's senior medical officers proffered sociological and cultural explanations. The first reason was that VD was a 'disease of leave', contracted mainly when BEF troops were on leave in the UK and especially in London. Butler pointed out the parallel between Australian soldiers in Egypt taking leave in Cairo and contracting VD and those on the Western Front becoming VD-infected during leave in London. They were similar scenarios. When the Australians were in France, he wrote, their VD rates were about double those of British troops; however, when they came to the UK on leave their rates soared to five times those of

British troops.[26] Whereas British soldiers took 'home leave', returning to families and home communities where they were less inclined to engage in risky sexual adventures, Australians and other 'Dominion' troops—Canadians, New Zealanders and South Africans—could not return home and accordingly spent their leave in the UK seeking diversions from the rigours of their life on the Western Front.[27]

Elaborating on this point, Butler argued that 'the Australian at home is not a loose-living man'. Sexual adventurism was to be expected, however, when 'some hundreds of thousands of men in the prime of life have been brought 12,000 miles from their homes, and kept there for several years under conditions of great restraint and frequently of great danger and hardship'.[28] Further, when leave in the UK was granted 'occasionally' and 'intermittently', VD rates would inevitably rise when soldiers took leave 'with money to spend, no home ties and few restraining influences'.[29]

The disparity between Australian and British soldiers' hospitalisation rates for VD were stark. Butler drew attention to this in a table he included in his official medical history. It is reproduced here as Table 3.6.[30]

Table 3.6-**Australian and British soldiers' VD hospitalisation rates compared (rate per thousand troops annually)**

Nationality and location	1915	1916	1917	1918	Average rate 1915–1918
Australian troops					
in Britain	134.1	148.1	129.2	137.1	137.1
in the BEF	58.7	72.6	59.6	63.7	63.6
British troops					
in Britain	23.5	29.7	31.9	33.4	29.6
in the BEF	29.7	18.2	25.6	32.4	26.5

Source: A.G. Butler, The Australian Army Medical Services, Vol.3, Special Problems and Services, p.180.

As Table 3.6 shows, on average Australian troops in Britain were hospitalised for VD at more than double their rate on the Western Front with the BEF. In the BEF their hospitalisation rate for VD exceeded that of the British by a factor of 2.4, while in Britain they were hospitalised at a rate 5.6 times that of British soldiers.

Detailed comparative figures for the other Dominions were unavailable to Butler and so he was unable to determine if the Australians in Britain and the BEF contracted VD at higher or lower rates than their Canadian, New Zealand

and South African comrades. The overall figures he did cite for the Canadian and New Zealand troops suggest that their VD hospitalisation rates were similar to that of the Australians. The overall rate for the Australians was 15.9 per cent of the AIF hospitalised for VD; for the Canadians the figure was 15.8 per cent, slightly lower than the AIF percentage; the New Zealand figure, about 13.0 per cent, was a couple of percentage points lower. The rates for the US and French armies were 9.1 per cent and 8.3 per cent respectively—appreciably higher than the British but well below the Australian, Canadian and New Zealand figures.[31]

A century afterwards, a historian cannot therefore conclude that AIF troops were the 'bad boys' of the war—the soldiers most likely to contract VD. All that can be said is that as an army they were much more VD-prone than British troops, more so than American and French soldiers, and not greatly different from their comrades in the Canadian and New Zealand armies.

A point to be emphasised here is that only a minority—less than 20 per cent—of Australian troops ever contracted VD. As Table 3.6 demonstrates, the 'worst' year and place for VD infection was 1916 in Britain, when the rate of hospitalisation for VD was 148 cases per thousand of troop strength. That was certainly high, but only relatively so—14.8 per cent of total AIF strength in the UK. The converse is equally true: the rate for troops *not hospitalised* for VD was 852 per thousand or 85.2 per cent of strength. As Butler rightly observed, 'the thousands of Australian soldiers who did *not* bow the knee to Baal were far more influenced by ideals of clean living and loyalty to their people in Australia'.[32] Their high moral standards, sense of duty and commitment to their families at home were what regulated their sexual behaviour while serving abroad with the AIF. Fear of VD and its medical and military consequences might also have motivated them, but for many these negative influences were outweighed by the positive effects of their personal codes of conduct.

The susceptibility of some Australians to contracting VD became obvious soon after the AIF's arrival in the UK and France in 1916. AIF commanders and politicians recognised that 'very systematic and definite measures would be required' if VD were not to compromise 'military efficiency' and threaten 'the future of the race'.[33] While the latter consideration was deemed crucial for 'a country like Australia, whose vital need [was] population', the more immediate concern was the former. General

Birdwood, his senior officers and medical advisers recognised that the AIF was confronted with the alternative of a heavy and uncontrolled incidence of disease, or of making use of every known method whereby it could be checked'. Arresting VD infection rates accordingly became a priority in which the AIF would use 'every means, moral, social and educative' as well as medical 'to prevent harm'.[34]

4. 'Moral, social and educative' anti-VD measures

The 'moral, social and educative' measures boiled down to the publication of anti-VD propaganda and monthly lectures to the soldiers to raise their awareness of the dangers that VD posed to them, their families, the AIF and Australia. An education program comprising at least two lectures was devised. The first lecture, dealing with the moral and social ramifications of VD infection, was delivered by Army chaplains. Army doctors gave the second lecture, which dealt with the nature of VD, its transmission, its treatment, and methods for avoiding infection.[35]

The lectures included 'a warning of the danger of alcoholic over-indulgence', which 'diminish[ed] self-control', allowing a soldier 'to be tempted and probably fall prey to some prostitute who is almost certain to be diseased'. As well as that, they '[denounced] the idea that continence is ever harmful, or that incontinence is an essential attribute of manliness'.[36] They also tried to encourage the troops not to think too long and longingly about sex:

> A false mental need for sexual gratification may be wrongly created by the mind dwelling constantly on sexual matters, by stimulating the imagination. Therefore, avoid unhealthy literature, obscene pictures, sexual conversation and association with street-walkers. The finest and healthiest man is he who is master of his passions, not their slave.[37]

Enjoining the troops to accept these strictures was probably a forlorn hope but nevertheless remained an essential element of the education program.

Most AIF units in the UK and in the BEF attended these lectures. What positive effect they had[9] in modifying soldiers' behaviour is difficult now to assess. Some chaplains were certainly

---

[9] Under the reorganisation, in February 1916 the original Australian and New Zealand Army Corps was replaced by two new corps, I Anzac Corps and II Anzac Corps. Further reorganisations followed after these two formations arrived in France.

well pleased with the outcome. For example, the AIF's Senior Chaplain, Lieutenant Colonel Frederick W. Wray, who took a leading role in the lecture program, reported enthusiastically to his CO on the lectures he had delivered to 5000 troops in training camps and depots in the UK. Senior Chaplain Wray described in his report what he said to his audiences and how they responded to his delivery. He wrote that:

> I talk to the men in the plainest possible language, of their duty to their country and its future. And appeal to them for the love of their country, for the sake of the women, the younger men, the children and their own happiness, to play the game and abstain ... Judging by experience so far ... the men are keenly interested and remarkably ready to listen to the advice given and are most responsive to the patriotic and moral appeal. I studiously avoid appealing to the men on strictly religious grounds ... The officers and men with whom I come in contact personally after the parades, are most demonstrative in their expression of approbation of this method of dealing with the trouble, and even amongst the cynical and sceptical, one notices a change of attitude and a disposition to concede to the

possibility of some real good being done ... It will be a splendid thing for the Army and still more for Australia, if the trouble can be reduced even if it is too optimistic to hope to wipe it out.[38]

Wray, a Church of England rector in civilian life, was a veteran of both the Boer War and the Gallipoli campaign, in each of which he had served as a 'front-line' chaplain. He was widely admired by the troops both for his sporting accomplishments and for remaining close to the action during combat. Known as 'the sporting parson', he ended the war with 'Mentioned in Despatches', CBE and CMG awards.[39]

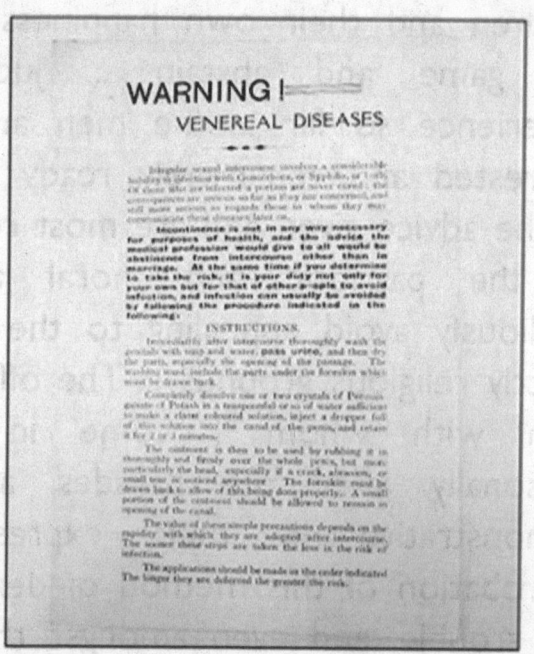

Figure 3.5: A World War I anti-VD propaganda leaflet distributed to AIF troops. It counsels readers to practise

'abstinence from intercourse other than in marriage' (AWM27 376/182).

Despite Wray's impressive personal qualities, Butler doubted the usefulness of the lectures that he and his fellow chaplains delivered. As the CO of the large No.3 Australian General Hospital at Abbeville and other units previously, Butler himself had been obliged to deliver the medical lectures of the program. Some 26 years later in his official history he opined that the chaplain's lectures he had heard were 'probably worse than useless'. The particular chaplain he had in mind was Archdeacon John W. Ward (1875-1938), who in civilian life was an Anglican archdeacon at Cooma, New South Wales.[40] In 1917 Ward undertook a four-week anti-VD lecture tour in France. Neither Ward nor his lectures 'were such as to impress Australian soldiers', Butler wrote, and even the medical lectures were of dubious value because 'no good results [were] reflected in the returns'[of hospital admissions for VD].[41] This was hardly surprising, Butler commented, because 'with Australians ... it is not the church parade and the sermon that count but the example of their leaders ... and most of all the home influence and the instinct of cleanness ingrained there'.[42]

Ward died at age 63 in 1938, five years before Butler published these adverse opinions. Safely dead, he could not respond to Butler's comments. If he had been able to, he might have said that he had done what he could to encourage the troops to avoid becoming VD-infected, that his lectures had been considered an indispensable component of the anti-VD education program, and that given the AIF's high wastage from VD any such program was necessary.

5. Medical anti-VD measures

The medical measures for attempting to prevent VD infection relied on a twofold program of, first, prophylaxis and, second, the early treatment of soldiers who thought they might have become VD-infected. 'Prophylaxis' consisted of issuing 'instruction cards' to soldiers going on leave, telling them how to avoid infection and what to do if they thought they might have contracted VD. They were also offered free 'prophylactic outfits' or kits.[43] Known as the 'Blue Label' or 'Blue Light Outfit', these contained a tube of calomel (mercurous chloride) ointment, a wad of cotton wool, several tablets of potassium permanganate (a compound used for treating dermatological conditions), a two-ounce

(56.82-millilitre) bottle and a 'card of directions' for using the kit. The card advised the user to rub the ointment on his penis before and after intercourse, fill the bottle with water post-coitus, dissolve one of the tablets in the water then wash his genitalia using the cotton wool and the solution from the bottle.[44]

The Blue Light kits did *not* contain condoms, but the soldiers were told they could buy them from the AIF's 'Blue Light Depots', which were clinics for treating VD soon after it had been contracted.[45] The AIF's principal venereologist, Lieutenant Colonel George Raffan, advised his fellow Army doctors that 'French letters [were] the only comparatively safe means of preventing [venereal] disease'.[46] His advice to soldiers was 'always have an adequate supply on hand'.[47]

The reason why condoms were not given away free with the Blue Light kits was probably a reflection of moral scruples within the AIF's command. General Birdwood had been lobbied by some of the AIF chaplains. A letter he received from Archdeacon Ward probably expressed the chaplains' shared view. Ward wrote saying he supported the anti-VD education program but he opposed the issuing of condoms to the troops because he believed that 'appeals to character and laying a moral foundation through education' were more worthy alternatives.[48] Perhaps as a concession to such opinion, soldiers wanting condoms were made to buy them instead of receiving them free.

Figure 3.6: A World War I 'Blue Light Outfit', i.e. a kit containing tubes of prophylactic ointment. One tube contained a 3 per cent concentration of Argyrol jelly, used as a precaution against gonorrhoea; the other contained Calomel ointment, a 33 per cent concentration of mercuric chloride for syphilis prophylaxis (image courtesy of Federation University Australia Historical Collection, image no. M14019-IMG_3842.JPG).

At this point Lieutenant Colonel Raffan needs an introduction. George Raffan MD, FRCS (Edinburgh) (1881-1941) was a Sydney physician and surgeon who joined the AAMC, then enlisted in the AIF in November 1915 at age 34.[49] At the time of his enlistment he was working as a specialist dermatologist and 'syphologist' at the Royal Prince Alfred Hospital. After arriving in the UK, he worked at the Great Peter Street VD clinic, joining I ADH when it arrived in England from Egypt and was located at Bulford. He spent much of his four years of AIF service with the hospital. During 1918 he was detached from I ADH to be the 'special adviser' on VD to the AIF's DMS, Major General Howse, at AIF headquarters in London. During this period he also worked in France, liaising with the AIF's medical officers. In Paris he collaborated with Ettie Rout, the anti-VD campaigner from New Zealand.[50] Raffan produced the detailed set of 'Instructions to Medical Officers regarding the prevention of Venereal Diseases', which, endorsed by Howse, became the AAMC's standard manual for managing VD. An appendix to the 'Instructions' contained the syllabus for the lectures on VD given to the troops by the medical officers, together with hints for teaching each topic.[51]

The Blue Light Depots were an idea borrowed from the UK War Office, which had established VD 'Early Treatment Clinics' in all British commands in May 1916 as a response to rising VD infection rates. They took their name from the blue light that shone above them at night to indicate their position within a unit. They were open day and night and operated on the basis of anonymity—'no names or questions regarding identity [were] asked'.[52]

The AIF set up its own Blue Light Depots staffed by medical officers and trained 'early treatment orderlies' who were 'constantly supervised' by the ADMS. Through agreements with the British, Canadian and New Zealand armies, Australian soldiers were also given access to those armies' Blue Light Depots as well. Howse recognised that the success of the depots would depend on the 'keenness and knowledge' of the staff. They were accordingly required to submit a weekly activity report ('Form AIF 587') to the ADMS.[53]

The principle of such clinics was that 'disinfection' procedures administered within 12 hours post-coitus to soldiers who thought they might have become VD-infected would greatly reduce the chances of infection. In the case of gonorrhoea, a cure was guaranteed in 90 per cent of cases if disinfection occurred no more than six hours after intercourse. 'Disinfection' involved first thoroughly washing the genitalia with antiseptic liquid soap and water. This was followed by a washing with a 1:2000 solution of bichloride of mercury. A wooden applicator wrapped in cotton wool and dipped in antiseptic was then inserted into the meatus (opening) of the penis for half an inch and kept there for two minutes. A drachm (3.7 millilitres) of 'Protosil' (a silver-based antiseptic) was then injected up the urethra and retained there for five minutes. After that the penis and scrotum were thoroughly rubbed with calomel ointment and a linen bandage applied.[54]

The Blue Light Depots offered eight days' treatment without loss of pay to soldiers who suspected they had been infected by gonorrhoea and had reported this promptly. If soldiers displayed symptoms of infection they received within the depots what was called abortive treatment, this being a regimen designed to 'abort' the disease, preventing it from advancing further. Butler's official history fell short of describing the procedures, but Lieutenant Colonel Raffan detailed them in the instructions he issued to the medical officers in the depots, as described in the previous paragraph.[55]

Whether or not these procedures deterred soldiers from undergoing disinfection at the Blue Light Depots is a matter for conjecture. The evidence, however, suggests that many did seek it. Of the 235,277 Australian soldiers who took leave in the 19 months to December 1918,

171,277 accepted 'cards of instruction', 142,699 accepted the free Blue Light kits and 168,563 attended the Blue Light Depots, presumably to collect kits or for post-intercourse treatment. The latter group, those who received abortive treatment, numbered 12,128.[56]

Prophylaxis generally, and condoms in particular, posed a dilemma for the Allied military commanders. On the one hand they might agree with Raffan that, short of abstinence, condoms gave the best protection against VD. On the other hand they could not be seen to be condoning immorality and sexual promiscuity among their troops by issuing free condoms. Whether or not VD prophylaxis and early treatment measures encouraged immorality, and indeed served to spread rather than confine VD, was a much-debated topic within the civilian community as well as in the armed forces. The debate flared in the UK Royal Commission into the Prevention and Treatment of Venereal Diseases and during a series of Imperial conferences on the VD problem and 'Temptation to Dominion Troops'.[57] Butler described it as 'a battle royal'.[58]

The contending viewpoints on both prophylaxis and the Blue Light Depots can be seen in several sharp exchanges between delegates at an Imperial conference on VD held in the Colonial Office in London on 19 July 1918. The Under-Secretary of State for War, Ian Macpherson, advised the conference that while the British government would continue conducting its early treatment clinics, it did not intend 'to advocate the use of prophylactics before connection'. That is, the government would run VD clinics for soldiers who had engaged in sex but would refrain from giving them condoms beforehand.[59] To the British authorities, early treatment of VD should be administered 'free from moral stigma', however, prophylaxis using condoms involved a deliberate intention to commit an act widely regarded in the community as a 'sin'.[60]

The Dominions were highly critical of the British approach. In response to Macpherson's comments, the New Zealand Prime Minister, William E Massey, said he 'hoped that his countrymen would never be degraded by the adoption of any system of prophylaxis' but nevertheless 'spoke with great emphasis on the necessity of doing all that is possible to prevent the spread of VD and the downfall of the Empire'.[61] Sir Joseph Ward, the previous (and later) New Zealand Prime Minister supported Massey, stating that 'the people of New Zealand [had] expressed considerable anxiety about sending their sons to [the war] to face the risks of destruction through venereal disease'.[62] An unnamed Canadian delegate declared that his government 'would never send another army for another war if they thought the troops would be subjected again to the same risks of [venereal] disease'.[63]

According to Butler, at these conferences the Dominion representatives made known 'with hysterical emphasis' their dissatisfaction with what they regarded as the British government's laissez-faire management of the VD epidemic.[64]

The AIF took a more pragmatic approach to VD than the British. Although the Blue Light Depots sold condoms rather than distributing them free in the Blue Light kits, unlike the British Army depots they *did* make condoms available. For the AIF commanders there was no 'moral difference' between issuing a free kit or selling condoms to a soldier before sex and 'disinfecting' him later.[65]

To ensure that the Australian troops were aware of the services provided by the Blue Light Depots, all soldiers in the UK taking leave and those from France travelling to Britain on leave had to parade before the medical officer at one of the depots. Leave could not be granted until the medical officer had initialled the leave form.[66] Making leave dependent on a Blue Light doctor's signature was, however, no guarantee that the soldier would use either his free Blue Light kit or a condom, if he had actually bought one. As soldiers often had intercourse when they were befuddled with alcohol, they might forget to use a condom or fail to follow the instructions in the kit.

6. No.1 Australian Dermatological Hospital at Bulford, 1916-1919

The main VD treatment centre for AIF troops in the UK was 1 ADH, which relocated from Egypt in August 1916. Departing Egypt, it passed its remaining 1200 'venereals' to other hospitals, mainly 2 ASH. In England 1 ADH was situated within the Bulford Army Camp on the Salisbury Plain, about 80 kilometres west of London. There it occupied a VD hospital of the British Royal Army Medical Corps (RAMC). The Bulford facility opened formally on 16 October 1916. Initially it had a 1040-bed capacity but this soon became inadequate. Additional huts were built to allow 1 ADH to become a 1200-bed facility. The Australian Red Cross equipped the hospital with the necessary instruments and appliances.[67]

1 ADH's relocation to Bulford arose from Major General Howse's dissatisfaction with the previous arrangements for treating the AIF's

VD-infected troops in the UK. When AIF troops began arriving in the UK in large numbers in early 1916, those who were VD-infected were sent to a VD convalescent home in Great Peter Street in Westminster, London. This unit worked in collaboration with a VD treatment centre in Dean Street, Soho, which, two kilometres to the north, was staffed by eminent British venereologists. As the number of Australian patients rose, more adequate and convenient provision became necessary.[68]

Various other factors also influenced Howse's decision to bring 1 ADH to Bulford and make that the centre of all the AIF's VD treatment programs in the UK.

First, the Australian VD patients were a generally truculent group who had been rendered uncooperative by their harsh treatment and pariah status within the AIF. No matter how good the British VD treatment centres were, the management of such Australian patients was more likely to be effective in an Australian-run hospital where they might be more at ease. The most fractious Australians were the 'military offenders'—those charged with committing offences and who also happened to be VD sufferers. They caused 'such vast trouble' at Bulford that eventually Howse arranged for them to be sent to the AIF's Detention Barracks at

Lewes in Sussex. A ward operated by AMS staff was established there for their treatment. It was kept busy, treating an average of 840 VD cases annually, or about 70 a month.[69]

Second, the Australian VD patients responded badly to being treated by British medical staff. The reasons for that probably reflected the antipathy of many Australians to upper-class English. Perhaps they were disconcerted by the 'posh' accents of the RAMC officers and disliked being condescended to as ill-disciplined 'colonials'. 'Treatment at a VD hospital,' as Butler pointed out, 'involved problems of discipline, and, for good discipline Australians required Australian officers.'[70] Howse appreciated that the AIF's already disgruntled VD patients were unlikely to submit to the discipline of the lengthy VD treatment regimen if they resented those providing it.[71]

An Australian VD hospital in the UK was therefore a necessity. After 1 ADH opened at Bulford in October 1916, all the AIF's VD sufferers in the UK were sent there. Howse also wanted the VD-infected Australians in France and Belgium sent there too. That, however, conflicted with British Army policy, which was for VD-infected soldiers serving with the BEF to be treated in France and not brought back to the UK. Treatment 'at home', Field Marshal Haig might have guessed, would be seen by malingerers as an inducement to contract VD. Instead of being sent to Bulford, the BEF's Australian VD sufferers had to be treated at one of the British treatment centres in France, either No.39 General (VD) Hospital at Le Havre or No.51 General (VD) Hospital at Étaples.[72] As a concession to Howse and AIF Commander General Birdwood, four Australian medical officers were attached to each of these hospitals to treat their Australian patients. Eventually an Australian wing was added to the VD hospital at Le Havre. In the end, Howse's wish was granted: the BEF's VD-infected Australians were sent to Bulford, but only in December 1918, the month after the war had ended.[73]

The caseload of 1 ADH was huge.[74] In the three years the hospital was operational at Bulford it admitted a total of 25,727 patients, equivalent to 8.7 per cent of the 295,000 AIF troops who served in the BEF and the UK.[75] The heavy annual caseload is indicated by the chart in Figure 3.7.

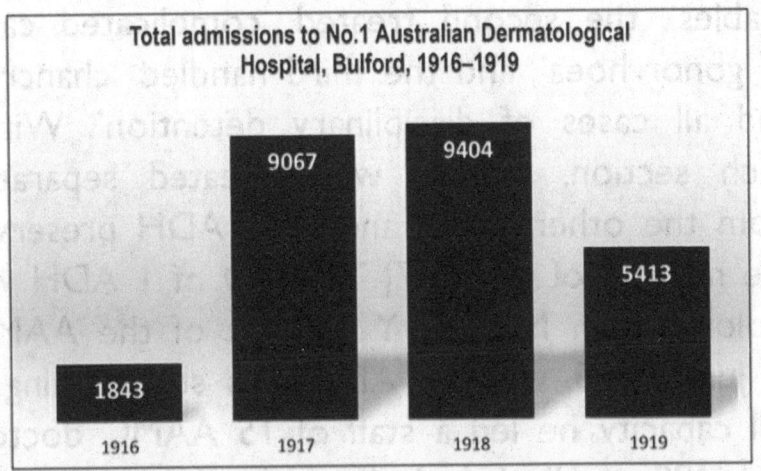

Figure 3.7: Admissions to No.1 Australian Dermatological Hospital during its 31-month period of location at the Bulford Army Camp, Wiltshire, 1916-1919 (derived from A.G. Butler, The Australian Army Medical Services, Vol.3, Special Problems and Services, pp.187-188).

The duration of treatment at Bulford varied according to the disease being treated. During 1917 and 1918, the average time for treating patients with both gonorrhoea and syphilis averaged 52 days; for gonorrhoea alone the average was 47 days, for chancroid 33 days, and for syphilis alone 12.5 days.[76] Any soldier sent to Bulford because of gonorrhoeal infection, by far the most common type of VD, could therefore expect to remain in hospital for almost seven weeks.

To undertake its large task, 1 ADH at Bulford was divided into three sections. The first managed cases of 'acute gonorrhoea, syphilis and scabies', the second treated 'complicated cases of gonorrhoea', and the third handled 'chancroid and all cases of disciplinary detention'. Within each section, officers were treated separately from the other ranks, and so I ADH preserved the niceties of rank.[77] The CO of I ADH was Colonel John Mitchell Y. Stewart of the AAMC. In June 1918, when I ADH was still running at full capacity, he led a staff of 15 AAMC doctors and 180 medical orderlies of other ranks.[78] This was appreciably fewer than the staff establishment for a 1040-bed General Hospital, which was what I ADH had become on relocating to Bulford. The establishment for 1040-bed Australian General Hospitals was 32 medical officers and 205 other ranks.[79]

I ADH was run in conjunction with the Convalescent Training Depot at the Parkhouse Army Camp adjacent to Bulford, which opened in May 1917. The depot's medical staff comprised an AAMC doctor assisted by four orderlies. As its name suggests, the function of this depot was to enable patients discharged from I ADH to convalesce while undergoing military training in preparation for their return to military duties. Like Bulford, it was a secure fenced facility patrolled by guards. When the dischargees entered Parkhouse their pay was restored, which would have served as an inducement to I ADH inmates to complete the treatment program in the shortest time possible.[80]

The average number of Convalescent Training Depot inmates was 388 over the two years it remained open. During the 18 months to December 1918, 7754 patients discharged from I ADH passed through the depot.[81] They, hopefully, had been rehabilitated, though many would bear the psychological scars of their VD treatment for years to come.

Bulford, unfortunately, never matched the happy success story of the Langwarrin VD Hospital in Australia (see the next chapter). Butler wrote that I ADH 'reflect[ed] the banal tragedy and social cruelty that surrounds venereal disease'. Bulford certainly undertook 'clinical work of conspicuously high standard', however, 'the forlorn and unhopeful outlook, imposed on these [VD] hospitals by social custom in civil life and continued in the war, was not relieved in this AIF unit by any obvious sympathetic consideration from AIF Headquarters [in London]'.[82]

News about Bulford filtered back to Australia in letters sent home by soldiers who knew about I ADH. One wrote a revealing letter to his father in Sydney. It gave a 'snapshot' of the problems VD posed for the AIF:

> [England] is miles worse than Egypt as all the prostitutes dwell on the Australian

soldiers with the result that most of them are left with a disease and also minus their cash ... At the main VD Hospital the inmates include ... Colonels, Majors etc with a sprinkling of Chaplains, so it is quite an establishment ... A number of chaps have the disease, but instead of reporting treat themselves privately ... One fellow was doing this for six weeks. His hair commenced to fall out, and a few other such symptoms occurred. The chaps in the same tent as him put his appearance down to the booze as he had been drinking quite heavily; they got a deuce of a fright when his true condition was revealed. Eating off the same plate as a man in this condition is rather risky, particularly if one has a sore lip ... Quite a number of men purposely get the disease to avoid going to the front. Rather an extreme course, isn't it, anyhow it is done, and openly boasted about ... I reckon that every girl who marries in Australia following this war should demand a blood test of her intended, otherwise she takes a great risk.[83]

While this particular letter was not a complaint about Bulford as such, it was significant because it eventually reached the Minister for Defence. That was after the father who received it passed it on to a friend who in turn was so outraged by the contents that he sent a copy to the minister. Demanding action, the friend told the minister that the situation described in the letter was 'disastrous'. He said he 'felt so strongly on the matter ... that I have declined today to subscribe to a local Roll of Honour unless arrangements are made to keep off the names of those who have so disgraced themselves'.[84] The adverse publicity in Australia was only one aspect of the enormously complex socio-medical problem that I ADH was expected to solve.

Figure 3.8: Administrative headquarters of No.1 Australian Dermatological Hospital, Bulford, April 1919 (AWM D00456).

Part of Bulford's problem lay with the DMS, Howse. According to Butler, Howse 'hated intensely VD in all its bearings—as he did alcohol; but on this, as on all other aspects of the problem of promoting military efficiency and saving the national purse, he was wholly objective and pragmatic'.[85] A DMS with puritanical views who emphasised military efficiency and economy was one with little sympathy for the unfortunates despatched to Bulford. Howse was also impatient with the time that 1 ADH took to treat its passing parade of VD patients. The hospital set criteria for 'cures' that were more demanding than those applying to civilian patients in Australia.[86] That of course made for lengthy patient through-put time at Bulford. Further, Howse believed that the specialist venereologists at Bulford were using 'refinements of technique' that were more sophisticated, and accordingly more time-consuming and costly, than was necessary—with little clinical advantage over simpler methods'.[87]

Discipline was always a problem at 1 ADH, both among the inmates and the staff. Indiscipline took many forms. The most common were failing to salute officers, being absent without leave, breaking out of the quarters in which offenders were confined, escaping from the camp, vandalism, and attempting to obtain liquor from the sergeants' mess. Punishments for such infractions ranged from 'admonition' to detention for up to 21 days.[88] Departing inmates frequently vented their animosities by trashing the quarters they had occupied. Vandalism was so common that the CO, Colonel Stewart, had a special 'Damage Voucher' (Army Form P.1960) designed for reporting deliberate damage to 1 ADH facilities and equipment. The cost of repairs, usually for amounts between £2 and £20, were met through claims submitted to the AIF's paymasters.[89]

Bulford's staff were also part of the problem. According to Butler, Stewart was appointed CO through seniority rather than expertise in venereology and did not contribute to the treatment programs. By inference, he possibly lacked the passionate commitment of a venereologist to curing and eliminating VD. The treatment was supervised instead by Lieutenant Colonel Grigor, a specialist in venereology. In addition, Bulford became 'the unhappy dumping ground for the disciplinary posting of medical officers and other ranks regardless of their special qualifications'.[90] Furthermore, most doctors posted to 1 ADH were captains, a junior medical officer rank, and so their opinions could be overlooked by senior AIF medical staff.

Staff turnover at Bulford was always high. The 1 ADH official war diaries show that as well as the inmate population continually changing, the medical staff came and went frequently as serving staff 'marched out' to appointments elsewhere and replacements 'marched in'. Colonel Stewart periodically recorded his frustration over the high staff turnover. In the 1 ADH war diary for April 1919, for example, he noted that:

> The frequent changes in the personnel of the medical staff greatly handicaps the prospect of recovery amongst patients ... I find a very considerable number of patients have had to be transferred to four or even six medical officers during their stay in this hospital, and the majority of these officers to whom they are transferred are only beginners and are naturally learning what they have to do. This is causing a great deal of grumbling amongst patients, and the OIC Treatment frankly admits that in all probability the cases would have done better if they had never come into hospital but [had] had private treatment.[91]

Perennial overcrowding exacerbated such tensions. At times 1 ADH refused to accept new patients because they could not be accommodated. In mid-August 1916, for example, Captain J.H. Wilson, the medical officer of the 6th Training Battalion asked for instructions from his unit's headquarters on what he should do with two of his VD patients. 'We rang up Bulford VD Hospital this morning,' he explained, 'and they informed us that the hospital is full and they are unable to take any more cases'.[92]

To those difficulties could be added the 1 ADH venereologists' knowledge that their DMS, Howse, was critical of their laborious treatment regimens, which he wanted undertaken in less time. On top of that, Bulford was understaffed. As seen, in June 1918 the staff total was 195 (15 doctors and 180 other ranks), or 18 per cent below its entitlement under the AIF's medical establishment of 32 doctors and 205 other ranks for a General Hospital of comparable size.[93] Worse than being below staff establishment levels was the gross shortfall in medical officers. With only 15 doctors, 1 ADH had fewer than half the medical officers to which it was entitled. The 1 ADH doctors consequently had double the workload of their colleagues in fully staffed General Hospitals. The hospital's under-appreciated and overworked medical officers accordingly had good reason for dissatisfaction.

1 ADH's peak year for admissions was 1918, when the hospital took in 9404 patients. On average, each 1 ADH medical officer treated 627 patients during the year—12 new patients a week on top of those he was already managing. Given an average six-week treatment regimen for gonorrhoea, in any week he could be responsible for 72 patients.[94] Was that being overworked? It might not seem so by comparison with general

practitioner workloads in Australia a century later, when a general practitioner in a suburban practice might expect to engage in about 160 'patient encounters' or consultations in a working week.[95] Such consultations, however, were just that—15-minute 'encounters', not six-week treatment programs for 72 patients.

A dissatisfied workforce treating resentful patients was a situation unconducive to either high morale or cooperative joint endeavour between the 1 ADH staff and the inmates. The Australian Surgeon General, Richard H.J. Fetherston, seemed to sense this when he visited 1 ADH during a tour of inspection of the AIF's overseas medical facilities in June 1918. 'Bulford,' he wrote, 'was generally depressing as a hospital.'[96] Bulford accordingly became another episode in the frequently sad saga of the AIF's experience of VD.

7. Conclusions

STDs remained a major problem for the AIF in the post-Gallipoli years in both Egypt and the UK. On average, the light horse regiments assigned to the EEF suffered losses to VD hospitalisations equivalent to 10 per cent of their strength. In the UK, the rate was appreciably higher for the AIF's infantry divisions—almost 16 per cent. The difference in the rates in the two theatres can largely be explained by 'opportunity' and 'propinquity'. During the EEF's desert campaigns, the Australians were most often deployed to areas well away from the cities and towns where prostitutes dwelt, whereas in the UK prostitutes were never far away from the army camps. Soldiers in the desert campaigns accordingly had fewer opportunities for consorting with prostitutes than their comrades in the UK.

The disparities were not only between theatres, however, because in both the desert campaigns and the UK, the Australian soldiers' VD hospitalisation rates were always much higher than those of their British comrades. The Australian rate was usually double the British rate and at times four or five times greater. Why that was so may be debated.

Various factors worked together to produce these gross disparities. Apart from those discussed in this chapter, they related to the nature of the AIF, how it had been recruited and the outlook of the men who had enlisted in it. Briefly, the following arguments suggest themselves:

> The higher Australian infection rates were a function of the youth of the AIF, which comprised mainly young, single,

physically fit men whose average age at enlistment was 24 years.

Perhaps the higher Australian rates of VD reflected the voluntary, non-conscripted nature of the AIF. The soldiers of such an army regarded their leave time as their own, to be used as they saw fit rather than spent as their officers dictated. If they wished to spend their recreation in bars and brothels, that was a choice for them alone to make.

Possibly the higher infection rates arose from the composition of the AIF, which was largely recruited from Australia's 'blue collar' classes. Arguably, men of that background were less inhibited behaviourally than Diggers of 'white collar' origin.

The higher Australian VD rates might also have stemmed from the Diggers' larrikin, egalitarian ethos. Soldiers imbued with those values resisted authority. They were consequently reluctant to allow the Army to impose its sexual mores upon them.

Such factors raise certain questions. First, did the AIF's commanders and senior medical officers fail their troops by not tackling VD more effectively? Second, could the AIF have better managed its VD epidemics in Egypt and the UK? The answer to both questions is a qualified 'yes', but only after viewing the VD epidemics retrospectively and with the wisdom of hindsight.

The refusal to distribute free condoms, and requiring soldiers to buy them, was an ill-advised strategy. If General Birdwood and Major General Howse had taken Lieutenant Colonel Raffan's advice about condoms seriously, they would have insisted that condoms be issued free of charge to all soldiers. They would also have ensured that the troops were given practical instruction in how to fit and use condoms efficiently. Further, Birdwood and Howse should have recognised early that punitive measures, such as cutting the pay of the VD-infected, instilling fear among them and shaming and stigmatising them, were counterproductive.

The reader in the 21st century can appreciate the common sense of the pragmatic approach. Given the prevailing mores, sexual prudery and general reticence regarding the topic of VD among the anglophone nations a century earlier, pragmatism and rationality might not have been an option for Birdwood and Howse. Many politicians, the morals campaigners and the churches in both Australia and the UK vehemently opposed the dissemination of information about VD prophylaxis. In particular, they would not countenance the distribution of free condoms to soldiers.

It could be argued that Howse and his AIF medical officers did their best within the constraints of their era. They were *obliged* to educate the troops about both the moral and medical ramifications of VD. Some of the chaplains who lectured the troops might have been unduly parsonical in dwelling on the 'sinfulness' of extramarital sex, but others could help the soldiers appreciate that VD infection often had unwelcome and unforeseen social consequences. Raffan's notes for the lectures delivered by the medical officers certainly spelt out the risks and consequences of VD, but they emphasised the practicalities of avoiding infection. Butler was sceptical of the value of either kind of lecture, but readers might agree that even indifferent lectures were ethically and practically preferable to none at all.

The reader might also appreciate that the AMS was itself on what a later era would call a 'steep learning curve' during World War I. Its medical officers certainly knew about VD and its treatment, but unless they were experienced in venereology they might never have been called on to manage VD patients previously. World War I was when large-scale VD epidemics confronted the Army for the first time, and those epidemics were of such magnitude that the AMS might not have foreseen what high wastage VD would cause. By the end of the war, the AMS's practical experience of venereology was extensive. The experience had been gained cumulatively through trial and error. World War I was accordingly a time of learning for the Army as it groped its way forward towards realistic and effective policies for managing VD within large military formations.

CHAPTER 4

Venereal Disease in the Australian Army, 1916-1919: Australia and the Western Front

1. Criminalising venereal disease

Under the King's Regulations No.462 and Section II of the *Army Act*, contracting VD was not an offence in itself; the offence was concealing the infection.[1] Despite that, during World War I the Army effectively criminalised VD infection. It did so by instituting lock-hospitals such as 2 ASH and 1 ADH and by cutting the pay of the VD-infected for the weeks they underwent treatment. The Army also permanently stigmatised the VD sufferers by entering the details of their treatment in their pay books and Army service files. In that form, their private experience of VD became part of official Army records and eventually public knowledge. In time, many such documents passed from the Department of Defence to the National Archives of Australia, where they are nowadays available to the public and are often digitised and open to online scrutiny.

Such stigmatisation had consequences that the Army's commanders might not have foreseen. First, the loss of pay and its recording in the pay book were deeply resented. (As a concession, the Army later adjusted the pay book's nomenclature to conceal the reason for forfeiture of pay because of VD infection.) Second, the resentment fuelled indiscipline and rebelliousness, which commonly revealed itself in acts of disobedience, vandalism, episodes of being absent without leave and even desertion. Third was a sense of shame and loss of self-respect among the VD-infected. This was more acutely felt in an era when most soldiers claimed affiliation with the Christian churches. Fourth was the social rejection that the VD-infected troops frequently experienced from their uninfected comrades. They were often shunned by other soldiers, their pariah status evident in petty acts of discrimination such as their comrades demanding that they use separate ablution and toilet facilities. And fifth, these other factors prompted many VD-infected soldiers to conceal their disease, heedless that doing so was an offence. The consequences of that included VD becoming more difficult to treat when it was eventually detected and the likelihood that the disease would be spread more widely.[2]

Figure 4.1: Shunning the VD-infected: the separate VD ablutions facility on the deck of the troopship Aeneas. The photograph shows AIF soldiers embarking on the Aeneas at Liverpool, England, on 31 May 1919 for repatriation to Australia. As they come aboard they file past the 'Venereal Washplace'. Separate ablutions facilities for the VD-infected were a concession to the non-infected troops, who objected to sharing facilities with soldiers suffering VD (AWM D00732).

The stigmatisation and rejection could also have long-term psychological effects. For example, after the war some formerly VD-infected soldiers eschewed reminders of their humiliation by never collecting their war medals, not joining the RSL or other veterans' associations, declining to attend unit reunions and refraining from participating in Anzac Day and Remembrance Day ceremonies. How they explained to their families this reluctance to enter into the life of the acclaimed 'returned Anzacs' is a matter for conjecture. Other returnees also refrained from taking part in the ex-Diggers' rituals because of their revulsion for the killing they had seen or done, but for many, VD infection left its own peculiar legacy of shame.[3]

That alternatives to the criminalisation of VD existed became obvious in a far-sighted, humane VD management program developed in Australia. The location was Langwarrin Army Camp south of Melbourne.

2. An alternative to criminalisation—Langwarrin Camp Hospital, 1915-1921

An enlightened alternative to criminalising the VD-infected was the treatment regimen instituted at the Army's Langwarrin VD Hospital in Victoria. Situated 42 kilometres south-east of Melbourne, Langwarrin during World War I was rural land still remote from the city. It was reached by the steam train from Melbourne to Frankston, the adjacent bayside resort, and then by car or horse and cart. The journey might take two-and-a-half hours.

Early in World War I, Langwarrin had been the site of an internment camp for about 500 German, Austrian and Turkish 'enemy aliens'. The camp, on Army land, changed functions on 13 March 1915, when it officially became the isolation centre for VD-infected soldiers identified by the medical officers at the Broadmeadows Army Camp, Victoria's main reception centre for AIF recruits. Within a couple of months, Langwarrin also began receiving VD-infected troops sent back to Australia from Egypt. The number of inmates built up rapidly as more ships arrived bringing back the VD-infected and as VD sufferers from other camps in Australia were sent there.[4]

For the rest of the war, Langwarrin would remain the Army's main VD isolation and treatment centre in Australia. The new arrivals from overseas tailed off after October 1915 because the Army's Director General of Medical Services (DGMS), Major General Fetherston, decreed that henceforth VD-infected soldiers would not be returned to Australia.[5] Despite that, a total of 7242 VD sufferers passed through Langwarrin up to June 1920. More than 6000 of those discharged as 'cured' subsequently returned to active military service overseas. Some then served with distinction, earning 400 military decorations for bravery.[6] These included two Victoria Crosses.[7]

During its years of peak activity from 1915 to 1919, Langwarrin admitted 6649 patients, of whom a remarkable 98.7 per cent were discharged as 'cured'. To what extent complete cures had been effected is uncertain. In the cases of gonorrhoea and chancroid, there was a good chance that full healing had occurred and that no sign of the infective bacteria could be discovered. Syphilis was more problematic because although the various tests for the disease might yield negative results, the disease enters a latent phase without obvious symptoms. The medical staff at Langwarrin and other Army VD treatment centres would not discharge VD-infected patients unless they were confident, within the limits of their knowledge, that a cure had been achieved. Table 4.1 shows the number of admissions to, and discharges from, Langwarrin.[8] As the table indicates, of the 6649 patients received at Langwarrin in the 52 months to the end of 1919, only 85 or 1.3 per cent had not been discharged as cured.

Table 4.1-**Aadmissions and discharges, Langwarrin VD Hospital, 1915-1919**

Period/Year	Admissions	Discharges
March–June 1915	733	668
1915–16	3161	2595
1916–17	1496	1879
1917–18	793	823
1918–19	466	599
Total	6649	6564

Source: A.G. Butler, The Australian Army Medical Services, Vol.3, Special Problems and Services, p.178.

Langwarrin VD Hospital began inauspiciously. It was a lock-hospital in which life for inmates was as grim as in any military prison. The Victorian government had been displeased to learn that the Army planned to develop a major facility for housing and treating 'venereals'. The Department of Defence circumvented these objections by promising that the Langwarrin Camp 'would be made so secure that the men could not get away from it while in a state of infection'.[9] In its first year, the Langwarrin facility was accordingly as much a gaol as a hospital. Butler's description conveys the sense of despair that overwhelmed inmates and staff alike:

> The men were herded behind barbed wire enclosures, and two hundred militia men were employed as guards. There were three or four officers (militia) and about as

many doctors. The accommodation was miserably unsuitable; the round tents then universally used were old and leaking and unfloored, and, in wet weather, damp and muddy. For bedding the men had only blankets and rubber sheets and they were dressed in oddments of uniform and plain clothes. The small medical staff found it impossible to treat the men adequately. There was no proper water-supply; all the water was carried by train from Mordialloc [22 kilometres south to Frankston] and thence by water-cart to the camp. The lack of bathing facilities implied habitual personal uncleanliness. The attitude of the public and authorities towards the men was that they were 'Untouchables'. Naturally [the men] were disgruntled, spiteful and insubordinate. Recovery under such conditions was difficult and slow—in some cases impossible. What the patients endured before treatment began to be remedial can only be conjectured and the unhappy men continually broke camp despite the barbed wire and armed guard.[10]

Langwarrin Camp was transformed after a new commandant, Captain (later Major) Walter Conder, was appointed in August 1916. Conder had been a teacher at Melbourne Grammar

School before enlisting in the AIF in 1914. Wounded at Gallipoli, he returned to Melbourne to convalesce. He was still only 27 years old when the commandant of the Third Military District (the State of Victoria), Colonel Robert Williams, appointed him as the CO at Langwarrin.

Colonel Williams had already dealt successfully with VD at the Broadmeadows Army camp, where he had 'routed' the prostitutes who congregated nearby. He had enlightened views about VD, which he saw as a medical rather than either a disciplinary or moral issue. His success as Army commandant in Victoria was subsequently acknowledged, among other honours and awards, by his promotion to brigadier and later major general. His appointment of Conder as the Langwarrin CO was part of his plan to 'clean up' the camp and rehabilitate its demoralised inmates.[11]

Supported by Williams, Conder began making sweeping changes to the Langwarrin regime. First, the inmates became 'patients' rather than 'prisoners'. Permanent wards and accommodation replaced the tents. Electric lighting and power were installed in all buildings. Bores were sunk to provide a permanent water supply. A spur railway line was extended from Frankston and a railway station built. The grounds were landscaped—lawns were laid out, gardens established, and 2000 trees planted; gravel drives and footpaths were constructed, and street lighting installed. A fountain and an imposing gateway were added. The buildings and fencing were freshly painted. The 24-hour guard of militiamen was removed, replaced by a guard drawn from among the patients. Pay was restored to the patients who worked on these various development projects. Sports were organised. The YMCA constructed, furnished and stocked a recreation hall replete with easy chairs, tables, library books, cupboards and billiard tables, and the Red Cross provided an entertainment hall in which movies were screened and weekly camp concerts held. The Red Cross also built a large bath house and furnace to provide hot showers. A military band was formed from among the patients and a band rotunda was built so that the band could present public recitals.[12]

The medical treatment of the Langwarrin patients also improved greatly. Instead of a haphazard roster of visiting part-time civilian medical practitioners, two permanent Army physicians were appointed, one of them a specialist venereologist.[13] Other doctors were appointed later, enabling VD research to be undertaken. This was credited with shortening the period of treatment required for gonorrhoea, chancroid and syphilis, thereby halving the average cost of treatment.[14] A permanent dental officer was also appointed, to conspicuous good effect.[15] VD treatment regimens were systematised and patient progress carefully monitored. As the VD therapies began taking effect, other benefits to the soldiers' health became obvious. Conder's biographer later observed that 'Langwarrin remained relatively free from diseases such as meningitis, so common in other [Army] camps'.[16]

Figure 4.2: Major Walter Conder (left) and Major Charles Johnson (right, a Medical Officer) in front of the band rotunda at Langwarrin Camp, about 1917 (Museums Victoria photograph MM 140031, reproduced with permission).

The historian of Langwarrin Camp, Raden Dunbar, detailed all these developments in his 2014 book, *The Secrets of the Anzacs: The untold story of venereal disease in the Australian Army, 1914-1919*. Langwarrin was transformed from a gaol into a hospital in which patients could regain self-respect in a congenial environment while recovering from their diseases. Seventy years before Dunbar, Butler had stated the situation nicely by observing that the hospital developed into a facility in which 'science and sympathy could triumph over righteousness'. The aim, and the result, he observed, was 'to mend and help every man sent there, to send him away a wiser human being, a decent citizen and a better trained soldier than when he entered the camp'.[17]

Despite some initial opposition, in time both the Victorian government and the local Frankston community came to appreciate the presence of the new hospital on the outskirts of the town. The politicians visited and declared themselves well satisfied. The band gave regular Sunday afternoon concerts, and the patients staged pantomimes to which Frankston's citizens were invited. One visitor who appreciated the transformation at Langwarrin was the Governor-General, Sir Ronald Munro Ferguson, who had visited the camp during 1915. He returned a year later, at Christmas 1916, when he declared it was 'the best military camp in Victoria'.[18]

Figure 4.3: The rotunda and the Red Cross hall at Langwarrin VD Hospital, about 1917 (AWM A03657).

The transformation of Langwarrin into an effective VD treatment centre was apparent in the high rate of patient discharges noted in Table 4.1. The humane regime also brought about a dramatic improvement in patient morale. This could be seen in the high rate of patients' return to active overseas service. As seen, about 6000 out of 7242, or 83 per cent, of 'Langwarrin men' did return to overseas theatres. Most obviously, a vast improvement in inmate discipline occurred under Major Conder's superintendency. Conder's predecessor as CO had been sacked because of a scandal involving gross breaches of inmate discipline.[19] Before Conder's appointment, many prisoners had escaped the camp and deserted, hundreds had absented themselves from the camp without leave, and almost 1500 disciplinary offences had been dealt with. The improvement under Conder can be seen by the figures set out in Table 4.2.[20]

Table 4.2-**Improvement in discipline at Langwarrin VD Hospital, as seen by the decline in desertion, absenteeism and punishable offences**

Year	Desertions	Absent without leave	Offences dealt with
1916	88	926	1487
1917	22	199	497
1918	nil	33	108

Source: A.G. Butler, The Australian Army Medical Services, Vol.3, Special Problems and Services, p.177.

What Williams and Conder had together demonstrated was that an enlightened approach to VD treatment was medically more effective and militarily more productive than punitive management. In a non-conscripted citizen army like the AIF, the 'carrot' was more likely to achieve desired results among the troops than the 'stick'. Langwarrin VD Hospital demonstrated that sympathy, patience and encouragement allied to 'best practice' medicine were more effective approaches than stigmatisation, coercion and punishment.

3. The AIF within the British Expeditionary Force, 1916-1919

The rate of VD infection among AIF troops in the BEF was only ever about half that of the AIF in the UK. Thus, of the AIF's 40,880 total hospital admissions for VD in Europe 1916 to 1918, fewer than half—18,615 or 45.5 per cent—were from the BEF.

This many VD-infected Australians was still a substantial number, and so adequate arrangements had to be made for their treatment. The DMS of the AIF, Major General Howse, wanted them treated at 1 ADH at Bulford, but Howse's jurisdiction did not extend to the BEF. He therefore had to accept the BEF policy stipulating that the BEF's VD-infected troops were to be treated in hospitals in France.[21]

The arrangement accepted by Howse was for the AIF's VD-infected troops in France and Belgium to be treated at No.39 British General Hospital at Le Havre, a VD hospital. By July 1917 Australians comprised no less than 46 per cent of all patients in the hospital. Pressure on accommodation available for the BEF's other VD patients was increasing. By August 1917 only

6100 beds were available for the BEF's 8028 VD patients.[22]

At this stage of the war, the AIF made some effort to offset its VD-induced wastage by using convalescent VD patients as stretcher-bearers. In September 1917 a group of recently discharged VD sufferers were sent to No.1 Australian Casualty Clearing Station as stretcher-bearers until they were fit enough to return to their units. Another batch went to No.2 Australian Casualty Clearing Station, where they were recorded as 'doing good work'. The 'frequent' practice of sending the convalescents to field medical units as bearers and general orderlies continued into 1918, even though the scheme proved 'troublesome'. Disciplinary issues and the need for some convalescents to undergo further treatment meant that difficulties beset the scheme.[23]

Because of overcrowding in the British VD hospitals, during 1917 the BEF commander, Field Marshal Haig, suggested to General Birdwood, the AIF commander, that the AIF should establish its own VD hospital in France. Birdwood referred Haig's request to his DMS, Howse, who disagreed because the only available accommodation for such a hospital would have been tents. Instead of a separate AIF hospital, he agreed to place four Australian medical officers at the two British

VD hospitals in France, 39 British General Hospital at Le Havre and No.51 British General Hospital at Etaples.[24]

The placement of AIF medical officers at the British VD hospitals proved unsatisfactory. As Butler explained, 'treatment at a VD hospital involved problems of discipline, and for good discipline Australians required Australian officers'.[25] Four Australian medical officers among as many as 1600 AIF patients were too few to maintain discipline. In May 1918 Haig again called for the establishment of a separate hospital for the Australians. At this time Howse had insufficient medical staff for that and as a compromise, a wing of 39 British General Hospital at Le Havre was staffed by AIF medical officers. Discipline nevertheless continued to be a problem there, so seven months later, in December 1918, the BEF command allowed the Australian VD patients to be sent to Bulford.[26] By that stage the war had ended and the repatriation of the AIF troops to Australia was beginning.

The Australian venereologists sent to France faced a thankless task. In January 1917 one of them, Major Edward Rae Cordner, wrote from 51 British General Hospital to a colleague on Howse's staff to describe his duties. In five weeks the caseload had increased from 1000 to over

1600 with more cases 'rolling in' daily. 'We shall soon be swamped,' he predicted. 'The hospital has orders to increase to 2,000 [beds], and it seems we will increase beyond that also.'[27]

Cordner also wrote that most of the hospital's cases could be sourced to Amiens. Of the 560 Australian cases of VD occurring in France during December 1916, half of them had been contracted in Amiens alone, the other half in the 'rest of France'.[28] Amiens was the principal city of the Somme, the region where most AIF units were deployed. The city soon became for Australians in France what Cairo was for the AIF in Egypt, and London in England—the place where they took local leave, congregated in bars, visited the *maisons tolérées* ('tolerated houses'—officially approved brothels), consorted with streetwalkers, and contracted VD.

The Army doctors routinely asked VD patients where they thought they might have become infected. Cordner's patients at 51 British General Hospital, who almost invariably had gonorrhoea, 'again and again' told him they had caught 'the clap' in Amiens. 'Really the incidence [of gonorrhoea] from there has been appalling,' he wrote.[29] The soldiers Cordner treated did not see things that way. They were generally unperturbed by the diseases they had picked up:

They get leave and go into Amiens and then come back and pass on to their pals the addresses of the houses where they have had connection. Their pals follow and each gets VD of some description. The men seem to think it is their duty to get VD. They really consider it a joke altogether and laugh and rag one another about it.[30]

Like Cordner, many Army doctors shocked by their patients' casual attitude towards VD might not have understood the underlying factors. Butler, who shared Cordner's concern about the Australians' attitudes, did allude to these in just two brief sentences in his official history. 'The Australian divisions,' he observed, 'were in the midst of the extreme trials caused by wintering in the mud of the battlefield.'[31] At another point he also referred to Dominion soldiers on leave in London 'with money to burn and without particular purpose save to obliterate the past and forget the future'.[32] As these sentences suggested, soldiers became fatalistic after living in the trenches for weeks on end, slopping through the mud of a soggy field of combat, seeing their mates shot and blown apart around them, knowing they themselves could be dead on the morrow.

Figure 4.4: Church Army amenities hut at No.39 British General (VD) Hospital, Le Havre, one of the two main VD treatment centres for AIF soldiers in France in 1917. About half the patients at the hospital were Australians. The Church Army, an Anglican outreach and welfare agency, was one of various civilian organisations providing support services to hospitalised Allied troops (IWM Q6365).

Unsafe sex with VD-infected prostitutes in Amiens, almost inevitably followed by gonorrhoea or syphilis, hardly mattered to men who stood a good chance of being annihilated in a trice a few days hence. If the individual soldier was still a virgin, 'trying it' with a prostitute before the next charge from the trenches across 'no man's land' might have been just the solace he needed. Thoughts of home, family, church and the civilian life post-war might have deterred many Australian soldiers from seeking out the fleshpots of Amiens, but for others even a squalid sexual encounter in a back alley might temporarily blot out the terrors of an imminent death.

A British military historian, Dr Clare Makepeace, has argued that the brothels and prostitutes of France fulfilled an essential service for the troops fighting on the Western Front. In an important 2011 article, 'Sex and the Somme: Officially sanctioned brothels on the front line', Makepeace wrote about the *maisons tolérées* and their clientele. The article shows that at least 137 officially sanctioned brothels, spread across 35 towns, were operating by 1917. Apart from them were non-sanctioned brothels, streetwalkers and 'amateur' prostitutes. With cafés and bars, the *maisons tolérées* offered soldiers a welcome relief from 'the slaughter and filth' of the trenches.[33] 'Bright and warm, light and jovial', the brothels 'provided an escape, a release' from 'the carnage of the front line'.[34] The queues of soldiers milling around outside the brothels, waiting for the switching on of the red light signalling 'open for business', were not depraved. They were simply buying 'a momentary release from the war'.[35]

The brothels as a social service? The AIF's medical officers might not have agreed. They, after all, had to manage the protracted treatment of the brothels' 'casualties'—the thousands of VD-infected troops.

Social services of another kind were provided by the voluntary civilian welfare agencies which offered amenities and support services for off-duty troops. These included the YMCA, the Australian Comforts Fund, the Red Cross, the Church Army and Ettie Rout's New Zealand Volunteer Sisterhood. The YMCA in particular worked hard at providing recreation facilities for soldiers on leave. In Paris, the 'Y' ran a popular hostel for troops on leave. Among its other offerings were daily excursions to Versailles and other places of cultural and historic interest.[36]

4. The women who helped spread VD

The women from whom the soldiers contracted VD were a continuing concern for both the military and civilian authorities in Australia. The AIF's commanders and senior medical officers accepted the 'market forces' reality that prostitution existed only because of men's demand for sex. As Butler coyly put it, 'common sense suggest [s] that the supply of women available for "illicit" indulgence by the promiscuous-minded male is created by the demand'.[37]

Butler and his colleagues also recognised that most VD-infected soldiers blamed the women with whom they had consorted rather than themselves for their episodes of infection. Alluding to the Biblical story of Adam and Eve, Butler wrote that:

> ...the attitude of man towards the problem of [venereal] disease has recalled his earliest plea: 'The woman tempted me and I did eat'.[38]

The AIF commanders were nevertheless surprised by the British government's attitudes to the sex trade and the women who were its purveyors. In some jurisdictions, notably Queensland and India, Contagious Diseases Acts had been in force to regulate prostitution and to attempt to reduce the risks of VD transmission. Such legislation allowed for prostitutes to be registered, regularly examined, and treated for gonorrhoea and syphilis. Regulation of that kind aroused fierce resentment, however, especially among women, because of its 'one-sided attitude' in 'plac[ing] on the female sex the whole onus of maintaining the public health'.[39]

Fearing a backlash from sections of the community which had a 'detestation' of regulatory legislation, the UK government steadfastly refused to control prostitution, though it made the sexual solicitation of soldiers an offence. Butler summed up official British inaction in regulating prostitutes as 'the attitude popularly ascribed to the ostrich'—a refusal to recognise a problem. Worse was the government's continuing to regard VD as a subject so taboo it could not be discussed, let alone become the subject of legislation.[40]

The result, according to Britain's critics in the Dominion armies, was that 'prostitution and solicitation were open and unashamed'.

The public, said Butler, had become 'accustomed to the importunity, reaching almost to violence, of women equipped with every device that experience and the struggle for existence could suggest'. The complacency with which British authorities accepted this situation 'astonished' the Army medical officers from the Dominions.[41]

Eventually the British government resorted to the law in an attempt to control the spread of VD among service personnel, but only in the last eight months of the war. In March 1918 a new regulation, number 40(c), under the *Defence of the Realm Act 1914*, was introduced to protect soldiers and sailors against VD-infected women. Regulation 40(c) specified that 'no woman who is suffering from venereal disease in a communicable form shall have sexual intercourse with any member of His Majesty's forces, or solicit or invite [him] to have sexual intercourse with her'.[42] Women disobeying the regulation were deemed guilty of a summary offence and were liable to detention for up to a week while undergoing medical examination to determine if they were VD-infected.[43] Whether or not the regulation did much to curb VD transmission is uncertain because the AIF continued experiencing high VD hospitalisation rates in both the UK and the BEF during 1918. As a coercive measure, it was probably a case of 'too little too late'. The major objection to it was that it threw the burden of responsibility of VD prevention solely on to the woman selling sex rather than the man seeking her services. As such, it could be seen as a misuse of the law', as one feminist historian later described it.[44]

A phenomenon that surprised the military commanders from the Dominions was 'the rise to prominence of the amateur prostitute'. Many women who normally did not work in the 'trade' entered it on a casual basis. Some probably did so opportunistically, because of the regional influx of hundreds of thousands of men with money to spend. Others seemed to offer their services out of curiosity, or because they regarded it as their patriotic duty to 'entertain' lonely soldiers from abroad. According to Butler, the commanders of all the armies on both sides of the war regarded the 'amateurs' as a serious problem because they were thought to be 'subversive to victory and inimical to national interests'.[45]

The 'amateurs' clustered around the camps where the troops were quartered. Periodically the local police moved them on, but that was not a long-term 'fix'. As Lieutenant Colonel Raffan pointed out at one of the London conferences on VD, the local police measures caused the women to 'travel from one camp area to another, and not [be] eliminated as a source of infection'.[46]

In the minds of the military commanders and visiting Dominion politicians, the 'amateurs' gave rise to a stereotypical view of the women with whom soldiers consorted. It was a stereotype in which 'hordes of female harpies' were waiting 'to exploit for gain the simple lads from overseas'.[47] Like all stereotypes, it was an over-simplification, one compounded from various influences, including these:

- the prevailing public prudery over sexual matters
- the exigencies of a war that had brought together hundreds of thousands of young men from across the world
- the social dislocation and economic hardship which the war caused in Belgium, France and the UK
- the time required to treat VD effectively

- the difficulties the armies experienced in recruiting troops to replace those away being treated for VD
- and, as Butler wryly observed, 'the desire to blame someone else'.[48]

The 'amateurs' consequently became a scapegoat for troop wastage and the disruption that VD caused in military formations.

On the other hand, and as in other stereotypes, the image of the predatory women lurking on the perimeters of military camps contained elements of truth. This was obvious in a memo that Colonel Douglas Murray McWhae, the ADMS of the AIF in the UK, sent to the Assistant Provost Marshal (APM at AIF Training Headquarters at Tidworth, Wiltshire, in May 1917. He wrote requesting action against the 'travelling women' frequenting the Army camps on the Salisbury Plain, where many Australian units were training. McWhae complained that:

> In investigating the source of VD locally acquired on the Plain, I am informed that a large proportion of this is acquired from 'travelling women'. These women arrive near a camp, remain several days only and stop men either returning to camp in the evening or else arrange a rendezvous for a few hours in a neighbouring paddock. Addresses

and names have not been obtained so far, and I should be obliged if you could see your way clear to helping me to limit the activities of these women. They are especially annoying at Codford, Hurdcott and in the neighbourhood of Lark Hill.[49]

McWhae would have been pleased with the prompt action taken to address his complaint. Nine days later he received a note from the APM advising him that:

> I have taken action, in cooperation with the local police. One girl was arrested and gaoled for a month. The owner of a house where two other women were lodging is being prosecuted; and the police are ordering 'suspicious women' to move on. The MPs [Military Police] have instructions to arrest loitering women and to hand them over to civilian police.[50]

The civilian police were not always so cooperative. On another occasion the APM at Tidworth obtained the names and addresses of 18 women in London whom soldiers being treated in I ADH at Bulford had blamed for giving them VD. The APM reported the women and their addresses to the City of London Police, requesting action against them. He received a reply from the police commissioner, who advised that he 'regret[ted] that the Police [were] not vested with the powers to deal with a matter of this nature'.[51]

Periodically the women who were thought to have infected soldiers with VD were identified, located, then medically examined and treated lest they transmit their diseases to others. One woman followed up in this manner was 'Josephine' of Erquinghem near Armentières in northern France. On 3 July 1917 an Australian soldier, Private O'Brien, complained during a medical examination that during a 'connection' with 'Josephine' on 27 May he had contracted gonorrhoea. She was duly tracked down by French authorities and on 12 July was examined at a local hospital, where she was found to be suffering neither gonorrhoea nor syphilis. She denied any 'connection' with O'Brien. Had O'Brien falsely accused her, and, if so, should he be court-martialled? AIF Third Division Headquarters investigated the matter but decided that no disciplinary action could be taken against O'Brien because he had neither committed an offence under the Army Act, nor could be prosecuted for libel in a civilian court because he had named 'Josephine' in the privileged circumstances of a private medical examination. A further consideration was that the character of 'Josephine' was such that no court would 'take her word against his'.[52]

The stereotypes of prostitutes soon found their way into the AIF's anti-VD educational and propaganda material. In their lecturers' notes, the Army doctors were enjoined to tell their classes that:

> No woman who will allow you to have irregular sexual intercourse can be regarded as safe. She has probably granted the same favour to others. The amateur, no matter how clean looking, is just as dangerous as the regular prostitute The streetwalkers of Leicester Square, Horseferry Road, Waterloo, and the Strand neighbourhoods [in London] are nearly all infected, and the same thing applies to any large towns you may visit.[53]

Appealing to Imperial patriotism, the lecture concluded with this advice:

> At this critical period, the Empire can ill afford to lose a man from disease that is preventable. For the sake of Australian womanhood and the welfare and happiness of the Commonwealth, keep your bodies and minds pure, for venereal disease is the great destroyer of national and individual happiness.[54]

The plea was also on behalf of the sanctity of Australian women, who by inference were placed on a pedestal, where they stood in contrast to the purportedly diseased, money-grubbing women of Britain, France and Belgium.

One Army doctor who was greatly concerned about women and VD was Major John ('Jack') W.B. Bean (1881-1969), the younger brother of the war correspondent, Charles Bean. As the RMO of the 3rd AIF Infantry Battalion, Jack Bean was twice injured and evacuated from Gallipoli. After his recovery he was posted to the Great Peter Street Hospital in London where he became greatly concerned by the incidence of VD among the AIF patients sent there. Following service in France, he spent 13 months, June 1917 to July 1918, on the staff of 1 ADH at Bulford.[55]

The Bean brothers corresponded frequently. Through Jack, Charles was kept well informed about the wastage caused by VD. The brothers' anxiety about the physiological, social and moral ravages of VD prompted them to become advocates for the 'Australian League of Honour'. This institution, which might never have progressed beyond the planning stage, seems to have been proposed by Charles. If the League had become active, it would have been similar to a British association known as the 'White Knights', founded by Beatrice Chase of Dartmoor, Devon.[56] Like the White Knights, the League aimed to encourage each soldier to 'treat all women and think of them as he wants his own Mothers and Sisters and Sweethearts treated and thought of by other men'.[57] Members of the League would be expected to 'show this honour and reverence to all women for the sake of our own women in Australia who have given us up freely to the war and who trust us to fight not only the enemy at the Front, but the brute which is in our own nature too'.[58]

Alluding to the prostitutes of Britain, the proponents of the League declared that 'the foolishness and weakness of so many of the City women thrusting temptation at us as they do, is yet not an excuse worthy of a man, since he is the stronger, and the chivalry in him should make him protect these women from their lower selves'.[59] Warming to the theme of foolish, weak, 'fallen' women, the proposal for the League declared that:

> We know they were all pure once, and we realise that each time they barter their bodies away for money or for sheer lust, with not a thought of anything approaching real love, they are degrading sexual intercourse, which should [be] a sacred and holy act of pure love, and they are degrading themselves still more. We feel we have no right to accept them because they

offer themselves and that if we do we are kicking them further into the mud from, which as men, we should try and lift them.[60]

The proposal concluded by observing that membership of the League would 'make all women sisters to us'. It then urged soldiers 'to join the League and to do their part in upholding the honour and race purity of Australia'.[61]

The League's view of the sanctity of sexual intercourse and of Australian womanhood was hopelessly idealistic. So, too, was its wish for the 'fallen' women to be raised through chivalrous Diggers refusing their blandishments. It was what might have been expected of brothers raised in the sheltered confines of Anglican boarding schools in which their protective priestly father had been the headmaster. At the same time, the League's manifesto expressed the deep concerns about VD that the Bean brothers shared with their close friends in the AIF. Those concerns were not only about the troop wastage caused by VD but about the wider ramifications of gonorrhoea and syphilis for British and Australian society. In this latter connection, despite its naivety the manifesto evinced genuine distress for the women who prostituted themselves in meeting the demand created for their services by the Diggers.

After the war, a conspiracy theory emerged among some medical officers to explain the part that prostitutes had played in helping the AIF soldiers attain their high rates of VD infection. The theory was one reported in the *MJA* by Dr James W. Barrett, who had served as a lieutenant colonel in Egypt and Britain with both the Australian AMS and the British RAMC. In post-war correspondence in the *MJA*, he argued that high VD hospitalisation rates among the troops had contributed to the defeat of the British Fifth Army by German forces on the Western Front in April 1918. 'We,' he wrote, referring to his fellow RAMC medical officers, suspected that the Germans had been 'subsidising infected women' to spread VD among the British and Dominion forces.[62]

VD as a form of 'germ warfare'? Prostitutes as 'enemy agents'? Barrett admitted that he had no proof but nevertheless regarded this as a possibility. He seems to have been the only former AIF medical officer to propound the notion publicly, and no one commented on his theory in subsequent correspondence. Whether or not his suspicion had any substance, it formed a bizarre postscript to the story of the women with whom the Australian soldiers had consorted.

5. Ettie Rout's 'safe sex' campaign

Ettie Annie Rout, leader of the New Zealand Volunteer Sisterhood, had toiled to alert the military authorities in Egypt to the dangers of VD among the troops.[63] In May 1917 she moved to London, where she began campaigning for 'safe sex'. Realising that the New Zealand Army Medical Corps was treating VD but doing little to prevent it, she took on the self-appointed task of controlling the spread of VD among troops overseas.[64]

Rout began by seeking out Britain's foremost venereologists to seek their views. She then developed her own 'prophylactic kit', which was similar to the AIF's Blue Light Outfit described in the previous chapter, though her kits also contained condoms. She sold her kits at the New Zealand Medical Soldiers' Club which she established in Hornchurch near the New Zealand Convalescent Depot. By the end of 1917 the New Zealand Expeditionary Force had adopted the Rout kit and was distributing it free and compulsorily to all New Zealand soldiers going on leave. Although she was never a member of the New Zealand Expeditionary Force, she received a 'Mentioned in Despatches' for this pioneering work.[65]

Rout approached her task pragmatically. A health and physical fitness advocate, she was appalled by the personal and public health ramifications of the high incidence of VD among soldiers, and especially those from the Dominions. She feared for the future of the 'white race' in Australia and New Zealand if VD infection rates among the Anzacs were not greatly reduced. She agreed with the stern moral strictures of the Army chaplains about abstinence being the best precaution against VD, yet neither conventional sexual morality nor religion figured in her campaign. Nor was Rout much interested in the post-infection VD medical treatment regimens managed by the Army venereologists, whom she accused of obfuscation by 'mak[ing] a Precious Mystery of sexual hygiene'.[66] She and the AIF's principal venereologist, Lieutenant Colonel Raffan, nevertheless seem to have collaborated[67] and one of her admirers was the official medical historian of the AIF, Arthur Butler.[68] She freely acknowledged the importance of all these influences in her public pronouncements and voluminous correspondence, but her focus was always on preventing VD through using the most effective forms of prophylaxis available—her safe sex kits. Promoting that cause, she was practical, realistic and non-judgemental, qualities which appealed to the Anzacs.[69]

Figure 4.5: Ettie Rout (seated second from left) with a group of Australian and New Zealand soldiers in Paris, September 1919 (AWM H03655).

In pursuing her goals, Rout was a tireless publicist for safe sex. An indefatigable correspondent, she badgered senior Army administrators, medical officers, politicians, government officials and the Anzacs themselves to promote her ideas and solicit their support. At the same time, she criticised them roundly and ridiculed them if she thought they were obstructing her. In one circular to AIF soldiers, couched in characteristically strident language, she averred that England was a 'cess-pool of venereal infection'. She then argued that 'the spread of venereal infection in the British Empire is due mainly to the following dangers: ... (1) Pious Prejudice, (2) Medical Claptrap, (3) Social Flapdoodle, (4) Official Delusions, (5) Political

Interference'.[70] In a letter to Major General Howse she claimed that VD-infected troops were avoiding the Blue Light Depots and self-treating rather than submitting to the ministrations of 'the so-called "expert" orderlies'. Further, the VD sufferers were 'sick to death of the meddlesome and impertinent interference of "the authorities" in their private affairs'.[71] The vehemence of her long letters, their intemperate language and her tendency to alarmist rhetoric enabled her critics to dismiss her views as those of a disruptive termagant.[72]

Rout relocated to Paris in April 1918. There she established her own 'one-woman social and sexual welfare service for soldiers'.[73] This took a radically proactive approach to VD prevention. Instead of simply distributing her prophylactic kits, Rout effectively sponsored her own 'safe' brothel. Her biographer described her modus operandi as follows:

> As troop trains arrived from the front, [Rout] stood on the platform of the Gare du Nord, greeted the New Zealanders—with her trademark kiss on the cheek—and handed out cards recommending the brothel of Madame Yvonne, who had agreed to run her establishment on hygienic lines. Rout regularly inspected it.[74]

After Rout publicised her methods in a newspaper in New Zealand, the government there imposed a ban on even the mention of her name in the press.[75]

Rout's manner of addressing officialdom is seen in a letter she sent from Paris to the New Zealand Expeditionary Force commander. 'The only way to teach the educated English is to insult them,' she wrote. 'If they are told enough home truths they may turn their C3 nation into an A1 nation, but I doubt it.'[76] This was a reference to British criticism of her work among the British troops sent to occupy Germany, where, she wrote, 'several thousand "tommies" are becoming [VD] infected every week', with the result that 'the homes of England are being blasted by the foulest of diseases'.[77]

Australian military officials kept Rout at arm's length. One whom she dealt with regularly was Major Burford Sampson, the officer commanding AIF troops in Paris in early 1919. He reported to AIF headquarters that 'the methods and activities of Miss Rout are objectionable and undesirable, however worthy her motives'. Sampson wrote that 'the advice she forces upon soldiers is harmful and bad for discipline'.[78] After Rout's death in 1936, Sampson changed his mind. By then a Senator for Tasmania in the Commonwealth Parliament, he wrote to Charles

Bean praising her. He said she had been an 'extraordinary character' and had done 'excellent work in Paris'.[79]

Undeterred by criticism, Rout carried on with her work, attributing her opposition to 'wowsers'.[80] At the end of the war she took on the role of soldiers' advocate to officialdom, lobbying politicians and senior military officers for the troops' swift repatriation to their homelands. Among those with whom she exchanged letters on this matter was W.M. Hughes, the Australian Prime Minister.[81] During 1919 and 1920 Rout also ran a Red Cross depot in the war-ravaged town of Villers-Bretonneux. For her various good works the French government awarded her the *Médaille de la Reconnaissance française* or 'Medal of Gratitude', an honour instituted to reward civilians for exceptional humanitarian achievement.[82]

A century later, historians struggle to determine what impact Ettie Rout might have had in reducing Anzac VD infection rates, which remained high during her campaign. She had a talent for antagonising military officialdom, but perhaps her one-woman campaign bore fruit unseen. Some Anzacs who might otherwise have contracted gonorrhoea or syphilis probably remained uninfected by using her prophylactic kits. On this issue, as on many others discussed in this chapter, Butler spoke with authority. 'The work of Miss Ettie Rout for the troops,' he wrote, 'has been much criticised but was a real help to many.'[83]

6. A note about VD statistics

This book includes much statistical data. The figures and tables presenting data are necessary because they tell an important story. In the present era of antibiotics, which usually cure VD sufferers effectively and quickly, the impact of VD in the pre-penicillin era is readily forgotten. Without considering the VD statistics of earlier decades, it would be easy to overlook the devastation caused by gonorrhoea and syphilis before the introduction of penicillin. VD could depopulate battalions as effectively as combat casualties did.

But how accurate are the figures?

The short answer is that the statistics are as accurate as wartime exigencies permitted. All such figures are probably somewhat suspect because they were recorded under wartime conditions. The soldiers compiling them were medical and clerical staff under the pressure of high caseloads, tight deadlines, often cramped and temporary office accommodation, staff shortages, frequent staff turnover and periodic changes of location. Under these circumstances, the figures might not always have been recorded accurately.

On the other hand, there is a strong possibility that the statistics *under* estimated the incidence of VD in the AIE The statistics are only those of hospitalisations for VD in *Army* hospitals. Some soldiers certainly managed to conceal their VD symptoms, and some received treatment privately rather than at the Army hospitals and Blue Light clinics. How many did is impossible to estimate, but the inducements for doing so were powerful. For some, the loss of pay for weeks on end, the public shame of being confined to a VD hospital, the ensuing stigmatisation and the fear of families at home learning about the infection were sufficient reasons to avoid becoming an official 'VD statistic'.

While the figures might be queried, it is important to recognise that the Australian Army has not only assembled statistics with an 'eye to history' but has been continually obliged to give a statistical account of itself to its own commanders, the Department of Defence, the government of the day and the Commonwealth Parliament. The AMS accordingly developed comprehensive bureaucratic procedures for ensuring that the statistics it needed were dutifully collected and recorded by its field units and hospitals.

Part of the author's archival research for this book was to examine the many files of monthly statistical returns from the Army VD hospitals of World War I. These often list patients by name and provide case-by-case details of laboratory test results plus the methods and length of treatment before discharge from hospital. The research also entailed reading Butler's own statistical files. A methodical historical researcher, Butler derived his statistics from the figures compiled by the VD hospitals for their monthly returns to the relevant ADMS or DDMS and the DMS. Even a cursory reading of Butler's files indicates that he worked carefully on his task of synthesising the statistical data available to him.

Confusingly for the present-day researcher, Butler's estimates of the number of hospitalisations for VD among AIF troops during World War I vary widely, and his figures are inconsistent. For example, in his statistical tables of diseases suffered by the AIF he gives a total of 62,050 VD cases, but that is only for the Western Front and does not include cases in the UK, the Middle East or Australia.[84] Elsewhere, in his summative comments on the incidence of VD, he gives a total of 52,538 cases for all theatres, yet further down the same page he sets out tables showing that the number of cases in Egypt-Palestine was 12,745, while the combined figure for the UK and the Western Front was 40,880—a total of 53,625 for the AIF overseas.[85] None of these figures include the VD cases in Australia, which later in his book he gives as 11,230 for 1915 to 1917, a total which does not include an estimated 495 cases in 1914. If the 1914 estimate is included, the number of cases in Australia would have been 11,725.[86]

Ignoring Butler's figure of 62,050 cases on the Western Front as being too high by comparison with his other statistical tables, a guesstimate of the approximate total VD infections for the AIF is possible.[87] This 'best guess' is set out in Table 4.3, indicating that an estimated 65,350 cases of VD were treated by Army medical units during the war. The figure is certainly an underestimate because it does not include the cases that occurred and were treated in 1919 after hostilities ended. Nor does it take account of the large but unknown number of soldiers who successfully concealed their symptoms, self-treated or sought treatment from civilian doctors.

Table 4.3-'Guesstimate' of total AIF VD cases in World War I

Theatre	Total VD cases
Australia	11,725
Egypt and Palestine	12,745
UK and the Western Front	40,880
Total	65,350

Source: Derived from A.G. Butler, The Australian Army Medical Services, Vol.3, Special Problems and Services.

A total of 65,350 VD cases among the 417,000 troops who enlisted in the AIF is almost 16 per cent of the total strength. Another way of expressing that statistic is to say that the equivalent of 16 out of every hundred soldiers who joined the AIF—one in six of them—became VD-infected at some stage of the war.

The proportion is higher when based only on the number of troops who served in overseas theatres—330,714. The 65,350 VD cases are then seen to be 19.8 per cent or one in five of embarkations.

Both proportions, one in six and one in five, seem inordinately high. Are they? They certainly are when compared with the figures from the next war, World War II, when an estimated five per cent or one in 20 of Australian troops suffered VD infections.

Adding to the confusion over the extent of VD in the AIF is the round figure of 30,000 cases of VD often quoted in the post-war decades.[88] The source of this very low estimate is never given, but various senior Army personnel commonly bandied the number around. Whether they were taking a blind guess or deliberately understating the number for political reasons is uncertain.

How might these wide discrepancies be explained? The probable answer is that the present-day researcher cannot always precisely determine what was being counted or excluded in the available statistical tables. Butler's figures certainly appear inconsistent. To him, they were possibly not so, and if called on to explain what they did or did not include, he could readily have done so.

Unfortunately, Butler did not write a treatise on the compilation and tabulation of his published VD statistics. In the absence of such a document, later historians must accept that his figures vary and that they include disturbing inconsistencies. At the same time, the historian must also realise that Butler's figures are the only comprehensive ones available because wide gaps exist in the VD hospitals' own statistical reporting.

Finally, even if Butler's VD statistics are only partially accurate, they are nevertheless useful indicators of the incidence of VD in the Australian Army during World War I.

7. Conclusions

STDs continued to be an issue of major concern for the AIF during its deployments to Egypt and Palestine, Belgium and France, the UK, and also in Australia. VD caused huge, if temporary, wastage. Whatever the exact figure for VD hospitalisations—65,350 or higher—if each case represented an individual soldier rather than a second or third hospitalisation of the same man, the total was the equivalent of between three and four AIF infantry divisions.

General Birdwood and Major General Howse could therefore be excused for their harsh measures against the AIF's VD-infected troops. First, being preventable, VD could be likened to a self-inflicted gunshot wound. As such it could be considered as a serious breach of discipline. Second, no army could sustain wastage of such magnitude for long. That being so, the AIF's punitive approach to VD management was a logical means of dealing with what was a military as well as a medical issue.

Criminalising VD and punishing the 'offenders' was only one approach. An alternative was the more humane, less alienating and militarily more constructive treatment regimen developed at Langwarrin VD Hospital. If Langwarrin's salutary methods had been adopted by the other Army

VD hospitals, the healing and rehabilitation of the AIF's VD-infected troops might have been effected more expeditiously and with better results for discipline. In addition, the personal costs to the VD sufferers might have been less adverse in both the short and long term.

Australians always suffered much higher rates of VD infection than their British comrades. Overall, between 16 and 20 per cent of AIF troops had to be hospitalised because of VD. The reasons stemmed from the composition of the AIF, the nature of Australian society and the manner in which these factors influenced Diggers' attitudes.

Finally, the nature of the war itself contributed to VD-related troop wastage. To many Diggers in the trenches on the Somme or in the Sinai desert, the war must often have seemed interminable. On the front line, wherever that was during the three years from 1916 to 1918, the soldiers must often have wondered if they would live long enough to return to their distant homeland. Doubts of that kind engendered the fatalism and moral nihilism that drove them into the arms of VD-infected prostitutes. Short of the unthinkable action of withdrawing the AIF from the war, the Army's commanders could have done little to combat such a mindset.

CHAPTER 5

Venereal Disease in Australia between the two World Wars, 1919-1939

In the two decades following World War I, the medical profession in Australia discussed VD more openly and widely than previously. Among doctors, VD was no longer the taboo subject it had been in some circles pre-war because the medical profession in Australia shifted from a 'moral-medical' towards a 'sociological-medical' view of VD. The incidence and management of VD was reported more often than previously in the medical press, principally the *MJA* and the *British Medical Journal*. By the early 1920s the six Australian states had all adopted Venereal Diseases Acts to attempt to control VD. The medical profession usually provided the impetus for such legislation, which included the establishment of government-run public VD clinics. A new generation of venereologists entered the field, many of them doctors who had learnt about venereology from firsthand experience as Army medical officers in the wartime VD hospitals. In the years immediately before the eruption of the next world war in 1939, the development of sulphanilamide, an antibacterial compound, gave the medical profession a powerful new drug for treating VD. diseases.

1. Anti-VD campaigners and the spectre of VD-infected returnees

World War I had barely ended when present and former AAMC officers began publishing articles in the *MJA* recounting their work on VD while serving with the AIE Among the first to do so was Major Zwar of 2 ASH. In July 1919 Zwar published an article in the *MJ A* that had begun as a report on his work at 2 ASH before the unit was deployed from Egypt for the Gallipoli campaign.[1] In the same *MJA* edition as Zwar's article was another by his colleague Arthur E. Morris, who had served with I ADH at Bulford in England. Morris's article was titled 'Army Medical Service: Prophylaxis and treatment of venereal disease'.[2] Two months later, Major W.L. Potter of 5 AGH published an article in the *MJA* titled 'The influence of treatment and rest in gonorrhoea'.[3] Another former I ADH officer, Lieutenant Colonel Piero Fiaschi, published a leading *MJA* article on 'The prophylaxis of venereal disease'.[4]

Articles and correspondence about VD from former AAMC officers continued appearing in the *MJA* thereafter. Among the most authoritative was 'Studies in Syphilis', published in 1921 by a rising star in Australian medical science, Major Neil Hamilton Fairley, formerly the senior physician at 14 AGH in Egypt but by 1921 a research scientist at the Walter and Eliza Hall Institute of Medical Research in Melbourne.[5] Fairley went on to a stellar career as a London-based international expert in tropical diseases.

A matter of common concern among the former AAMC medical officers and the Australian medical profession more generally was the possibility that VD-infected troops returning home from abroad would transmit their infections to the women of Australia. They believed that would be a catastrophe—a terrifying threat to the health and welfare of the nation.

Such a view had been expressed earlier by Dr Richard Arthur MD (1865-1932), an influential medical practitioner, social reformer and New South Wales parliamentarian.[6] In 1915 and 1916 Arthur chaired a select committee of the New South Wales parliament inquiring into the prevalence of VD; he was the architect of the

New South Wales *Venereal Diseases Act 1918*; and he served for three years from 1927 to 1930 as Minister for Health.[7] In 1916 Arthur lectured AIF officers on the danger to the Army and the nation of uncontrolled VD. He told them that it was 'difficult to over-estimate the injury' that VD was causing to the AIF in both Australia and Egypt. Apart from the wastage of military manpower and the financial cost to the Commonwealth, there was a 'further lamentable aspect' to the AIF's high rates of VD infection. This was:

> ...the ease that men from the backblocks of Australia, who, had there been no war, would never have become infected, will now return home and carry infection far and wide, with disastrous results to the next generation.[8]

Arthur's lecture to the AIF officers had been published as a leading article in the *MJA* in May 1916. Five months later, the *MJA* published another article by Dr Arthur, this time drawing attention to 'the menace of venereal disease' in Australia. He argued that 'of all the racial poisons which make for national degeneracy, there are none more potent in their effects than syphilis and gonorrhoea'. Australia's future, he warned, 'holds the promise of grave and sinister possibilities that call for a numerous and virile population to meet them'. Turning to recent events, notably the failed Gallipoli campaign in 1915, he claimed that, but for VD, the war in the Dardanelles could have resulted in an Allied victory! 'A tremendous number of Australian troops were more or less incapacitated by VD,' he asserted, 'and had these men been available, the history of the ... campaign might have been very different.'[9]

The AIF's commanders might not have agreed with Dr Arthur that the 5924 Australian soldiers hospitalised for VD in Egypt between December 1914 and January 1916 could have tipped the balance during the Dardanelles campaign if they had remained uninfected.[10] Transforming the Gallipoli debacle into a victory might have required more than that. What they might have agreed on was the necessity for anti-VD legislation to halt the post-war transmission of VD to the civilian population of Australia from the ex-servicemen returning home.

The fear that VD would spread from VD-infected veterans throughout the nation was one shared by many civilians. In a 1920 *MJA* article titled 'The treatment of gonorrhoea by the general practitioner', Dr J.G. Avery, a dermatologist-venereologist[10] at the Brisbane General Hospital, expressed the public mood. 'Since the outbreak of the war,' he wrote, 'the venereal diseases have been occupying the minds of the general public and of the medical profession to a far greater degree than previously'.[11]

Various organisations sprang up to defend the community. Among the first was the University Society for Combating Venereal Diseases, which formed at the University of Sydney in October 1916, having been initiated by final year medical students. The University Chancellor became its patron and the dean of the medical school its president. The society's objectives included 'the study of the problems of venereal disease, prostitution and kindred evils', and 'educat[ing] public opinion to secure suitable legislation'.[12] Among other activities, over the

---

[10] In the period before the 1920s, venereology was considered to be a subset of dermatology. Dermatologists were consequently expected to have expertise in venereology because of the dermatological aspects of VD. The link between dermatology and venereology was the reason behind the naming of No. 1 Australian Dermatological Hospital, one of the Army's major VD hospitals during World War 1.

next two years the society conducted a series of lectures on VD for the students of the university and another series for the members of the Trades Hall.[13]

Another Sydney group that was active during the war was the Council for Civic and Moral Advancement, the leaders of which comprised representatives from the major religious denominations and leading private schools. Among its causes was 'the grave question of the spread of venereal disease'. It hoped to 'discover some method by which the public conscience might be aroused and the public mind impressed with a sense of the seriousness' of VD spreading further.[14] How much it achieved is unclear, but its existence reflected public disquiet about VD.

In Melbourne during the war the social reformer and eugenicist, Angela E. Booth (nee Plover, 1869-1954), had formed the Association to Combat the Social Evil. 'The Social Evil' was a term she borrowed from the Women's Political Association (WPA), an organisation led by the feminist activists Vida Goldstein and Adela Pankhurst.

In May 1916 the WPA had conducted 'The Social Evil Women's Convention' in Melbourne to discuss the Victorian government's Venereal Diseases Bill of 1916, which in December that year became law as the *Venereal Diseases Act 1916*. The WPA strongly opposed the criminalisation of VD implicit in the Bill, which, it argued, would result in the 'civil rights' of women being 'abrogated'.[15] For the WPA, 'The Social Evil' was 'code' for prostitution, but Mrs Booth extended the meaning to include 'prostitution and its inevitable consequence of VD'—perhaps a convenient euphemism at a time when neither subject could be discussed openly.

Angela Booth was an immigrant from Liverpool and the wife of a medical practitioner in Broken Hill and later North Melbourne. A feminist and an activist, she had become interested in what women could do to improve their social, economic and political conditions.[16] Like members of the WPA, she was confident that the 'sex problem' could be remedied by social reform. She founded the Association to Combat the Social Evil with the ambitious objective of eliminating prostitution and eradicating VD.[17] As her biographer observed, she believed that 'women were forced into prostitution through economic necessity and that prostitution was encouraged by a double standard of morality'—one standard for women, another for men.[18] Her threefold solution was for women to receive equal pay, become active in government and for the public to be educated in 'racial responsibility'. The last of these required sexual restraint outside marriage and planned parenthood within to produce healthy, wanted children.[19]

During the 1920s, Angela Booth and her husband, Dr James Booth, emerged as leaders of the Australian eugenicist movement. They became convinced that 'the proliferation of mental defectives in society was the greatest single cause of unemployment and crime'.[20] They and their supporters believed that prostitution and VD were at the root of this problem. VD-infected prostitutes, they maintained, were generally 'feeble-minded', and so when they reproduced, their offspring were feeble-minded too. 'Moron breeds moron' was one expression they used.[21] 'It is no exaggeration to say that over 75% of prostitutes are either feeble-minded or high grade morons [because] prostitution, like all other unnatural vice, is chiefly practised by mental degenerates,' one like-minded contributor to the MJA correspondence columns had written in 1919.[22] The Booths' remedy for this 'stain on the national honour' was the 'sterilisation of the unfit'.[23]

Yet another group which campaigned against VD was the Victorian Branch of the Australian Association for Fighting Venereal Diseases (AAFVD), a Melbourne-based organisation of which Sir James W. Barrett was the instigator and president. (The AAFVD, which seems only to have had the one branch, in Victoria, was also known as the Association for Combating Venereal Diseases.) Barrett was the most frequent contributor of *MJA* letters-to-the-editor on VD during the 1920s and 30s. He served as the Vice-Chancellor and then the Chancellor of the University of Melbourne during the 1930s but continued contributing correspondence about VD to the *MJA*. Barrett wrote about the AAFVD in several of his letters to the *MJA*. 24 According to these, the association was modelled on similar organisations in the UK, namely the British Society for the Prevention of Venereal Disease, and the National Council for the Combating of Venereal Diseases.[25]

Barrett announced his intention of forming the AAFVD in a letter-to-the-editor in the *MJA* on 1 October 1921. He indicated that he was doing so as a member of the council of the British Society for the Prevention of Venereal Diseases.[26] Barrett succeeded in recruiting into the AAFVD an extraordinarily wide cross-section of individuals and representatives of institutions and organisations. They included Dr John H.L. Cumpston (head of the Commonwealth Department of Health); Dr Edward Robertson (head of the Victorian Department of Health);

representatives of the churches, the Department of Education, the Association of Secondary Teachers, the Society for Combating the Social Evil, the YMCA, YWCA, the Trades Hall Council, the Labor Party, the Australian Natives' Association, the National Council for Women, the Women's Christian Temperance Union, the Pharmaceutical Society of Victoria, the Inspector-General of the Insane, the Farmers' Union of Victoria, the Women's Medical Association, and the RSL.[27]

The AAFVD began by issuing a manifesto—*The Venereal Diseases Problem: A Memorandum Issued for the Information of All Responsible Citizens*. This set out four objectives for the AAFVD: (a) public education through lectures on VD by medical experts, (b) the dissemination of information about VD to medical practitioners, (c) the issuing of literature on VD to the public, and (d) the promotion of 'legislation bearing on the notification, prevention and treatment' of VD. After describing syphilis and gonorrhoea, this pamphlet emphasised how widespread VD infection was and what it was costing Australia. It quoted a Professor Atkinson who had estimated that VD was costing Australia £50 million annually, or about $3498 million in 2020 values. The pamphlet proceeded to outline the attitude of the British Medical Association

(BMA) to VD and then provided a list of the hospitals and clinics in Melbourne that provided treatment for VD.[28]

How active the AAFVD was is uncertain. Perhaps it did conduct lectures and distribute literature about VD, but not much evidence of that has survived. Possibly it did little more than produce its manifesto, *The Venereal Diseases Problem*. The very existence of the AAFVD, as well as the Council for Civic and Moral Advancement, the Association to Combat the Social Evil and others of their ilk was nevertheless a measure of the widespread post-war community concern about the threat of VD.

2. The 1922 Melbourne conference on venereal disease

Concern about the spread of VD also found expression in a conference sponsored by the Commonwealth and state governments. The Conference on Venereal Diseases, which had prime ministerial approval,[11] took place in the Senate Club Rooms of the Commonwealth Parliament on 1 February 1922. Dr Cumpston,

---

[11] The Prime Minister was W.M. Hughes, who held the position from October 1915 to February 1923.

recently appointed as the inaugural Commonwealth Director-General of Health (a position he held from 1921 to 1945), was conference chairman and the Commonwealth Minister for Health, Mr (later Sir) Walter Massy-Greene was present to welcome the delegates formally.[29]

Figure 5.1: Portrait of Dr John H.L. Cumpston (1890—1954), the inaugural Commonwealth Director-General of Health 1921—1945, who chaired the 1922 Melbourne Conference on Venereal Diseases (National Library of Australia PIC/9249).

The conference was attended by 24 representatives of the Commonwealth and state departments of health, the state VD commissioners, the government-sponsored VD clinics, the medical faculties of Melbourne and Sydney universities, the states' quarantine officers, the Commonwealth Serum Laboratories, and an agency called the International Health Board.[30] The council of the BMA was represented by Major General Fetherston, the Army's wartime DGMS, who had perforce been obliged to grapple with the AIF's disconcertingly high VD infection rates from 1914 to 1919.[31]

In opening the conference, the minister (Massy-Greene) explained that the Commonwealth was subsidising the states to the amount of £15,000 ($1.24 million in Australian values a century later) 'to enable them to carry out a scheme aiming at the control of venereal diseases'.[32] As Commonwealth ministers customarily do when dispersing largesse to the states, he told the delegates that he expected 'the best results [would be] obtained for the expenditure of the money'.[33] He then handed over the chairmanship to Dr Cumpston, who had organised the conference, which was probably also his idea.

Cumpston was already an authority on VD as a public health issue. Three years earlier, in 1919, he had published Australia's first book on VD—*Venereal Disease in Australia*.[34] That had been when he was the Commonwealth's Director of Quarantine. His slim 44-page book had been published by the Quarantine Service. It summarised the history of the states' legislation on VD and then considered the intention of the various Venereal Diseases Acts. The tenor of such legislation is indicated by the series of 16 subheadings under which Cumpston discussed the scope of the legislation. These were as follows:

1. Treatment by medical practitioners only
2. Patient's obligation to obtain medical treatment
3. Treatment to continue until cure effected
4. Notification
5. Action taken where patients fail to continue treatment
6. The detention of prisoners
7. Knowingly affecting other persons
8. Owners of brothels
9. Indecent and forbidden advertisement
10. Prostitutes
11. Facilities for the treatment of infected persons
12. The influence of alcohol in affecting the incidence of venereal diseases
13. Prophylactic measures
14. Source of infections
15. Distribution of venereal diseases

16. Cases occurring in the military forces enlisted or mobilised in the Commonwealth.[35]

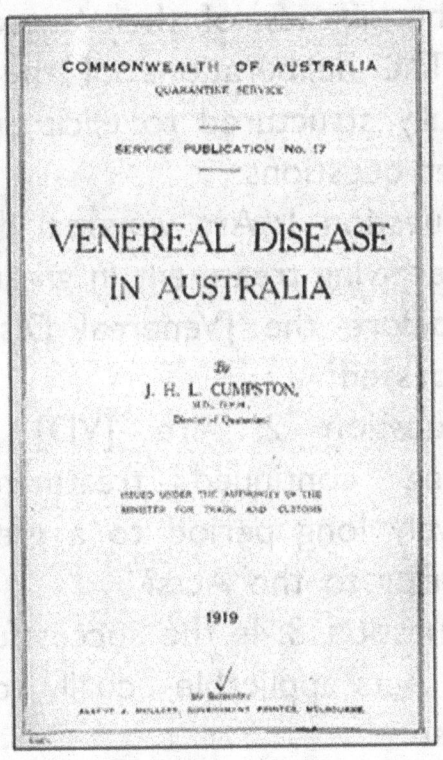

Figure 5.2: An Australian 'first': Dr John H.L. Cumpston's 1919 book, Venereal Disease in Australia. The title of the book was a misnomer because the contents had little to do with venereology but was rather a digest of Australian legislation relating to VD. The book was written when Cumpston was still serving as the Commonwealth Government Director of Quarantine (author photo courtesy of the National Library of Australia).

In organising the conference, Cumpston had clearly done some agenda-setting because most of the issues discussed had been the topics covered in his book *Venereal Disease in Australia*. The main business of the conference was to consider 'the efficacy of the Venereal Diseases Acts'.[36] The deliberations of the conference were carefully structured to elicit answers to a series of set questions:

> Question 1: Are venereal disease cases now receiving treatment in greater numbers than before the [Venereal Diseases] Acts were passed?
>
> Question 2: Are [VD] cases now receiving continued treatment for an effectively long period to a greater extent than prior to the Acts?
>
> Question 3: Is the successful operation of the Acts applicable equally to males and females?
>
> Question 4: Has the passage of [the Acts] resulted in the reduction of the prevalence of [VD] in the community?
>
> Question 5: Has the passage of this legislation resulted in the reduction of congenital [VD] infections?
>
> Question 6: Has the operation of [these Acts] produced a more complete appreciation by the practising section of the [medical] profession of the national gravity of [VD] or a valuable cooperation between

the general [medical] profession and the health authorities directed towards the control of [VD]?[37]

The resolutions adopted by the conference in response to these questions were a mix of affirmative and negative answers. The 'scorecard' was as follows: 'Yes, more people are now seeking treatment and for longer' to Questions 1 and 2'; 'more applicable to males than females, because more men are being treated' for Question 3; 'insufficient time has passed to know if VD is less prevalent' to Question 4; 'no evidence yet for a reduction in congenital VD' for Question 5; and 'generally yes, the medical profession better appreciates the seriousness of VD' to Question 6.[38] Whether or not this was the feedback that Cumpston and his minister might have hoped for is uncertain. The conference, however, had served one useful purpose by bringing together for the first time the state health authorities and the medical profession to consider the threat that VD might pose to the Australian community.

One consequence of the conference was its 'knock-on' effect in encouraging the medical profession and the state health agencies to be more proactive about VD. One of the conference resolutions was a request for the federal committee of the BMA to issue a circular to all its Australian members 'appealing for their cooperation and emphasising their legal responsibilities in connexion with [VD]'.[39]

The BMA circular was prepared and distributed during the second half of 1922. In turn, it prompted lively discussion. The council of the Victorian branch of the BMA discussed the circular at length then 'affirm [ed] that chastity is the only absolute safeguard against [VD]'.[40] More realistically, and recognising that chastity was a virtue not sustained by the VD-infected, the council recommended that people at risk of contracting VD should either consult a medical practitioner or visit a VD clinic within eight hours of their exposure to infection.[41]

Another conference outcome was the establishment of the Australian AAFVD, which has been described above.[42] As seen, the AAFVD gave Sir James Barrett a platform from which he could promote his views on VD control. Although Barrett had given notice of the formation of the AAFVD in a letter to the *MJA* in October 1921, it was the Melbourne conference that prompted him into action during 1922.[43]

3. Australian legislation to control venereal disease

Laws endeavouring to control the spread of VD had been enacted by some pre-federation colonial parliaments. Usually called the Contagious Diseases Acts, these instruments were modelled on the British *Contagious Diseases Act 1864*, which had aimed to curb VD by suppressing prostitution.[44]

By World War I, the emphasis was shifting from the prostitute to the disease and to measures for reducing its incidence. The passage of legislation directly addressing VD in Australia was an achievement of the six state governments during the wartime years. Independently of each other, their parliaments had all passed Venereal Diseases Acts between 1915 and 1920. Western Australia had been the first, in December 1915. Victoria followed in December 1916, and then came Tasmania and Queensland in February 1917, New South Wales in December 1918 and South Australia in December 1920.[45]

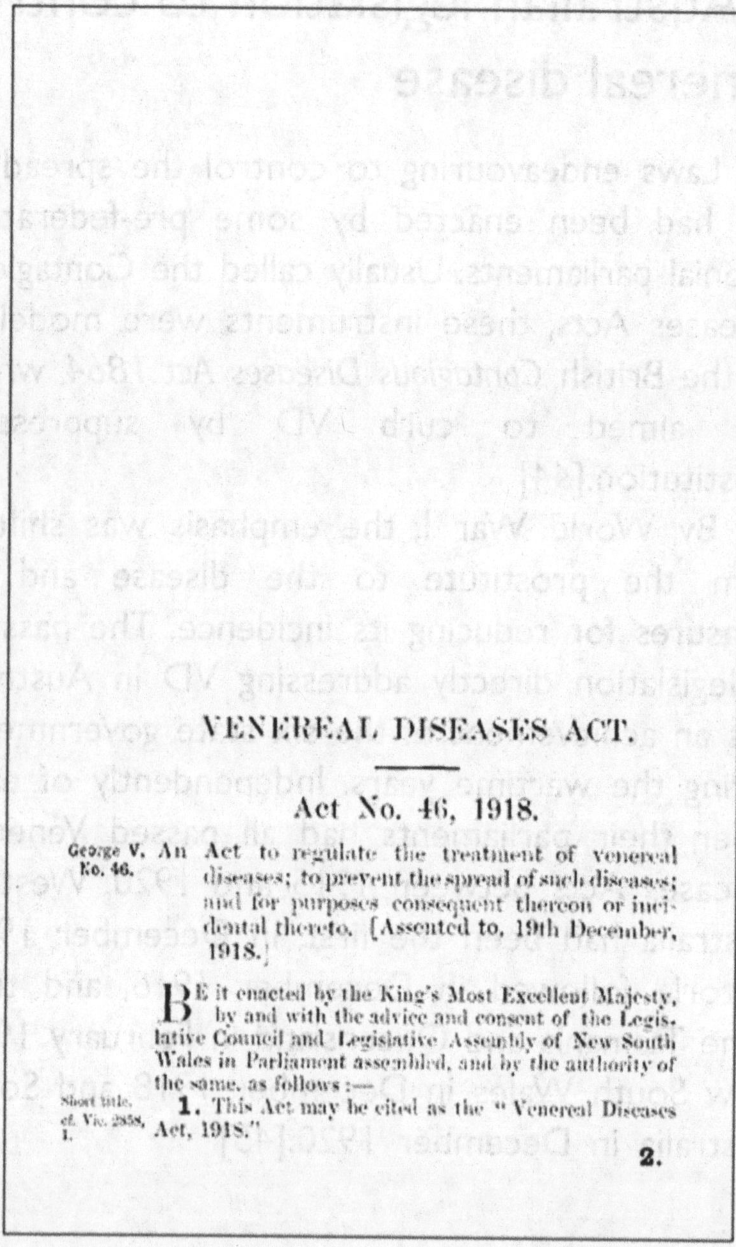

VENEREAL DISEASES ACT.

Act No. 46, 1918.

George V, No. 46. An Act to regulate the treatment of venereal diseases; to prevent the spread of such diseases; and for purposes consequent thereon or incidental thereto. [Assented to, 19th December, 1918.]

BE it enacted by the King's Most Excellent Majesty, by and with the advice and consent of the Legislative Council and Legislative Assembly of New South Wales in Parliament assembled, and by the authority of the same, as follows:—

Short title. cf. Vic. 2858, 1. **1.** This Act may be cited as the "Venereal Diseases Act, 1918."

2.

Figure 5.3: First page of the New South Wales Venereal Diseases Act 1918, which aimed to regulate the venereal diseases (NSW

Government legislation, https://legislation.nsw.gov.au/acts/1918-46.pdf).

The NSW legislation in 1918 was fairly typical of such Acts. In common with parallel legislation in the other states, it aimed to 'regulate the treatment of venereal diseases in order to prevent the spread of VD'.[46] It endeavoured to do so through these means:

1. Only a registered medical practitioner was permitted to treat and prescribe drugs for VD patients.
2. Every person suffering VD was obliged to report to a medical practitioner or hospital and undergo the treatment deemed necessary.
3. A medical practitioner who had diagnosed or was treating a VD sufferer was required to 'give notice' of the case by providing written notification about it to a VD commissioner appointed under the Act to maintain a register of people deemed to be VD-infected.
4. The doctor diagnosing and treating a case of VD was required to alert the patient to the infectious nature of the condition.
5. A doctor managing a VD patient who wished to marry was empowered to advise a prospective marriage partner that

the person they intended marrying was VD-infected.
6. Someone who married knowing they were VD-infected would be committing an offence. (The penalty was up to five years' gaol or a fine of up to £500—the equivalent of $45,000 in 2020 values.)
7. Where a patient had been cured of VD, their doctor was obliged to issue a certificate attesting that they had been cured. Issuing such a certificate when the patient had not been cured was an offence.
8. VD-infected people were debarred from working in jobs requiring them to handle food.
9. Press censorship was applied to matters relating to VD infection that came before the courts. This was to safeguard the confidentiality of the parties to the case.
10. Allowing someone who was VD-infected to use premises for prostitution became an offence.
11. Hospitals receiving government funding could be required to provide treatment to VD sufferers.
12. The advertising of patent medicines claiming to prevent or cure VD was prohibited.

13. Magistrates were empowered to authorise police to enter premises to search for and seize any medicines or materials that could be used to treat VD.
14. The Minister for Health was required to:
    a. establish hospitals or places for the reception and treatment of persons diagnosed as suffering from VD
    b. arrange for the examination or treatment by medical practitioners of persons suffering from VD
    c. provide for the reception, examination, and treatment of such persons free of charge at such hospitals
    d. arrange for chemical, bacteriological and physical examinations for VD to determine whether a person was suffering from, cured of, or free from VD, or was no longer likely to transmit infection
    e. arrange for the supply of drugs, medicines, and appliances for the treatment of VD where the VD sufferer was unable to pay for the drugs used in treating VD
    f. provide for the preparation and distribution to the public of information about VD.

15. It became an offence under the Act to accuse someone of being VD-infected without legal justification for doing so.
16. If a Children's Court established that a child was VD-infected, the child could be declared neglected and required to undergo treatment in a secure facility.[47]

In short, the Venereal Diseases Acts endeavoured to restrict the treatment of VD to the medical profession and specialised VD clinics in order to prevent quacks and charlatans trying to 'cure' VD with their own nostrums. VD became a 'notifiable' disease, with sufferers' names entered in a government-maintained register. The Acts provided coercive legal machinery to force VD sufferers to seek treatment, and they ensured that the appropriate clinics existed for that to happen. The rights to freedom of employment and marriage for VD sufferers were severely curtailed. Legal safeguards for the privacy of VD sufferers were also introduced.

The introduction of the Venereal Diseases Acts was a direct result of pressure on state governments by the medical profession. In the decade before World War I doctors had lobbied governments through the BMA to adopt measures like those outlined above. The need for such legislation had also been a continuing theme at successive meetings of the Australasian Medical Congress.[48] And the presence in the state and Commonwealth parliaments of doctor politicians such as Dr Richard Arthur, and later Dr Earl Page and Sir Neville Howse, ensured that the medical profession's point of view was always heard by the legislators.

Once the legislation was in place, the *MJA* monitored its effectiveness. During the inter-war years the *MJA* frequently editorialised on the extent to which the Acts were achieving their purpose.[49] In addition, the *MJA* correspondence columns became a lively forum in which medical practitioners discussed how effective the legislation was from the perspective of their own experience of VD management.[50]

The system of official coercive management of VD attracted critics. One was Dr Alex Goldstein of Sydney, who in March 1922 wrote to the *MJA* pointing out that coercion was proving ineffective. Goldstein claimed that:

> ...evasion of the Venereal Act, both in New South Wales and Victoria, is an everyday occurrence, and many chemists and unqualified men openly supply drugs for and treat venereal diseases. Seldom do medical men notify patients who default from treatment. In spite of this, prosecutions

under the Venereal Diseases Act are almost unheard of in either State.[51]

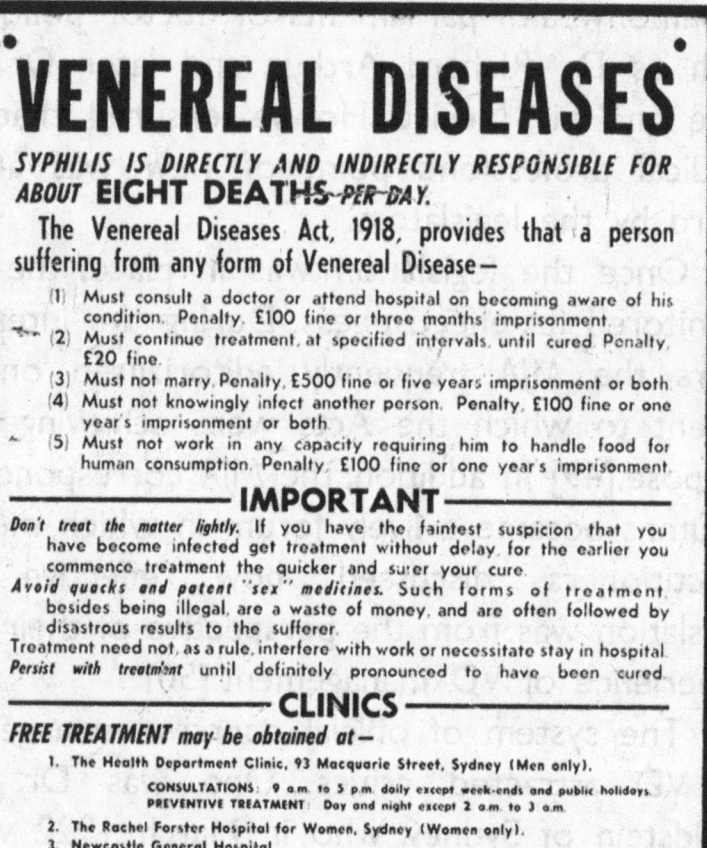

Figure 5-4: 'Venereal Diseases' information sign used by the New South Wales Health Department from 1950 to 1965. Such signs, printed in enamel on sheet metal, were commonly fixed to the walls of public toilets to remind the public of the provisions of the state's Venereal Diseases Act 1918. Similar signs adorned the walls of public toilets in other states (Picture no. DS-3399 of the Museum of

Applied Arts and Sciences, Sydney, reproduced with permission).

Another critic was Dr J. Cooper Booth, who later became the New South Wales State Director of Venereal Disease Control and then the Director-General of Social Hygiene. In July 1922 he wrote to the *MJA* to argue that the *Venereal Diseases Act 1918* was 'a menace'. According to Booth, the Act had the opposite effect to what the legislators had intended because it drove VD-infected people 'into the hands of quacks'.[52] Fearing detection, public shaming and being reported to the state health authorities, they sought out pharmacists and 'various laymen' who would sell them unlabelled medicaments of dubious efficacy. 'I know that [VD] is very common in Sydney,' Booth wrote, 'and I doubt that if even half the infected persons are being treated by legally qualified medical practitioners.'[53]

For its part, the *MJA* asserted that 'notification [was] an effective weapon if it [was] properly applied'.

> In our opinion, the strict enforcement of all the provisions of the Venereal Diseases Acts and the establishment of prophylactic depots and of treatment centres and of [VD] clinics on a large scale, with

ample indoor accommodation for persons of both sexes would prove of far greater value in reducing the amount of infection than educational measures.[54]

Sir James Barrett wrote two of his many letters-to-the-*MJA* -editor to affirm the effectiveness of public VD education programs. Alluding to his time as an RAMC lieutenant colonel and senior Red Cross official in Britain during World War I, he argued that the British Army had successfully reduced the incidence of VD through a combination of complementary measures. These included both the moral and medical education of the soldiers, the provision of adequate recreational facilities, the availability of medical prophylaxis, the notification of VD cases and appropriate VD treatment regimens. By contrast, in the USA the punitive, non-education-based management of VD in rural populations by government agencies had led to an increase in the incidence of VD.[55]

The *MJA* continued defending the Venereal Diseases Acts staunchly. It maintained its position throughout the inter-war years, periodically editorialising to the effect that:

> ...venereal disease affects the nation as a whole. It takes its toll in the lives, the physique and in the health of the community. It affects those who have

contracted the disease through carelessness, those who are affected through no fault of their own, and it makes its appearance in the new born [sic]. This being so, it is necessary that the State should make efforts by legal enactment to prevent and eradicate it.[56]

Debate over the Venereal Diseases Acts continued during the 1920s, 1930s and beyond. Depending on which particular jurisdiction was under discussion, the Acts were periodically amended but remained law until the 1960s.[57] After that they were generally subsumed within public health and infectious diseases legislation although certain of their coercive provisions remained in place.[58] In 2016, for example, notification of a group of four STDs remained obligatory under the Commonwealths *National Health Security Act 2007*. These were chlamydia, donovanosis, gonorrhoea and syphilis—all 'old' infectious diseases in that medical science had known about them for many decades.[59]

One direct outcome of the Venereal Diseases Acts was the establishment of State-sponsored VD clinics in the capital cities and some major regional centres. In Melbourne, for example, separate government-run clinics were set up for men and women. Under various names and at different locations, the clinics continued receiving and treating patients during all the century that followed. By 2017 they had conducted a total of 87,719 consultations—77,290 gonorrhoea, 9381 syphilis and 1048 chancroid cases.[60]

4. Incidence of venereal disease in Australia 1919-1939

In view of the debate over the effectiveness of the Venereal Diseases Acts, a pertinent question is how successful the Acts were in arresting the spread of VD among Australia's civilian population. To answer that question would require a set of tabulated statistics showing the annual number of infections state by state for each of the VDs across a long time period, for example from the end of World War I to, say, the end of World War II. Unfortunately, such statistics might not exist or if they do they might be fragmentary and perhaps not accessible to the general public. The most accessible STD statistics are those published in *Year Book Australia*.[61] This is an annual national statistical compendium covering many fields—demography, education, health, trade, industry, agriculture and forestry, science and technology, defence, government and administration among numerous others.

The *Year Book* statistics for STDs are intermittent and fragmentary. The only figures published for this present chapter's period of study, 1919 to 1939, are deaths from syphilis, of which there were 3185 (2270 males and 915 females).[62] Unfortunately, the number of annual cases of syphilis infection were not published for that period, an omission that might well have been politically motivated. 'Causes of death: Syphilis' was a category included in successive *Year Books* for the 104 years from 1907 to 2010, but after that the *Year Books* stopped reporting national mortality from syphilis.

Under 'Notifiable diseases', the *Year Books* published the annual number of reported cases of both syphilis and gonorrhoea—but only for the 50 years 1961 to 2010. (The totals across that period were 99,476 cases of syphilis and 367,139 of gonorrhoea.[63]) From 1988 the *Year Books* published the annual number of notified cases of HIV (a total of 23,950 from 1988 to 2010), and from 1991 the chlamydia cases (535,860 from 1991 to 2010).[64]

People wishing to write about the history of STDs in Australia accordingly receive little help from the one national publication in which they might expect to find a comprehensive suite of statistics. The anonymous author of the 'Health of Australians: Morbidity' entry in the fourth

(1983) edition of *The Australian Encyclopaedia* realised this. The brief note, 'the extent to which venereal disease is widespread throughout Australia is unknown, due to incomplete statistics', reads like an admission of defeat.[65]

After the advent of extensive online publishing in the mid-1990s, the Australian Bureau of Statistics was able to make available a much wider range of STD statistics. Unfortunately, historical figures were still not available, but even one year in the 21st century, 2012, presents a 'snapshot' of the kind of material that would have been collected by the states as soon as STDs were declared 'notifiable'. The number of notifications and the rate per hundred thousand of population for each of chlamydia, gonorrhoea, syphilis and HIV infection that year were as indicated in Table 5.1.

Table 5.1 -**Notification rate of four STDs, Australia, 2012**

Disease	Number of notifications	Rate: notifications per 100,000 of population
Chlamydia	81,214	357.3
Gonorrhoea	12,183	53.6
Syphilis	1250	5.5
HIV	1068	4.7

Source: Australian Bureau of Statistics 2012

If such data were available as a time series for the entire inter-war period, 1919 to 1939, that would give researchers a clear view of the trends in STD infections. That in turn would enable them to judge if the authors of articles and letters-to-the-editor in the *MJA* in the 1920s were presenting an alarmist view when they voiced concern about purportedly rising VD infection rates and the widespread ramifications of these for Australian society.

For example, how sustainable were the opinions of Dr William A.T. Lind, the pathologist to the Victorian Lunacy Department, on the nexus between VD and insanity? Dr Lind once claimed that syphilis was 'rampant' in *all* the patients admitted to the state's lunatic asylums, and that the disease had been present in all the autopsies he had performed in the asylums. He also said syphilitics comprised more than 10 times as many inmates in asylums as nonsyphilitics.[66] Dr Lind, a eugenicist, advocated the compulsory sterilisation of 'mental defectives' to prevent them from breeding, but he also believed that sterilising them would not halt the spread of VD because they were habitually promiscuous.[67] Dr Lind presented a paper on 'Venereal Disease and the Abnormal Mind' at the Australasian Medical Congress in Perth in November 1922. His paper argued that as well as being a major factor in 'certifiable insanity', VD also played a part in producing 'abnormal-mindedness' and dementia in the general community. Further, gonorrhoea was 'a more important factor in the production of insanity than was generally supposed', while 'gynaecological diseases were more prevalent in the insane than among the sane'.[68]

A comprehensive set of statistics showing trends in VD infection rates during the 1920s and 30s could neither confirm nor disprove Dr Lind's assertions. Such figures would, however, demonstrate whether some doctors' scepticism about the effectiveness of the Venereal Diseases Acts in reducing the incidence of STDs was justified.

The fragmentary VD statistical data that are available suggest that in the pre-penicillin era the coercive legislation was indeed necessary. The Acts gave the states an instrument for tackling the spread of STDs, which, for both social and medical reasons, were difficult to eradicate, rendered many thousands infertile, afflicted many innocent sufferers and were a needless drain on government finances. The Acts were certainly coercive and intrusive on personal freedoms. In individual cases they were probably administered harshly and insensitively, with little respect for the sufferer's personal dignity, and they would have had the effect of stigmatising VD sufferers. Nonetheless, that did not negate the need for such legislation.

Contemporaneously in 1921, two important studies of syphilis were conducted in Melbourne by former AIF medical officers, Dr Neil Hamilton Fairley and Dr Robert Fowler. Each had served with distinction in the 1st AIF during World War I and would do so again with the 2nd AIF in World War II.[69] In December 1921, when Fairley was on the staff of the Walter and Eliza Hall Institute for Medical Research in Melbourne and Fowler was a surgeon at the Melbourne Women's Hospital, they published separate but complementary research papers on syphilis in the same edition of the *MJA*. Fairley's had the simple title 'Studies in Syphilis' and Fowler's was called 'Familial Syphilis'.[70] These two studies were among the most sophisticated and scientifically rigorous of any on VD that the *MJA* had yet published. Both papers yielded instructive figures which gave a clearer view of the epidemiology of syphilis while also filling in some blank spaces in the inter-war VD statistics.

What the Fairley and Fowler studies revealed was a tendency for syphilis to run in families. Their research was carried out among all the women attending the maternity department of the Women's Hospital in Melbourne. They found that a tenth (9.8 per cent) of 380 women examined in the study showed a 'strongly positive Wassermann reaction' to the syphilis antibody test developed by the German bacteriologist, Dr August P. von Wassermann, in 1906. Further, a slightly higher proportion (11.2 per cent) of the babies born to them tested positive, in other words, were suffering congenital syphilis. This demonstrated 'the persistence of syphilis in the offspring of syphilitic mothers'.[71] When the studies were extended to the other members of the syphilitic women's families, Fowler and Fairley found that 50 per cent of the women's husbands and other children also tested positive for syphilis. 'Some families,' Fairley observed, '[were] universally syphilised, all the members being infected.'[72]

Fairley and Fowler recognised the sociological implications of their findings. 'The subject of familial syphilis is not one purely of medical interest,' Fairley observed, 'it is also of vital importance to the whole community.'[73] With reference to the congenitally syphilitic offspring of syphilitic mothers, he argued that 'it is a deplorable fact that no legal measures exist [to enable] children to receive the benefits of anti-syphilitic treatment in the event of the parents refusing to assist the physician'.[74]

When Fairley and Fowler reported their findings to a meeting of the Victorian branch of the BMA at the Melbourne Hospital in September 1921, their presentation provoked lively discussion. Dr Cumpston used the occasion to emphasise the necessity of the coercive provisions of the Venereal Diseases Acts. Cumpston had recently published an *MJA* article in which he had pointed out that in both Victoria and Western Australia the current rate for VD notifications was 113 per hundred thousand of population for syphilis and 350 per hundred thousand for gonorrhoea. Moreover, 16 per cent of the notifications were married people, which had ramifications for 'the wastage of infant life from venereal infections'.[75] After Fairley's and Fowler's presentations Cumpston commented that their evidence confirmed the need for, first, 'a certificate of freedom from syphilis before marriage' and, second, 'the provision of compulsory powers for the examination of other members of the family of which one member was found to be infected'.[76] Sir James Barrett rounded off the discussion by commending Fairley and Fowler for their studies, which, he averred, 'marked another milestone in progress of the campaign against venereal diseases'.[77]

Another senior medical administrator who attended the Fairley-Fowler presentations was Dr Edward Robertson, head of the Victorian Department of Health. Robertson took the opportunity of providing the meeting with some recent statistics. He said that in Victoria in the four years from July 1917 to June 1921, a total of 28,297 cases of VD had been reported—24,234 (86 per cent) of these being males and 4063 (14 per cent) females. The vast majority of these, 92 per cent (26,032 of the 28,297), were from metropolitan Melbourne, with much smaller percentages from the three main regional cities (Geelong, Bendigo and Ballarat) and the rest of the state.[78] The number of cases treated at the governmentrun VD clinics had been 8224, with the breakdown between diseases and sexes as indicated in Table 5.2.[79]

Table 5.2-**Patients treated at Melbourne's government VD clinics, 1917-1921**

Disease	Males	Females	Total	Disease as proportion (%) of total	Males as proportion (%) of total	Females as proportion (%) of total
Gonorrhoea	4996	251	5247	64%	95%	5%
Syphilis	2254	282	2536	31%	89%	11%
Chancroid	434	7	441	5%	98%	2%
Totals	7684	540	8224	100%	93%	7%

Source: 'British Medical Association News: Syphilis', report in Medical Journal of Australia, 24 December 1921, pp.611-612.

As Table 5.2 demonstrates, the great majority, more than nine-tenths, of patients were males; about two-thirds (64 per cent) of the cases were gonorrhoea and a third (31 per cent) syphilis, with chancroid comprising one in 20 cases.

The figures for notifications and treatments were only for the four-year period ending in 1921. They cannot be extrapolated to the other five states or to periods later in the inter-war decades. They nevertheless give those researching STIs a glimpse of the epidemiology of VD in Australia in the early inter-war years. They also enable scholars to make general inferences and ask questions, such as the following:

- The 28,297 VD notifications in Victoria over the four years 1917 to 1921 were the equivalent of 7074 annual notifications. In a state population of about 1.53 million, the annual notifications therefore amounted to one in 212 (0.47 per cent) of Victoria's citizens.[80]
- Was that a high notification rate? It was by comparison with later national figures. For example, some six decades later in 1981, notifications for VD (gonorrhoea and syphilis) in Australia totalled 14,113 in a population of 14.93 million—a notification rate of 0.1 per cent or one in 1053 of all Australians.[81]

One remarkable historical VD statistics retrieval project was carried out in 2016 and 2017 by a research team associated with the

Melbourne Sexual Health Centre, formerly called the 'Government Clinic'. The project results were published in 2017. The team used the clinic's admissions registers, which covered the period 1918 to 2016, to retrieve data that had not been previously reported. Team members were able to tabulate and chart the admissions for gonorrhoea, chancroid and syphilis over that entire 99-year period. What the data generally reveal for the period of study covered in this chapter (1919 to 1939) is that the number and rate of VD admissions fell during the early to mid-1920s before rising to a peak in the early 1930s. After that the number and rate fell steadily during the late 1930s, 40s and early 50s to levels appreciably lower than in 1919.[82] These trends are illustrated in the charts at Figures 5.5 and 5.6, for gonorrhoea and syphilis respectively. The charts are from the study published in 2017 under the title 'Sexually Transmitted Infections in Melbourne, Australia, from 1918 to 2016: nearly a century of data'.[83]

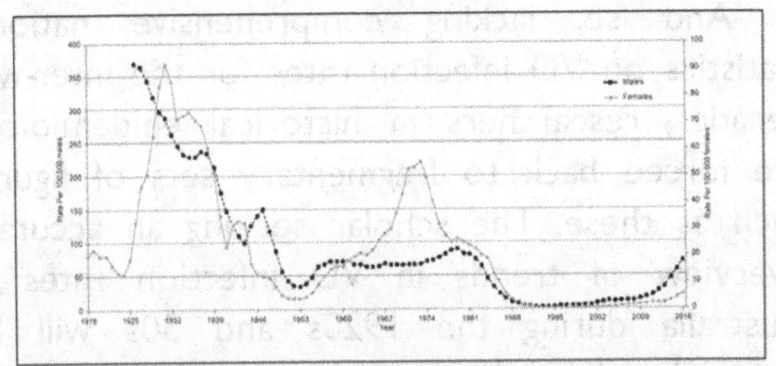

Figure 5.5: Average rate (diagnoses per 100,000 of population) of gonorrhoea diagnoses for males and females in sexual health clinics in Melbourne, 1918-2016 (Emile Jasek et al., 'Sexually Transmitted Infections in Melbourne, Australia, from 1918 to 2016: nearly a century of data, Communicable Diseases Intelligence, Vol.41, No.3, 2017).

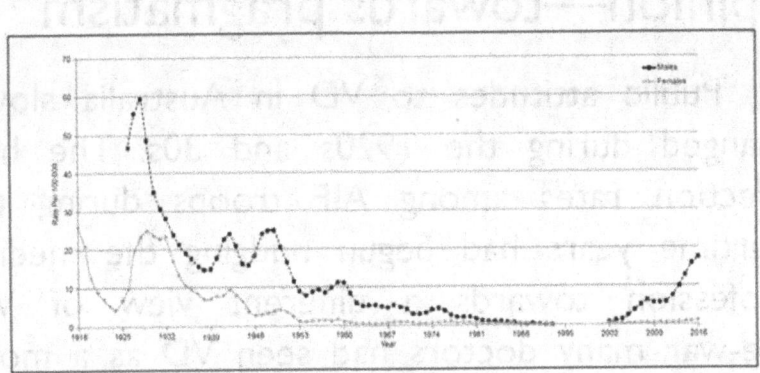

Figure 5.6: Average rate (diagnoses per 100,000 of population) of syphilis diagnoses for males and females in sexual health clinics in Melbourne, 1918-2016 (Emile Jasek et al., 'Sexually Transmitted Infections in Melbourne, Australia, from 1918 to 2016: nearly a century of data', Communicable Diseases Intelligence, Vol.41, No.3, 2017).

And so, lacking comprehensive national statistics on VD infection rates for the inter-war decades, researchers in historical epidemiology are forced back to fragmentary sets of figures such as these. The scholar seeking an accurate overview of trends in VD infection rates in Australia during the 1920s and 30s will be disappointed by the huge gaps in the data. The reader accepting that only a partial view is available, as afforded by the charts above, might settle for the microcosmic glimpses they offer.

5. A shift in medical opinion—towards pragmatism

Public attitudes to VD in Australia slowly changed during the 1920s and 30s. The high infection rates among AIF troops during the wartime years had begun nudging the medical profession towards a different view of VD. Pre-war, many doctors had seen VD as a moral issue as much as a medical problem. 'Weak-willed', 'feeble-minded' and 'immoral' people contracted VD; 'clean-living' people of 'good character' did not. Doctors who served overseas with the AMS during the war had generally come to realise that such a dichotomous view was unrealistic. VD infection occurred for many reasons which most often arose from the exigencies of war and the situation in which the war had placed individual soldiers.

The old attitudes towards VD nevertheless continued beyond the inter-war decades into World War II. The persistence of the World War I-era punitive measures for VD-infected troops within the Army was obvious to Alan S. Walker, the official Australian medical historian of World War II. Walker began his special chapter on VD in *Clinical Problems of War*, the first book of his four-volume series, by observing that 'before the 1914-1918 war ... powerful taboos still imposed an obstacle to the fullest realisation of scientific methods in the prevention and treatment of venereal diseases'.[84] 'The old rigid disciplinary measures,' he wrote, 'were still being applied with unwise rigour.' For example, as late as February 1941, 107 AGH at Puckapunyal north of Melbourne still had a 'VD isolation wing' which was effectively a separate 'compound under armed guard'. The Puckapunyal VD ward accordingly had 'the atmosphere of a prison camp'. Further, 'there were still non-medical officers in the Army who [regarded VD-infected soldiers] as criminals'.[85]

The medical profession led the way in the Australian public's changing perceptions of VD. The 'swing from the predominantly moral outlook to one which was predominantly medical', as Walker termed it, was an achievement of the medical profession.[86] The *MJA* reflected doctors' changing attitudes. A more pragmatic acceptance of the reality of VD could be seen in an early post-war editorial. In March 1919, the *MJA* looked back on the way the war had tempered public opinion about VD. 'The war has taught the community many things,' the editorial noted. 'It has been the means for educating public opinion on matters that formerly were regarded as unworthy of recognition or too unsavoury to warrant free discussion.'[87] The editorial then described the pre-war situation as one where:

> ...formerly the Bishops in the [UK] House of Lords led a campaign of opposition to any endeavour to limit the incidence of venereal disease, on the grounds that each and every proposal to this end must imply a condoning of vice. The public was kept in absolute ignorance as to the nature, frequency and consequences of these diseases; and since these infections were never spoken of, they were allowed to spread through all classes unchecked and unchallenged.[88]

Turning to the war and post-war era, the editorial went on to suggest that:

> ...the war has forced the world to realise that venereal disease was one of the most important facts to be reckoned with in the establishment of armies. It was evident to those in authority that unless special means were adopted, the loss of effective [troops] as a result of venereal infections might make the difference between victory and defeat ... It is probably true that danger, hardships and prolonged restraint induce in the majority [of soldiers] a desire to throw off the bonds of discipline and to follow natural inclinations ... We feel that it is only the exceptional male to whom this dictum does not apply. Consequently, the hygienist is compelled to recognise the fact that, despite all appeals to conscience, despite all preaching and moral teaching, illicit sexual intercourse will remain a serious cause of disease until the rational prophylactic measures are applied throughout the community.[89]

Two-and-a-half years later, in October 1921, the *MJA* editorialised on these topics again in an 'opinion piece' headed 'A Public Question'. More stridently than previously, it declaimed to the effect that:

> A few years ago the subject of venereal disease and that of the sexual relations

between men and women was taboo in the daily press and in public discussion. These matters were regarded by Mrs. Grundy[12] as non-existent, or, at worst, of no concern to the community as a whole. False modesty was the order of the day and no one was courageous enough to face a condition which was undermining the health and happiness of our race.[90]

Not all *MJA* readers could accept the editorial thrust towards this more practical or sociological view of VD and its management. One dissentient voice was that of a mysterious correspondent identified only as 'M.S. Wallace', who wrote to protest the opinion of an earlier correspondent who had argued that 'prostitution [had] existed from time immemorial, all effort to abolish it [had] failed, and therefore it must be accepted as inevitable'.[91] Wallace rejected that view, arguing that prostitution and its inevitable concomitant of VD infection were 'a

---

[12] 'Mrs Grundy': 'a person with very conventional standards of propriety' (Concise Oxford Dictionary). Wikipedia extends the definition to: 'a figurative name for an extremely conventional or priggish person, a personification of the tyranny of conventional propriety'.

stain on the national honour'. He or she advocated a punitive approach:

> When suitable provision ... has been made for the prevention of venereal disease, members of the public who are too dirty or too lazy to avail themselves of these certain preventive measures, and who thereby endanger their fellow citizens, should be punished as other criminally careless persons are...[92]

Another dissident was Dr John Brady Nash, a surgeon and parliamentarian who spent 24 years as a member of the Legislative Council of New South Wales. Presumably with leave of absence from the parliament, Nash had served as a lieutenant colonel with 2 AGH in Egypt from January to December 1915 before returning to Sydney.[93] Taking exception to the drift of MJA editorial comment on VD generally, and to the views of Sir James Barrett in various letters to the MJA in particular, in 1922 Dr Nash wrote to the MJA to state an alternative, traditional and Christian viewpoint. His letter is worth quoting from at length because it ran against the tide of MJA comment.

> In every moral code that holds place amongst the advanced races of mankind, fornication is a major crime ... Before one can accept the teachings of Sir James Barrett

and of those agreeing with him in regard to prevention of venereal disease, [one] must be prepared to deny the correctness of the Christian moral code. Christian morality and immorality cannot be separated from the sexual organs, because they are attributes of these organs. Sir James may reply, 'But, be practical amongst the sons of men!' To which can be made answer: 'When to be practical requires connivance at immorality, no Christian can subscribe thereto.'

Is not the crux of the subject compassed by the Mohammedan gibe, so often heard in Egypt: 'You Christians do not look after your women!' Can one wonder at this gibe when [one] has seen the *rendez vous* [sic] of the white Christian women, who were brought purposely from the south of Europe to cohabit with the men of the army of occupation? Not one of those women could have entered Egypt if the military authorities had forbidden them...[94]

Dr Nash's protest might have jogged the memories of Army doctors who had fretted over VD infection rates among Australian troops in Egypt. In 1922, however, four years after the war, it elicited no response at all in the *MJA's* correspondence columns. His and M.S. Wallace's were apparently lone voices crying in a wilderness of post-war pragmatism.

The clearest enunciation of the pragmatic approach came from the later official medical historian of World War I, Dr A.G. Butler, and a Brisbane colleague, the provocative pathologist Professor James Vincent Duhig,[95] in a letter to the *MJA* editor in April 1922.[96] The Butler-Duhig letter put forward a series of arguments explaining the complexities of VD management and what was required for its success. They argued as follows:

1. 'True prevention' of VD must embrace both 'moral' and 'sociological' measures.
2. VD would not exist without 'promiscuous sexual intercourse', which was largely 'inevitable and uncontrollable'. The factors influencing such promiscuity included these: (a) the relaxation of communal attitudes towards sex; (b) general ignorance about both sex and VD; (c) a preoccupation with hedonistic diversions; (d) alcohol and prostitution acting in tandem; (e) industrialisation and the concentration of the population in large cities; (f) the growth of slums; (g) a dearth of opportunities for healthy recreation; (h)

a distaste for marriage; and (i) poorly developed civic ideals.
3. The effective control of VD must depend on the collaborative engagement of a wide range of government, municipal, medical, and community development agencies 'whose concern is social and civic order and elevation'.
4. US-style 'medico-social clinics' should be among the services offered by the state social welfare authorities.
5. The Venereal Diseases Acts should be administered by commissions of experts, who, drawn from medical and community health agencies, should be given powers 'to coordinate the social and sanitary [aspects] of preventive efforts'.
6. 'Preventive efforts' must embody public education about VD.[97]

The Butler-Duhig scenario for VD management was more or less what eventuated some 50 to 60 years later, after the grim post-World War I 'Government Clinics' had evolved into the 'Sexual Health Centres' of the 1970s and 80s. In the meantime, progressive doctors such as Butler and Duhig had led the Australian medical profession towards more enlightened attitudes to STDs.

In time the general community followed the progressive doctors, but not until the 'penicillin' era after World War II. Penicillin could not prevent the almost inevitable STDs resulting from promiscuous 'unsafe sex' but it effectively cured those of bacterial origin. That had ramifications for the epidemiology of STDs which a later chapter will explore.

6. Introduction of the sulpha drugs

The development of effective medicaments for STDs began during the first decade of the 20th century as doctors and pharmacologists sought out chemotherapies that were less injurious than 'the wretched' mercuric, arsenical and antimonial compounds customarily used to treat VD.[98]

The first breakthrough came in 1907 when the great German physician and medical scientist, Professor Paul Ehrlich, developed 'No.606', one of over 600 arsenical compounds he had synthesised and had been testing on the syphilis-causing spirochaete bacterium, *Treponema pallidum*. Ehrlich, who won the 1908 Nobel Prize in Physiology or Medicine, patented 'No.606' but did little more with it. In 1909 a Japanese bacteriologist, Dr Sahachiro Hata joined Ehrlich as an assistant at the German National Institute for Experimental Therapeutics in Frankfurt am Main. Hata retested all of Ehrlich's arsenical compounds, finding that 'No.606' was 'very active'. A group of Ehrlich's physician collaborators who tested the compound intramuscularly on some of their most hopeless patients' were 'surprised at the improvements engendered by a single injection'.[99]

By September 1910 'Preparation 606', or 'Arsphenamine 606' as it became known, had been used to treat some 10,000 syphilitics. Marketed as 'Salvarsan', Ehrlich's and Hata's arsenical compound 'transformed syphilis treatment', especially after a modified form called 'neoarsphenamine' and 'neosalvarsan' were introduced in 1914. As the medical historian Roy Porter later observed, the use of neosalvarsan represented 'a considerable advance' in the treatment of syphilis. It was, however, toxic. Moreover, 'many painful injections into the bloodstream over a long period [were still required] before a cure was complete'.[100]

An Australian historian of the treatment of syphilis, John Frith, has shown how 'arsenic, mainly arsphenamine, neoarsphenamine, acetarsone and mapharside, in combination with bismuth or mercury, [remained] the mainstay of treatment for syphilis until the advent of penicillin in 1943'.[101] As seen in earlier chapters, a

Salvarsan regimen was followed in the Australian Army's VD hospitals and treatment centres during World War I. It was then used in the state-run VD clinics established under the Venereal Diseases Acts of the mid to late 1910s. The 'arsenic' regimen would be used again in the Army's VD treatment units during World War II.

Figure 5.7: Salvarsan treatment kit for syphilis, Germany 1909—1912 (Science Museum, London, Wellcome Collection, L0057814, CC BY)

The next advance in treating STDs flowed from the research of another German Nobel Laureate, Professor Gerhard J.P. Domagk. A pathologist and bacteriologist, Domagk was awarded the 1939 Nobel Prize in Physiology or Medicine for discovering the anti-streptococcal properties of a red dye known as 'suffonamidochrysoidine'.[102]

In 1932 Domagk, the research director of the Bayer pharmaceutical firm in Wuppertal, found that sulfonamidochrysoidine, also called 'sulphonamide', cured mice injected with a fatal dose of haemolytic (red blood cell-destroying) streptococcal bacteria. He treated his own daughter successfully with the compound after she contracted a streptococcal infection. Sulphonamide was a 'bacteriostatic' compound, meaning that it did not kill bacteria but prevented them from multiplying in the body of the host, whose immune system then destroyed them. After further development, Domagk commercially released sulphonamide under the brand-name 'Prontosil'. Doctors who used Prontosil at Queen Charlotte's & Chelsea Hospital in London declared it a 'miracle drug' after using it to treat puerperal (childbed or postpartum) fever. It had the effect of reducing mortality from puerperal infection by a factor of five, from 20 per cent to 4.7 per cent.[103]

Meanwhile, a research team at the Pasteur Institute in Paris further developed Prontosil. Led by the chemist Ernest Fourneau, they discovered that within a patient's body the 'sulpha' compound divided into two parts, one of which, sulphanilamide, was responsible for the drug's bacteriostatic action.[104]

Although Prontosil proved highly effective against streptococcal bacteria, it did little to inhibit pneumococcal infections. Further development of the sulphonamide was undertaken at May & Baker (also called 'M&B'), a British pharmaceutical firm in Dagenham, East London. In 1938 a research team led by Dr Arthur J. Ewins developed a drug called 'M&B 693' or 'sulfadiazine 693', later called 'Sulphapyridine'. This was not only effective against pneumococci, but was even better than sulphonamide when used against streptococci.[105]

By the end of the 1930s, the new sulpha drugs were being widely used to treat bacterial infections successfully. The range of complaints being treated included erysipelas, mastoiditis, meningitis, skin infections, pneumonia and urinary infections. Sulphanilamide was found to be particularly effective in treating gonorrhoea. It cured a 'typical' case of the disease in five days—unheard of in the 1st AIF's VD hospitals in World War 1, when the treatment regimen took seven or eight times that long to complete.[106]

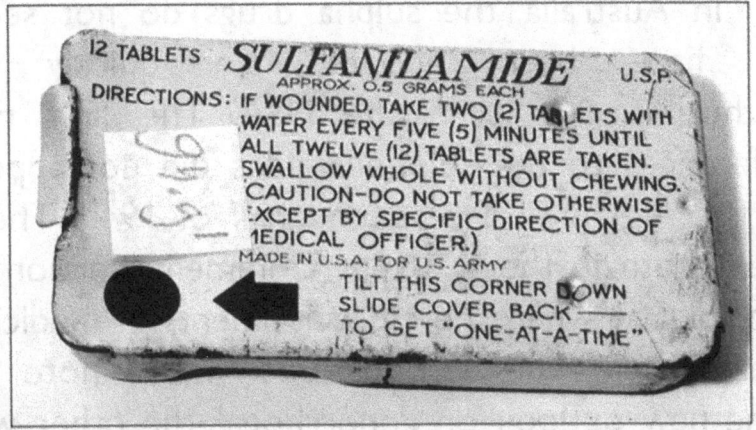

Figure 5.8: A can of Sulphanilamide ('Sulfanilamide') tablets from 1944-1945. Issued by the US Army for self-medication by wounded soldiers, the tablets came in a dispenser with a slide-back cover (KingaNBM, CC BY-SA 4.0).

In the USA in the late 1930s and early 40s a 'craze' for sulpha drugs seized both the medical profession and the pharmaceutical industry. Thus, by 1941, 1700 tons (1727 tonnes) of sulphonamides were being prescribed for 10 million Americans. The disadvantages of such widespread usage were that the sulpha drugs could have serious adverse side effects and became less effective as sulpha-resistant strains of bacteria emerged. Despite that, as Roy Porter observed, 'they nevertheless represented a major step towards the control of bacterial diseases, and their development spurred research into other antimicrobial agents'.[107]

In Australia, the sulpha drugs do not seem to have been adopted so quickly or enthusiastically as in the USA. The first two references to the sulphonamides did not appear in the *MJA* until the second half of 1940. These were both in the 'Current Comment' section of the journal, where new developments in medicine were briefly summarised. One was a note on 'The new outlook on gonorrhoea'; the other was on 'The use of sulphanilamide in gonorrhoea in the male'.[108] After that, the *MJA* made little reference to the sulphonamides in relation to STDs until the 1970s, the reason perhaps being that penicillin had largely eclipsed the sulpha drugs for that purpose.

7. The inter-war decades in retrospect

By the time the sulpha drugs came on the market in Australia, the nation was at war again. The 2nd AIF had formed in late 1939 and its advanced units were being despatched to Palestine, Southeast Asia and the archipelagos of the South-West Pacific by the end of that year. AMS doctors who had learnt venereology as junior officers in the VD hospitals and bacteriological laboratories of the 1st AIF in Egypt, the UK and France would soon become senior medical officers in theatres such as Palestine, Egypt, Libya, Greece, Syria, Ceylon, Malaya, Singapore, Java, Ambon, Papua and New Guinea. They would be joined by a new generation of medical officers who had graduated from Australian medical schools during the inter-war decades.

The 1st AIF's harrowing experience of VD overseas during World War I had not been wasted effort because it had produced positive results in Australia during the 1920s and 30s. These included the Venereal Diseases Acts, Australia's first systematic attempt to deal with the medical and societal impact of VD. The AIF's experience also engendered a ferment of research, discussion and debate that continually surfaced in the doctors' forums—the Australasian Medical Congresses, the meetings of the BMA and the pages of the most-read doctors' mouthpiece, the *MJA*. Much of this was led by doctors who had seen the huge wastage that VD had caused within the Australian Army during the war.

But perhaps the most worthwhile outcome of the AIF-wide experience of VD was the more realistic, more objective and more pragmatic view of STDs that emerged during the inter-war decades among medical professionals, administrators and legislators. Mrs Grundy still hovered, but she was now on the sideline rather than centrestage. Most of those responsible for managing STDs in Australia still espoused the moralistic rhetoric of yore, but they could now appreciate the sociological as well as medical aspects of STD epidemiology.

One important outcome of that attitudinal sea change was that the commanders of the 2nd AIF and their medical support staff could pragmatically manage the STD infections that lay ahead unencumbered by the moralistic and religious 'baggage' of an earlier era.

In this, its second worldwide conflict in only two decades, the AMS would have new pharmacological weapons for the next major campaign against STDs.

CHAPTER 6

The Army and Venereal Diseases during World War II, 1939-1941

During World War II, VDs were never the serious problem for the Australian Army as in World War I. Reasons included the introduction of sulphanilamide to treat gonorrhoea from 1932 and the advent of the 'wonder drug', penicillin, after it became available late in 1943. Another contributing factor was greater candour and reduced prudery in publicly discussing sexual matters. This in turn followed the anti-VD proselytising by campaigners such as Ettie Rout and Angela Booth in earlier decades. The passage of the Venereal Diseases Acts by the six Australian states between 1915 and 1920 had also played a part. The legislation made gonorrhoea and syphilis notifiable diseases, obliging sufferers to undergo treatment. The Acts also required the state health departments to educate the public about VD.

The sum of these influences was greater public awareness of VD, better identification of

VD sufferers, and more effective treatment regimens.

1. VD infection statistics in the Army during World War II

By theatres of war, the estimated number of cases of VD treated in the Army during World War II is indicated in Table 6.1.[1]

Table 6.1—**Estimate of cases of VD treated in the Australian Army 1940-1945**

Region	Period	Total estimated cases
Middle East, Mediterranean and North Africa	1940–1942	11,000
United Kingdom	1940–1943	number unknown
South-East Asia (including Ambon, Malaya, Singapore and Timor)	1941	1488
Ceylon	1942	110
South-West Pacific (including Papua, New Guinea, Moratai and Borneo)	1941–1945	230
Australia	1942–1945	21,350
Total	1940–1945	34,178

Source: A.S. Walker, Clinical Problems of War, Vol.1, Australia in the War of 1939—1945, 'Venereal Diseases', Chapter 22.

What might the reader conclude from this table?

The first observation is that the total number of VD cases treated in the Australian Army during World War II was appreciably lower than in World War I. The estimate for VD cases in World War I was about 65,350. Those figures were for a war in which a total of 417,000 Australian soldiers were engaged over a four-year period. The World War II figures, by contrast, are for a war which lasted six years and in which 730,000 Australian troops were involved.[2]

Can the VD figures for the two wars be compared? For the purposes of this discussion they will be. The comparison is shown in Table 6.2.

Table 6.2-**World War I and World War II VD case rates compared**

	World War I	World War II
Total Army enlistments:	417,000	730,000
Total VD cases:	65,350	34,178
VD cases as proportion (%) of total enlistments:	15.7%	4.7%

Sources: A.G. Butler, The Australian Army Medical Services, Vol.3, Special Problems and Services-; A.S. Walker, Clinical Problems of War, Vol.1, Australia in the War of 1939-45, 'Venereal Diseases', Chapter 22.

As the table suggests, the Army in World War II was 75 per cent larger than it had been during World War I, yet it suffered 48 per cent fewer VD cases. As a proportion, the Army's VD cases in World War II were 4.7 per cent of enlistments, whereas the figure in World War I had been 15.7 per cent or 3.3 times the World

War II rate. VD was clearly not the massive problem for the Army in World War II as it had been in World War I.

The second observation is that the numbers in Table 6.1 require some qualification, which is given in the endnote to this paragraph.[3]

2. The Army's preparations for the expected occurrence of VD

The 2nd AIF was the Army formation established for overseas service during World War II. Like its World War I counterpart, such a formation was necessary because the *Defence Act 1903* precluded the deployment overseas of members of either the permanent full-time Army or the part-time militia unless they volunteered for service overseas. Only volunteers could be sent overseas, and so both AIFs were all-volunteer forces.

Recruitment of the 2nd AIF began soon after the declaration of war on 3 September 1939. On 13 September the Prime Minister, R.G. Menzies, announced its formation and the appointment of the Commander, Sir Thomas Blarney. Recruiting depots opened within the next week. The first of the 2nd AIF's five divisions, the 6th Infantry Division, was raised on 28 September. The advance units of the 6th

Division were despatched to Palestine in December 1939. Most of the division's remaining units followed in early 1940.[4]

From the experience of World War I the Army Medical Directorate (AMD) anticipated that VD would probably be as much a problem in World War II as in the previous war. Based at Victoria Barracks in Melbourne, the AMD was under the command of the DGMS, Major General Rupert M. Downes, who had held the position since 1934. Downes, a paediatric surgeon, knew much about VD because he had been responsible for its management as DDMS for the 1st AIF in the Middle East during World War I.

As DGMS, Downes's principal responsibility in late 1939 was to mobilise the AMS for the war ahead. It was a frantic time for him. He had been overseas on a study tour when war was declared. He hurried home, arriving in early October, to take charge of the mobilisation. His first tasks were to establish and equip the Army hospitals that would accompany the 2nd AIF overseas, supervise the appointment of their staff, and secure their supplies. He described these activities in a 13-page internal AMD summary of the mobilisation that he wrote in January 1940 under the title 'Observations on the administration of the Army Medical Services in the first 4 1/2 months of the War'.[5] A present-day reader is struck by the bureaucratic obstacles he had to negotiate as the mobilisation proceeded.

Concerning VD, the Minister for the Army, Brigadier Geoffrey A. Street MG, assured Downes that 'no expense was to be spared whatever in carrying out' the arrangements for VD prophylaxis in the Army hospitals.[6] He phoned Downes with this directive, which Downes immediately implemented. Street had given distinguished Army service during World War I. He had enlisted as a private, then risen through the ranks to major in a military career in which he saw active service in New Guinea, Gallipoli, the Middle East, France and Belgium.[7] He was one soldier-politician who knew what a threat VD was to Army efficiency; as a personal friend of Downes he wished to help his DGMS ensure that VD would not cause the wastage in World War II that it had in the previous war.

Downes could consequently write that because 'full prophylactic facilities were provided by a direct order from the Cabinet ... as compared with the last war, Venereal Disease was almost negligible'.[8] This happy situation pertained only during the months in late 1939 and early 1940 while the 2nd AIF was being mobilised and despatched overseas.

Downes was not the only senior medical officer to comment on the low levels of VD infection among troops in Australia. Colonel Samuel Roy Burston, ADMS for the 6th Division, wrote from Melbourne to a colleague in Palestine that 'so far, in Australia, thanks to the very thorough manner in which prophylactic treatment has been used and carried out, and thanks also to the thorough education that the rank and file of the Force had in the necessity of prophylaxis and the methods of prevention, incidence of Venereal Disease has been extremely low'.[9]

When Downes and Burston had proudly written that the occurrence of VD had been 'negligible' because of the 'full prophylactic facilities' provided by the AMS, they were referring to the Prophylactic Ablution Centres (PACs, also called 'Prophylactic Clinics') established by the AMS. The PAC of World War II fulfilled a similar function to the Blue Light Depot of World War I: it was a place where soldiers could seek early treatment if they thought they had exposed themselves to the risk of VD infection. During World War I the AMS had conducted depots at the main army camps and in cities frequented by soldiers on leave. The Blue Light Depots had also sold condoms and distributed free self-medication Blue Light kits to soldiers as a precaution against unsafe sex.

By late 1939, PACs were being run in association with the medical units at all the major army camps in Australia. In addition, the AMS had set up central PACs in Sydney and Melbourne in collaboration with the state health authorities.[10] As well as providing post-coital ablutions and medication, the PACs supplied soldiers with pre-coital Prophylactic Outfits, the packets of condoms and ointments known earlier as Blue Light kits.[11]

The basic procedure followed in the PACs was one frequently described in communications between the senior officers of the AMS and the Army Board, between the AMD and the Deputy and Assistant Directors of Medical Services, and between the AMS venereologists and the RMOs in the field. As if all that was insufficient, summaries of the PAC procedures were distributed throughout the AMS units. Copies were also placed in all the PACs.[12] The procedure was, briefly, as follows:

1. Soldiers who thought they might have risked VD infection were advised to attend a PAC within 12 hours of coitus.
2. The soldier attending the PAC began the procedure by removing his tunic (which guaranteed initial anonymity) and trousers and tying his shirt around his waist.

3. The soldier was first examined for symptoms of VD by a medical officer. If he displayed symptoms, he was not treated in the PAG but referred to his RMO.
4. If the soldier did not display symptoms of VD his anonymity was assured; he was not required to give his name or the name of his unit. His treatment in the PAG then proceeded.
5. The treatment began when a medical orderly thoroughly washed the soldier's genitals with an antiseptic solution. This was referred to as 'irrigation'.
6. Wearing rubber gloves and using a sterilised syringe, the orderly injected five cubic centimetres of a five per cent solution of Argyrol through the meatus (opening) of the penis into the urethra.
7. The soldier then held the meatus closed with his fingers for three minutes.
8. After three minutes, the soldier voided the solution and dried his penis with sanitary paper.
9. Next, the soldier was given a teaspoonful of calomel (commonly used in the treatment of syphilis). Watched by the orderly, the soldier then massaged the

ointment into the head, foreskin and shaft of his penis and his scrotum.

10. Finally, the soldier was instructed not to urinate for four hours. He then washed his hands thoroughly with soap and water, dressed himself and departed.[13]

As indicated, the PACs also distributed free Prophylactic Outfits and condoms to soldiers. The instructions coming with these kits advised soldiers to take the following precautions:

a. **French Letters** [condoms]:

   i. These are provided by all Units and by Blue Light Depots. Test them by blowing them up beforehand.

   ii. They are a comparatively safe way of preventing VD, but they have certain pitfalls. They may break and allow contamination; and they leave bare parts above the rubber. To overcome this, rub your Blue Light Outfit cream all over your penis and surrounding parts before putting on your French Letter.

   iii. Remember that bare parts of your penis must never come in contact with bare parts of the woman before, during or after connection, so remove it by its rim, and don't allow your contaminated hands to come in contact with your bare penis until you have had a wash.

    iv. Lastly, attend the Blue Light Depot at earliest possible moment.

b. **Blue Light Outfits:**

For foolhardy soldiers who will NOT use the protection of French Letters, the following procedure is advised:

    i. **Before connection**—Apply Blue Light Outfit Cream [i.e. Calomel] all over your penis and adjoining parts, taking care to draw back the foreskin and level out all folds before application. Insert a little cream into the eye of the penis.

    ii. **After connection**—Pass your water [urinate] in gushes. Wash your penis and surrounding parts. WASH YOUR HANDS. ATTEND THE BLUE LIGHT DEPOT AT EARLIE POSSIBLE MOMENT.[14]

When Major General Downes described the AMD's anti-VD preparations for the war ahead as 'full prophylactic facilities', he was referring to a complex military-medical infrastructure and an elaborate series of procedures which his minister had endorsed.[15]

Gaining ministerial approval for a project was one matter, but implementation was something else again. Unfortunately, Downes and the AMD experienced much frustration with the Army bureaucracy as they tried to give effect to their minister's directive. Downes summed up the situation in a half-page satirical statement under the title 'The house that Jack built'. A parody in the style of the cumulative nursery rhyme 'This is the house that Jack built', it ran like this:

The house that Jack built
1. The Federal Cabinet has said that VD prophylaxis treatment is to be given to the troops.
2. Calomel is required for this.
3. The Melbourne Hospital, where some of the treatment is to be done, has no Calomel.
4. There is no Calomel to be bought on the market.
5. The Equipment Control Committee have one ton of it at Portsea.
6. The contract to bring it from Portsea cannot be let because there is no Treasury Authority to pay a contractor.
7. There is £7,000-odd available for this Committee when a Treasury Warrant is transferred.
8. So the Soldiers cannot have the VD prophylactic treatment that Cabinet has ordered.[16]

The title of Downes's parody was also a double entendre that might have amused his readers. 'Jack' was a contemporary slang alternative for 'gonorrhoea'.

The situation Downes lamented was, unfortunately and perhaps inevitably, part and parcel of the hasty mobilisation of a large military formation for overseas service. In this respect, Jan McLeod, a historian who has written about Downes's service as DGMS, has observed that 'strained relationships within military departments, clashes between civilian and army administrations, inter-governmental power struggles, and the historically pervasive British influence punctuate the history of Australian military medicine'.[17] Downes's experience in mobilising the AMS, McLeod suggests, pointed to 'challenges [which] persisted throughout the war and directly impacted medical personnel as well as the soldiers in their care'.[18]

3. The VD epidemic in the 2nd AIF in the Middle East

Three of the 2nd AIF's four infantry divisions, the 6th, 7th and 9th, were sent to the Middle East, where they served in Palestine, Egypt, Libya, Greece, Crete, Syria and Lebanon, during the period 1940-1942. Depending on the campaigns to which they were assigned, they fought against the forces of Italy (in Egypt and Libya), Germany (in Greece, Crete, Libya and Egypt) and the Vichy French (in Syria and Lebanon). The 8th Infantry Division was not sent to the Middle East but to South-East Asia, where nearly all its units were swiftly overrun by Japanese forces after Japan entered the war in December 1941.[19]

Most units of the 6th, 7th and 9th divisions were withdrawn from the Middle East and returned to Australia during 1942 to meet the Japanese threat to northern Australia and the Australian dependent territories of Papua and New Guinea. Japanese forces invaded these territories in early 1942. Henceforth the Army's focus was on a series of campaigns aimed at defeating the Japanese in Papua and New Guinea and elsewhere in the South-West Pacific theatre.[20]

The troops of the 2nd AIF in the Middle East gave the Army its first long-running VD epidemic of World War II.

VD was the third most common infectious disease suffered by the 2nd AIF after it arrived in Palestine. The chart in Figure 6.1 shows the rate of its occurrence per thousand troops in relation to the other eight most common diseases in 1940, the first full year of the Australian presence in the Middle East.[21] The official medical historian of the war, Allan S. Walker, was surprised that VD 'outscored' dysentery, 'which was recognised to be the principal endemic disease in Palestine', and one of the historic diseases which could influence the success or failure of a military campaign.[22]

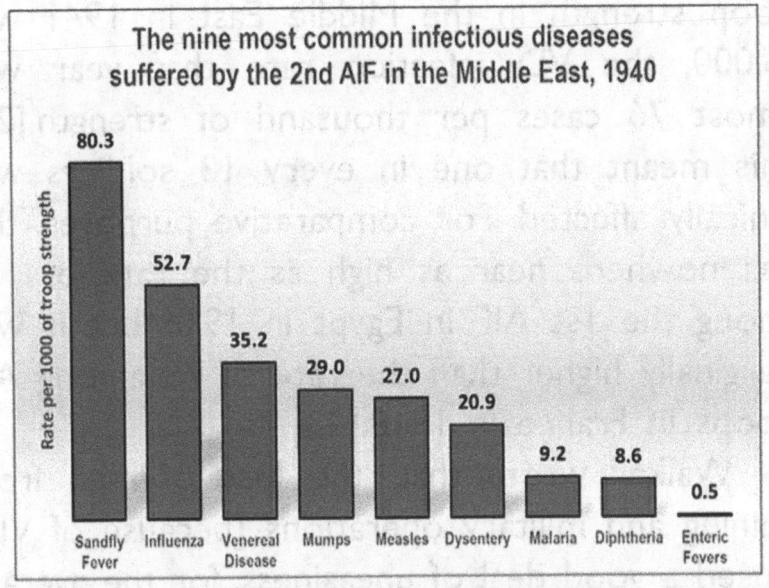

Figure 6.1: VD was the third most common infectious disease for 2nd AIF troops in the Middle East in 1940 (A.S. Walker, Middle East and Far East, Australian War Memorial, Canberra, 1953, pp.104, 106).

Were the 11,000 VD cases in the Middle East an 'epidemic'? One definition of 'epidemic' is 15 cases per 100,000 people for two consecutive weeks'.[23] Under those criteria, the 2nd AIF's VD cases in the Middle East were certainly an epidemic. Distributed across the 2nd AIF's three years in the Middle East, the 11,000 VD cases averaged 3667 cases a year or 70 a week. The worst year was 1941, when the 8th Special Hospital treated 5774 cases, or more than half the three-year total. That year's weekly average was 111 cases. Because the average troop strength in the Middle East in 1941 was 76,000, the VD infection rate that year was almost 76 cases per thousand of strength.[24] This meant that one in every 13 soldiers was clinically affected. For comparative purposes, this was nowhere near as high as the rate of 138 among the 1st AIF in Egypt in 1916 but it was marginally higher than the rate of 75 among AIF troops in France in 1918.[25]

Walker wrote that 'the loss of men from training and military operations [because of VD] caused a good deal of uneasiness, for the average time they spent under treatment was nearly four weeks, during which the men were virtually useless'.[26] An average treatment time of four weeks would have entailed a loss of 44,000 'man-weeks' or 846 wasted 'man-years' for the 2nd AIF in the Middle East. Because VD was preventable, the high sick wastage from VD was a matter of deep concern for the AIF commanders and especially for the head of the AMS in the Middle East, DMS Brigadier Burston. He assigned the task of managing the VD epidemic to the 2nd AIF's consultant physician, Colonel Neil Hamilton Fairley.

4. No.8 Australian Special Hospital and the other VD units

Initially, the VD patients were assigned to an annexe of the 2/1st Australian General Hospital, which had been established at Gaza in Palestine during February 1940.[27] This annexe continued treating the 2nd AIF's VD cases for the next nine months, until November 1940, when a recently established specialised VD hospital, No.8 Australian Special Hospital (8 ASH), took over the annexe's functions and patients. Henceforth all VD cases were sent to 8 ASH, which became the main VD treatment centre for the 2nd AIF in the Middle East.[28]

The idea for a special VD hospital had begun with Burston when he was still ADMS of the 6th Division in Melbourne. In January 1940, he wrote to his friend Colonel Clive H. Disher, who had led the division's advanced medical units to Palestine. 'I have got Ministerial approval for a special hospital for VD to be sent [to Palestine] with the next "Flight".' The VD hospital would 'be specially staffed and equipped and be capable of dealing with 500 cases'. He added that he hoped this would 'prevent the regrettable failure in this direction in 1915'.[29]

The VD hospital for which Burston (and Major General Downes) had obtained approval was not 8 ASH but No.3 Australian Special Hospital (3 ASH), the formation of which was agreed to by both the Military Board and the Treasury in mid-February 1940.[30] It was a generously endowed establishment comprising seven officers and 45 other ranks. Including salaries, rations, uniforms, equipment and supplies, the estimated cost was a total of £19,625 or more than $1.7 million in the values of 2020.[31] Commanded by Major Derby Loudon, 3 ASH was not sent to Palestine but England. It was located at Tidworth in Wiltshire, where it functioned as a tent hospital for a month before being absorbed within the 2/3 AGH.[32]

To replace 3 ASH in Palestine, another short-lived VD hospital was formed. This was No.2 Australian Special Hospital (2 ASH). The CO was Major Neil Francis, who had been in charge of the VD annexe at 2/1 AGH, and 2 ASH was raised in Palestine in July 1940 from among personnel of 2/1 AGH. For some reason this arrangement did not prove satisfactory, and so 2 ASH became the nucleus around which 8 ASH formed.[33] 8 ASH was consequently the 2nd AIF's third specialised VD hospital established in less than a year.

As 8 ASH's first CO, Major Francis returned from Palestine to raise the unit in Brisbane in August 1940. He then brought it to Palestine in mid-October. Under his command, 8 ASH became established as a 400-bed hospital occupying its own complex of barracks and huts at the Kilo 89 Camp at Gaza Ridge.[34] It remained at Gaza Ridge until it returned to Australia during February 1943.

From 26 March until 6 May 1941, Captain John O'Connor was temporarily the CO of 8 ASH while Major Francis was in Greece serving with 'Lustre Force', which fought against the Germans there during that period. A week after Francis's return a new CO took command of 8 ASH. He was Lieutenant Colonel Loudon, previously CO of 3 ASH and now promoted. A specialist in venereology, he became the CO of 8 ASH on 13 May 1941.[35]

Meanwhile, Major Francis was detached from 8 ASH and assigned the task of opening a new 300-bed VD hospital, No.14 Australian Special Hospital (14 ASH) near Beirut in September 1941. This unit was set up for the treatment of VD patients after the campaign against the Vichy French in Syria and Lebanon during June and July 1941.

Lieutenant Colonel Loudon remained the CO of 8 ASH for the rest of the hospital's time in

Palestine. He brought the unit back to Australia in February 1942. He continued as CO until July that year, when he was posted to Land Headquarters in Melbourne as the Army's consultant in venereology.[36] The estimate of 11,000 Australian troops treated for VD in the three years the 2nd AIF spent in the Middle East from 1940 to 1942 was the figure Loudon provided to the official historian, A.S. Walker.[37]

In all 8 ASH s time in Palestine, the hospital was kept busy with a high caseload. It measured its workload by its 'bed-state'—the number of patients occupying beds. By the time the bed-state reached 397 on 27 May 1941, the hospital was running at full capacity. The continuous arrival of new patients kept the hospital full. There were 639 and 428 admissions in January and February 1942 respectively, the new patients taking the place of those being discharged.[38] Over time the staff expanded to meet the caseload. Initially 8 ASH comprised four medical officers and 31 other ranks, but by the time the unit reassembled after its return to Australia it had nine officers and 101 other ranks.[39]

An important aspect of 8 ASH's task in the Middle East was to develop pathological and serological tests for detecting the presence of VD-causing organisms. This proved 'greatly to the benefit of accurate and speedy diagnosis' and became an important part of the 2nd AIF's pathology service in the Middle East.[40]

During its time in Palestine, 8 ASH developed a corporate life of its own. The hospital had its own canteen and a YMCA amenities hut, where weekly film shows and regular concerts were run. The staff played rugby matches against other units and visited nearby Jewish settlements. There were regular church parades, and Easter and Christmas were celebrated. For the first Christmas, in 1940, the patients formed a committee to organise their own celebrations. At that stage only 90 patients were in the hospital. During the afternoon they held a euchre party, and before dinner at 5.00pm the Red Cross presented each of them with a 'Christmas box'. The Red Cross also distributed presents among the staff. At 3.00pm the Commander of the 2nd AIF, Lieutenant General Sir Thomas Blarney, had arrived to inspect the wards and wish everyone well. He chatted with each of the patients.[41] As well as spreading Christmas cheer, perhaps the commander's visit was intended to demonstrate to the patients that he had not forgotten them and appreciated their human frailty. Whether or not that was his intention, such a visit to a VD hospital would have been inconceivable during World War I.

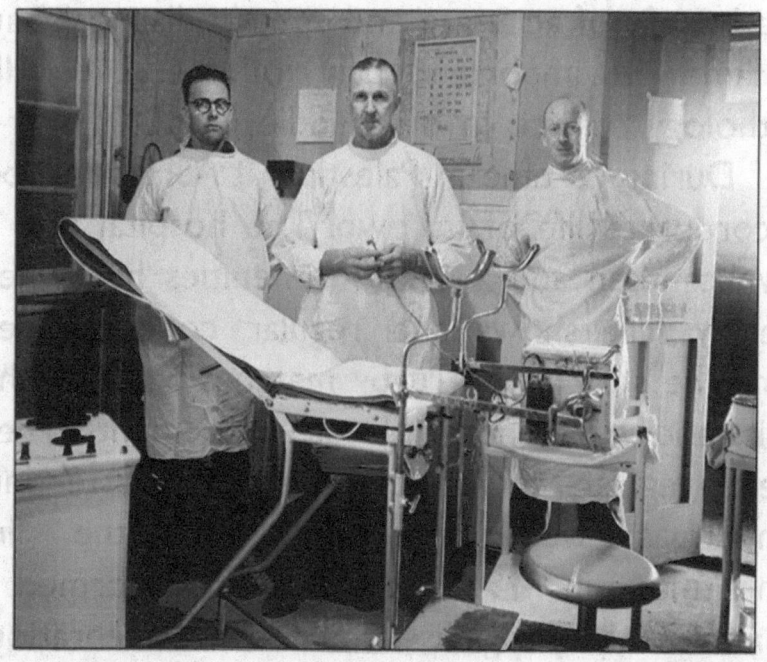

Figure 6.2: Staff of No.8 Australian Special Hospital (8 ASH), Kilo 89 Camp, Gaza Ridge, Palestine, December 1941. Left to right: Staff Sergeant D. McDonald, Lieutenant Colonel D.B. Loudon (Commanding Officer) and Lance Corporal C. McHale. 8 ASH was the 2nd AIF's principal VD treatment centre in the Middle East during World War II (AWM 100325).

Through activities of this kind, 8 ASH maintained staff and patient morale, which in turn elicited the patients' cooperation and the success of the treatment regimens. According to A.S. Walker, 'diagnostic and therapeutic work of a high standard was carried out' at 8 ASH.[42] That might not have been possible if both staff and patients' attitudes were hostile.

8 ASH continued functioning at Gaza Ridge until early 1942. Along with most other medical units of the 2nd AIF in the Middle East, 8 ASH was shipped back to Australia in an operation undertaken during January and February 1942 under the code-name 'Movement Stepsister'.[43]

In addition to the Special—'code' for VD—Hospitals such as 2 ASH, 3 ASH and 8 ASH, the AMS operated various PACs. After the 2nd AIF arrived in Palestine, PACs were opened in Jaffa, Tel Aviv, Jerusalem and Haifa, the four cities frequented by soldiers on leave. A PAC was already operating in Cairo in the Birka red-light area, jointly staffed by British and Australian orderlies. The British DDMS for the Middle East, Colonel J.C. Sproule, and his Adviser in Venereology, Lieutenant Colonel Robert Lees, inspected it at 11.00pm one night in early October 1940. They found a queue of 40 soldiers waiting their turn to be treated while eight men were already being processed by the four orderlies on duty there. They recommended that the staff be doubled.[44] PACs were later established in Syria and Lebanon when the campaigns in those nations ended in an Allied victory in July 1941.

Because Palestine was still a British mandated territory, at first the PACs were conducted by the British authorities with the assistance of AMS medical orderlies. Later the PACs became a 2nd AIF responsibility.[45] The DMS of the 2nd AIF in the Middle East, Burston, and his consultant physician, Fairley, regarded the PACs as a critical element in their strategies to contain the spread of VD infection among the Australian troops.

5. Management of the 2nd AIF s VD epidemic in the Middle East

At first the numbers of VD cases among the Australian troops in the Middle East were low. As more troops arrived during 1940, and more soldiers were granted leave, the rate of infection rose.[46] On leave, the soldiers visited the adjacent cities of Jaffa and Tel Aviv as well as Jerusalem in Palestine and later Cairo and Alexandria in Egypt, Beirut and Tripoli in Lebanon, and Latakia in Syria. All were cosmopolitan cities 'full of temptation for soldiers on leave'. Most had large numbers of prostitutes, 'practically all infected', as well as numerous 'amateurs' who were 'at least an equal source of danger'.[47]

The management of VD during World War II was rendered more effective than in World War I by the availability of the new 'sulpha' drugs. Syphilis was treated with injections of the arsenic-based drug arsphenamine (in the form of the commercially available 'Novarsenobillon'), an unspecified sulpha drug, and a bismuth compound.[48]

Gonorrhoea was treated at first with sulphapyridine and later with sulphathiazole. The use of these sulphonamides reduced the time required treating the disease from the six weeks common in World War I to as little as a fortnight.[49]

That was a huge saving in 'sick wastage' due to VD. What the total saving in time was in 'man-weeks' and 'man-years' is impossible to calculate because there is no way of knowing how many gonorrhoea cases there were. Walker did not provide estimates of the numbers of cases of the different types of VD as A.G. Butler did in the disease statistics published in his World War I official history. As seen, Walker did indicate that the average time taken to treat a VD patient in the Middle East during World War II was about four weeks. That was a fortnight less than the World War I average; if that difference were applied to the 11,000 estimated World War II VD cases in the Middle East, it would mean a total of 44,000 'treatment-weeks' rather than the 66,000 that would have been necessary in World War I for the same number of patients. The difference—22,000 'treatment-weeks'—was the equivalent of 423 'treatment-years'. The sulphonamides clearly had a beneficial impact in reducing VD-induced troop wastage.

Disturbingly, however, sulphonamide-resistant strains of gonococci emerged among the Australian VD cases in the Middle East, and that added to the time required to cure the gonorrhoea-affected soldiers. The rate of 'primary cures' of gonorrhoea, that is, the number of cures effected solely by sulphonamide medication, fell from between 60 and 75 per cent in 1940 to between 40 and 55 per cent in 1942. Patients who did not experience a primary cure would therefore have to remain in hospital longer to undergo further treatment.[50]

The overall VD infection rate was worst in 1941, the year when the 2nd AIF fought four campaigns in the Middle East-Mediterranean theatre—in Libya, Greece, Crete and Syria. The 5774 VD cases that year represented a rate of 76.0 per thousand of strength in the theatre. These rates, Fairley pointed out to Burston, were 'unnecessarily high and caused a constant drain on manpower'.[51]

This realisation forced Burston and Fairley to take action. They were both based at 2nd AIF headquarters in Cairo. To apprise himself of the full extent of the threat, Burston instructed Fairley to tour Palestine to assess the mounting

VD problem. Fairley spent a week on a motor tour of 2nd AIF facilities in Palestine. He left Kantara on the Suez Canal at 2.00 am on 7 May 1941 and arrived in Tel Aviv at 10.30 am. He was met by Lieutenant Colonel John Walstab, the 2nd AIF's APM, and motored through the brothel area in Jaffa. In the afternoon he was escorted to inspect 'Marie's', a popular brothel. He then 'discussed the whole question of prostitution in Tel Aviv and Jaffa from a police and medical viewpoint'. The next day, 9 May, he was driven to Gaza. In the afternoon he visited 8 ASH with Colonel Joseph Steigrad, the ADMS (and later DDMS), inspected the facilities, and held discussions with the staff. While there he obtained the admissions figures for the months of January to April. Fairley spent his third day in Palestine, 10 May, discussing with Steigrad issues in relation to VD.[52]

These were the only days that Fairley spent working on VD. For the rest of his week in Palestine, he spent his time visiting other hospitals and discussing with their senior staff a series of other pressing medical issues, including anxiety neurosis, meningitis, dysentery, diphtheria and desert sores.[53]

Fairley, however, had seen enough to provide Burston with a realistic, pragmatic report free from moral censure and religious scruple. Its main points were these:

- According to figures provided by Lieutenant Colonel Robert Lees (the British Adviser on Venereology at Allied Headquarters in Cairo), 'a definite rise in the incidence of VD' occurred among Australian troops in the Middle East. The number of cases had risen from 192 in January to 424 in March 1941.[54]
- The admission figures of 8 ASH confirmed Lees's claim about the increase; 8 ASH had admitted 1229 patients between January and April 1941. In that period the number of monthly admissions had risen by more than 100. Much of this increase could be attributed to the troops in Palestine taking leave in Jerusalem, Tel Aviv and Jaffa.[55]
- The 'unnecessarily high' incidence of VD called for 'every possible remedial measure—medical, social and ethical'.[56]
- 'Despite everything that can be done, a proportion of troops will continue to have sexual intercourse with women of the prostitute class.'[57]
- Policy on VD should therefore be guided by these four principles:

1. Every prostitute should be assumed to have VD and this fact must be communicated to the troops.
2. Routine weekly examination of prostitutes by doctors should be undertaken, but troops must be advised that that was no guarantee that the women were uninfected, because especially in Jaffa the prostitutes were each servicing up to 20 soldiers a night. If one of those soldiers was infected, the prostitute would transmit VD to all her subsequent clients.
3. The rubber sheath or condom should be 'universally advocated and distributed among troops'; brothels that did not routinely insist on their use should be placed out of bounds for Australian soldiers.
4. PACs should be located within the brothel areas, but the PACs should be regarded as subsidiary to and not a substitute for condoms.[58]

Fairley concluded his report with a set of pragmatic recommendations. They were mainly made for Jaffa and Tel Aviv because he did not regard Jerusalem as a serious problem. Prostitution, he thought, was much less an issue there because of the 'religious' nature of the city: 'Being a holy city,' he wrote, 'prostitution was officially discouraged ...[and he was] informed there were no large brothels'.[59] Fairley was realist enough to know that no necessary link existed between religiosity and the apparent absence of overt prostitution. Whatever his true beliefs about Jerusalem, his recommendations were that:

a. an additional PAC be established in Jaffa close to the brothels and hotels frequented by the troops
b. the restrictions on 'suitably run brothels by military and civilian police should be relaxed, 'suitably run being defined as: (a) 'reasonable standard of cleanliness and sanitation', (b) 'use of rubber sheaths insisted upon', (c) 'weekly medical inspections of the prostitutes made by a suitable civilian or army doctor', and (d) cases of VD contracted in the brothel are infrequent'
c. the area in Jaffa where 'suitably run' brothels were located should be placed in bounds for soldiers.[60]

What happened then? Were Fairley's recommendations implemented and, if so, did they make much difference to the VD infection rate? The short answer is that Fairley's common-sense recommendations were adopted and implemented. The situation was about to change in surprising ways, because only three weeks after Fairley submitted his report to Burston the Allied invasion of Syria began. With that, new approaches to the VD problem were essayed.

As well as emphasising the critical importance of the PACs, the 2nd AIF in the Middle East launched an anti-VD propaganda offensive directed at the troops. Among other things, this campaign included the ubiquitous unit lectures by the RMO and chaplain on the medical and moral hazards of VD. An anonymous 7th Division RMO left behind an entertaining account of his experiences in dealing with VD from the time he joined his unit at the Ingleburn Army Camp south of Sydney until after its arrival in the Middle East. In summarising how he handled the lectures, he explained that 'the language used is necessarily of a colloquial and even coarse type, as otherwise the lectures would not be understood'.[61] He outlined the five main points he tried to communicate in his lectures:

1. An indication of the symptoms and signs of the several diseases. These were actually news to many of the troops.
2. A resume of the course and sequelae of the diseases followed and it frightened some of the troops but only for a day or so.

3. An exhortation that the best way of not getting it was not doing it.
4. The advice that if they wished to indulge in sexual intercourse, they should use a condom. This advice was generally taken.
5. The best method of prophylaxis was soap and water, with the use of calomel and protargol as subsidiary preventatives. And never let anyone wash their urethras out with KM No.4 Solution [potassium permanganate, also known as Condy's Crystals], which was ineffective, unsterile and had probably been hanging in an uncovered bottle for weeks [and caused] renal tract infections.[62]

'The moral aspect of the question from both private, public and religious point of view I did not touch upon as I considered this to be the province of the Padre.' Almost as a postscript, he added that the unit's first padre ignored VD's societal consequences because 'he considered that no such thing as sex existed and also, I fancy, believed in Santa Claus'.[63]

After the USA entered the war in December 1941, the Army secured various American 'scare' films produced by the film units of the US War Department with the express purpose of frightening audiences into practising what a later generation would call 'safe sex'. The films were 'found most valuable'.[64] Health authorities in Australia also published graphic and unabashed anti-VD posters. The Army seems to have obtained supplies of these for display in the PACs and the brothels. An example is the poster in Figure 6.3.[65]

Without going into any detail, A.S. Walker noted that the measures to combat VD included 'intimate group talks with men', 'amenities for sport and diversion', 'physical training', 'discipline through control and penalty', 'prophylactic centres in all more or less settled areas', 'availability of preventives on request' and 'control of prostitutes'.[66] He observed that 'sometimes it was possible to identify infected persons [particular prostitutes] and to hand them over to civil police'.[67]

Figure 6.3: Anti-VD propaganda poster used in Melbourne early 1940s. Posters of this kind were intended for display in brothels. Their target was American servicemen stationed in Melbourne. Copies of this poster seem to have found their way into the Army-controlled brothels in the Middle East during 1941—1942 (maker unknown, poster Dont risk it feller, early 1940s, lithographic print on paper, courtesy of City of Melbourne Art and Heritage Collection, no.1646752).

One measure that does not seem to have been adopted was the disciplining of persistent 'offenders'—particular soldiers who experienced multiple infection episodes. Walker pointed out that such individuals were a problem because they 'appear [ed] to be either more promiscuous or more careless'.[68]

Forfeiture of pay was a disciplinary measure introduced in the Middle East after much debate, but it was never as draconian a penalty as in the 1st AIF during World War I. That was because loss of pay while being treated for VD was imposed only on men 'who had contracted the disease other than accidentally in the course of duty or congenitally and then only after 35 days'.[69] That measure, Walker wrote, 'encouraged men to report early, and was of undoubted value'.[70]

Some soldiers avoided loss of pay by self-medicating with sulphonamide drugs. The troops discovered that soldiers with NSU, later known to be caused by the bacterium *Chlamydia trachomatis*, were exempted from forfeiture of pay. Some men suffering from gonorrhoea took sulphonamide tablets 'to mask the true diagnosis'.[71] To what extent this subterfuge achieved its purpose is uncertain, but the practice demonstrated ingenuity on the part of those trying to avoid detection as VD sufferers.

Another aspect of the anti-VD campaign was the distribution of information pamphlets and booklets aimed at educating soldiers about VD. One booklet was the pocket-sized, six-page *Notes on the Prevention of Venereal Disease* published in 1942 by Brigadier Joseph Steigrad, DDMS of the 2nd AIF in the Middle East. The booklet he produced was a model of clarity and brevity. Simple, direct and informative, it would have given any soldier who read it a 'short course' on VD. Copies were distributed to every soldier still serving in the Middle East and later to all troops in Australia as well.[72]

6. The situation in Syria and Lebanon from July 1941

The short and hard-fought five-week campaign against the Vichy French regime in Syria and Lebanon resulted in a victory for the Allied force. Under the terms of the peace treaty between the Allies and the French administration, an Allied occupation force, including units of the Australian 7th Division, was garrisoned in Syria and Lebanon.

As soon as the treaty was signed on 13 July 1941, the Australian members of the force began visiting the cities and villages of the region on leave. VD soon became a problem; Beirut and

Tripoli in Lebanon, and Latakia in Syria, became hot-spots for infection. Having learnt from their experience with VD in Palestine, the 7th Division medical officers endeavoured to give effect to the spirit of Fairley's recommendations to Burston.

An unsigned, undated handwritten summary of the situation, possibly in Walker's handwriting and perhaps compiled in the early post-war period as research notes for his official history, described the situation that had developed:

> **Brothels**
>
> In towns of Egypt and Palestine and particularly Syria, efforts were made to establish and control brothels and to bring prophylaxis within easy access of troops.
>
> In certain cases suitable buildings were set aside and 'staff' obtained from local professionals. In a few cases 'going concerns' were taken over for exclusive Australian use. Women were examined once or twice weekly, by pelvic exam, cervical smear, W.R.[the Wassermann Reaction test for syphilis] monthly & a gynaecologist if possible. Infected women were sent to hospital.

Price was controlled—1 Syr. Pound.[13]

PACs established in or close to houses [brothels]. Prophylactics [condoms] were readily available here and in unit posts. Attendance voluntary but virtually compelled by men themselves.

Control of alcohol and inebriates most important.

Attendance amazing. From 5-11p.m. soldiers thronged in queues waiting for door to open. 50-60 (even once 100) per girl per night.

Most VD was contracted from amateurs or in villages.

Troops will cooperate if treated in way they understand.[73]

The summary went on to say that similar Army-sanctioned brothels had been established in the Jaffa and Tel Aviv area in Palestine. It then described how the control of the Army brothel was working there:

PAC civilian staff being supervised by AAMC officers. Operatives identified by photographs, frequently checked by DAPM [Deputy Assistant Provost Marshal] Tel Aviv, who will inspect premises frequently.

---

[13] A Syrian pound had roughly the same value in Syria in 1941 that $86 would have in Australia in 2020.

Provosts will be posted near for general control if needed. Condoms to be supplied, operatives to insist on their use. PAC in the building. Printed slips emphasising its use and other precautions supplied. MO at Tel Aviv [does] the examinations.

Control of the establishment was by DAPM ME [Middle East]. Medical supervision by ADMS-DADH [Deputy Assistant Director Hygiene]—CO 8 Special Hospital—MO in charge.[74]

In other words, rather than leave the control of VD in the brothels to chance, the 7th Division commanders, senior medical officers and military police accepted the reality that their troops were going to consort with prostitutes and frequent brothels. Rather than run the risk of soaring VD infection rates, they took pre-emptive action by collaborating in the establishment of the 2nd AIF's own medically controlled network of brothels. This was a radical departure from previous practice.

Military-controlled brothels were a 'first' for the Australian Army. They were not, however, mentioned in any of the three official general war histories by Gavin Long and Barton Maugham dealing with the campaigns in the Middle East.[75] The first and second volume of A.S. Walker's official medical history, *Clinical Problems of War*

(1952) and *Middle East and Far East* (1953), alluded to the Army brothels briefly. In the former volume Walker wrote that 'the most controversial feature of this war was brothel control'.[76] In the latter volume he prefaced his remarks by observing that 'venereal disease caused anxiety soon after the Syrian campaign ended'.[77] In just two sentences, he commented briefly on 'the remarkable experiences in Beirut and Tripoli' involving 'the successful experiment of permitting brothels under strict disciplinary and medical supervision'.[78] The sanctioned brothels 'saved many men from taking almost certain personal risks in villages, though the figures of the attendances at the prophylactic centres form a sad social commentary'.[79]

7. Social impact

Why was more not written about the Army brothels at the time? In all the many dozens of World War II Army files on VD retained in the archival collections of the Australian War Memorial and the National Archives of Australia, the only reference to them is the three-page undated, unsigned summary quoted above. Scrawled hastily as notes, it is a critical document because it demonstrates the determination of the commanders of the 2nd AIF in the Middle East to control the spread of VD by resorting to whatever measures seemed most effective.

The reason why the Army-controlled brothels have not become better known lies perhaps in Walker's observation that the need for them and the PACs was 'a sad social commentary'. The resort to controlled brothels was an 'achievement' of which few senior Army officers could have been proud, even though they must have been gladdened by the outcome. No one stepped forward to claim the credit for the idea. As again in Vietnam 30 years later, it was not an accomplishment to brag about because it reflected poorly on the Army and its troops. Service personnel returning home could hardly have boasted that the Army had introduced its own brothels to curb a VD epidemic among the Australian soldiers. Nor was it a subject proudly reported in the dozens of unit histories so lovingly produced in the post-war decades. The very idea of brothels and PACs as necessary appendages to the AMS's hospital system would simply have been too shocking for the Australian public to accept. After all, the troops queuing for hours outside the brothels of Beirut and Jaffa were sons, brothers, husbands and fiances from families in Australia who were toiling at home to support the war effort. What might *they* have thought if they had known that 'their boys' were debauching themselves in Army-run bordellos and afterwards being forced to anoint their genitals liberally with toxic mercury-based ointment?

And what of the so-called 'operatives'—the overworked prostitutes obliged to satisfy dozens of sex-starved Australians every night? Could they be numbered among the ancillaries necessary for keeping the Army in the field? A good case can be made for considering them to be in the same category as the civilian workers hired locally for labouring jobs around the army camps. In a later age, that of the early 21st century, they would also be regarded as grossly abused victims of the war.

If the Army-controlled brothels can be accepted as a 'necessary evil', were they effective in reducing VD infection rates?

The fragmentary surviving evidence suggests that the Army's controlled brothels did indeed help fulfil their intended purpose. In the Jaffa and Tel Aviv area, for example, the number of VD cases among the troops fell from '70-80' in November 1941 to 45 in January 1942.[80] In the Tripoli area in Lebanon, where some 13,000 members of the 7th Division were based, in the 12 weeks from 14 September 1941 the controlled brothels recorded 11,955 'attendances'. Even though many of the attendances were probably repeated visits by a few, that number was the equivalent of 92 per cent of the Australians serving there. In addition to those attendances, an unknown number of troops consorted with 'outside' or 'non-controlled' prostitutes. The total number of VD cases among the troops was 134 or one case for every 89 'attendances'.[81] The rate per thousand troops was 11.2 or a quarter of the 48.5 which was the overall rate for the AIF in the Middle East in 1941.[82]

Although the VD infection rates were gratifyingly low after the Syria-Lebanon campaign, the presence of a dedicated VD treatment centre was still considered necessary. In the first couple of months after the campaign ended, VD cases were treated in a clinic within the 2/3rd Casualty Clearing Station in Beirut, but in September 1941 the recently promoted Lieutenant Colonel Francis was assigned the task of raising the new 300-bed VD hospital, 14 ASH.[83] Opening at the end of November, 14 ASH was sited at Bhamdoun in Lebanon, 23 kilometres from Beirut on the Damascus road. It functioned there for two months until withdrawn at the end of January 1942 and sent back to Australia the next month. After the unit's withdrawal, VD cases in Syria and Lebanon were sent to 8 ASH in Gaza.[84]

An entertaining account of the anti-VD effort among the troops of the 7th Division in Syria and Lebanon was written by Colonel Frank Kingsley Norris, the 7th Division ADMS. Norris, who was responsible for the program to minimise VD infection during and after the Syrian campaign, later wrote a long report on the anti-VD measures which he reproduced in his lively 1970 autobiography, *No Memory for Pain*.[85]

Figure 6.4: The 2/3rd Casualty Clearing Station in Beirut, July 1941. The building, formerly an Italian girls' school, had just been occupied by 2/3 CCS. A VD clinic set up within 2/3 CCS treated the VD-infected troops until No. 14 Australian Special [VD] Hospital under Lieutenant Colonel Neil Francis opened at Bhamdoun on the road to Damascus in November (AWM 119042).

In one section of his report, Norris related his dealings with 'Madame Olga', the proprietor of one of the Army-controlled brothels in Tripoli. He visited the brothel with the DAPM to inspect it and to explain to Madame Olga that her girls must be examined and tested regularly by a gynaecologist, that only girls carrying an identity pass would be allowed to work in the brothel, that no alcohol could be brought on to the premises and that the price for using a prostitute would be fixed at one Syrian pound. All this seemed too onerous for Madame Olga, who attempted to haggle with the two Australian officers. Eventually 'Madame with alternate tears and smiles accepted the conditions,' Norris wrote, 'offering all sorts of concessions and exclusive personal attention to ADMS and DAPM.'[86]

Norris was soon to receive a salutary lesson in other aspects of the Middle Eastern sex trade. All went well at the brothel for a week or two, until the local Lebanese police arrested Madame Olga and her girls, imprisoned them and closed the brothel. The reason for this action was that, with her brothel under Army control, Madame Olga had not continued paying the police their accustomed 'rake-off'. Fearing that with the brothel closed the troops would start using 'uncontrolled' prostitutes, Norris and the DAPM spent two hours persuading the police to allow the brothel to reopen.[87]

Looking back on the 7th Division's experience of VD, Norris came to these seven realistic conclusions:

1. The problem of VD will arise in any army. The problem cannot be adequately solved with lectures and PACs.
2. Soldiers' alcohol intake must be controlled. This was the most important single factor in the incidence of VD.
3. Recreation amenities must be developed. Units must organise their own amenities.
4. Adequate medical supplies must always be available.
5. Every soldier must understand the nature of VD and its prevention.
6. In foreign countries where prostitution was rife, it was more sensible, however distasteful this might be, to organise and adequately control certain brothel areas than to ignore the problem and trust to luck.
7. The success of anti-VD measures depended on adequate supervision. Reliable collaboration with the provosts was essential in any attempt to control VD.[88]

Norris's time with the 7th Division in the Middle East was a learning experience in his understanding of VD. Like many of his senior

AMS colleagues, his encounter with the realities of VD in an army in the field taught him pragmatism.

8. The Loudon plan

Lieutenant Colonel Derby B. Loudon, CO of 8 ASH, was another Army medical officer whose experience of VD in the Middle East led him to write about its management. In February 1942 Loudon was given the additional title of Adviser in Venereology to the DMS of the AIF in the Middle East. After his return to Australia in February 1943, Loudon was appointed as Adviser in Venereology to the DGMS at Army Headquarters in Melbourne.[89]

In his capacity as Adviser in Venereology, Loudon produced a 'Plan for the Control of Venereal Disease in the AIF (Middle East)' in October 1942. Although two of the 2nd AIF's divisions, the 6th and the 7th, had returned to Australia by then, the 9th Division remained in the Middle East. Loudon had become sceptical about the AIF's VD management measures, which he believed were failing. He devised his plan in order that 2nd AIF headquarters and the AMS in the Middle East might improve on their system of control.[90]

Loudon introduced his plan by reiterating the VD statistics—11,000 VD cases treated in the 2nd AIF in the Middle East, all of them preventable and 'enormous loss to the fighting strength' of the Army, with 373 years of manpower lost to syphilis alone. He then went on to enumerate the reasons why he thought the present VD control measures were failing, listing eight issues:

1. PAC techniques had not changed since World War I despite advances in venereology.
2. The controlled brothels had failed to 'check the ravages' of VD because many soldiers did not visit the brothels but consorted with streetwalkers and 'amateurs of easy virtue'.
3. The troops were not using condoms. One study by 8 ASH indicated that only 22 patients out of 200 had used them.
4. The Blue Light Outfits were ineffective. Another 8 ASH study indicated that out of 200 patients, 103 had used the kits but had still been infected.
5. Chemical analysis of the Blue Light kits being issued showed that the chemical content of the ointments had decomposed.
6. Lectures on VD in the units were ineffective because the lecturers often

knew little about VD and the lectures were too infrequent.
7. The troops often did not know where the PACs were located so did not bother visiting them.
8. The PACs were failing 'by virtue of present techniques to give adequate protection'.[91]

Regarding better VD management as an urgent priority for the AMS, Loudon proposed the formation of a small 'Venereal Disease Control Unit'. It would be staffed by a major, who would be a venereological specialist; a warrant officer, who would be a trained VD orderly; and a sergeant trained in VD recordkeeping procedures. The unit would take responsibility for VD education, prepare and distribute literature about anti-VD methods, supervise the activities of all the PACs, and train medical orderlies in the preventative treatment of VD. The VD education program would emphasise the benefits of abstinence, but soldiers who would not abstain would be taught 'what to do immediately before, during and after exposure', and they would be advised of 'the absolute necessity of going to the Blue Light Depot within 12 hours'.[92]

Loudon's plan envisaged a hierarchy of PACs comprising 'stationary large town depots', 'stationary small town depots', 'mobile leave depots' and 'mobile unit depots'. All would be adequately equipped and staffed with trained functionaries. 8 ASH would provide the training according to an agreed schedule as laid down in one of the DMS's periodical 'Technical Instructions'.[93]

The Loudon plan also proposed a series of disciplinary measures to ensure that soldiers taking leave would depart from camp forewarned and prepared. Each soldier proceeding on leave would have to sign a register attesting that he had received an adequate supply of condoms and kits of prophylactic ointments, a VD information pamphlet with his name upon it, the addresses of PACs in the towns he was visiting on leave, and that he had received a 'final word of advice' from his unit medical officer. On visiting a PAC, the soldier would be issued with a counterfoil that he must retain for three months as evidence that he had used the PAC's services. If he contracted VD and could not produce the counterfoil, he would incur 'total loss of pay during his period of treatment'. Further, it would become 'a Court Martial offence to contract venereal disease unless a proved attendance at a Blue Light Depot could be sustained'.[94]

What Loudon's superiors made of his plan is uncertain. His proposed Venereal Disease

Control Unit does not seem to have been established. Walker's first volume, *Clinical Problems of War*, notes that Loudon had proposed the unit but his recommendations were 'never fully adopted'.[95]

Why were Loudon's proposals not implemented? One obvious factor was the end of the 2nd AIF's three-year deployment to the Middle East. Most of the 9th Division, the last division to leave the Middle East, returned to Australia in February 1943. Loudon's own unit, 8 ASH, had quit Gaza a year earlier. Without his personal presence in the Middle East, was anyone left there interested in or capable of introducing his scheme?

Another probable factor was the administrative complexity of the plan. A system relying on the signing of leave registers and the issuing of attendance counterfoils by the PACs was one requiring additional clerical resources and complicated record-keeping systems.

A further factor was the coercive nature of the Loudon plan, with its threat of loss of pay and court martial action against VD sufferers. The Australian Military Force (AMF) was endeavouring to reduce the penalties for contracting VD. The rationale for that was the realisation that punitive anti-VD measures prompted the VD-infected to try to conceal their infections. Encouraging them to seek early treatment was considered a more productive tactic. Loudon's coercive strategy may have been seen as running counter to prevailing thought on the best means for managing VD.

Loudon himself seems to have left no record of his attitude to the non-implementation of his plan. Within several months of returning to Australia he was appointed as Adviser in Venereology at Army headquarters in Melbourne. With that, his focus shifted to the rising problem of VD among the troops in Australia.

9. Conclusions

STDs in World War II were once again a problem for the Australian Army, though not as devastatingly so as during World War I. Shorter treatment regimens made possible by the sulpha drugs was one reason why VD did not produce the great wastage it did in the earlier war. Another reason was that many of the Army's senior medical officers were veterans of the 1st AIF. They could remember the wreckage that VD had caused in World War I and were determined it would not again impede the Army. In helping mobilise the 2nd AIF, they accordingly took precautions to minimise its impact. The establishment of PACs early in the war was one such measure. Another was the early formation of the Special or VD Hospitals staffed by specialist venereologists.

Despite such precautions, once the 2nd AIF arrived in the Middle East VD did become a problem. Indeed, during the Army's second year in the region, 1941, the VD infection rates rose to epidemic proportions. That called for drastic measures and for the first (but not the last) time, the Army took the radical action of sponsoring its own brothels, run in association with the PACs. The public back in Australia never heard of this and so the Army-controlled brothels did not become the great national scandal they would otherwise have been.

The management of the 2nd AIF's VD epidemic in the Middle East eventually proved effective. After the campaign in Syria and Lebanon ended in July 1941, the threat from VD was greatly reduced.

Most of the Australian forces in the Middle East were withdrawn and returned to Australia in early 1942. After that, the Army in Australia experienced its own epidemic of VD as troop numbers built up rapidly to repel the Japanese advance through Australia's island territories to the near north. Fortunately for the AMS, the Allied commanders and the seemingly VD-prone troops, penicillin, the new 'wonder drug', was about to revolutionise the treatment of STDs.

CHAPTER 7

The Army and Venereal Diseases during World War II, 1942-1945

Japan dramatically entered the war on 7 December 1941 (8 December in Australia) with simultaneous pre-emptive air attacks in Hawaii, Malaya, the Philippines and other targets in the Asia-Pacific region. Over the ensuing weeks, Japanese forces rapidly advanced across this vast region. On 23 January 1942 a Japanese invasion force landed at Rabaul on New Britain, the main town in the Australian mandated Territory of New Guinea. Port Moresby, capital of the Territory of Papua, was bombed for the first time on 13 February. Singapore fell on 15 February. Darwin suffered the first of its 65 bombings on 19 February. That same day, Japanese forces landed on Timor, and they landed in Java on 28 February. On 8 March Japanese troops invaded the New Guinea mainland, capturing Salamaua and nearby Lae, which had become the territory's capital. By the end of

March almost the entire chain of archipelagos to Australia's near north was under Japanese control.

The Australian government responded by bringing home the 2nd AIF from the Middle East to defend Australia and its nearby island territories in New Guinea and Papua. The 6th and 7th divisions came first, beginning in early February 1941. The 9th Division followed in January and February 1943, after fighting in both the first and second Battles of El Alamein in July and October to November 1942.

In the four-year period 1940 to 1945, military hospitals in Australia treated 21,350 soldiers for VD. That was almost double the number of VD cases treated in the Middle East and 62.5 per cent of the World War II VD caseload of 34,178 for all theatres of the war. Before considering that second epidemic in detail, however, the reader needs to know about VD among Australian troops in the other theatres, namely those in South-East Asia and the Pacific Islands.

1. VD among Australians in South-East Asia and the Pacific Islands

VD occurred among Australian troops in all the theatres in which they were engaged during World War II. This section considers its occurrence during the campaigns in South-East Asia, Papua New Guinea and Morotai-Borneo.

Ceylon

Ceylon (Sri Lanka) served as a staging post for Australian troopships travelling to and from the Middle East. The Australian 6th and 7th divisions called in there for stopovers on the voyage home from the Middle East in early 1942.

VD cases emerged among Australian units in Ceylon during the short time they stayed there. A.S. Walker, the official medical war historian, wrote little about them other than to note that 'venereal disease occurred in disappointingly large numbers'.[1] According to Walker, 110 cases were treated in 'a special wing of a camp hospital'. The patients were later sent back to Australia in a shipboard hospital on one of the troopships returning to Australia.[2]

The number of VD cases treated in Ceylon was small by comparison with the number hospitalised in the Middle East, where an average of 106 new cases a week had been hospitalised over the two-year period 1940 to 1941. It was nevertheless so many that one of the AMS medical officers, Major (later Lieutenant Colonel) Clive H. Selby, requested that a PAC be established. This was agreed to, but how many soldiers used the PAC is uncertain.[3]

Meanwhile, the 2/12th Australian General Hospital (2/12 AGH), established in Australia in June 1941, was sent to Ceylon as a semi-permanent Australian military hospital for the island. Its purpose was to receive Australian soldiers passing though the colony and needing treatment. It remained in Ceylon until early 1943, after the 9th Division had returned home, following which it, too, returned to Australia and later saw service in Borneo. The hospital treated many Australian and British malaria patients in Borneo, and probably VD cases as well.[4]

Ambon, Malaya, Rabaul, Singapore, Timor

The 2nd AIF troops sent to South-East Asia in 1940 and 1941 comprised mainly units from the 8th Division, which were variously deployed to Ambon, Malaya, Singapore, Timor and Rabaul. Although Rabaul, on the island of New Britain, was within Australia's mandated Territory of New Guinea, early in the war the town was garrisoned by an 8th Division battalion.

Except for the few who managed to escape, the 20,000 troops of the 8th Division were rapidly overrun by Japanese forces. Most of those surviving the initial Japanese onslaught became prisoners of war (POWs) by the end of February 1942. Many died in captivity from the combined effects of malnutrition, infectious diseases, overwork, brutal treatment and the extreme deprivation of life as prisoners under Japanese rule.

The estimated 1488 VD cases among the 8th Division's troops treated during 1941 were all the result of infections contracted in Malaya before the Japanese invasion at the end of 1941.[5]

Figures for Ambon, Singapore, Timor and Rabaul are unavailable. Walker did not include them in his official history. If, as likely, there were VD cases during those deployments, the documents recording them do not seem to have survived.

What proportion of the POWs from the 8th Division might have suffered from VD while in captivity is unknown. Some were thought to have had VD and to have been treating themselves. After liberation in August 1945, a number of ex-POWs contracted VD in Singapore and Thailand before their repatriation to Australia. Walker provided no figures to suggest how many suffered VD and did not indicate which hospital(s) treated them.[6]

The territories of Papua and New Guinea

The campaigns against the Japanese forces in the territories of Papua and New Guinea continued for 43 months, from January 1942 to August 1945. In that time an estimated 193 VD cases were treated in the two territories. The 193 cases were the equivalent of an average of 4.5 cases a month—the lowest averages among Australian troops in any of the theatres of the war.

The chart in Figure 7.1 compares the rates in Australia over the four years 1942 to 1945 with those in the South-West Pacific Area (effectively the two territories of New Guinea and Papua for all of 1942 to 1944 but including Morotai-Borneo as well in 1945).

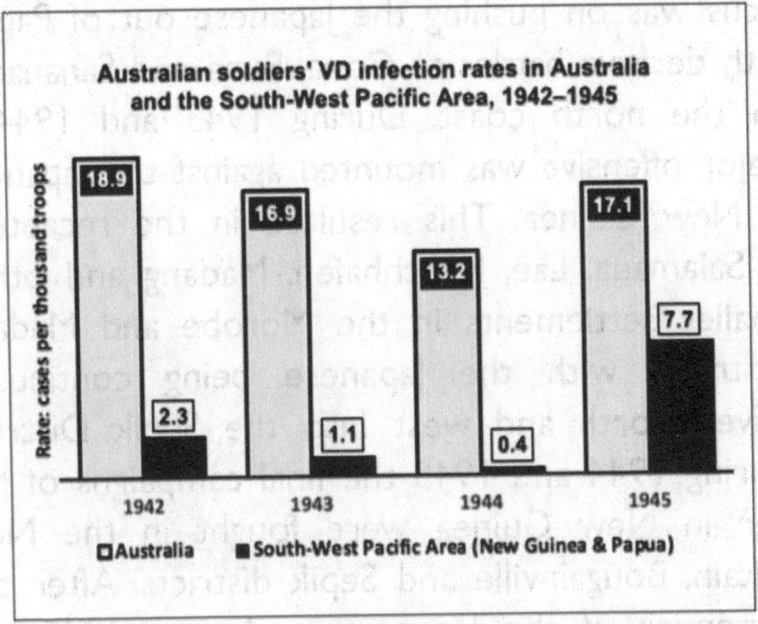

Figure 7.1: Comparison of VD infection rates among Australian soldiers in Australia and in the South-West Pacific Area, 1942-1945 (A.S. Walker, Clinical Problems of War, pp.268-269).

As the chart demonstrates, the rate in Australia was always much higher than that in the two territories. The Australian rate exceeded that in the territories by a factor of eight in 1942, of almost 16 in 1943, of more than 36 in 1944 and double the territories' rate in 1945.

The lower but varying rates in the two territories may be correlated to the stages of the war. In 1942, the Australians were fighting major defensive battles against the Japanese at Wau in New Guinea, and along the Kokoda Track and at Milne Bay in Papua. In 1943 the focus was on pushing the Japanese out of Papua, with decisive battles at Gona, Buna and Sanananda on the north coast. During 1943 and 1944 a major offensive was mounted against the Japanese in New Guinea. This resulted in the recapture of Salamaua, Lae, Finschhafen, Madang and other smaller settlements in the Morobe and Madang Districts, with the Japanese being continually driven north and west into the Sepik District. During 1944 and 1945 the final campaigns of the war in New Guinea were fought in the New Britain, Bougainville and Sepik districts. After the surrender of the Japanese in August 1945, the troops remaining in the two territories undertook garrison duties.

The higher VD rate in 1945 included both the VD cases in Morotai and Borneo between April and September 1945 as well as those in Papua and New Guinea for the whole year. The estimated total number of VD cases for the South-West Pacific Area for the period 1942 to 1945 was 230.

Very few VD cases occurred in Papua and New Guinea. According to Walker's figures, there were 159 cases from 1942 to 1944.[7] To this tally an estimated 34 cases in 1945 must be added, giving a 1942 to 1945 total of 193 cases.[8]

According to Walker, the stark differential in the VD infection rates in Australian and Papua New Guinea could be explained by the 'lack of opportunity of acquiring infection' in the two territories and the 'absence of settled areas where soldiers might spend leave'.[9] In addition, and especially during the later stages of the war, the nature of the fighting was also an influence. Many of the battles in Papua and New Guinea took place in widely dispersed jungles, swamps, kunai grasslands, plantations and mountainous terrains distant from settlements. The towns, mission stations and patrol posts being fought over had been deserted by their usual civilian populations, and village communities often fled their homes to seek temporary refuge elsewhere while battles were being fought across their lands.[10]

US Army lore recognised these realities. According to Dennis Shanks, an ADF malariologist who once ran a US Army VD clinic, 'it was said in the US Army that VD rates were inversely proportional to combat and that disease rates reflected boredom with routine activities'.[11] Soldiers' pay was also a factor, because 'soldiers were often not paid in the field and thus could not purchase sex'. So, too, was proximity to towns because 'infections were directly proportional to time spent in local towns'. When soldiers were kept in camp for security reasons and could not make trips into town, 'infections stopped'.[12]

Walker gives no indication where the 230 VD cases in the South-West Pacific Area were treated, or in what hospitals. Presumably the military hospitals in the major centres, mainly Port Moresby and later Lae, Rabaul, Morotai and Borneo, provided whatever treatment was deemed necessary by the medical officers.

Morotai and Borneo

Morotai, in the Maluku Islands in eastern Indonesia, was the base used by Allied forces in the recapture of the Philippines by the Americans, and of Tarakan, Brunei and Balikpapan in Borneo by the Australians.

The Australian landings and swift capture of Tarakan, Brunei and Balikpapan took place during May, June and July 1945. According to Walker, during and after these brief campaigns a sharp increase in VD infections occurred because 'known sources of infection existed among the natives in various areas in Borneo'.[13] Walker attributed the sharp rise in the rate to the 'state of idleness' of the soldiers left occupying Borneo after the campaigns there had ended.[14]

The number of cases of VD in Morotai and Borneo was very small—17 in Morotai and 20 in Borneo between April and September 1945—a total of just 37.[15] Expressed as a rate, that figure gives a very low rate of one case per thousand of strength. (Six brigades from the 7th and 9th divisions took part in the Borneo campaigns, a total of some 37,000 troops.) That rate was very much lower than the rate of 17.1 among troops in Australia in 1945. It contrasts even more strongly with the rate of 48.5 in 1941, the peak VD year in the Middle East.

Although the VD case rate was gratifyingly low among the Australians in Morotai and Borneo, a worrying aspect of the infections was the emergence of drug-resistant strains of gonorrhoea and chlamydia. Walker noted that 'trouble was experienced with sulphonamide-resistant forms of gonorrhoea and that 'intractable forms of non-specific urethritis also appeared, unquestionably of venereal origin [caused by chlamydia]'.[16] Treatment of the latter condition did not in some cases result in a cure 'even after 70 to 80 days of treatment, including the use of penicillin and sulphonamides'.[17]

2. VD among the troops in Australia during World War II

After the Middle East, Australia was the locus of the Army's second VD epidemic of World War II. The figures for 1939 to 1941 are unavailable, but during the four-year period 1942 to 1945 an estimated 21,350 VD cases were treated in military hospitals in Australia. The figures for each of those years are set out in Table 7.1.[18]

Table 7.1-**VD cases in the Army in Australia, 1942-1945**

Year	1942	1943	1944	1945	Total
Army strength	350,779	380,289	345,004	219,843	—
Estimated cases	6640	6408	4547	3755	21,350
Rate: VD cases per 1000 troops	18.9	16.9	13.2	17.1	—

Source: A.S. Walker, Clinical Problems of War, p.269. As the table indicates, the case rate fluctuated from year to year, between a high of 18.9 in 1942 and a low of 13.2 in 1944. Although the rate of 17.1 in the last year of the war was little lower than in 1942, the decline in the number of cases was striking. The hospitalisations fell from 6640 to 3755, a drop of 43 per cent. The decline can be seen clearly in the chart at Figure 7.2.

The steady decline in hospitalisations for VD reflected three influences. First was the continued strenuous effort of the AMS, strongly supported by the Army command, to reduce the number of VD infections through a combination of anti-VD strategies. Second was the fact during 1944 and 1945 the Army reduced its strength as the war against the Japanese was clearly being won. In addition, proportionately more soldiers were serving out of Australia in theatres where they were less likely to become infected. Third, penicillin was having an impact. As Walker observed, 'penicillin changed the whole therapeutic outlook in the venereal diseases'.[19]

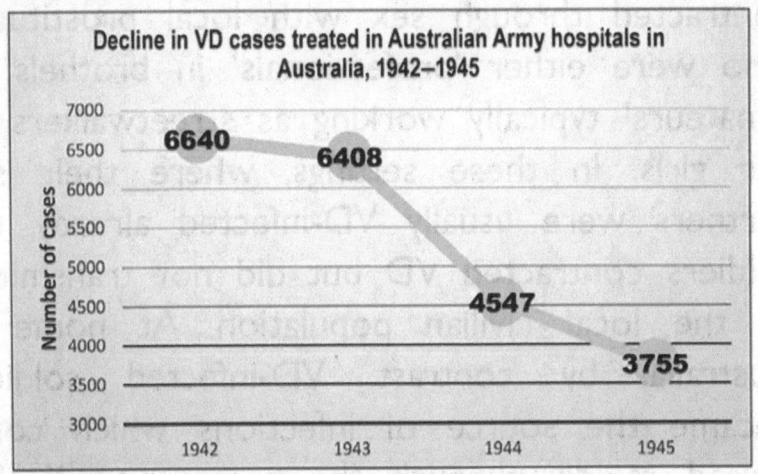

Figure 7.2: Number of VD cases treated in Australian Army hospitals between 1942 and 1945 (A.S. Walker, Clinical Problems of War, p.269).

Disconcertingly, the spike in the rate in 1945, up from 13.2 to 17.1, probably reflected a more relaxed attitude among the troops as the end of the war approached. Even though the trend in VD cases was downwards, as far as the AMS was concerned the VD statistics remained a cause for anxiety. For the AMS and the civilian authorities, VD in Australia was a more serious issue than overseas because in Australia VD infections could readily be transmitted to the civilian population.

In most of the Army's overseas deployments, on the other hand, the troops were posted to 'colonial-type' societies in which VD was contracted through sex with local prostitutes, who were either 'professionals' in brothels or 'amateurs' typically working as streetwalkers or bar girls. In these settings, where their sex partners were usually VD-infected already, the soldiers contracted VD but did not transmit it to the local civilian population. At home in Australia, by contrast, VD-infected soldiers became the source of infections which could spread rapidly through the community. If that occurred, unwelcome societal and political consequences would follow.

To avert that possibility, the AMS established its PACs 'near all camp areas and in all population centres'. Particular care was taken to select and train the PAC staff.[20]

The AMS also established in Australia a series of 'Special' or VD hospitals, as it had done earlier in the Middle East. At least six Special Hospitals were formed and functioned in Australia during World War II They were the:

- 81st Australian Special Hospital at Evandale on the Gold Coast south of Brisbane, operational 1944 to 1945 (previously the 81st Camp Hospital)
- 120th Australian Special Hospital, initially at the Sydney Showgrounds as 1st Australian Special Hospital then as 120 ASH from January 1941 at Little Bay, Sydney, operational 1940 to 1946
- 122nd Australian Special Hospital at the Melville Army Camp, Fremantle, Perth, operational 1942 to 1945
- 123rd Australian Special Hospital at Athelstone, Adelaide, operational 1942 to 1945
- 124th Australian Special Hospital at Puckapunyal north of Melbourne, operational 1942 to 1946
- 126th Australian Special Hospital at Kangaroo Point, Brisbane, operational 1943 to 1946.[21]

In addition to the Special Hospitals, some of the Army's General Hospitals and Camp Hospitals included 'Special Annexes' of 'Special Detachments' which admitted and treated VD patients. Such hospitals would have included 101 AGH at Katherine; 119 AGH and 129 AGH at Darwin; the 55th Australian Camp Hospital at Tennant Creek; 2/7 AGH at Lae in New Guinea; 2/9 AGH at Port Moresby in Papua; and 2/4 AGH, 2/5 AGH and 2/6 AGH on Moro tai and in Borneo.

Whichever Army hospitals treated VD, 'a high standard of cure was insisted upon'.[22] Whereas an average period of hospital treatment of 28 days had sufficed for a 'cure' in the Middle East, an average of 52 days was the norm in Australia.[23] That, of course, made for many more lost 'man-years' among VD-infected

3. Reactions in Australia to the reality of VD-infected troops within the community

The Army's and public health authorities' concern about soldier-transmitted VD was evident in joint conferences attended by representatives of the armed services and civilian health agencies in Brisbane and Melbourne in 1942. These conferences emphasised the need for research on VD and high standards of prophylaxis and diagnosis, and especially 'social control' measures.[24]

The Commonwealth Government took responsibility for 'social control' by promulgating coercive regulations under the *National Security Act 1939-1940* and the *National Emergency Act 1941*. The National Security (Venereal Diseases and Contraception) Regulations issued under the former Act on 1 September 1942, empowered civilian health authorities to 'detain and examine persons suspected of carrying infection'.[25]

This strategy targeted brothel-based prostitutes and particularly 'amateurs' working alone. According to one study conducted by 120 ASH in Sydney, 'amateurs' were responsible for 85 per cent of the VD cases the hospital was treating and 'professionals' only 15 per cent.[26] The study was conducted by Lieutenant Colonel Norman Gibson, the CO of 120 ASH, a venereologist and one of the Army's three principal advisers in venereology.[27] Gibson was a specialist with long Army experience during two world wars. He was appointed CO of 120 ASH in December 1940 and remained in the position as a lieutenant colonel until his retirement in August 1946.[28]

In September 1942 Gibson published an article in the *MJA* under the title 'Control of Venereal Disease in the Army', reporting the findings of his study at 120 ASH. Gibson pointed out that VD infection rates fluctuated over time. During times of prosperity and wars, much money is in circulation and more alcohol is consumed, the incidence reaches its highest peak, and the contrary is true in times of depression'.[29] In discussing 'sources of infection', Gibson observed that 'the enthusiastic amateur was the great source of danger'. Sydney was the epicentre of VD infection among troops on leave. There, 'alcohol played a very large part in the causation' because while soldiers were 'under its influence they became careless and indifferent to risks and failed to take the necessary precautions'.[30] troops in Australia. For example, in 1942, the last 'pre-penicillin' year, the 6640 cases in Australia represented 345,280 'hospital treatment days' or 946 'man-years'.

Gibson had already made similar points to a soldier audience in a series of three articles in *Salt*, the weekly journal of the Australian Army Education Service. Significantly, the title of the first was 'The Second Front'. Gibson began it by arguing that 'in every war there have been two fronts—one against the human enemy and one against venereal disease'.[31]

'What is the Army doing about it?' Gibson asked rhetorically in his *MJA* article. In a section headed 'Prevention of Venereal Disease', he summarised the Army's current strategies in Australia for attempting to reduce the risk of soldiers becoming infected. Briefly, these seven anti-VD measures were in place:

1. **Medical inspections** after soldiers were admitted into camp, at various stages during their training and before they were deployed to war theatres.
2. **Short-arm parades** conducted every week as a routine of camp life, with every effort made to preserve soldiers' privacy while identifying cases of VD infection.
3. **Lectures** to the Army medical officers at the Army School of Hygiene and the School of Public Health and Tropical Medicine at the University of Sydney, and lectures to combat officers and non-commissioned officers at the Army School of Hygiene. Those lectured were then expected to impart what they had learnt to the troops of their units.
4. **Articles** about VD in simple layman's language were being published in *Salt*, the Army education journal.

5. **Training** in VD prophylaxis routines for medical staff were being conducted at 120 ASH (of which Gibson was the CO).
6. **Condoms** and Blue Light self-treatment kits were being issued free from the many PACs.
7. **Prophylactic depots**—PACs—staffed by trained personnel were operating in all the Army camps and towns where there were nearby concentrations of troops.[32]

The article concluded by describing the current methods of diagnosis and treatment for soldiers who had become VD-infected. Patients with gonorrhoea were treated with injections of one gram of sulphonamide four times daily for five days. The patient's urine was then examined for 'threads' of gonococci-produced pus. If the urine was clear, which occurred in 75 to 80 per cent of cases, the patient was discharged and returned to his unit. If the urine still displayed 'threads', the procedure was repeated after ten days.[33]

Patients with test-confirmed diagnoses of syphilis, about 5 to 8 per cent of those admitted to 120 ASH, were 'boarded out' from the Army as medically unfit, reported to the state health authorities and directed to undergo treatment. 'Boarding out'—making the soldier appear before a medical board to determine if he was medically unfit for further service—was a serious step. It meant the loss of a trained soldier who had to be replaced. The reason for 'boarding' the syphilitics was the time taken to cure them. According to Gibson, 'it was considered necessary for them to receive continuous treatment for eighteen months to two years'.[34] In that time they were of no use to the Army. Before being discharged to civilian life, the syphilis-infected were treated in the Special Hospitals to the stage where their lesions had healed and they were considered 'temporarily non-contagious'. The treatment comprised intramuscular injections of the arsenic-based drugs combined with intramuscular injections of one of the bismuth compounds.[35]

In tackling VD, the medical services of the Navy, Army, and Air Force endeavoured to adopt a cooperative, joint approach. They formed a VD Sub-Committee of the Standing Committee of the Service Medical Directors. The Standing Committee comprised the Director of the Naval Medical Service, DGMS Army and DGMS Air Force. The VD Sub-Committee, a panel of about eight members, all senio military medical officers, included representatives of all three armed services and the Controller of VD of the United States Armed Forces in Australia. Lieutenant Colonel Gibson of 120 ASH became a co-opted member. The sub-committee held a series of conferences at which it considered matters such as measures for the prevention of VD, regulations for curbing the spread of VD, the standardisation of VD treatment regimens and the determination of uniform criteria for what was deemed a 'cure'.[36]

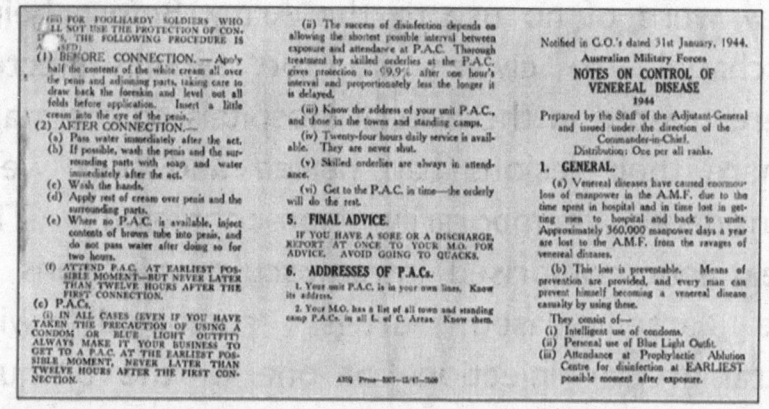

Figure 7.3: 'Control of VD' card issued to all Australian military personnel in 1944 (AWM114 267/6/17 Part 3).

According to A.S. Walker, the control of VD in the Army improved after Lieutenant Colonel Loudon was appointed in July 1943 to the new position of 'Adviser in Venereology'. As such, he was attached to the staff of the DGMS, Major General Burston.[37] Loudon worked in the position at Land Headquarters in Melbourne for a year, until he was placed on the retirement list in July 1944. Two months after that, he was promoted to honorary colonel and appointed as the Army's 'Consultant in Venereology', a position he retained for the next two-and-a-half years, until February 1947.[38]

As the Army's most senior venereologist, Loudon travelled extensively to visit the hospitals which treated VD patients. He began his duties as Burston's venereological adviser by touring the hospitals to investigate their current practice. At the end of the tour he reported to Burston that he had discovered a lack of adherence to the guidelines laid down in the booklet *Standards of Prophylactic Treatment and Cure of Venereal Diseases* (published by AMS headquarters in March 1943 with a foreword by Burston).[39] He found that the location of the PACs was little-known to troops. The soldiers did not have access to up-to-date pamphlets about VD. The implementation of the DGMS's Technical Instructions on VD was unsatisfactory. There was poor liaison between the Special Hospitals and other Army hospitals and insufficient communication with the civilian health authorities. Finally, there was no standard syllabus for instructing the medical orderlies who staffed the PACs.[40]

Loudon recommended the appointment of a threefold hierarchical structure of venereological supervisors. At the national level there would be a Director of Venereology based at Land Headquarters in Melbourne. In each of the major

Army Line of Communication Areas (the states) there should be an Assistant Director of Venereology, ideally the CO of the Special Hospital in that area. A Deputy Assistant Director of Venereology should be appointed in each of the minor Line of Communication Areas (regions within states), the appointee to be the CO of a Special Hospital if available, or the officer commanding a Special (VD) detachment of an Army General Hospital. Loudon set out a schedule of duties for the appointees at each of the three levels of his proposed VD organisation.[41] Whether the DGMS accepted and implemented these recommendations is unclear, however, Loudon's proposals indicated a more systematic approach to controlling VD was being sought.

In early 1944 Loudon visited all states and then submitted another report to the DGMS. He found in South Australia that the DGMS's Technical Instructions on VD were being implemented. In Queensland, particularly in Cairns and Townsville, the VD control procedures were being efficiently managed. In Western Australia a local anti-VD campaign was proving effective, with increasing numbers of troops visiting the PACs. In Victoria there was close liaison between the Special Hospital, the General Hospitals and the US Hospitals. In Tasmania the Red Cross was cooperating by providing additional amenities and equipment. In New South Wales the military and civilian health authorities were cooperating closely, particularly in the compulsory treatment of the VD-infected.[42]

The DGMS would have expected his Adviser in Venereology to collaborate with the Army's other two leading venereologists, Loudon's colleagues—Lieutenant Colonels Gibson at 120 ASH in Sydney and Francis at 126 ASH in Brisbane. Loudon, Gibson and Francis produced a series of important reports on VD, which Walker subsequently used as the basis of his chapter on VD in the first of his official histories, *Clinical Problems of War*. Because of their reports, much is known about how the AMS managed VD in Australia in the period 1942 to 1945.[43]

The advice that these senior venereologists gave the DGMS was periodically disseminated to medical officers in the Army hospitals and field units through a series of edicts termed 'Technical Memoranda' and 'Administrative Instructions'.[44] These communications kept reiterating the information provided by Gibson in his article in the *MJA* in September 1942. The venereologists' advice also reached the Army's RMOs in publications such as the booklet *Standards of Prophylaxis, Treatment and Cure of Venereal*

Diseases, which, as seen, was intended to provide prescriptive guidelines for managing VD cases.[45]

The Australian public knew little of this literature. Their source of information about VD, its spread and its impact on the armed forces was the popular press. The newspapers of the day, whose currency was scandal and sensation, often published stories about VD running rampant among armed service personnel and spreading through the community. Two brief examples are given here, confined to the headlines and the introductory paragraphs. Both from early 1943, they illustrate the type of reportage VD received in the popular newspapers of the day.[46]

- ***The Sun*** **[Sydney], 1 March 1943:**
  GIRLS BLIND TO V.D. PERIL
  Rising figures for venereal disease were a flagrant example of the effects of ignorance, Sir Charles Bickerton Blackburn, the well-known consulting physician said today. Sir Charles, who was giving evidence today before the Parliamentary Committee on Social Security, recommended immediate education of parents and a campaign in schools to inculcate in children a sense of responsibility to their own health and that of the community.

  'If all these unfortunate children—girls of 16 and 17 who are becoming infected—had been better educated,' he said, 'a large proportion of these V.D. cases could have been prevented.'

- ***Truth* [Melbourne], 3 April 1943:**
  ALL-OUT WAR ON V.D.

  Despite Army Minister Forde's recent disclosure that the venereal disease rate in the Australian Army had dropped 40 per cent below last year's figure, the American Army officials have started on a blitz against the scourge, particularly in Melbourne. Urging that drastic measures are imperative, they point out that, in one month alone, 10,000 fighting hours were lost by U.S. troops suffering from V.D.

  The American authorities have suggested measures against women which would virtually amount to compulsory checks and quarantine.

The threat of VD to the military forces and the general community was real enough, but ordinary Australian citizens would have learnt little about it from the newspapers of the day. The frequency of newspaper reportage was nevertheless a barometer of community concern about VD's societal impact.

Politicians were better placed to know more about VD than their constituents. Parliaments received the annual reports of the departments of health with the latest statistics of VD infection, and the ministers for health were periodically questioned about VD infection rates and what governments were doing to control VD. In addition, the Commonwealth Government's Advisory War Council was kept briefed on the incidence of VD among military personnel by the Armed Forces Joint Chiefs of Staff.[47]

On at least one occasion, discussion of 'the VD problem' by the Advisory War Council captured prime ministerial attention. The matter of young women contracting VD was considered by the Council in early 1944. In March the Prime Minister, John Curtin, referred this issue to his Minister for Health, James M. Fraser. Curtin asked Fraser for his views, and then expressed his opinion that the matter should be discussed by representatives of the Services and the Commonwealth and State Health authorities as soon as convenient'. He directed Fraser to convene a meeting to consider the issue and take appropriate further action.[48]

Figure 7.4: A poster produced for the Commonwealth Government's anti-VD campaign in 1943—1944. The poster was designed to shock by contrasting happy, secure family life with disease and death after the sordid contracting of VD (Venereal Disease is a Killer, NAA: A1861).

The outcome of the meeting was a decision to spend £25,000 ($1.7 million in 2020 values) on an anti-VD publicity campaign. On 24 May 1944 the Acting Prime Minister (and also Army minister), Frank Forde, announced the campaign and the money to be spent.[49] Among other things, the money was expended on anti-VD publicity posters such as those depicted in Figure 7.4.

4. Policy on women in the armed services who contracted VD

Female Army personnel who contracted VD became a special concern for the AMS. During World War II, the Army had four female branches—the Australian Army Nursing Service (AANS), the Australian Army Medical Women's Service (AAMWS), the Australian Women's Army Service (AWAS) and the Australian Women's Land Army (AWLA). Members of the AANS provided the professional nursing staff of the Army hospitals. AAMWS members undertook medical ancillary work as nursing aides and laboratory technicians. AWAS members undertook a variety of tasks including work as drivers, cooks, canteen workers, typists, clerks and signallers. AWLA members worked on farms, substituting for the men of farming communities who had enlisted in the armed services. Eventually, almost 50,000 women served in the Army's female branches: 5000 in the AANS; 8500 in the AAMWS; 24,000 in the AWAS; and at least 3400 in the AWLA.[50]

With some 50,000 women in Army uniform, most of them in Australia, almost inevitably some among them contracted VD. How many is uncertain. Walker gave the matter only half a page in *Clinical Problems of War*.[51] His source was a three-page memorandum from the DGMS, Burston, to the Adjutant General (the Army's principal administrative officer) in March 1943, describing how the AMS intended managing what was a novel situation. The memo is the only known record in which the issue was discussed by the Army during the war.[52]

According to this memo, no VD cases had so far been recorded in either the AANS or the AAMWS; the AWLA was not mentioned, so presumably no cases had been detected there either, but nine cases had occurred in the AWAS. The AWAS cases, seven in Queensland and two in Victoria, represented infection rates of 8 per thousand and 2 per thousand respectively in those states, much lower rates than among male soldiers.[53]

No known statistics exist to indicate long-term trends in the VD rate in the Army women's services. Whatever the levels, Burston's memo did not signal these as a serious problem. The AMS had nevertheless developed a policy for handling female VD cases. The AMS, Burston wrote, 'felt that the low incidence of VD in

Army women can be regarded as evidence of the sense of responsibility and self-respect possessed by women of the Services; and these factors will continue to prevent VD becoming a major problem among Army women personnel'.[54] The DGMS set out a simple six-point plan for managing VD in the women's services:

1. No further legislation or regulations were required because the Army already possessed 'ample authority to require any suspected member of the forces, either male or female, to undergo any form of examination or treatment considered necessary'.
2. No punitive measures would be instituted because that would encourage VD sufferers to try to conceal their symptoms, which, in women, were more difficult to detect than in men.
3. Education in general personal hygiene would be given to all female personnel but not specifically VD education (such as male soldiers received). The reason was that explicit VD education might 'convey the impression that promiscuity was receiving official recognition'.
4. The rates of VD incidence within the women's services would be monitored

and any rise in the rates would be reported to the DDMS 'for investigation' and, presumably, appropriate action would be taken.

5. Where syphilis was diagnosed among Army women, similar procedures would be followed as for male syphilitics. Following diagnosis, initial treatment would be provided to the 'temporarily non-contagious' stage, after which the case would be considered by a medical assessment board, the patient discharged as medically unfit and referred to the civilian health authorities for further treatment.

6. Gonorrhoea presented particular difficulties in women because its symptoms in the early stages of infection were often so mild that sufferers might not suspect they had been infected, however, early treatment was essential to prevent subsequent complications. Encouraging women to seek early treatment 'without minimising the seriousness of contracting the disease' accordingly required 'a balanced and wise' approach. Women suspected of gonorrhoeal infection were subject to 'rigid bacteriological control';

those who refused treatment were 'not retained in the service'.[55]

When Army women did become VD-infected, they were treated in special annexes of the Army's women's hospitals, of which there were three. All established in 1942 and 1943, and operational until 1945, they were the 1st Australian Women's Hospital at Claremont, Perth; the 2nd Australian Women's Hospital at Yeronga, Brisbane; and the 3rd Australian Women's Hospital at Concord, Sydney.[56]

Figure 7.5: 3rd Australian Women's Hospital, Concord, Sydney, March 1943. Originally a private mansion, 'Yaralla', it had served as a convalescent home before being redesignated as a women's hospital in 1942-43. Female VD patients were treated within an annexe of the hospital (AWM 126467).

5. The Mapharsen episode at 126th Australian Special Hospital

During 1944 both the 126th Australian Special Hospital (126 ASH) in Brisbane and its CO, Lieutenant Colonel Neil Francis, were at the centre of a controversy over the experimental use of the arsenic-based drug Mapharsen in treating 126 ASH's syphilis patients.

In the eight-month period January to August 1944, thirteen of 40 patients being treated with Mapharsen for 'early' (Stage 1) syphilis developed a condition called 'toxic jaundice'. Two of the 13 died, the first on 30 June, the second on 23 August. After the second death the treatment regimen was no longer administered to new patients but continued for those who had already started the course.[57] The CO, Francis, was removed in mid-July and placed on 'Reserve'. He was discharged from the Army on 9 September.[58]

The Adviser in Venereology, Colonel Loudon, was sent to Brisbane to investigate. He conducted a seemingly thorough inquiry, but did not take direct evidence from the medical officers who had been supervising the treatment program because they had been posted elsewhere. He submitted a detailed nine-page report to the DGMS on 12 December.[59]

Loudon's report found fault with the Mapharsen treatment under Francis's supervision at 126 ASH. Guidelines for using Mapharsen were laid down in the AMS booklet, *Standards of Prophylactic Treatment and Cure of Venereal Diseases*. The *Standards* stipulated that:

1. When diagnosis [of early syphilis] is established, treatment will commence immediately as follows—bi-weekly [twice weekly] intravenous injection of Arsenicals for 20 injections. The first dose will be at the rate of .45 grams Neosalvarsan type, or .04 Mapharsen type. Subsequent doses will be at .6 grams [neosalvarsan] and .06 grams [Mapharsen] respectively. The persistence with the course will be decided by the progressive condition of the patient. During the course, the patient will be an in-patient of a Special Hospital.
2. A Wassermann or Kline test will then be taken.
3. Irrespective of the result of the test there will be given a course of bi-weekly intramuscular injections of an approved bismuth salt, preferably an iodobismuthate of quinine preparation, for a period of 10 weeks.

4. The Wassermann or Kline test will then be taken. Should Wassermann or Kline test be positive, the arsenical course will be repeated. Should the test be negative, the course of bismuth will be continued bi-weekly for a period of 12 months from the commencement of treatment. During this period, a Wassermann or Kline test will be taken every three months.[60]

The use of Mapharsen was permitted at the rate of 0.04 grams for each of the 20 injections administered over the first 10-week course of treatment. For the second 10-week course the dosage was raised to 0.06 grams per injection. The medical officer managing the treatment was allowed some discretion because he had to decide whether to continue the treatment based on the 'progressive condition' of the patient.

Loudon discovered that, under Francis's direction, the 126 ASH regimen had departed from the guidelines. Instead of administering 0.04 grams of Mapharsen per injection for the first course of treatment, 126 ASH had administered 0.06-gram injections from the outset. Further, instead of alternating between the courses of Mapharsen and bismuth injections, 126 ASH had administered the bismuth treatment at the same time as the Mapharsen treatment.[61]

It seemed that under Francis, 126 ASH had tried to follow US Army practice. Whereas the AMS *Standards* provided for treatment to extend across a period of 12 to 18 months, the US regimen was completed in six months. The reason for the shorter US regimen was apparently to achieve a 'mass saving of manpower days' that would otherwise be lost in treating syphilis cases.[62]

The 126 ASH regimen was also foreshortened to six months or 26 weeks.[63]

This meant that the 126 ASH patients were not only receiving a higher dosage of Mapharsen than specified in the AMS *Standards* but were receiving it in a third to half the time. Because the Mapharsen injections were given intravenously rather than intramuscularly, the drug would soon enter the liver from the bloodstream, whereas the intramuscular bismuth injections were absorbed more slowly by the patient's body. Apparently the higher dosage impacted adversely on the patients' livers, causing the 'toxic jaundice' condition.[64]

From 19 July 1944, 19 days after the death of the first patient, the 26-week 126 ASH treatment regimen was not used with new patients, who were treated instead according to the AMS *Standards*. Patients who had already started the 26-week course of treatment continued with it. After the death of the second patient on 23 August, the DDMS of the Queensland Line of Communications Area ruled that no patient could receive more than one 'arsenical' injection a week.[65]

In reporting on his investigation of the episode, Loudon stated that 'CO 126 ASH'—Francis was not named in the report—had 'exercised his discretion in his choice of method of treatment in accordance with ... *Standards of Prophylaxis, Treatment and Cure of Venereal Diseases 1943*'.[66] Loudon went on to make a series of recommendations, which included a review of the section of the *Standards* dealing with Mapharsen. He also recommended that injections of the drug should only be administered twice a week in the first fortnight of treatment, after which one injection a week should be given.[67]

Loudon's report condemned 126 ASH's routines for sterilising the equipment used in giving injections. At 126 ASH only the needles of the syringes were being boiled. The rest of the syringe was washed in 'spirit' (presumably alcohol). He recommended that all the equipment be boiled.[68]

Although Loudon could not determine whether the 126 ASH patients' jaundice resulted from the toxicity of the Mapharsen or from infective viral hepatitis, he raised the possibility that the latter might have been the cause. Noting that infectious hepatitis was endemic in Queensland at the time, he suggested that infectious hepatitis could have been transmitted from one patient to another by infected syringes.[69]

Walker wrote little about the episode. He mentioned 'intensive treatment of syphilis by Mapharsen given in massive doses continually over a brief period', but gave few details and did not name the hospital where the treatment took place.[70] He mentioned that 'a death occurred in a series of forty patients so treated, the cause of death being toxic jaundice and encephalopathy; therefore a ban was promptly placed on this method'.[71] That was not quite accurate because *two* of the patients had died. Further, the procedure was *not* banned immediately because patients who were already undergoing the shortened form of Mapharsen treatment continued with it.

Loudon's report seems to be the only surviving record of the irregular Mapharsen regimen. Apart from Walker's paragraph about the episode, no other reference to the episode appears in any of the many archival files on VD consulted in research for this book.

The 126 ASH official war diary makes no mention of the Mapharsen episode. The diary runs from December 1942, when the hospital opened, until its closure at the end of February 1946. It reveals that at its peak in 1944 the hospital had a staff of eight officers and 108 other ranks. Over its three-year period of operation, the hospital treated several hundred patients; at its closure it was still treating 92. No details of the clinical treatment programs are included, but there are many references to the tennis and cricket matches played by the staff, the weekly distribution of cigarettes, and the concerts, films, lectures and band recitals arranged for the patients.[72]

Significantly, perhaps, the diary's entries for August 1944 are missing. That was the month when the second Mapharsen-treated patient died. The diary mentions a visit of inspection by Lieutenant Colonel Loudon in March that year, another by a Lieutenant Colonel W. Crisp from Army Land Headquarters in Melbourne in May and a third by an unnamed officer from Land Headquarters in July. It does not mention Loudon's inquiry into the Mapharsen episode, which was conducted during October. The only reference to the departure of Francis is an entry noting that on 15 July 1944 Maj or Tom C. Anthony marched in as CO' to replace 'Lieutenant Colonel N.W. Francis who has been placed on the Reserve of Officers'.[73]

What, then, might present-day readers conclude about *l'affaire* Mapharsen? More than seven decades later, many questions about 126 ASH's shortened treatment regimen remain unanswered, among them these:

- Was the 126 ASH shortened treatment regimen a scandal that first Loudon and then Walker swept under a military-medical carpet?
- If it was not a scandal, why was Lieutenant Colonel Francis removed so soon? And why were the other medical officers involved in the treatment program promptly reposted elsewhere?
- Did the AMS headquarters in Melbourne have foreknowledge of and condone the treatment regimen introduced at 126 ASH? If so, did Francis become the scapegoat?
- Were the 40 patients undergoing the shorter, more intensive Mapharsen regimen ever informed that their treatment was not in accordance with AMS protocols?
- Did anyone explain to the 13 patients who suffered toxic jaundice that the treatment they had received was poisoning them?
- Were the families of the two soldiers who died ever told the full story of their deaths?

The critical question is why Francis and his medical staff had departed from the AMS

Standards by implementing the shortened, intensive Mapharsen treatment regimen. Did they believe that the US Army regimen was better? Had they been conducting an unauthorised experiment unbeknown to AMS headquarters? Alternatively, had it been an experiment carried out with the knowledge and approval of headquarters? If so, was it an experiment-gone-wrong? Had they behaved unethically by using their patients as experimental subjects without the patients' knowledge or consent?

Although patient foreknowledge and consent might not have been principles as strictly adhered to in 1943 as seven decades later, it is interesting to note that those principles *were* adopted in Australia's greatest military medical experimental program of World War II. That was the research on malaria and anti-malarial medication undertaken at the Land Headquarters Medical Research Unit at Cairns from 1943 to 1946, conceived and implemented by Brigadier Neil Hamilton Fairley. In that program, which in its first year coincided with the Mapharsen treatment episode at 126 ASH, soldier volunteers were infected with malaria for the effects of various dosages of a series of anti-malarial drugs to be assessed. The purpose of the program was to identify the most effective drug and dosage. Volunteers were advised what the experiments would entail and 1189 gave their consent. Ethically, the experimental program was considered 'world's best practice' at the time.

Another critical question about the Mapharsen episode is whether Loudon's report on the shortened Mapharsen treatment regimen at 126 ASH amounted to a whitewash—a deliberate attempt to conceal the truth of what had happened. Loudon was certainly critical of aspects of 126 ASH's practice. He did not, however, apportion blame for the toxic jaundice episode and the two deaths. Nor did he name names', attributing responsibility to particular individuals, as might have happened in a judicial inquiry. Significantly, Loudon provided no evidence from Francis or the other medical officers involved. His excuse for not interviewing the officers was that they had been posted elsewhere. He gave no explanation for leaving Francis out of his report. Perhaps he wished to protect Francis, a colleague from the time they had worked together at 8 ASH in Palestine three-and-a-half years earlier.

Amidst these questions-without-answers, several verifiable aspects of the 126 ASH regimen stand out. First, arsenic is highly toxic. The lethal dose for an adult is 200 milligrams. Second, the full 10-week program of twenty 0.06-gram injections meant that 1200 milligrams of

Mapharsen were being injected into a 126 ASH patient's bloodstream, which entailed risk of liver damage. Third, 13 cases of toxic jaundice out of 40 cases at 126 ASH in 1944 was 30 per cent of the caseload. That was a very high proportion; a much higher rate than in the contemporary medical literature available to Francis and Loudon. A percentage that high negates the basic principle of medical treatment —*Primum non nocere*, the Latin phrase meaning 'First, do no harm'. Fourth, two dead patients out of 40 represented a treatment mortality of five per cent. That, too, was an unacceptably high rate and should have prompted the immediate cancellation of the intensive Mapharsen treatment regimen.

Walker commented on none of this in *Clinical Problems of War*, so perhaps he, too, helped extend a whitewash. Walker had been an AMS lieutenant colonel who had commanded a hospital on Gaza Ridge in Palestine in 1940 and 1941. He would have known both Loudon and Francis well from their time with 8 ASH at Gaza. By writing little about either of these colleagues in his history, was he, too, protecting friends' reputations? Answers are unlikely to be found because Walker died in 1958, Loudon in 1963, and Francis in 1964.

The final question is whether the Mapharsen treatment episode at 126 ASH in 1944 was a scandal. It certainly is in retrospect, but it was not at the time because it was effectively hushed up. The newspapers and the public never knew of it. Many AMS medical officers probably remained unaware of it. It did, after all, occur in August 1944 at a time when the Australian Army was beginning its final campaigns against the Japanese. Australian soldiers were dying in combat in New Guinea, so few Army personnel would have worried much about the deaths in an obscure Army hospital of two syphilitics suffering from a preventable, essentially self-inflicted disease.

The great irony of the Mapharsen episode was that penicillin would have obviated the need for such a toxic medication. Penicillin was already available for other infections. It soon became the safe, sure means of treating syphilis as well.

6. Forfeiture of pay by VD-infected troops

The forfeiture of pay of soldiers being treated for VD was a disciplinary measure introduced in the 2nd AIF in the Middle East but never enforced as punitively as in the 1st AIF during World War 1. The reason for greater leniency was to encourage VD-infected troops to seek treatment early.

The issue of whether soldiers suffering VD should also suffer the whole or partial loss of their pay while being treated continued being debated throughout the war. In May 1941 the Military Board proposed to the War Cabinet that 'any member of the Australian Military Forces absent without leave suffering from venereal disease, shall forfeit one-half of his daily pay and pay allowances unless he satisfies his Commanding Officer that he received treatment at a prophylactic centre ... before the infection became apparent'.[74]

After this proposal had been accepted and included in War Financial Regulation 25, the regulation was revised in December 1943. The revision was in the direction of greater leniency. It provided that there would be 'no reduction in pay for the first occasion [infection], or relapses from the first occasion, up to a period of 35 days'. For 'second or subsequent occasions' the reduction would be one-third of pay.[75] The view of the Commander-in-Chief, Allied Land Forces in the South-West Pacific, General Douglas MacArthur of the US Army, was that the regulations should include no financial penalties.[76] His reasoning was that loss of pay simply encouraged soldiers to conceal their VD symptoms, which meant that when they had been detected they took longer to be cured and returned to their units. The abolition of War Financial Regulation 25 would 'aid early disclosure of the disease and [lead to] successful and speedy treatment'.[77]

The financial penalties for VD infection were abolished in May 1945 in the last three months of the war. The three main reasons for abolition were, first, that loss of pay 'militated against early disclosure and speedy treatment, and encouraged members to obtain illicit treatment'. Second, 'the introduction of Penicillin treatment had greatly reduced the incidence of VD and shortened the period of treatment'. Third, 'with the abolition of the penalty, expense and manpower were being saved as considerable clerical work was involved in maintaining individual records of all personnel treated for venereal diseases for the purpose of determining the date at which forfeiture of pay would operate'.[78]

And so after a six-year debate, the forfeiture of pay as an anti-VD measure was abandoned in the AMF. In retrospect, it can be seen as a naive and counterproductive strategy. Ironically, in the end it was not given up for reasons of preventive medicine, military discipline or public health. Post-penicillin economics had been the deciding factor. The cost of the clerical and accounting systems required to dock VD-infected soldiers' pay proved more expensive than the foreshortened VD treatment programs.

7. The impact of penicillin

A story often told is the discovery of the bacterium-inhibiting properties of the *Penicillium notatum* mould by Alexander Fleming in 1928. So, too, is the subsequent development of penicillin, a derivative of the mould, as a highly effective antibiotic drug by an Australian medical scientist, Howard Florey, and his colleague Ernst Chain at Oxford University in the period 1938 to 1943.[79] Of particular interest in this book is how penicillin impacted on the treatment of VD in the AMF during the last two years of the war.

Initially, the military use of penicillin was confined to treating infected wounds. Clinical trials of penicillin were completed at 115 AGH at Heidelberg in Melbourne. By that time, penicillin was being produced for general AMF use by the Commonwealth Serum Laboratories in Melbourne.[80] Florey himself returned to Australia at the invitation of the Prime Minister in August 1944 to deliver a series of lectures to both military and civilian audiences. 'This visit,' according to Walker, 'was most stimulating and helpful, and did much to further knowledge of antibiotic therapy in the Services and the civil medical profession'.[81]

The potential of penicillin for treating syphilis and later gonorrhoea was not discovered until October 1943, when a researcher at the US Department of Agriculture's research laboratory at Peoria, Illinois, announced to colleagues that penicillin offered 'a quick easy cure for syphilis' because the drug was highly active against the *Treponema pallidum* spirochaetes. The drug was soon shown to be effective against sulphonamide-resistant gonorrhoea as well, and so the Peoria laboratory, which had been producing penicillin on an industrial scale, proposed using penicillin against VD as well as infected wounds.[82]

According to one source, HistoryNet, diverting scarce penicillin supplies to treat VD led to a debate in Britain over who should have priority in receiving penicillin treatment — wounded or VD-infected soldiers. In an online article, 'Penicillin: Wonder Drug of World War II', HistoryNet has argued that:

> Venereal diseases were rampant in wartime, and the discovery of a cure immediately raised debate about whether scarce supplies should go first to treat soldiers wounded 'on the battlefield or in the bordello'. The bordello actually made

more practical sense, since you could cure a soldier and send him back to the front in a matter of days. And astonishingly, some politicians made the common-sense choice, with the Prime Minister, Winston Churchill, ordering medical staff to put battlefield readiness foremost.[83]

One historian quoted by HistoryNet has even suggested that giving priority to VD treatment was a war-winning decision because 'the resulting advantage in troop strength tipped the balance in favour of Allied forces during key engagements late in the war'. German forces, on the other hand, had no penicillin and continued suffering high wastage from VD.[84]

In the Australian Army, penicillin 'changed the whole therapeutic outlook in the venereal diseases'.[85] As Walker observed, 'the value of this antibiotic in both gonorrhoea and syphilis was soon established; treatment was simplified and made safer, with lessened risk of heavy metals; the time lost in hospital was also much reduced'.[86]

In the case of syphilis, instead of the protracted treatment with toxic arsenic and bismuth-based compounds across a period of 10 weeks and more, treatment was reduced to an eight-day cycle of twice-daily injections of penicillin. The new treatment regimen was set out in Technical Instruction No.125. This required that after the penicillin treatment had ended, the patient be retained in hospital for another fortnight while receiving bismuth medication twice a week. After that the patient was assigned to a works company while he continued attending hospital regularly as an outpatient.[87]

Clinical trials of the treatment of gonorrhoea with penicillin demonstrated that 'a great saving in manpower' would be gained from using the new drug. Penicillin was trialled in 300 cases of acute gonorrhoea. Of these, 90 per cent were 'clinically and bacteriologically cured' after receiving 100,000 units of penicillin; 95 per cent were cured with double that dosage; and when sulphamerazine (a sulphonamide) was administered twice daily for five days as well, the rate of cure was raised to 100 per cent.[88] Penicillin in combination with sulphamerazine reduced the average time spent in hospital by gonorrhoea patients from seven weeks to about three.[89]

8. Epilogue to Allan S. Walkers essay on VD in World War II

Dr Allan Seymour Walker, official medical historian of World War II in Australia, has been the reader's guide through this book's two chapters on the war. Walker's four-volume history comprises Series 5 ('Medical') in the five-series, 22-volume official Australian history of the war, published under the overall title of *Australia in the War of 1939-45*. The Walker volumes have provided most of the signposts and the pathways the reader has been following in this book's account of VD during World War II.

Walker, who had no training as a historian but became one of Australia's greatest doctor historians, learned his craft as he researched, drafted and published his four-volume series. He took on the task of the official medical historian at the urging of Gavin Long, the general editor *Australia in the War of 1939—45*, after the previous medical historian, Major General Rupert Downes, was killed in a plane crash in March 1945.

In concluding his discussion of VD in World War II, Walker reflected that 'a review of the venereal diseases during the war gave satisfaction from the scientific point of view'. He pointed out that 'suffering, danger of complications and of risk of transmission of infection have undoubtedly been lessened'.[90]

That was Walker the medical practitioner talking. Walker the concerned citizen could not be so sanguine. He was not optimistic that the armed services could ever be rendered VD-free.

That was because although 'medical instructions designed to prevent venereal disease attempt to build on the sure foundation of continence and personal responsibility, it was evident that neither such considerations nor those of caution nor fear would act as deterrents'.[91]

Walker's chapter on VD in *Clinical Problems of War* constitutes an erudite 13-page essay on VD in the Australian Army during World War II. It is a treatise that has been much quoted and referred to in this present chapter and the previous one. Walker ended his essay elegiacally, referring briefly to the Army's experience of VD in Japan as part of the British Commonwealth Occupation Force (BCOF), a deployment immediately following the end of the war.

Almost as soon as World War II had ended, Australian troops were committed to Japan as a major component of BCOF. The availability of penicillin notwithstanding, that deployment would achieve the dubious distinction of yielding the Army's highest rates of VD infection ever. In the year after World War II ended, 1946, the Australians serving with BCOF accounted for 73 per cent of the Force's VD infection, even though they comprised only a quarter of all BCOF troops.[92] Ironically, the reason was the very availability of the sulphonamides and penicillin. Publicity about the new drugs had convinced many Australian soldiers they had nothing to fear from VD, and so the elaborate pre-coital precautions of yesteryear no longer seemed necessary.[93]

As Walker had feared, the BCOF experience of VD demonstrated that 'underneath the medical achievements with the new drugs, few changes had been effected in the social milieu'. He seemed convinced there were 'intrinsic causes for the high incidence of VD in the men themselves', but did not elaborate.[94] He left readers to draw their own conclusions about flaws in the Australian national character that might underlie the epidemics of VD suffered by the Army during World War II and the BCOF deployment.

Walker wished that the AMS could 'build a sure edifice of prophylaxis on a moral basis'. That remained a forlorn hope. The reality was that 'evil opportunity waited for many, aided by such influences as alcohol, distance from home, personal risk in war, and most recently the relative ease with which cure of venereal disease could be accomplished'.[95]

9. Conclusions

VD occurred in each theatre in World War II where Australian soldiers served, and in epidemic proportions in the Middle East and Australia itself. The need to control the epidemic in the Middle East drove the 2nd AIF command and the AMS to sponsor their own 'controlled' brothels. Though successful in reducing the VD caseload of the Special Hospitals, the controlled brothel was not a measure introduced in Australia. The prospect of the opprobrium that would have engulfed the Army if it had attempted to open its own brothels in Australia was sufficient deterrent for no senior Army officer to mention the idea.

In the end, no need existed for Army-controlled brothels to manage VD in Australia because for the last two years of the war, penicillin proved more effective. Penicillin certainly saved the AMF hundreds of 'man-years' lost to VD. It also spared many VD sufferers the embarrassment and humiliation of months spent receiving treatment in the Special Hospitals. As the scandal of the Mapharsen syphilis treatment regimen at 126 ASH demonstrated, penicillin also spared patients a treatment that could be more lethal than the disease it was designed to cure.

The disadvantage of penicillin was that by freeing soldiers from the fear of the long-term consequences of becoming VD-infected, the new wonder drug encouraged a recklessly irresponsible attitude to sex. 'The clap? The pox? She'll be right, mate! A shot of penicillin will clear it up in no time!' The bar-room conversations are not difficult to imagine.

CHAPTER 8

The British Commonwealth Occupation Force in Japan, 1946-1952

Immediately after the end of World War II, the Australian Army undertook the first of its many post-war overseas deployments. In the six-year period 1946 to 1952, Australian soldiers were a major component of the BCOF in Japan.

At the end of World War II hostilities in August 1945, a US-led Allied army occupied Japan. Commanded by General Douglas MacArthur as Supreme Commander for the Allied Powers, most of its troops were American.

The British Commonwealth also contributed to this army. Comprising Australian, British, Indian and New Zealand units, the BCOF formed a relatively minor segment of the occupying army with a total strength of some 45,000. About 16,500, 36 per cent, were Australians from the 65th, 66th and 67th battalions of the 34th

Australian Infantry Brigade Group plus associated support units.[1]

1. The British Commonwealth Occupation Force in Japan

BCOF was assigned to a mainly rural region centred on the devastated Hiroshima prefecture at the southwest end of the main Japanese island, Honshu. The prefecture was remote, with Hiroshima being 680 kilometres from Tokyo. The first BCOF units began arriving in the allocated area during February 1946. The component groups of the force occupied different zones. The Australians took over the Hiroshima zone, the New Zealanders occupied the Yamaguchi zone immediately to the west, the Indians the Shimane and Tottori zones to the north and north-east, and the British the Okayama zone to the east and Shikoku Island to the south. The US 8th Army occupied the prefectures to the east of the Indian and British zones.[2]

BCOF was led by Australians, initially Lieutenant General John Northcott, and from April 1946 by Lieutenant General Horace Robertson. As well as providing the BCOF commanders, Australia provided many of the headquarters staff, while the force's activities were overseen by the Joint Chiefs of Staff in

Australia, based in Melbourne, and augmented by British, New Zealand and Indian representatives.[3] BCOF headquarters were located at Kure, 20 kilometres south-east of Hiroshima. The Australian Army component was based at nearby Hiro.[4]

Australia provided all the supplies and rations for BCOF, including medical and surgical equipment. Medical supplies were the responsibility of an AMS unit, the 112th Advance Depot Medical Stores, which was based at Kure. The medical units supporting BCOF included the 130 AGH, 20th Australian Field Ambulance, 116th Australian Convalescent Depot and the 89th Australian Dental Unit. The Australian contingent was supported by four hospital ships.[5]

During 1946 BCOF achieved its main purpose, which was to assist the Americans to democratise the Japanese government, demilitarise the occupied area and demobilise Japanese troops.[6] By early 1947 BCOF was beginning to wind down. After the British, Indians and New Zealanders had withdrawn during 1947 and 1948, BCOF was composed entirely of Australians. By mid-1950 many fewer than the official establishment of 2750 Australian soldiers remained in BCOF, and reinforcements were no longer being sent to Japan.[7] BCOF was formally disbanded on 28 April 1952, when the Japanese

Peace Treaty came into effect. BCOF responsibilities were then passed over to a successor, the British Commonwealth Forces Korea. By then the Korean War was almost two years old and Japan had become a support base for Commonwealth units serving in Korea.[8]

During the six-year BCOF sojourn in Japan, medical services came under the command of a DDMS. The first appointee was a British RAMC officer. After the British withdrawal in 1947, an AMS medical officer, Brigadier Joseph Stubbe, took the position. Stubbe reported regularly to the DGMS at Army Headquarters in Melbourne, Major General Burston, who had spent a month touring the BCOF bases in Japan during September and October 1946.[9]

Burston's 38-page report on his tour gives the present-day reader a comprehensive overview of the early work done by BCOF medical units.[10] By far the most serious health threat was VD, which 'immediately became a major problem' when BCOF troops began arriving in Japan in February 1946.[11] By June 1947 a total of 10,469 BCOF soldiers had been admitted to hospital because of VD infection. That was almost a quarter of the entire force. Australians comprised almost 57 per cent of that number and were consequently the national grouping within BCOF which was by far the most heavily infected with VD.[12]

Most of the Australians hospitalised for VD were treated at 130 AGH on Etajima Island, in Hiroshima Bay 12 kilometres south of Hiroshima City. Unlike Australian practice in World Wars I and II, no separate or special hospital was established in Japan for Australian VD patients.

Figure 8.1: 130th Australian General Hospital on Etajima Island in Hiroshima Bay, October 1946. For a time the hospital shared this building with the headquarters of the Australian BCOF contingent (AWM 132233).

2. VD among the Australians serving with BCOF

The BCOF commanders arrived in Japan knowing they would probably have to deal with high VD infection rates. They had received forewarning from the 2nd AIF's senior hygiene specialist, Lieutenant Colonel Cecil E.A. Cook, who was based on Morotai Island with the Army's Advanced Land Headquarters. Cook was sent to Japan on 19 August 1945, several days after the Japanese surrender, to investigate the medical and hygiene situation. He spent several weeks there and wrote a long (23-page) hygiene assessment report, which included an 11-page draft set of standing orders for managing hygiene in BCOF.[13]

Cook's report contained a three-page section dealing with VD. It pointed out that 'no effective system of VD control exist[ed] in Japan'. Further, 'VD cases were not notifiable and reporting the source of infection is repugnant to the Japanese concept of chivalry'.[14] The report explained that prostitution in Japan was common, being 'a recognised and registered entertainment trade'. As well as the professional prostitutes working in officially recognised brothels, part-time prostitutes commonly worked as waitresses in bars and cafés. 'Street girls' also plied their trade. VD infection rates among the prostitutes were normally high, with an estimated 70 per cent of the brothel prostitutes being syphilis-infected and 50 per cent gonorrhoea-infected.[15]

Cook suggested that the best means of minimising the risk of high VD rates among

BCOF troops would be to implement a system embracing:
- education of the troops in the risks involved in sex with Japanese women
- generous provision of troop recreation amenities and of attractive evening entertainments
- establishment of PACs in unit lines, with free provision of the Blue Light prophylactic kits
- enforcement of a 'non-fraternisation' rule, with military police patrols to enforce it
- placing brothels out of bounds for troops
- establishing within the Japanese Ministry of Health an efficient organisation for controlling VD in the civilian population, including: (i) prompt notification of infections, (ii) weekly medical inspections of prostitutes and monthly serological testing for syphilis, and (iii) efficient modern VD treatment clinics.[16]

All of these measures were subsequently adopted, but with mixed success.

The accuracy of Lieutenant Colonel Cook's predictions about the likelihood of high VD infection rates was proved as soon as the BCOF contingents began arriving in Japan five months later. VD among the Australian soldiers in Japan continued to cause great concern to their commanders for as long as they served with BCOF. The VD problem was obvious almost from the outset. In April 1946 the British DDMS circulated a report to all BCOF medical officers to advise them that the VD infection rate was 'alarmingly high'.[17] By June 1946, four months after the Australians arrived in Japan, it was clear that the Army had a major VD problem. The commander of the Australian contingent, Brigadier Ronald N.L. Hopkins,[18] issued a memorandum to his unit commanders pointing out that '34th Australian Infantry Brigade venereal disease figures are rising steadily'.[19] In October BCOF advised the Joint Chiefs of Staff in Australia that 'VD could be regarded as existing in epidemic form' among the BCOF contingents.[20]

The Hopkins memo proved its point with a graph showing how the number of confirmed new cases per thousand troops had risen from 11 a week in mid-April to 16 a week by mid-June. Hopkins wrote that a monthly rate of 10 VD cases per thousand troops was 'considered NOT unreasonable in present circumstances', but only four units had rates that low. The major units—65th, 66th and 67th infantry battalions—had monthly rates of 222, 135 and 167 per thousand troops respectively. The highest rate was that of Brigade Headquarters, with a rate of 550. That medical units were not immune was evident in the rate of 268 in the 20th Australian Field Ambulance, which might have embarrassed the unit commander.[21] The chart in Figure 8.2 reproduces the Hopkins graph. Table 8.1 shows the comparative infection rates for the Australian units, listed in the 'order of merit' in which Hopkins arranged them.

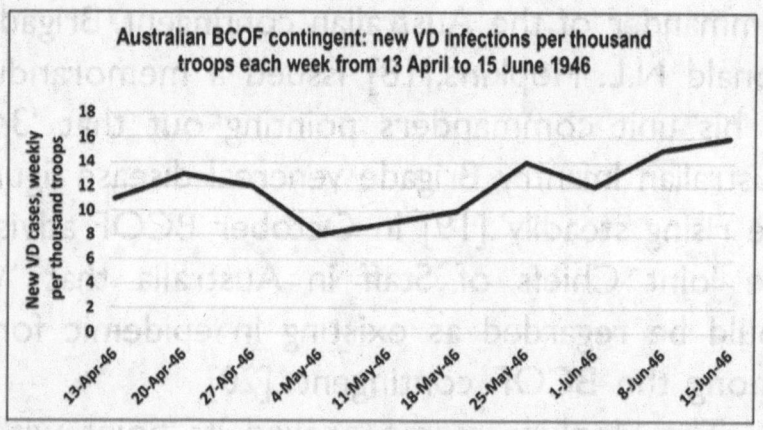

Figure 8.2: VD infection rate within the Australian BCOF contingent, April to June 1946 (Brigadier R.N.L. Hopkins, 'Control of VD,, 28 June 1946, AWM114 267/6/17 Part 1).

Table 8.1-Unit VD figures (monthly rate per thousand troops), April to June 1946

Unit	Monthly VD rate per 1000 troops, April–June 1946	'Order of merit'
140th Australian Ordinance Field Park	47	1
1st Australian Armoured Corps Squadron	50	2
140th Australian Brigade Workshop	60	3
34th Australian Infantry Brigade Signals Section	63	4
34th Australian Infantry Brigade Provost Company	80	5
169th Australian General Transport Company	90	6
A Field Battery	97	7

Source: Brigadier R.N.L. Hopkins, 'Control of VD,', 28 June 1946, AWM114 267/6/17 Part 1.

Unit	Monthly VD rate per 1000 troops, April–June 1946	'Order of merit'
343rd Australian Light Aid Detachment	117	8
66th Australian Infantry Battalion	135	9
67th Australian Infantry Battalion	157	10
28th Australian Field Company	214	11
65th Australian Infantry Battalion	222	12
345th Australian Light Aid Detachment	222	12
20th Australian Field Ambulance	268	14
252nd Australian Supply Depot Platoon	483	15
HQ 34th Australian Infantry Brigade and attached units	550	16

As well as providing the statistics of infection, the Hopkins memorandum of June 1946 gave notice of a set of anti-VD control measures which were to be immediately implemented. First was the establishment of an 'Anti-VD Team' in each unit to organise, supervise and conduct the anti-VD program.[22] In addition, a series of compulsory control measures would be introduced. These were:

- regular anti-VD lectures by the medical officers, chaplains and unit officers
- regular showing of anti-VD films
- continued anti-VD propaganda
- strict supervision of ex-VD patients for 15 days after their discharge from hospital; they would be confined to barracks for that time, during which they must report *hourly* to their anti-VD Teams and consume no alcohol
- frequent checks on absenteeism between Tattoo and Reveille (the times signalled by evening and morning bugle calls)
- a weekly VD report to Brigade HQ 'covering all anti-VD activities'
- institution of a 'pass sheet' system for troops going on leave, showing what 'preventative equipment' had been issued to them
- a weekly written examination in venereology for all members of all units—a 'tick-the-correct-box', short-answer test

- periodic short-arm inspections of all troops plus *daily* short-arm parades for all ex-VD patients
- introduction of a scale of punishments for contracting VD, including the 'loss of proficiency pay', 'loss of leave privilege for three months', 'automatic confinement to barracks for 14 days', 'stoppage of late pass for 28 days', 'reduction in substantive rank', 'reprimand'.[23]

The tone of the memorandum was didactic and the proposed measures were prescriptive and punitive.

An appendix to the memorandum justified the measures by pointing out that 'these regulations have been framed with one object in mind—it is essential to maintain the health of the regiment'.[24] The appendix also warned all ranks that 'penicillin treatment is NOT, repeat NOT, the 100% cure it was supposed to be'.[25]

Most of the measures foreshadowed in the Hopkins memorandum had been tried previously, during World Wars I and II, but one innovation was the weekly written examination in venereology. Sample questions and correct responses were:

- What is the common name for gonorrhoea?
- *Answer:* Any of clap, jack, gleet or strain
- Is gonorrhoea common in Japan?

- *Answer:* Yes
- If a woman has gonorrhoea in the neck of the womb, are you likely to see it if you have intercourse with her?
- *Answer:* No
- What skin disease can you get by physical contact with Japanese women?
- *Answer:* Any of lice, scabies or tinea
- What disease sometimes causes weakening of the wall of the blood vessels, followed by bursting and sudden death?
- *Answer:* Syphilis.[26]

The point of the exercise was not so much to assess the troops' medical knowledge but to ensure they knew the basic facts of VD transmission and prevention.

In announcing the anti-VD measures to his unit commanders, Hopkins emphasised 'the moral factor as the keystone of the campaign'. He told them that 'the growth of a healthy morality which steadfastly condemns illicit relationship with women is the greatest single factor in stamping out VD'.[27] Recognising that some troops might not attain the ideal moral standard—conscious abstinence—he stated that the campaign would aim 'to reduce temptation and limit the risk of infection for men whose moral standard is inadequate to prevent their seeking illicit relationships with women'.[28]

Seven weeks after introducing the anti-VD campaign, Hopkins wrote to his unit commanders to express his satisfaction at the outcome. 'Since the inception of the Brigade anti-VD campaign, the plan has met with a considerable amount of success and the incidence of VD has dropped considerably in most units'.[29] As proof, he noted that the overall brigade infection rate in early July 1946 had been 51 cases per thousand troops per month, whereas during the month ending 7 September the rate had fallen to 30. In addition, only three units had been VD-free in July but seven were VD-free by the end of August.[30]

Hopkins recognised that the September rate, 30 new infections per thousand troops a month, was unsatisfactory because it was triple the 'acceptable' rate. 'It is clear a large proportion of personnel [were] risking VD infection' because 'one Australian in every five in Japan has contracted VD'.[31] In a second memorandum to his unit commanders, dated 12 September 1946, he gave notice that the anti-VD campaign must move into a new phase in which:

- 'neurotic types' would be removed from their units, such soldiers being those 'whose influence and encouragement of immorality offer [ed] a specific temptation to others'

- in cooperation with the Military Government, 'raids on brothels and streetwalkers' would be instituted, as well as the obligatory medical examination of women working in the sex trade plus the 'segregation' and compulsory treatment of such women
- troops who contracted VD would be charged with disobedience of orders if they could not demonstrate they had undertaken prophylactic treatment at a PAG.[32]

In other words, the 'rotten apples' would be expelled, punitive action would be taken against the prostitutes, and VD would become a disciplinary matter as well as a medical condition.

The new, harsher regime seems not to have produced the desired effect. Fifteen months later, little seemed to have changed. In December 1947 Brigadier Hopkins prefaced a new set of orders with the observation that 'during the past few months there has been a noticeable and disturbing rise in the incidence of VD within 34 Australian Infantry Brigade'.[33]

Hopkins did not summarise the latest VD infection figures, but he canvassed reasons for the increase. They included:
- the arrival of reinforcements from Australia who had not been fully 'indoctrinated' in

the threat from VD and who had not been present for the 'all-out' anti-VD campaign the previous year
- the posting of some units to localities 'hitherto not rigidly policed'
- the slackening of anti-VD measures in the units in relation to the consumption of alcohol, the granting of leave, insistence on PAG attendance, punishment for non-attendance at the PACs, and bed checks.[34] (The last of these referred to unannounced and random inspection of dormitories to ensure that all personnel were present in their quarters between Tattoo and Reveille.)

In introducing even harsher anti-VD measures, Hopkins had advice from his chaplains. On 5 December 1947 they wrote to him pleading for renewed emphasis on the part religion must play in asserting the moral values that should underlie any anti-VD campaign. Their petition began by stating that 'the only reliable and safe guide to human conduct is the Law of God'. They reminded him of the 'commandments and the teaching of the Church', pointing out that 'whatsoever contravenes this Law is both wrong and indefensible'.[35] They then advocated that:

- Chaplains should be members of all BCOF's Anti-VD Committees and whatever means were used for tackling VD should be decided upon in consultation with them.
- Lectures on 'the spiritual, moral and social aspects of sexual promiscuity' should be separated from the medical lectures.
- Increased facilities should be granted for conducting courses in moral leadership designed to help troops see themselves as 'responsible individuals who [were] required to take an active part in combating the great moral and social evil of our day'.
- Publicity material used in the anti-VD campaigns should not simply emphasise a fear of VD but should appeal to the 'higher aspirations' of 'love of God, home, wife, children and decent manhood'.[36]

For good measure the chaplains went on to recommend that greater prominence be given to their role; to attendance at the Sunday church services they conducted; and that entertainments, excursions and sporting events not be conducted in competition with church services.[37]

Meanwhile, one emerging problem was VD among BCOF officers. Eventually a policy for handing such cases was required. There was a suggestion that a special facility should be established for treating VD-infected officers, but that was ruled out as 'impracticable'. At the same time, it was agreed that officers could not attend the PACs for treatment because the effects on general discipline would be 'unacceptable'. Treating the officers in the privacy of their quarters was one option 'to ensure secrecy', even if medically inconvenient. An adverse report written into the individual officer's personnel file was considered but possibly not implemented because no one wished to harm a brother officer's career prospects. The best option seemed to be to re-post the officer to another unit in which his indiscretions would not be common knowledge.[38]

To reinvigorate the anti-VD campaign, Hopkins issued Administrative Instruction No.22. The Anti-VD Control Teams were reactivated in all units. The anti-VD lectures were reintroduced and made a part of each unit's 'normal training syllabus'. The PACs were publicised and clearly signposted so that troops knew where they were. Soldiers deemed under the influence of alcohol were refused leave passes because they were thought likely to expose themselves to infection. Roll calls were conducted in every unit at the sounding of the Tattoo. Bed checks were carried out at least three times a week after lights out. Soldiers returning to their units after hospital treatment for VD were not allowed to take leave for 15 days and were not permitted to consume alcohol in that time. Soldiers who had suffered gonorrhoea were prohibited from having sexual intercourse for 90 days after their discharge; for those who had been treated for syphilis the period was 180 days. How such a prohibition could have been implemented or enforced is uncertain, but disobeying it was regarded 'as a serious offence and appropriate punishment imposed'. They were also denied the privilege of staying at the BCOF Holiday Hostel on Lake Biwa near Kyoto for 180 days after the end of their treatment. Japanese workers employed at Australian Army bases were to be closely supervised, and the women among them were to be medically examined to ensure they were not the source of VD infection among the troops. Finally, the provosts were to establish 'Anti-Vice Squads' to patrol the camps and adjacent areas and arrest Japanese women suspected of soliciting for prostitution.[39]

Hopkins ended Administrative Instruction No.22 optimistically. 'The rigid adherence by units to the provisions of this instruction should lessen considerably the present high incidence of VD and ensure that the satisfactory results already achieved in combatting [sic] this evil are maintained.'[40]

The optimism was premature. Fifteen months later, in February 1948, the situation apparently had changed little. The Principal Administrative Officer of the Australian contingent issued 'Administrative Instruction 108'. This document announced that 'the Commander in Chief [Lieutenant General Robertson] has expressed the gravest possible concern at the continued high incidence of Venereal Disease in the Force'. The commander-in-chief accordingly directed that 'all Commanders ... are immediately to take the most energetic, practical and positive measures to reduce ... the present tragic rate of Venereal Disease, which is the highest in the world wherever British Commonwealth Forces are serving'.[41] To emphasise the point, the Instruction went on to claim that 'all other problems ... at the present time fade into insignificance compared with the problem of Venereal Disease'.[42]

Like the previous instructions, Administrative Instruction 108 sought to impose more stringent measures to curb VD. As usual, this Instruction began by promoting the notion that VD had a 'moral and spiritual aspect'. It gave notice that the chaplains would be emphasising this point in their lectures and discussions with the men. The 'medical aspect' of the renewed anti-VD campaign would include further lectures by the medical officers, more films about VD, more 'posters, booklets, pamphlets, waxwork models [and] preserved and live VD exhibits'—all of which would be marshalled in the 'indoctrination' program. Hopkins's own scepticism about the value of such measures was evident in his comment that 'the troops have been lectured, shown pictures etc ad nauseum'. 'In my opinion,' he wrote, 'they all know the risks they run and the comparative protection they can ensure themselves by prophylaxis.'[43]

As well as the lectures, Administrative Instruction 108 called for renewed emphasis on personal anti-VD prophylaxis, with condoms and Blue Light kits being made freely available. Records of attendance at the PACs would be scrupulously maintained. Anti-VD discipline would be tightened and 'firmly enforced'. Brothels would be placed 'out of bounds' and there would be no 'tolerated houses'. 'Vice Squads' would be formed to remove prostitutes and 'other undesirable persons' from the neighbourhood of barracks, and the squads would also return inebriated soldiers to their quarters. Leave would not be given for periods after lights out at 10.30pm in the barracks. Fraternisation with the Japanese would be restricted and tightly controlled. Women found to be the source of VD infection would be reported to the Japanese authorities, who would be expected to examine them medically and provide treatment. The Japanese police would be supervised to ensure they were carrying out 'anti-vice' measures within the Japanese civilian population. The troops would be strongly encouraged to use the recreational facilities established for them. And, finally, 'statutory deductions from pay' would be reintroduced to penalise VD-infected soldiers for the time they spent being treated.[44]

Some of these measures were standard anti-VD controls and had been used in previous campaigns. Others were new and more authoritarian measures. Administrative Instruction 108 justified the latter by pointing out that the VD rate in BCOF was the highest among British Commonwealth troops anywhere in the world. The Instruction ended by observing that 'that is a staggering and disastrous fact and is to be remedied at once'.[45]

Administrative Instruction 108 was issued with an eye on public opinion in Australia. As one historian of BCOF later observed, the 'Supreme Commander Allied Powers [General MacArthur], Joint Chiefs of Staff in Australia and BCOF were very aware of the public and political sensitivity' of high VD rates, abundant brothels and proliferating prostitution in Japan.[46] The historian George Davies, who served in Japan with BCOF's New Zealand contingent, argued that the most sensible strategy would have been for BCOF to establish its own 'properly supervised and medically controlled brothels'.[47] That, of course, had been a strategy adopted by the 2nd AIF in the Middle East with some success in 1941. In Japan, however, public and political pressure from home constrained the [BCOF] authorities'.[48]

3. The Australian BCOF contingent s VD infection rates

Was the Australian VD rate in Japan as appallingly high as Administrative Instruction 108 averred? Was the VD situation really so dire?

Unfortunately for present-day students of historical epidemiology, the VD statistics for the Australians serving in BCOF are fragmentary and incomplete. There is no single set of comprehensive figures showing the number and rates of infection. Regrettably, no official history of Australian involvement in BCOF was ever produced, and so there are no authoritative and accessible statistical tables for the historian to draw upon. BCOF was covered only briefly in the final 'Army' volume of the multi-volume official history of World War II—*Australia in the War of 1939—1945*.[49] Allan S. Walker's official medical history of the war made only fleeting reference to BCOF. Walker confined his comment to the observation that 'during part of 1946 Australian troops, though only 25 per cent of the total [BCOF] force, supplied 73 per cent of the venereal disease'.[50]

The Australian figures were always high in comparison with those of the other BCOF contingents. This first became apparent in the earliest statistics to come from the BCOF deployment. In December 1946, BCOF's DDMS sent a long report on VD to the War Office in London. He provided the figures for just one week in November, set out in Table 8.2.[51] Although his report focused on VD in the British contingent, he concluded by pointing out that 'the Australian problem overshadows even the British ... and the Australian incidence earlier in the occupation was double those shown [in Table 8.2]'.[52]

Table 8.2-BCOF venereal disease cases for the week ending 15 November 1946

Formation	Strength	VD cases in week ending 15/11/1946	Proportion (%) of total	VD Incidence per 1000 per week
Australian Army	9106	72	42.9%	7.9
British Army	7171	31	18.5%	4.3
Indian Army	11,176	38	22.6%	3.4
New Zealand Army	4311	3	1.8%	0.7
Royal Air Force	1860	2	1.2%	1.1
Royal Indian Air Force	277	2	1.2%	7.2
Royal NZ Air Force	278	0	0.0%	-
Royal Australian Air Force	2052	18	10.7%	8.8
[Royal] Navy	497	2	1.2%	4.0
Total	36,728	168	100.0%	

Source: Brigadier C. Scales, 'Venereal disease, BCOF', 19 December 1946, AWM114 267/6/17 Part 1.

As the table demonstrates, in that one week, the total Australian VD hospitalisations, for both Army and Air Force, were 90 cases out of 168, or 53.6 per cent of the total—once again double the infections in the rest of BCOF. The Australian infection rates per thousand were also the highest—8.8 for the Air Force and 7.9 for the Army. The Indian Air Force excepted, each was greatly in excess of the rates for the other BCOF formations. This was an unenviable achievement, given that the Australians comprised less than a third (30.4 per cent) of BCOF personnel at the time.

The evidence that the Australians were the 'bad boys' of BCOF kept accumulating. A further set of comparative figures compiled in June 1947 indicated that until then the Australian Army contingent, the worst affected, had experienced 5960 VD episodes since the arrival of BCOF in Japan. The Indians were second with 2344 episodes, then came the British with 1590 and the New Zealanders with 575. Of the BCOF total of 10,469 episodes, the Australian share was almost 57 per cent, so the situation was worse than in the previous November.[53] The chart in Figure 8.3 shows each army contingent's number of VD episodes and proportion of the total.

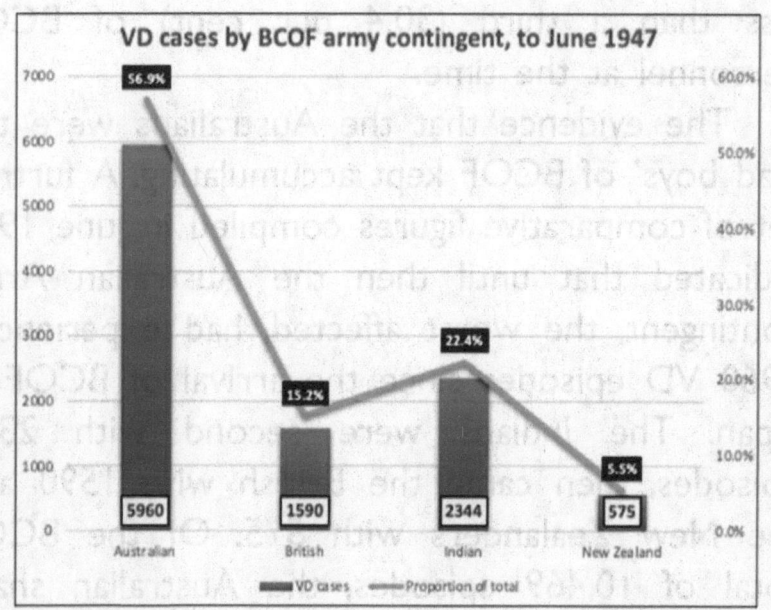

Figure 8.3: Number of VD cases among BCOF army contingents and their proportion of the total ('Brief History of the Medical Services [of] BCOF', 21 July 1947, AWM114 481/11/2).

The Australian case load was so high by April 1947 that 130 AGH opened a 200-bed VD annexe.[54] This became known as 'the house that Jack built', an allusion to a currently popular colloquial term for gonorrhoea.[55] The annexe was also dubbed 'Jack College' and the discharged soldiers its 'graduates'. Those obliged to make a return visit were said to have undertaken 'Higher Education'.[56]

The most complete set of BCOF VD figures is contained in a large graph in a slim file in the Australian War Memorial. It has the simple title

'Venereal Diseases—BCOF (Japan)'.[57] A highly complex, detailed and beautifully hand-drawn coloured chart, it was produced in the Central Army Records Office at Army Headquarters in Melbourne, probably in late 1949. It sets out a summary of the monthly VD infection rates within the Australian BCOF contingent across the 40-month period from March 1946 to July 1949. The chart yields these statistical facts:

- A total of 16,497 Australian troops served with BCOF in the 40-month period covered by the chart.
- Of those Australian soldiers, 4768 were infected with VD, that is, 29 per cent of the Australian contingent were infected.
- A total of 7350 separate VD cases or 'episodes' were treated, which means that 2582 soldiers suffered more than one episode of VD. (Elsewhere the evidence indicated that 25 per cent of the VD cases were re-infections.[58])
- The 7350 separate VD episodes were the equivalent of an overall contingent infection rate of 446 cases per thousand troops. Those episodes also amounted to the equivalent of 45 per cent of Australian enlistments in BCOF.
- The average time spent in hospital by Australians undergoing treatment for VD

was 16 days. (Thanks to penicillin, this was a great improvement on the six weeks that was common during World Wars I and II.)
- A total of 75,781 'man-days' were lost by Australian troops being hospitalised with VD, that is, 4.6 man-days per Australian in BCOF were lost. The man-days were the equivalent of 208 man-years.
- Putting a monetary value on the loss of that many days is difficult. The easiest means of doing so is to express the amount in soldiers' pay. Assuming seven shillings a day for a private, the lost days were the equivalent of at least £26,520 or $1.8 million in present-day values.
- Gonorrhoea was by far the most common form of VD suffered by the Australians in Japan. It comprised 62 per cent of all their VD cases treated. This compared with 6 per cent for syphilis and 32 per cent for 'other VD' (which included chancroid, non-gonococcal but sexually transmitted urethritis, genital warts, scabies, pubic lice, granuloma venereum and lymphogranuloma inguinale).[59]

The rate of 446 VD cases treated per thousand troops was spectacularly high by any measure. That rate was three times greater than the 138 cases per thousand troops among the

1st AIF in Egypt in 1916. It was almost six times as high as the 76 per thousand in the 2nd AIF in the Middle East in 1941, and it was 23 times the 19 per thousand among Army personnel in Australia during 1942. In short, the VD epidemic among Australians serving with BCOF was by far the most serious of any the Army experienced during the 20th century.

4. The Anti-VD Advisory Committee

In order to oversee and review the progress of the campaign against VD, BCOF established an Anti-VD Advisory Committee. The committee referred to its meetings as 'conferences'. These were conducted about every two months and were attended by delegates with a direct interest in BCOF's anti-VD programs.

The first conference seems to have been held on 13 May 1947 at 34th Infantry Brigade Headquarters in Hiro. The conference began by reviewing 34th Infantry Brigade's latest VD infection figures. Of the 98 new infections since 1 April 1947, 32 had been contracted in Kure, 20 in Shikoku, 14 in in Hiroshima, 11 in Hiro, and lesser numbers in Onomichi, Tokyo, Fukuyama, Otake and Kaitaichi. Of these cases, 45 per cent were soldiers recently arrived in

Japan as reinforcements. The next topic discussed was the activities of the Hiroshima Vice Squad, the performance of which was reported as having 'vastly improved'. Then came the statistics of women treated at the VD hospital in Kure. Since 1 April the hospital had admitted 715 patients, of whom 619 were suffering gonorrhoea, 78 syphilis and 18 chancroid. The final agenda item was a progress report on the examination of the female labour forces employed at the various BCOF army bases. A total of 35 women had so far been identified as VD-infected, and VD examinations were to be repeated every three months.[60]

A later conference, which took place at BCOF Headquarters in Kure on 7 June 1948, is worth reporting here in detail because it shows something of the range of issues the attending officers considered. It was chaired by the DDMS, Brigadier Stubbe, and was attended by 10 other senior officers, including the Assistant Adjutant General, the APM, and representatives of the New Zealand contingent and the Military Government. Stubbe advised delegates that the VD infection rates in both the Australian and New Zealand contingents were trending upwards. This prompted a discussion of the average age of each contingent—23 for the Australians and 22 for the New Zealanders. Delegates agreed that BCOF was clearly 'a young force and thus the task of controlling the VD incidence rate was made more difficult'.[61]

Discussion of various other related matters followed. One delegate reported on a study which had found that whereas 90 per cent of the New Zealand soldiers had previous sexual experience before contracting VD, the figure among the Australian troops was 96 per cent. Although the difference between those percentages might not have been statistically significant, the delegate thought it was worth reporting. The next topic was cultural influences in the use of condoms. One delegate asserted that in Australia it was the female sexual partner who usually initiated the use of a condom, whereas in Japan the male partner decided whether or not to use one. Stubbe then reported on a study of non-gonococcal urethritis in which soldiers had been asked to volunteer for examination. Of the 78 volunteers, 28 were found to be suffering a mild form of the disease. His explanation for the mildness was that many soldiers were self-treating with sulpha drugs. The conference then moved on to consider women released from the Kure VD Hospital after being treated. The conference recommended that after their discharge such women should relocate to prefectures outside those occupied by BCOF.[62]

The final topic for discussion was the matter of the medical examination of Japanese 'house-girls' (young female servants), who were required to undergo a medical examination for VD at a hospital. A group of them had complained that the examinations were being conducted by medical students rather than licenced medical practitioners. Not unreasonably, this practice embarrassed them, causing them to leave their employment. In the ensuing discussion the Liaison Officer of the 34th Infantry Brigade indicated that he had investigated the complaint and had found 'the examinations were carried out capably and with more privacy afforded patients than is usual in a normal Australian hospital'.[63]

5. Fears that VD would spread from Japan to Australia

A great fear of the BCOF commanders and their superiors in the Department of Defence in Melbourne was that undetected VD would return to Australia with military personnel whose period of service in Japan had ended. The surviving BCOF archival files are accordingly replete with correspondence, memoranda and instructions about preventing VD-infected troops from returning home from Japan until they had been cured.

At Brigadier Hopkins's direction, 34th Australian Infantry Brigade developed a policy on 'Return to Australia [of] personnel who have contracted VD'. Hopkins announced it in a memorandum dated 17 August 1946. He pointed out that from October that year large numbers of Australian soldiers would be returning to Australia either for leave or discharge from the Army. Of necessity, 'positive action should be taken to prevent the introduction of venereal diseases into Australia'.[64] Those troops who had not yet been pronounced cured or who had not yet undergone the obligatory 'examination for cure', undertaken three months after the end of their treatment, would be regarded as 'medical evacuees'. They would be accompanied by their medical records. As soon as they reached Australia they would be transferred under escort to a Special [VD] Hospital in their home states. They would then become the responsibility of the Special Hospital, which would continue observing or treating them until they were pronounced cured and discharged. This system was designed to minimise their chances of transmitting their diseases while travelling to their home states and to ensure that their treatment was completed successfully.[65]

In November 1946 Lieutenant Colonel John W.H. Merry, the Senior Medical Officer of 34th Australian Infantry Brigade, drew attention to the importance of a strict 'Return to Australia' policy. He advised BCOF headquarters that VD-infected troops had recently returned to Australia. According to Merry, no fewer than 29 soldiers who had suffered *two* VD episodes had gone to Australia on leave and would be returning to Japan. Merry said he 'considered that this is an unduly high number of undesirables accepted for further service in Japan'. He suggested that soldiers who had experienced multiple VD episodes should be 'definitely excluded from re-enlistment'.[66]

As problems like those identified by Merry were considered, the policy was refined over the following months. There had also been complaints in Australia that soldiers who had been cured of VD in Japan were not checked before returning home.[67] In January 1947 the BCOF commander-in-chief issued a directive aimed at addressing such criticisms. Henceforth, troops drafted for return to Australia would be medically examined as soon as joining the draft and again immediately before embarkation. Anyone found to be VD-infected would be removed from the draft and treated in Japan. 'Nominal rolls'[lists of names] would be drawn up to show which draftees had been treated for VD within the previous six months. The rolls would be sent to the DGMS at Army Headquarters in Melbourne so that suitable follow-up checking could be undertaken by Army medical officers in the soldiers' home states.[68]

Various difficulties with the policy emerged over the next two years. One problem was sloppy management of medical records. There were cases where VD patients' records were lost. One outcome of that was that some troops were returned to Australia while still infected. There were also cases where some soldiers' personnel records gave no indication that they had contracted VD, but after cross-checking their unit records it was discovered they had suffered multiple VD episodes.[69]

Another difficulty arose in the Army's Eastern Command [New South Wales], where soldiers on leave were not permitted to return to Japan if they were known to have contracted VD there during their BCOF service. This practice was not welcomed by unit commanders in Japan, who were then reluctant to grant leave to former VD patients because that meant losing militarily experienced soldiers. If 20 to 30 per cent of BCOF personnel had experienced VD episodes, many otherwise efficient soldiers would be lost to BCOF by going on leave to Australia and being debarred from returning.[70]

It subsequently emerged that the Minister for the Army, Cyril Chambers, had ruled that no soldier who had suffered from VD would be 'permitted to proceed or return to Japan'. Further, any soldier who contracted proven VD in Japan must be returned to Australia after receiving treatment and showing no evidence of infectivity after medical examination.[71]

Meanwhile, the Australian newspapers could be relied on to sound the alarm about the threat to Australia of BCOF's VD-infected soldiers whenever the opportunity arose. In 1948 the press found good copy in the public pronouncements of Barry McDonald, the national president of the Legion of Ex-Servicemen. On one occasion McDonald was widely quoted as saying that the BCOF troops were 'spiritually leaderless' and on another that they were 'morally rotting'. Another critic was a Melbourne barrister, Edward J. Thwaites, who served as a captain in Japan with the 2nd Australian War Crimes Section. On returning home he was quoted as saying that the VD rates among the Australians were very high and many of their illegitimate offspring were being cared for in a Hiroshima orphanage. The Australians, he said, were 'ill-disciplined, ill-trained troops with too much time on their hands [who were] indulging in a range of unhealthy activities'.[72]

In editorialising, The Sydney Morning Herald asserted that the Australians in BCOF 'were not a good advertisement for their country'.[73] The BCOF troops, however, were not without their defenders. One was the federal Labor politician, Les Haylen, who toured Japan with a parliamentary delegation in July 1948. Back home again, he protested in parliament about the 'vicious and unsubstantiated reports of the misbehaviour of lonely, homesick men'. He called on his fellow Australians to 'cease libelling the fighting men of our country'.[74]

Other defenders were the three Chaplains General—the Reverends Allen Brooke and Alexander H. Stewart and Father Timothy McCarthy—who the Minister for the Army, Chambers, had sent to Japan to investigate in April 1948. Soon nicknamed the 'Sin Busters', they subsequently reported to Chambers that recent press coverage had 'grossly defamed the Australian troops'.[75] They found that 'the degree of promiscuity in Japan [among the troops was] no greater than would have been the case in Australia'.[76] The Sin Busters might not have appreciated the irony of this back-handed compliment.

Another delegation that Chambers sent to Japan at much the same time was a two-man team comprising Major General Charles E.M. Lloyd, a recently retired career Army officer, and Massey Stanley, a Sydney journalist who had been the managing editor of *Salt*, the World War II Army journal. Lloyd and Stanley were appointed to inquire into the administration of BCOF then report to the Joint Chiefs of Staff in Australia. Chambers tabled their findings, the 'Lloyd-Stanley Report', in the House of Representatives on 2 June 1948.[77]

Among other matters that Lloyd and Stanley investigated were allegations about black-marketing and immorality among Australian soldiers in Japan. The report found that the former was a 'negligible' problem but the latter, especially the high incidence of VD, provided 'serious grounds for disquiet'. The report stated that 'incidence rates of VD in the BCOF area were very high from the beginning of the occupation and, despite control measures, are still high'. The report went on to criticise the Joint Chiefs of Staff in Australia for 'failing to take positive action' against VD among the Australians in Japan.[78] Finding fault with the Joint Chiefs of Staff was easy enough for the newspapers, but what the Joint Chiefs of Staff could have done which the BCOF commanders were not already doing was not clear.

6. The difficult relationship with Japanese authorities

In attempting to contain VD, the BCOF commanders were obliged to deal with the both the Military Government and the Japanese civilian authorities, particularly the police and health agencies. Two main issues concerned the Australians: the control of prostitution, and the treatment of VD in Japanese hospitals and by Japanese doctors generally. Because the Americans, Japanese and BCOF commanders had differing priorities, these were areas in which policy was often inconsistent.

Under Japanese law, prefectures and municipal authorities were obliged to provide public education on the prevention and treatment of VD, and to conduct VD treatment clinics.[79] VD prevention law defined a series of offences and a scale of penalties that matched the severity of the offence (Table 8.3).[80]

Table 8.3-**Offences and penalties relating to VD under Japanese law**

Offence	Penalty
Assisting, soliciting or providing a place for prostitution with knowledge of presence of infectious VD	Imprisonment up to three years. Fine up to 20,000 yen (¥)
Knowingly performing prostitution when suffering infectious VD	Imprisonment for up to two years or a fine up to ¥10,000
Knowingly acting so as to infect others with VD	Imprisonment up to one year. Fine up to ¥5000
Evading treatment for VD	Fine up to ¥5000

Source: 'The Japanese Venereal Disease Prevention Law' and 'Disposition of cases in the Tokyo area involving violation of ... the VD Prevention Law', 23 June 1949, AWM114 267/6/17 Part 4.

For purposes of comparison, at the time ¥20,000 was worth about £20 sterling and £25 Australian, the equivalent of AUD$1246 in 2020. Fines of ¥10,000 and ¥5000 would accordingly have been the equivalent of $623 and $312 respectively in Australian values in 2020. These were presumably large amounts for poverty-stricken prostitutes in post-war Japan.

The Military Government of Japan took a stern approach to the spreading of VD to soldiers via prostitution. The Occupation Courts established by the Military Government were empowered to impose penalties for 'acts prejudicial to the security of Occupation Forces'. Japanese citizens soliciting troops for 'immoral purposes' were liable to a penalty of 30 days' imprisonment. VD-infected Japanese women who solicited or transmitted VD to occupation personnel were liable to six months' imprisonment. After their imprisonment the offenders could be returned to their 'legal residence' (home prefectures). Brothelkeepers of houses declared 'out of bounds' to occupation personnel were liable to six months' imprisonment unless they immediately reported the presence of troops to the police. The Military Government also pressured the Japanese judges, prosecutors, police and prison officers to adopt a similar hard line against prostitution targeting occupation personnel.[81]

At first the BCOF commanders were disconcerted that the Japanese civilian authorities seemed uncooperative. A long memorandum to the BCOF VD Control Officers pointed out that:

> There is an attitude of passive resistance on the part of the Japanese authorities to the control of venereal disease. The subtlety of such resistance is apparent ... It is difficult to detect and causes great lowering of morale and efficiency among the Force ... The Australian troops have ... been played for suckers'[because] at the moment it would appear that the war is being slowly lost in the brothels.[82]

The author of this memorandum possibly did not appreciate that the Japanese authorities were themselves uncertain and confused about controlling the brothels because of the recent abolition of what had been a well-established Japanese institution—licenced prostitution. Licenced brothels, in which prostitutes were bound by contract to the proprietors, had been conducted under an ordinance of the Japanese Home Ministry since 1900. In January 1946, however, the Home Ministry revoked the ordinance on the order of the Supreme Commander for the Allied Forces, General MacArthur, who had declared that licenced prostitution was 'in contravention of democracy and inconsistent with the development of individual freedom'. The Home Ministry subsequently advised the police and municipal authorities in the prefectures that licenced prostitution had been abolished and that the prostitutes in the brothels were released from their contracts.[83]

A perhaps unintended consequence of the abolition of licenced prostitution was that prostitution and the brothels were effectively deregulated. Attempting to contain the sex trade and the spread of VD, the BCOF commanders advocated that in any city or town the brothels should be all confined to the one area. Such red-light districts could be more easily policed, especially if the red-light areas were declared 'out of bounds' to the troops.[84]

In May 1948 the Australian BCOF Commander-in-Chief, Lieutenant General Robertson, wrote to General MacArthur to request the reintroduction of Home Ministry Order No.16, a regulation from 1908 which enabled women deemed likely to transmit VD to be arrested, summarily tried and convicted and subsequently moved back to their home districts. The order was designed to prevent soliciting for prostitution. In early 1948 the Home Ministry replaced the order with a 'Minor Offences Act' which did not encompass soliciting and prostitution. According to Robertson, under this Act the Japanese courts were no longer imposing penalties for simply soliciting but only in cases where a woman could be proved to have transmitted VD. Robertson protested that he 'consider [ed] it essential for the effective control of VD ... that the powers under the Home Ministry Order No.16 be restored'. VD, he argued, was 'probably the most serious and vital problem that the Occupation Forces [had] to face'. He therefore requested MacArthur to instruct the Japanese government to 're-proclaim the offences of prostitution and soliciting as previously enacted'.[85]

When required, BCOF and civilian police could take concerted action to reduce VD transmission rates. In September 1946, for example, the BCOF Deputy Provost Marshal advised senior BCOF officers that the Military Government in the Hiroshima prefecture had directed the civilian police to conduct 'an organised check and medical examination of female Japanese suspected of subjecting themselves to prostitution'. This exercise would be carried out over the three days 26 to 28 September. The military police of 34th Australian Infantry Brigade were made available to assist. 'Anti-Vice Teams' comprising one BCOF provost and two Japanese police managed the operation and were provided with trucks for transporting the women to the hospitals and depots where they were examined. Nominal rolls of all women apprehended were compiled. Those found to be VD-infected were sent to the Asahi Hospital in Kure for treatment and detention until pronounced cured.[86]

Insofar as treating VD-infected prostitutes was concerned, the management of VD cases in the Japanese hospitals appears to have been efficient. Their treatment regimens had been specified by the US-controlled Military Government. For gonorrhoea the standard treatment after confirmation of diagnosis by smear test was a 1-gram dose of sulphathiazole or sulphadiazine six-hourly for five days. In cases where there was resistance or sensitivity to the sulpha drugs, 500,000 units of penicillin were administered two-hourly for four doses. The patient was hospitalised for 10 days and discharged after three negative successive daily smears.[87]

For syphilis the standard was confirmation of diagnosis through all three (Wassermann, Murata and Ide) blood tests, followed by combined arsenic and bismuth treatment. The regimen was two injections a week of 0.06 grams of Mapharsen (arsenic compound) for 40 injections plus 20 injections of 130 milligrams of bismuth at the rate of one a week. (This was a regimen similar to that used controversially, and proven to be lethally toxic for some patients, at 126 ASH in Brisbane in 1944.) Penicillin was only used for syphilis when the patient responded poorly to the Mapharsen or suffered from its toxic effects. Hospitalisation was for 21 days. Monthly serological tests for syphilis then continued for 18 months after discharge.[88]

A matter of concern for the medical officers serving with BCOF was that some VD-infected soldiers, seeking to conceal their diseases to avoid disgrace, privately sought treatment from Japanese doctors. The senior medical officer of the 34th Brigade, Major David Harvey Sutton, expressed the concern of his colleagues in a minute circulated to BCOF commanders in April 1947. He advised them that one of his junior officers, Captain William Inglis, had recently attended a conference on VD at which Japanese doctors were present. They seemed surprised when Inglis warned them 'that they must NOT treat BCOF personnel suffering from VD'. From his discussions with them, he learnt that BCOF personnel were being treated privately to avoid admission to the BCOF hospitals. The Japanese doctors were obtaining their anti-VD medications from BCOF dispensaries, moreover, some of their patients were officers and 'NOT all low-ranking'; British rather than Australian troops were those mostly involved.[89] Again, the 'nonofficial' treatment of VD-infected BCOF troops suggests that the reported VD rates were underestimated.

Figure 8.4: Two police of the 1st Australian Provost Company serving with BCOF in 1950 escort a young Japanese man in a military police jeep. Wearing their slouch hats, they are driving along a street in Kure accompanied by two Japanese police officers. A female police officer is sitting next to the driver while a male Japanese officer sits behind the driver helping guard the prisoner (AWM HOBJ0249).

Sutton pointed out that the dangers of the practice included the likelihood of inadequate treatment and the probability of poor-quality post-treatment surveillance. To remedy the problem, he recommended the tightening of regulations protecting VD patients' confidentiality and the disciplining of troops who spread rumours about particular soldiers being VD-infected. That would have the effect of minimising the sense of shame of the VD-infected in seeking treatment at the BCOF VD clinics. To prevent Japanese doctors from treating BCOF personnel, he suggested that the Military Government should order them not to treat BCOF troops for VD. In addition, Occupation Forces should be directed not to seek or accept VD treatment from Japanese doctors. Finally, the BCOF provost and Japanese police should work together to prevent the doctors from accepting patients from BCOF.[90]

7. Australian soldiers and Japanese women

At first the Occupation Forces discouraged their troops from fraternising with Japanese women. The first Australian BCOF Commander, General Northcott, banned fraternisation outright. One historian of BCOF, George Davies, has argued that this policy was justified during the early period of the occupation, at least until the Japanese and the occupation troops had established a workable modus vivendi. That fraternisation was occurring soon became obvious; thereafter 'the non-fraternisation policy should have been abandoned'.[91] Keeping the policy in place proved counterproductive because it 'forced men into illicit relations with the streetwalker'.[92]

One major obstacle to the non-fraternisation policy was that for many soldiers, Japanese women were irresistibly attractive. According to another historian of BCOF, Robin Gerster, 'the chance of picking up an infection was an insufficient deterrent' to seeking out such alluring women.[93] Clifton Pugh, an Australian artist who served with BCOF, was one who appreciated the gracefulness of Japanese women. He wrote home to his mother to say that he had 'never seen a fat unsightly body yet and never will for they don't get fat; quite a lot of the women have really beautiful figures—there is no denying they are very attractive'.[94] After citing Pugh and other examples, Gerster observed that 'from a long historical perspective, some BCOF veterans sentimentalised the raw sexuality of [their] Japan days in lyrical, almost romantic terms'.[95]

In time the BCOF commanders realistically recognised that many soldiers would seek out prostitutes despite 'disciplinary measures and prohibition'—and contract VD as a result.[96] As Gerster commented, 'sex had been immediately established as the dominant form of human currency between Occupier and Occupied' and the troops 'took to the sexual hospitality with enthusiasm'.[97] The non-fraternisation policy effectively lapsed through its well-nigh universal breaching. In its place the close and harsh control of the Japanese prostitutes became and remained a key strategy for the Occupation Forces in endeavouring to manage the VD epidemics among their troops. A BCOF report to the Australian Joint Chiefs of Staff in October 1946 advised that 'the main radical line of attack was to reduce the amount of VD among the Japanese women'.[98]

The Japanese women responsible for transmitting much of the VD to occupation troops were derogatively called 'Panpan girls' in Japanese. The term 'Panpan' referred to the mainly young street prostitutes who serviced the troops of the Occupation Forces.[99] According to one of their historians, the Panpan girls 'with their red lipstick, cigarettes, nylon stockings and high-heel shoes, often holding on to the arms of tall, uniformed American GIs ... became the symbol of the occupation'.[100]

The Panpan girls were a phenomenon of the early post-war years. As soon as the war had ended and the troops of the Occupation Forces began arriving, the Japanese national authorities established the Recreation Amusement Association (RAA). Like the term 'Comfort Women' so recently used during the war in the nations overrun by the Japanese, the RAA was a euphemism for state-organised prostitution. The RAA 'employed several thousand women to provide sexual services for foreign soldiers, ostensibly to protect Japanese women of middle and upper classes from rape and other violence'.[101] The RAA, however, had a short life; it was shut down in 1946 because of US fears that it would spread VD. Many of the women who lost their jobs took to the streets to work illegally as *Panpan* girls.[102]

Much BCOF effort went into trying to control the *Panpan* girls and eliminate VD-infected women from the areas frequented by occupation troops. The surviving BCOF archival files are replete with references to them. Many a file describes the way in which the BCOF military police, often working in concert with the Japanese civilian police, took punitive action against them, raiding their premises, rounding them up, charging them, having them convicted, gaoled and subjected to compulsory treatment.[103]

For example, one file held by the Australian War Memorial contains a memorandum circulated on 23 April 1948 by BCOF's Deputy Adjutant

General under the title 'Campaign against spreaders of VD: Progress report'. The report described two raids recently undertaken, the first on 'Asahi Machi' (a prostitutes' association in Kure) at 6.00 am; the second at 6.30 am on 'Otame Kai' (another Kure prostitutes' association).[104] Table 8.4 sets out what the raids had yielded.

Table 8.4-**Results of anti-prostitution raids, Kure, 1948**

	Arrests		
Action	Prostitutes	Proved to be VD-infected	Brothel keepers & procurers
Already arrested & in VD hospital on 21 April	115	115	—
Raid on 21 April	122	31	30
Raid on 23 April	66	8 (medical examinations not yet completed)	29
Total	303	154	59

Source: 'Campaign against spreaders of VD: Progress report as at 23 April 1948', AWM114 267/6/17 Part 12.

Of the prostitutes arrested in the raid on 21 April, 94 were sentenced to periods of between 20-and 29-days' imprisonment, but most had been given suspended sentences and returned to their home districts. All the brothel keepers and procurers were still in prison and awaiting trial. The report ended by noting that further 'systematic raids' would soon be conducted in four other nearby towns and cities—Hiro, Hiroshima, Kaidaichi and Yoshiura—with the aim of 'cleaning up all areas'.[105] Meanwhile, the houses being used as brothels would be confiscated by the Japanese civilian authorities and 'allocated to Japanese families engaged in essential industries'.[106]

Other files discuss at length the activities declared to be punishable offences, including soliciting members of the Occupation Forces, infecting them with VD, and procuring service personnel for prostitutes.[107] For example, in Iwakuni, a city south-west of Hiroshima, under the 'Municipal Ordinance for the Control of Prostitution' all of the following were offences punishable by imprisonment or heavy fines:

- sexual intercourse with any person picked up at random and receiving for such act remuneration or with intention of receiving remunerations
- acts of inducement to prostitution, on highways and other public places such as obstructing passages of, pestering about, or hanging on to or likewise molesting a stranger
- to obstruct passages of, to loiter about, to hang on to or likewise molest a stranger with the intention of assisting prostitution

- to offer a place for prostitution, receiving remuneration for such accommodation.[108]

One case suffices to illustrate the persistence of the *Panpan* girls and the problems they caused. 'MN' was a 30-year-old resident of Kure who was convicted in a Summary Court at Kure in May 1949 of 'carrying on prostitution while being infected with VD'. Found guilty, she was fined ¥2000, a surprisingly light fine considering that she had 'a particularly bad history and [had] been admitted to Kure VD Hospital eight times with gonorrhoea and seven times with syphilis over the past few years'. Apart from that, she had a previous VD record in Okayama. Only seven days after her conviction, she was readmitted to the Kure VD Hospital suffering another episode of gonorrhoea 'in all probability contracted after the termination of her trial'. The previous month, April 1949, two Australian soldiers had become VD-infected after intercourse with her.[109]

Captain E Nicholas of the BCOF Provost Unit, who reported MN's case to the APM, noted that 'almost nightly this girl can be seen loitering and soliciting in the vicinity of the 3rd Battalion unit lines at Hiro'. In concluding his report, Nicholas opined that 'a fine of ¥2000 will be no deterrent' and that 'more severe action should be taken in future'.[110] Nicholas shared his CO's views. Brigadier Hopkins generally believed that 'women found in or around [unit] lines should be brought before the courts and salutary punishment inflicted'. He instructed his VD Control Officers accordingly.[111]

Another difficulty was the semi-permanent relationships formed between some soldiers and particular prostitutes. These soldiers were continually reinfected with VD unless their women were treated and cured. The BCOF commanders were inclined to dismiss such men as 'feeble-minded' and to have them 'weeded out'.[112]

Encounters between Australian soldiers and Japanese women also produced many 'military' children—fathered by Australian soldiers and born to Japanese mothers. According to one historian, the Australians of BCOF left behind 'hundreds' of children in Japan.[113] During the late 1950s and 60s the Australian government received many petitions asking that they be allowed to settle in Australia.[114] Decades later, after the dismantling of the 'White Australia Policy' between 1967 and 1975, the Australian Embassy in Tokyo advertised the possibility that Japanese children of Australian parents could be granted Australian citizenship 'by descent'.[115]

Numerous marriages were also contracted between Australian soldiers and Japanese women, despite the earlier strictures against fraternisation.

Many of the couples settled in Australia, the women becoming 'war brides'. In the period 1952 to 1956 some 650 Japanese women migrated to Australia as war brides. Their successful integration into Australian society in turn became a factor in the abandonment of the White Australia Policy.[116]

In an effort to control prostitution, the government issued 'Health Cards' to prostitutes who had been medically examined and declared free from infection. The difficulty was that the women could become VD-infected again after being issued with their cards and pass on their infections. Soldiers wrongly assumed that Japanese women with the cards were 'clean'. The prostitutes regarded the cards as a 'licence to practise' because the military police would not arrest them if they could produce their cards on demand.[117]

Figure 8.5: Japanese female civilian employees ironing clothes at the BCOF Base Laundry, Hiro, Japan, June 1952. BCOF was obliged to employ a large Japanese labour force. So many Japanese civilians worked at the BCOF bases that fraternisation between the workers and soldiers inevitably occurred (AWM 147948).

Another strategy was to trace the women thought to have infected particular soldiers and then subject them to the process of arrest, prosecution, imprisonment or fines, and compulsory treatment. To that end, the Occupation Forces developed a detailed 'Venereal Disease Contact Questionnaire' which had to be completed by military personnel who had contracted VD. The questionnaire required a VD-infected soldier to name the woman who had allegedly transmitted VD to him, provide her address, description, their place of contact, the manner by which he had been procured for prostitution and the price he had paid for his sexual encounter. When the military police 'Vice Squads' had this information, they were supposed to find the prostitutes and ensure that they were prosecuted.[118]

Figure 8.6: Sergeant T.R. MacQuin of the Australian Army Education Service with a class of Japanese war brides who will soon depart for Australia, Kure, Japan, 1952. He is imparting information about Australia (AWM 148580).

As officials of the Occupation Forces conducted their campaigns against the *Panpan* girls, they had the enthusiastic support of many Japanese women's organisations. Throughout

BCOF's time in Japan, its commanders continued receiving petitions from women's organisations requesting that they take action to suppress prostitution. One such petition, dated 20 November 1950, was signed by Mitsuko Yoshida on behalf of the Iwakuni branch of the Japan Christian Women's Moral Reformation Association. Her plea ran as follows:

> PETITION FOR THE CONTROL OF PUBLIC MORAL
>
> It is to be gratified that the Occupation Force officers and men are exerting their best for the sake of this country.
>
> Recently we have confronted with hundreds of misguided women who have found their way into Iwakuni encroaching upon the virginity of priceless youths. The ill effect suffered by the people in the town in general deserves a serious attention and there is little to be wondered but that it will entail a serious social question of no mean magnitude, if let alone.
>
> I am asking you kind consideration for the enforcement of a control over the said prevalence.[119]

Despite the deferential tone and the tortured prose, the petitioners' wish was clear. They wanted the *Panpan* girls removed from Iwakuni lest they corrupt the young men of the city.

There was perhaps a subtext to the petition as well, a plea to the BCOF commanders to restrain their troops in order to halt the spread of disease into the Japanese community.

This last point is one that BCOF commanders might not have appreciated. In their anxiety over their troops' soaring VD infection rates, and their preoccupation with containing prostitution, they seem to have overlooked the damage their men were inflicting on Japanese society as it struggled to emerge from the wreckage of war. They also ignored the obvious fact that their men were spreading VD as much as Japanese women. The Occupation Force troops and the *Panpan* girls together became a self-fulfilling prophecy; a vicious circle in which the sexual appetite of the one called forth and magnified the promiscuity of the other.

8. Why were the Australian VD rates so high?

The consistently high Australian VD infection rates in Japan demand explanation and invite speculation. Why was it that the Australians became more VD-infected than their British, Indian and New Zealand comrades?

It was a question that BCOF's Australian commanders pondered. The Australian DDMS,

Brigadier Stubbe, attributed the cause to two main factors: the source of infection (the Japanese), and the troops themselves.[120] In relation to the first, he opined that five reasons existed:

1. 'Very high' VD infection rates prevailed in the Japanese population, among men and women alike.
2. The Japanese generally were 'not particularly concerned' about VD.
3. Prostitution was not 'dishonourable' in Japan, and because the war had destroyed many female jobs, it had become the only means of livelihood for many women.
4. The Japanese medical profession was 'well below normal world standard in numbers and proficiency', as a result of which a high proportion of patients treated for VD were not cured.
5. The combined effect of these factors was that 'a spreading pool of infected women' had accumulated, particularly in bombed-out industrial and port cities such as Kure, in and around which most of the Australian units were based.[121]

Among the troops, a further four influences played a part:

6. Most of the original members of the 34th Australian Infantry Brigade, veterans of the

2nd AIF, had returned to Australia. They had been replaced by much younger troops who were generally 'adventurous and irresponsible youths, unused to discipline and unheeding of advice'. The British contingent, by contrast, comprised mainly Regular Army veterans who were much better disciplined.

7. Most of the Australian units were located in city areas, where 'it [was] well-nigh impossible to keep troops within non-existent boundaries'.

8. The scarcity of Australian civilian workers necessitated the employment of a Japanese labour force at each military base, many of whom were 'girls whose presence and promiscuity are constant reminders of sex to the troops'.

9. Much police work had to be delegated to the 'untrustworthy Japanese civil police', who were 'not concerned about illegal fraternisation' between the soldiers and Japanese women.[122]

Were other factors at work? One very senior Australian BCOF officer, Brigadier Hopkins himself, speculated about this in a September 1946 memorandum on 'Control of VD'. He raised the possibility that the comparatively high incidence of syphilis among the Australians and the 'incorrect certificates given by the Jap medical officer' might be linked. 'There may be some substance in the charge that the health of our force is being deliberately destroyed'.[123] Japan's revenge on the victors of World War II? Syphilis as biological warfare to subvert the Allied Occupation Forces?

A counterargument would be that the Australians' sexual adventurism in Japan was one way of getting even with the Japanese for their invasion of Malaya, New Guinea and the archipelagos in between, as well as for the brutalities suffered by the Australian POWs. Even at the cost of contracting VD, denigrating the Japanese by prostituting their women could be seen as an expression of Australian schadenfreude at the squalor to which the Japanese had been reduced. This is an argument that cannot be quantified, but there remains the possibility that some Australians wished at least subconsciously to humiliate the Japanese. If so, casual promiscuous sex with Japanese women could have been self-justified by contemptuous soldiers.

Other factors readily suggest themselves to scholars who have taken the trouble to pore over the BCOF files preserved in Australia's national archives collections. Briefly, they include these:

- Japanese *Panpan* girls regarded the well-paid Australians as a reliable source of ready cash. The Japanese prostitutes were cheap and abundantly available. Under these circumstances prostitution thrived.
- Off-duty, there were few recreational facilities for Australian soldiers, at least in BCOF's first year or two. Gymnasiums, tennis courts, cricket pitches, swimming pools, football ovals and athletics stadiums were not provided. Booze and sex were the two most accessible off-duty recreations, and the two usually went together.
- Unlike in Papua New Guinea and Borneo in the recent past, the Australians in Japan were not fighting a war and so the pressures and constraints of combat were a burden lifted from them. The VD infection rates in Papua New Guinea had been exceptionally low because of the constant strain of war and a lack of opportunity for sexual escapades. The opposite was true in Japan.
- In relation to this last point, a former Army venereologist observes that one of the 'key principles' of military venereology is that VD rates are 'inversely related to amount of battle activity'.[124] BCOF experienced no

battle activity, and so the VD rates were inevitably high.
- Many of the Japanese prostitutes were VD-infected. Consorting with Japanese prostitutes accordingly incurred a strong risk of contracting VD. The Army propaganda material continually reiterated this point.
- Penicillin and its effectiveness in curing VD made the soldiers blase about the risks of venereal infections, which in turn encouraged them to be sexually reckless. The instructions to soldiers about how to avoid VD consequently stressed the point that penicillin was not a fail-safe anti-VD medication.
- The type of soldiers sent to Japan was possibly also a factor. There were allegations that some troops went to Japan mainly for its easy money-making potential, for example in racketeering and black-market operations. Few character assessment filters or other safeguards seem to have been applied to prevent 'bad types' from signing up with BCOF. The Army used the word 'undesirables' and its various policy memoranda spoke of 'weeding them out'.
- Finally, there was one key factor that is only hinted at in the BCOF files: the BCOF officers who contracted VD. The Army

venereologist quoted above has observed that another 'classic' principle of military venereology is that 'the military hierarchy is part of the problem rather than contributing towards the solution'. 'Cooperation of the troops is reduced by the sexual activity of senior officers, including the military police, who often have [taken] their own mistresses from the prostitute population'.[125] And so if the BCOF senior officers and military police set a poor example to the troops, and were as derelict in observing BCOF anti-VD protocols as the 'other ranks', they, too, were certainly 'part of the problem'.

The great unanswerable question is whether flaws in the Australian national character or Australian culture caused the troops serving with BCOF to incur higher VD rates than their allies. That question might contain contentious assumptions, but as in World War I and later in Vietnam, in Japan the Australians contracted VD at appreciably higher rates than the military personnel of other nations. It was a question implied but left unanswered by Allan S. Walker in his great official medical history of World War II, in which he briefly touched upon BCOF's high VD infection rates. He hinted at such faults without elaborating, allowing his readers to draw their own conclusions on the evidence he presented.

An epidemiologist considering why the Australians in BCOF 'outscored' the other contingents might find other explanations. One who did was Professor Dennis Shanks, a malariological epidemiologist.[14] Reviewing the VD infection rates of the 34th Infantry Brigade, he commented that 'when gonococcal infections continue within a defined population such as a body of soldiers using sex workers, the reason for high rates is usually failure to cure the infections'. The consequence is that 'suppressed infections carry over into the next contacts and continue the cycle, which is never broken by adequate, fully curative treatment'.[126] If that was the case among the Australians of BCOF, their infection rates remained high because they were not fully cured.

But that still does not explain why the Australian VD rates exceeded those of the British, Indians and New Zealanders in Japan. Perhaps the reason lay in the regions where the BCOF contingents were deployed. As seen, the Australians were consigned to the Hiroshima

---

14 In 2020 Professor Shanks was the Director of the Australian Defence Force Malaria and Infectious Diseases Institute.

prefecture, the British to Okayama and Shikoku, the New Zealanders to Yamaguchi, and the Indians to Shimane and Tottori. Of all these, nuclear-blasted Hiroshima was the most devastated and accordingly the most poverty-stricken in the immediate post-war years. Hiroshima prostitutes might therefore have been the most desperate.

If so, market forces would have been a factor in the Australians' higher VD rates. 'Prostitutes have to earn a certain amount of money to get by,' Professor Shanks pointed out, and 'those whose services are less expensive have to have more contacts in order to earn the same amount of money.'[127] Supposing that the Australians served in a region of 'down-market' sex providers who accepted higher numbers of customers to survive, the chances were that many of the prostitutes were VD-infected despite periodic sessions of compulsory treatment. Their clients accordingly faced high risks of infection and re-infection.

9. Conclusions

The occupation of Japan generated the Army's highest sustained rates of VD infection during the 20th century. It also taught lessons to anyone prepared to heed.

First, the Australians' experience in Japan proved yet again that a punitive approach to VD control was counterproductive. Punishing soldiers for contracting VD simply drove the problem further underground. It encouraged the VD-infected to try to conceal their diseases by self-medicating, using whatever nostrums were available, and seeking help from doctors whose expertise was questionable. That in turn meant that their infections might not be completely cured, leaving them liable to transmit their diseases to others, including women in Australia.

Second, the experience in Japan demonstrated once more that the sex drive of virile, libidinous young men could not readily be sublimated, especially when recreational activities alternative to booze and sex were not provided. Channelling the sex drive by providing the amenity of 'safe' Army-run brothels was not possible in the late 1940s and early 50s. The Army-sponsored brothel had been tried with some success in Palestine and Syria in 1941, but the Australian public had not known about that particular experiment in VD control. Army-run brothels in the Hiroshima prefecture would have been unacceptable in early post-war Australia. Political, religious and cultural considerations precluded that idea. Meanwhile, the soldiers in Japan took their chances with the *Panpan* girls.

Finally, anti-fraternisation proscriptions could never hope to be effective because they defied human nature. As the large number of Japanese war brides in Australia suggested, linguistic, cultural and racial differences were obstacles that people attracted to each other could overcome. The war brides and their husbands might not have recognised it at the time, but their marriages helped diversify Australian society in the post-war era. They were a step towards the multi-ethnic kind of society which Australia increasingly became during the remaining decades of the 20th century.

CHAPTER 9

Korea and Malaya, 1950-1963

Australia's involvement in BCOF in Japan overlapped its participation in the Korean War of 1950 to 1953. The AMF commitment to the Korean War followed a call from the United Nations (UN) to defend South Korea from North Korean aggression. The Army fought in Korea as a member of British Commonwealth formations, successively the 27th and 28th Commonwealth brigades within a wider UN force.[1]

Simultaneously with the Korean War, the AMF was involved in another war in Asia. This was the Malayan Emergency, a war against the Malayan government by communist insurgents from Malaya's large ethnic Chinese population. The Australian commitment to this war began in 1950, when RAAF Dakota aircraft from the 38th Squadron were deployed to Malaya to transport cargo and assist with paratroop and propaganda leaflet drops. The Australian Army deployment to Malaya began in 1955, when the 2nd Battalion Royal Australian Regiment (2 RAR) was sent to

Malaya to support the support the Malayan and British troops in their fight against the communists. Although the Emergency officially ended in 1960, Australian troops remained in Malaya until August 1963, assisting in 'mopping-up' operations against remnant communist forces who had continued guerrilla activities in the northern jungles along the border with Thailand.[2]

1. The Korean War

The Korean War began on 25 June 1950, when troops from communist North Korea crossed the 38th parallel to invade South Korea in strength. Within a week they had pushed the South Korean forces south down the Korean Peninsula and had captured the South Korean capital, Seoul.[3]

The two Koreas resulted from the occupation of the Korean Peninsula by the Soviet Union and the USA following the defeat of the Japanese and the subsequent end of World War II. Japan had annexed and ruled Korea since 1910. Both the Soviet Union and the USA installed Korean governments to their liking. The 38th parallel became the line of demarcation between what quickly became two separate Korean nations.[4]

With the invasion of South Korea by North Korean forces, US President Harry Truman immediately committed the American military forces to supporting South Korea. The UN also pledged support for South Korea despite a Soviet boycott in the Security Council. Following a UN call for willing nations to assist, 21 sent troops, aircraft, naval vessels and medical units to South Korea.[5]

The Australian contribution to this multinational force initially comprised two Royal Australian Navy ships, No.77 Squadron of the RAAF and the 3rd Battalion of the Royal Australian Regiment (3 RAR). Transferred to Korea from Japan, where it had been serving with BCOF, 3 RAR was formerly known as the 67th Battalion, before being reformed and renamed as 3 RAR in November 1948. On 28 September 1950, 3 RAR arrived in Pusan, South Korea, where it joined the 27th British Brigade, which was renamed the 27th Commonwealth Brigade. Over the next three years the Commonwealth force incorporated Canadian, Indian, New Zealand and South African units as well.[6]

The Commonwealth troops fought within the UN force led by General Douglas MacArthur of the USA, who in July 1950 was appointed Supreme Commander of the UN forces. Confined at first to the port city of Pusan, a combined US, South Korean and Commonwealth force thrust out from that perimeter, led by the US 1st Marine Division, which landed at Inchon, 26 kilometres south-west of Seoul, on 15 September 1950. Seoul was recaptured on 25 September. The North Korean army was driven back across the 38th parallel. US and South Korean troops took Pyongyang, the North Korean capital, on 19 October. The thrust north continued. By the end of the month the UN forces were approaching the Yalu River, the border with China.[7]

China entered the war on 25 October 1950 after its troops crossed the Yalu River. They pushed the UN forces back across the 38th parallel. Communist forces retook Seoul in January 1951, but in a counter-offensive the US Eighth Army recaptured the city on 14 March. Seoul had changed hands four times in 10 months. MacArthur was relieved of his command in April 1951 because of disagreements with President Truman, including MacArthur's wish to invade China and use nuclear weapons. He was replaced by General Matthew Ridgway, Commander of the US Eighth Army, the main army of the UN force. By the end of May the communist armies had been pushed back north of the 38th parallel again.[8]

3 RAR participated in a series of hard-fought battles of the war. Among the most celebrated was the battle for the Kapyong Valley, 55 kilometres north-east of Seoul, in April 1951. The Chinese army had begun a spring offensive with a thrust towards Seoul. After a South Korean division was driven back down the valley, 3 RAR and the 2nd Canadian Battalion engaged the Chinese. Supported by US tanks and New Zealand artillery, they halted the Chinese in a four-day battle fought between 22 and 25 April. The battle helped save Seoul from changing hands yet again. 3 RAR suffered heavy losses: 32 killed, 53 wounded and three taken prisoner.[9]

After the see-sawing fortunes of both sides during its first year, by July 1951 the war entered a period of stalemate. Although at least 11 major battles were fought over the next two years, neither side captured much territory. The fighting continued as both sides sought to negotiate an end to the war. An armistice was agreed to on 27 July 1953. A Demilitarised Zone (DMZ) was established across the Korean Peninsula close to, but crossing, the 38th parallel. The DMZ ran along the border between the North and South; effectively the agreed 'demarcation line' between the North and the South. The DMZ has continued to be one of the most heavily guarded boundaries on earth. Numerous incidents and casualties on both sides have periodically occurred as the security forces of the two Koreas confront each other across the DMZ.[10]

Korea was a costly war for both sides. The UN forces lost 178,405 dead, 32,925 missing and 566,434 wounded. North Korea and China are thought to have lost at least 398,000 dead (though estimates are as high as 750,000), 145,000 missing and somewhere between 686,500 and 789,000 wounded. Total civilian casualties were an estimated 2.5 million killed or wounded; 991,000 in South Korea, 1,550,000 in North Korea.[11] Australia's losses were small by comparison. Over 17,000 Australians served in the war. Of these, 340 were killed, 1216 were wounded and 29 became POWs.[12]

2. Medical arrangements for the UN ground forces in Korea

In a break with previous practice, the Korean War was one to which the Australian Army sent no major medical units. Starting with Captain Bryan Gandevia, it sent a succession of RMOs, usually captains or majors. The RMO was responsible for running a Regimental Aid Post (RAP) behind the line of battle. He was supported by a sergeant and corporal from the Royal Australian Army Medical Corps (RAAMC).

Wounded troops were brought to the RAP from a series of companylevel Collecting Points. These were located as close to the front line as possible, preferably on a road. The wounded were stretchered to the Collection Points for preliminary first aid. At each Collection Point was an RAAMC corporal and four stretcher-bearers, who were usually 3 RAR military bandsmen. Following initial treatment, the wounded were driven from the Collection Points to the RAP in 4-wheel-drive jeeps for further emergency treatment before evacuation to a Field Ambulance in the rear.[13]

Instead of the accustomed field ambulances provided by the national armies of each Commonwealth country participating, as in previous wars, only one such unit, the 60th Indian Field Ambulance (60 IFA) was deployed to Korea. The RAPs sent their casualties to 60 IFA, which consequently received many of the Commonwealth patients, including numerous Australians.[14]

In the early months of the war, during late 1950 and early 1951, each RAP was assigned several jeeps for transporting wounded troops from Collection Points to 60 IFA.[15] The casualty transport system improved dramatically during 1951 as US-managed evacuation of the wounded by helicopter became the norm. The

US provided a helicopter evacuation shuttle service for the Commonwealth forces as well as its own. Casualties were swiftly moved back from the front line to a US Mobile Army Surgical Hospital (MASH) or to 60 IFA in the rear.[16]

After initial treatment in a MASH or 60 IFA, casualties expected to be under treatment for longer than three weeks were flown aboard RAAF Dakota (DC3) aircraft to Japan, where they were admitted into one of the major military base hospitals. In Japan the Australians were sent to either the American Army Hospital in Tokyo or the British Commonwealth General Hospital at Kure. This hospital had absorbed 130 AGH, which had been located in Etajima during the occupation of Japan. The Commonwealth General Hospital was staffed mainly by British, Canadian and Australian medical personnel, who worked harmoniously together. Cases needing prolonged treatment were airlifted to hospitals in their home nations. For Australians that meant repatriation hospitals such as Greenslopes, Heidelberg and Concord.[17]

The swift evacuation of casualties, together with the increased use of antibiotics and plasma resulted in higher survival rates for Korean War soldiers than those in previous wars. The mortality rate among wounded Australians who reached a forward medical post was 2.5 per cent, compared with 5 per cent a decade earlier in World War II, and 10 per cent in World War I.[18] The lower death rate reflected the reality that instead of many wounded troops dying from their injuries during long, slow, uncomfortable and painful transfers to treatment points, they received life-saving surgery in specialised emergency hospitals fairly soon after being wounded.

The introduction of helicopter-based retrievals transformed military patient transport and treatment procedures. Rapid aerial evacuation obviated the need for patient transfers between the World War I and II-style chain of RAPs, field ambulances, Casualty Clearing Stations and Stationary Hospitals, each progressively further from the front line. In reducing the need for locating large surgical teams near the line of battle, use of helicopters also minimised the risk of medical units coming under fire and of their personnel becoming battle casualties.[19]

Figure 9.1: Indian medical personnel loading wounded troops aboard a US Sikorsky S-51 Dragonfly helicopter, Korea, August 1952. The wounded were possibly soldiers of the 1st Battalion Royal Australian Regiment (AWM HOBJ3545).

3. VD and other diseases within the Australian Army in Korea

The Korean War was one of the few in the 20th century in which the AMF participated without systematic and comprehensive health statistics apparently being compiled and made available via official war histories. It seems that with so many nations handling the Australian casualties, no central medical statistics repository was maintained. The statistics are accordingly sparse and fragmentary.

The Korean War was also one for which no Australian official medical history volumes were subsequently published. A comprehensive two-volume official history of the war was compiled by Robert O'Neill and published by the Australian War Memorial under the title *Australia in the Korean War 1950—53*.[20] The second volume included a chapter by the historian Dr Darryl McIntyre on 'Australian Army Medical Services', but there was no separate medical volume.[21]

Given the paucity of source material, McIntyre dealt as effectively as possible with the topic of VD in the AMF in Korea. Scholars interested in gaining a comprehensive overview of the impact of VD during the war accordingly need to start with McIntyre's account. After that, other secondary sources should be considered, mainly what Army medical officers later wrote about VD, for example in the *MJA*. The Australian DGMS during the Korean War, Major General F. Kingsley Norris, who toured Korea twice, also wrote about the war. While there, he interviewed Australian VD patients in order to determine why VD had become a problem. He later reported his findings briefly in his 1970 autobiography.[22]

Though the VD rates in Korea were comparatively high, the medical officers who dealt with it regarded VD infections as a nuisance rather than the catastrophe of earlier conflicts. Captain Gandevia described how he and his colleagues managed it:

> Venereal disease was not a serious problem, although occasional fresh cases were seen in reinforcements from Japan. Only one of the patients admitted to sexual intercourse in Korea. Treatment of gonorrhoea or urethritis consisted of the intramuscular injection of 300,000 units of penicillin in oil on two successive days with a further injection on the fifth day if the discharge [of pus] had not completely cleared. Evacuation of these patients was not considered unless the discharge persisted; but in practice two doses were usually found sufficient.[23]

A treatment period of two days for most gonorrhoea patients was a huge advance on the 16 days common in BCOF in Japan three or four years earlier. A treatment regimen so short would have been unimaginable a decade earlier during World War II, when six weeks' treatment was common, even if sulphanilamide was being administered.

The shortened treatment time eliminated the need for the 'Dermatological' and 'Special' VD hospitals of World Wars I and II. VD-infected soldiers in Korea were most often treated as far forward as possible, usually in 60 IFA.[24]

During the Australians' first year or so in Korea, most of the VD infections were contracted in Japan rather than Korea. The official historian, McIntyre, concluded that the main reason for high VD rates was the practice of sending the troops to Japan for recreation leave. As seen in the previous chapter, prostitution was commonplace in Japan and most prostitutes were VD-infected. Resort to prostitutes, McIntyre wrote, was 'the normal reaction of young men spending five days' leave in a big city, far from the hazards of war'.[25]

Another factor was the availability of penicillin, which had greatly lessened the burden of treating bacterial infections. In treating gonorrhoea and syphilis, penicillin had ended the previous messy, painful, protracted, toxic and sometimes lethal VD treatment regimens. Soldiers soon learned that several injections of penicillin would cure VD. That in turn fostered a blasé attitude. On his second tour of Korea, in

November 1951, the DGMS, Major General Norris, discovered this for himself when interviewing VD patients. In his autobiography he recalled that he 'gained the impression that since the dramatic introduction of penicillin fear of VD was rapidly fading and exposure to infection overseas was seldom a new experience'.[26] The soldiers Norris interviewed seemed to be continuing in Korea sexual habits acquired in Australia. These included periodic VD infection. For those he spoke with, contracting VD seemed to be only a minor inconvenience.[27]

In 1952 and 1953, locally contracted VD became more common among the Australians in Korea. In March 1953 a sharp rise in the infection rate, with 83 new infections that month, coincided with 3 RAR's period at Camp Casey, a US base 64 kilometres north of Seoul. In the nearby town of Dongducheon was a precinct known to the troops as 'Little Chicago', a 'notorious' locale for contracting gonorrhoea.[28] After March the infection rate fell away because 3 RAR returned to the front line, adding further credence to the maxim that VD rates were inversely proportional to the amount of combat activity.[29]

As seen, some 17,000 Australians served in Korea and 340 were killed. The Army's share of these statistics included these:

- A total of 10,657 Army personnel served in Korea between August 1950 and July 1953.
- 276 soldiers were killed in action and one died as a prisoner of war.
- Non-fatal battle casualties totalled 1210.
- 23 soldiers were captured and became POWs.
- Between January 1951 and December 1953, the RAAF Nursing Service escorted 12,762 patients from Korea to Japan, of whom 728 were subsequently evacuated to Australia.[30]

It is uncertain whether the 12,762 patients flown to Japan from Korea were all Australians or included personnel from the other Commonwealth contingents. Whoever they were, the great majority were probably the victims of diseases and complaints arising from environmental conditions. Korea in the early 1950s was an unhealthy country which, in the words of a British medical officer serving there, Major Felix Jackson Ingham, was 'comparatively uncivilised, ravaged by war, with a population in which disease [was] rife'.[31] Diseases common in Korea included 'intestinal diseases, typhus, relapsing fever, encephalitis, tuberculosis and venereal diseases'.[32] Many Commonwealth troops suffered from frostbite during their first harsh winter in Korea. Other common complaints were respiratory diseases, dysentery, infective hepatitis, malaria and a previously unknown, sometimes lethal viral disease which the medical officers called 'acute epidemic haemorrhagic fever'.[33]

Where did VD fit among this array of infectious diseases? The one set of surviving figures for the Commonwealth troops was provided in a 1953 article in the *Proceedings of the Royal Society of Medicine* by Major Ingham, the British medical officer quoted above. Ingham's figures are only for 1952 and are for the Commonwealth force as a whole rather than for its national contingents. The total number of VD cases treated was 10,535 and the overall rate was 376 cases per thousand troops for the year.[34] The chart in Figure 9.2 shows the 1952 cases month by month.

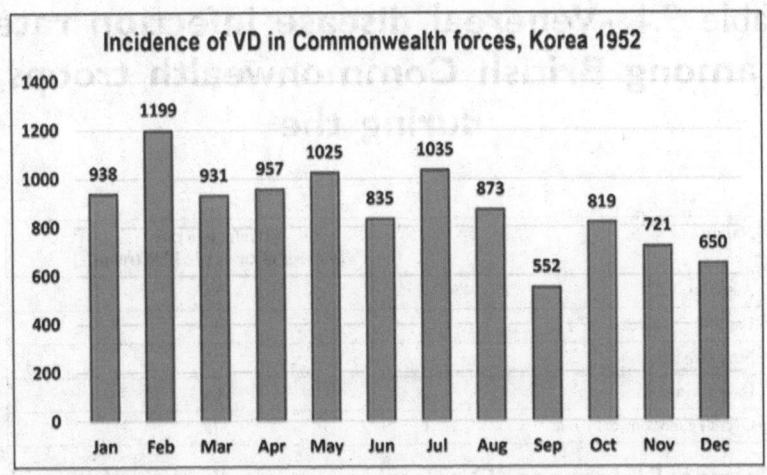

Figure 9.2: Number of monthly VD cases among Commonwealth forces in Korea, 1952 (F.J. Ingham, 'Discussion on medical problems in Korea: Army health problems', Proceedings of the Royal Society for Medicine', Volume 46, 1953, pp.1041-1046).

Major Ingham did not provide separate figures for the monthly tally of VD infections by each of the national contingents within the Commonwealth force. He simply stated what the annual infection rates were for the Australian, Canadian, New Zealand and UK contingents (Table 9.1). Although the rates were high, with one in three Australian soldiers contracting VD, perhaps the Australian commanders were mollified by knowing that for once the Australians did not 'outscore' their comrades from the other Commonwealth contingents.

Table 9.1 - Venereal disease infection rates among British Commonwealth troops during the

Nation	VD infection rate (number of cases per 1000 troops)
Australia	386
Canada	616
New Zealand	410
United Kingdom	264
Overall Commonwealth rate	376

Source: EJ. Ingham, 'Discussion on medical problems in Korea: Army health problems', Proceedings of the Royal Society for Medicine', Volume 46, 1953, pp.1041-1046.

As the table shows, the Australian rate of 386 was slightly above the overall Commonwealth figure but appreciably lower than the Canadian and New Zealand rates. It was nevertheless a historically high figure for Australian troops because it was 2.8 times higher than the rate in Egypt in 1916, 2.6 times higher than in the UK in 1917, and eight times higher than in the Middle East in 1941. All of those had been VD epidemics for the Australians; Korea in 1952 was as well.

Ingham had no explanation for the discrepancies between contingents. Possibly they represented time in combat, with the Australians and British having spent more time fighting than the Canadians and New Zealanders. Ingham did, however, provide a brief explanation of how the Commonwealth contingents were tackling their high VD rates:

> Efforts have been made on all sides to educate men in the dangers of these diseases and to discourage them from running the risk of infection. Lectures are given by chaplains, medical officers and commanding officers. Propaganda films are also frequently shown. Particular attention is directed to newly arrived drafts. It has been found that the incidence of VD can be reduced by cutting down to a minimum the periods spent in transit in base towns where the risk of infection is high.[35]

Major Ingham might not have known much of the history of VD in the Australian Army. If he did, he would have been aware that all these measures had been tried before with no discernible effect in lowering infection rates.

But if, as Ingham believed, VD rates could be reduced, how many Australians became infected during the war? No overall number is known but an extrapolation is possible. Thus, when Ingham's 1952 infection rate, 386 per thousand or 38.6 per cent, is applied to the total of 10,657 Australian soldiers who served in Korea, a figure of 4114 may be derived. It is only a guesstimate and it assumes the infection rate remained more or less the same across the three years of the Army's commitment to Korea, but it provides a credible ballpark figure.

4. The American army's experience of VD during the Korean War

Unlike Australia, the USA did publish an official medical history of the Korean War. This enables Australian readers to gain a broader appreciation of the impact of VD during the war than is available in their own official war history. The author was Albert E. Cowdrey. He called his book *The Medics' War*. Cowdrey saw the Korean War as an extension of the post-war US Occupation of Japan and Korea. He began his account of the US medical arrangements in Korea by considering those in Japan. With a flair for the apt phrase, he observed that 'American troops celebrated victory in immemorial fashion: almost immediately they found means to visit prostitutes, and a lively venereal disease problem began to take shape'.[36] 'Young soldiers,' he wrote, 'flocked to [prostitutes] with the pertinacity of lemmings and in similar numbers'.[37] VD infection rates rose steadily among the Americans in Japan. By December

1947 the rate had reached 94 cases per thousand troops per annum. Cowdrey regarded that as high by American experience but low in comparison with 'European' figures.[38] If he had known that the US figure was only a fifth that of the Australians in BCOF, he might have been surprised.

Turning to South Korea, which the US had occupied in 1945 following the Japanese surrender, Cowdrey pointed out that 'sex, like food and drink, brought soldiers and civilians together'.[39] The Americans in Korea resorted to prostitutes as enthusiastically as in Japan. Not surprisingly the VD infection rate rose from 22 cases per thousand troops to 102 per thousand during 1946 and to 185 per thousand by mid-1948.[40] The US Army's strategies for reducing the infection rate included 'indoctrination, sermons, establishment of prophylactic stations and issuing condoms', but none of these served to contain the burgeoning VD rate.[41] Australian military commanders had often sung this lament before.

When the Korean War erupted in June 1950, it had an immediate impact on the VD rates. The rate among American troops in Korea fell from 183 cases per thousand in 1949 to 103 per thousand during 1950.[42] After this initial fall, the rate rose again over the next two years, reaching 202 cases per thousand troops in November 1952. By then, 'infection [was] on the average of one man out of five once a year', but, thanks to antibiotics, even such a high rate did not 'represent a very serious drain on job performance'.[43]

Figure 9.3: MASH: A Novel About Three Army Doctors, the 1968 account of the fictional 4077th US Mobile Army Surgical Hospital in Korea by 'Richard Hooker'. The novel was the inspiration for the long-running television comedy-drama, M*A*S*H. In its day, M*A*S*H was the most popular TV series in the USA. (Image: book cover from MASH by Richard Hooker. Copyright 1968 by William Morrow Co. Used by permission of HarperCollins Publishers.)

According to Cowdrey, VD during the Korean War was 'an annoying though not militarily significant problem'. The US commanders came to see VD as 'an occupational disease of soldiers'.[44] They nevertheless insisted on a series of measures to try to keep it under control. As in both the US and Australian armies in the past, these included divisional VD clinics, continuously updated registers of the VD-infected, frequent lectures 'of the sort that emphasised man-to-man candour', appeals to moral sentiment, prophylactic kits and condoms, and 'that staple of ribald and rueful GI memory', the short-arm inspection.[45]

Perhaps indulging himself, at this point Cowdrey quoted from the novel from which the popular, long-running TV comedy-drama M*A*S*H grew. The novelist, Richard Hooker (nom-de-plume of Dr H.R. Hornberger Jr, an army surgeon), based his 1968 novel, *MASH: A Novel About Three Army Doctors,* on his own experiences in the 1055th Mobile Army Surgical Unit in Korea. The chief protagonist of *MASH* is Dr Benjamin Franklin ('Hawkeye') Pierce. In one episode of the novel, Hawkeye Pierce lectures newly arrived army doctors on how to conduct a successful short-arm inspection:

> It's very simple. You get a chair. You sit on it backwards with your arms clasped behind its back and your chin resting on the top. You gotta have a big cigar in your mouth. You sit there and look. Most of the

guys will know what to do. If they don't you growl, 'Skin it and wring it, soldier.' Sound mean when you say it. If you think there is a suspicion of venereal disease, you make a gesture with your thumb like Bill Klem calling a guy out at the plate. Then somebody hauls the guy off somewhere. I never found out what happens to them. Every now and then, just so they know you're alert, you grunt, 'Don't wave it so close to my cigar, Mac!' If you follow these simple rules, you can't go wrong.[46]

Hawkeye's instructions, Cowdrey averred, could 'hardly be improved upon'.[47]

5. The Malayan Emergency

The Malayan Emergency was a war waged largely by ethnic Chinese communists for regional communist strategic purposes in South-East Asia. Opposing them were the forces of the Malayan Federation and contingents from Commonwealth nations—the UK, Australia, New Zealand, Fiji and Southern Rhodesia. The communist force, which called itself the Malayan Races Liberation Army (MRLA), was essentially an army led and dominated by communist insurgents of mainly Chinese ethnicity. The MRLA conducted a guerrilla campaign against Malaya and its Commonwealth allies.

For a time Australia's involvement in Malaya ran concurrently with its engagement in the Korean War. The RAAF was active in Malaya from 1950, however the Australian Army did not commit troops to Malaya until 1955. Australian troops continued serving there until August 1963, a period which overlapped the Army's participation in the Vietnam War.[48]

The Emergency began in mid-1948 after the resumption of British civilian rule in Malaya. The British response to the threat of the 'communist terrorists' was vigorous. Starting in the south, the British military commanders removed the insurgents' power base by systematically driving them northwards, away from settlements and into jungle areas where living was difficult. The British also relocated village communities in strictly supervised 'New Villages', thus denying the guerrillas their principal support base. British troops continued patrolling the settlements and jungle areas thoroughly, cutting off MRLA supply lines, breaking up concentrations of MRLA forces and denying them refuge.[49] The guerrillas were pushed out of Malaya into Thailand, where their dwindling numbers were no longer a threat.[50]

Australian support of the British forces began in June 1950 when the RAAF sent a bomber squadron and a flight of transport planes, which were based at Butterworth on the mainland of Penang state in northwestern Malaya.[51] Australian ground forces from 2 RAR were sent to Malaya in October 1955. Once there, they became a part of a formation called the British Commonwealth Far Eastern Strategic Reserve. They were operating in what was still a British colony, within a British Army region where the major formation was the Far Eastern Land Force.

2 RAR was based at first on Penang Island and then at Butterworth on the mainland nearby. The unit guarded the New Village perimeters and patrolled the rubber plantations and jungles, mainly in Perak state to the east of Butterworth and immediately south of the border with Thailand. 2 RAR saw little action and was withdrawn in August 1957, replaced by 3 RAR which arrived in October 1957. 3 RAR had more active engagement with the MRLA guerrillas, whose overarching organisation had largely been destroyed. In October 1959, 1 RAR replaced 3 RAR. 2 RAR returned for a second tour of duty in October 1961, by which time the Emergency had officially ended. Some Australian troops remained in Malaya until 1963.[52]

The AMF lost 51 dead in Malaya, 15 of whom were killed in action. About 7000

Australian soldiers fought in Malaya; the Army's losses were 33 dead and 135 wounded.[53]

6. Disease among the Australian troops during the Malayan Emergency

The jungle campaigns of the Malayan Emergency produced tropical medical conditions similar to those in the campaigns in New Guinea during World War II. The medical officers in the field used to refer to the 'Death Dealing Seven'—falciparum malaria, scrub typhus, leptospirosis, dysentery (both bacillary and amoebic), Japanese 'B' encephalitis, snake bite (from cobras and vipers), and gunshot wounds (both from enemy action and unauthorised discharge of weapons).[54] In addition to this potentially fatal seven, skin conditions (mainly tinea) and infectious hepatitis were common among the Australian soldiers.[55]

As in Korea, the Australian Army sent no medical units to Malaya other than the RMOs and their RAPs. Instead, the Army in Malaya relied on British military medical units or, in an emergency, the local Malayan and Singaporean hospitals. Australians requiring hospital treatment for relatively minor injuries and illnesses were usually sent to the nearest British Army Medical Receiving Station. Those with more serious conditions went to one of four major British Hospitals: Kamunting near Taiping, Kinrara near Kuala Lumpur, Kluang in Johore state, and in Singapore, which received patients with more complicated conditions requiring longer treatment. As well as these, the British Army maintained a convalescent hospital in the Cameron Highlands of central Malaya. Those requiring evacuation to Australia usually travelled on commercial flights.[56]

The most common infectious diseases during the Emergency were STDs. In Malaya the total number of Australian VD cases between October 1955 and September 1961 was 2902. The VD cases amounted to 47 per cent of all 6192 Australian hospital admissions in that period; the equivalent of two-fifths (41 per cent) of the Australian soldiers in Malaya contracted VD.[57]

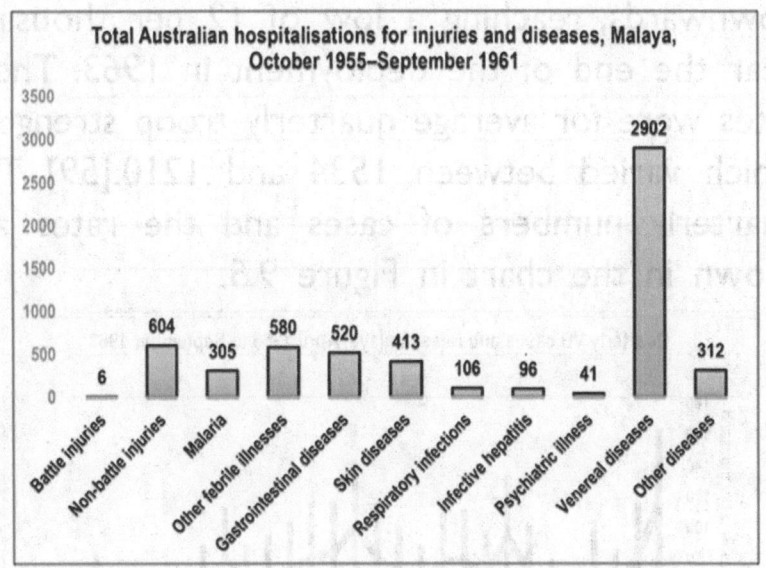

Figure 9.4: Reasons for hospitalisation of Australian troops in Malaya, 1955-1961 (Brendan O'Keefe, Medicine at War, 1994, pp.376-379).

The disease situation among Australian troops in Malaya is summarised in the chart in Figure 9.4. As the chart indicates, the 2902 VD cases were by far the single most common reason for hospitalisation. They comprised half of all hospital admissions between October 1955 and September 1961. VD was always the chief cause of sick wastage among Royal Australian Regiment soldiers in Malaya.[58]

The Australians' VD infection rate in Malaya fluctuated. The rate was higher earlier in the deployment, rising to a high of 116 cases per thousand troops during the April to June quarter of 1956. It fluctuated thereafter but trended downwards, reaching a low of 12 per thousand near the end of the deployment in 1963. These rates were for average quarterly troop strengths, which varied between 1534 and 1210.[59] The quarterly numbers of cases and the rates are shown in the chart in Figure 9.5.

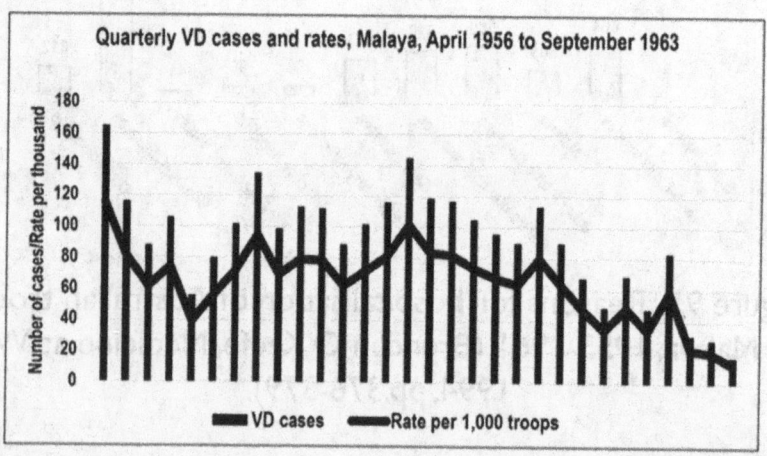

Figure 9.5: Australian quarterly VD infection rate in Malaya, 1956—1963 (Brendan O'Keefe, Medicine at War, 1994, pp.376-379).

At first sight these rates appear much lower than the rates in either the Korean War previously or the Vietnam War later. Appearances are deceptive, however, because they are *quarterly* rates. It is only when the *overall* rate is derived from the total number of VD cases and the total number of troops who served in Malaya that the 'big picture' is seen. About 7000 soldiers served in Malaya, of whom 2902 became VD-infected. This means that the overall VD infection rate was 415 cases per thousand troops—higher than the rate of 386 in Korea several years earlier.

As in previous wars, the chief military problem with VD was the loss of manpower caused by high infection rates. Even though antibiotics had greatly reduced VD hospitalisation times, all VD-infected troops were routinely admitted to one of the British Army medical centres for tests and treatment. The time off duty was usually four days for gonorrhoea, eight for non-gonococcal urethritis and ten for chancroid.[60]

Assuming that gonorrhoea comprised the majority of cases, say 62 per cent, as in BCOF in Japan, a notional number of days lost to gonorrhoea alone can be estimated as follows:

62 per cent of 2902 VD cases = 1799 gonorrhoea cases
Therefore days lost to gonorrhoea = 1799 cases × 4 days each = 7196 total days lost.

Arithmetic of this kind perturbed the DGMS in Melbourne, Major General Sir William Refshauge, who demanded that the medical officers in Malaya take decisive action to reduce the infection rates. Recognising that VD infection was mainly a result of soldiers going on leave, he proposed that troops taking leave be compulsorily issued with condoms. This immediately aroused opposition among the chaplains, especially the Catholic chaplains because of the Catholic Church's proscription of artificial means of birth control. The commander of the Australian force in Malaya, Colonel Frank W. Speed, pointed out to Refshauge that 'no possibility' existed for controlling prostitutes in Malaya as had been the case earlier in Japan. Further, 'antibiotics had practically extinguished any fear of contracting the disease among the soldiers'.[61] The only strategy left, Speed wrote, was 'to prevail upon the soldier, by all means possible, to sublimate his urge'.[62] Whether or not Speed knew it, appeals for sublimation had often been tried before, with no success.

Meanwhile, Major General Refshauge and the senior Australian officers in Malaya were 'stunned' by a change of policy on VD by the UK War Office in early 1958. The new policy required the British Army to abolish its PACs, which had been among the Australian Army's principal anti-VD strategies since World War I. The British Army also abandoned its disciplinary approach to VD control, for example by doing away with penalties for soldiers who concealed their VD infections. Instead, the British Army shifted to 'educational' means for controlling VD, hoping to convince its troops that VD was a 'social disgrace'. At the same time, the British retained measures of 'proven effectiveness' such as issuing free condoms, tracing the women thought to have transmitted VD to soldiers, and policing brothels declared 'out of bounds'.[63]

The British policy shift on VD perturbed Major General Refshauge and the new Australian commander in Malaya, Colonel Ernest G. McNamara, who believed it would cause them to relinquish VD control measures they regarded as effective. McNamara remonstrated with the British Far East Land Forces headquarters, which refused to re-establish the PACs but agreed that the Australian contingent could continue pursuing its discipline-oriented control policy.[64]

McNamara and Refshauge were alarmed by the high Australian VD rates, which again greatly exceeded those of the British troops. In 1957, for instance, the Australian annual VD rate had been 251 cases per thousand troops, compared with only 68 per thousand among the British.[65] In view of such rates, McNamara pointed out that 'we are all quite certain that a return to strong disciplinary measures is the only way in which we will reduce the incidence'.[66]

Major General Refshauge officially toured Malaya in June 1958. While there he reviewed the Army's position on VD. He realised that because of the reliable, swift treatment of VD with modern antibiotics, the Army's field operations were not being greatly hampered by VD. As a result, his concern shifted to the societal consequences of high VD rates. He feared what effect the rates might have on public opinion in Australia. If the rates became public knowledge, the Army's reputation would suffer and that in turn could lead to the withdrawal of the Australian contingent. He also worried about what the government of newly independent Malaya[15] might think of playing host to VD-infected Australians. He concluded that such political issues 'demanded a continuation of energetic efforts to control [VD]'.[67]

Refshauge decided that Army-controlled brothels should be introduced, of which he had firsthand experience. His service in the Middle East during World War II had included a period running a hospital facility in Syria that examined and treated VD-infected prostitutes. For various reasons, however, he was unable to go ahead with this idea in Malaya. The small scale of the

---

[15] Malaya achieved independence from the UK as the Federation of Malaya on 31 August 1957. The name was changed to Federation of Malaysia in 1963 when Singapore and the North Borneo states of Sabah and Sarawak joined the Federation. Singapore subsequently withdrew from the Federation in 1965 to become a separate nation.

Australian contingent, the more tolerant view of VD in the War Office and the opposition of the chaplains stymied his plans.[68]

Another idea proposed by Refshauge included recreational venues called 'Soldiers' Clubs'. The membership would include 'wholesome Australian women', the wives of married soldiers who were living on the Army bases in Malaya. He had seen something similar among the British troops in Korea, where the social life of such clubs had provided an alternative to booze and prostitutes.[69]

Refshauge also contributed a novel idea of his own to the armoury of anti-VD measures. Why not introduce an inter-platoon competition, the winner of which would be the platoon with the lowest VD infection rate? The suggestion was duly implemented, but with little perceptible impact on the incidence of VD.[70]

Anecdotal evidence suggests that the inter-platoon competition might well have produced the opposite effect to what the DGMS intended. For example, one enthusiastic young lieutenant keen for his platoon to win the 'lowest VD rate' prize called his men together for a pep-talk. He said he earnestly wished them to win. To emphasise the importance of their doing so he advised them that, far from having the lowest VD rate, they currently had the highest.

His men received this news by cheering lustily.[71]

Further evidence that the competition was not taken seriously was that the infection rates of some battalions rose rather than fell in the months leading up to the end of their tours of duty.[72] The prospect of VD infection clearly held few fears even for those soldiers about to return home to their families in Australia.

7. Indonesian-Malaysian Confrontation

Indonesia opposed the 1963 expansion of the Federation of Malaya to embrace Singapore, Sarawak and Sabah within a wider Federation of Malaysia. Indonesia regarded the federation as a facade behind which the UK would retain control of its former colonies in the region. In an undeclared war which the Indonesian government termed *Konfrontasi* ('Confrontation'), Indonesia sent armed troops across the borders it shared with Malaysia in Borneo (Kalimantan) in an attempt to destabilise and break up the expanded federation.[73]

At first the Australian government rejected requests from Malaysia and the UK to send troops to support Malaysia. Australia feared that an involvement in Borneo could lead to retaliatory cross-border Indonesian raids into the Australian territories of Papua and New Guinea.[74] In March 1965 the Australian government finally agreed to send 3 RAR to Sarawak to help the British Commonwealth Far Eastern Strategic Reserve protect areas threatened by infiltration from Indonesian irregulars. In April 1966, 4 RAR replaced 3 RAR. Confrontation ended in August 1966 after the Malaysian and Indonesian governments negotiated a settlement.[75]

In addition to the troops from 3 RAR and 4 RAR, signallers and engineers plus Royal Australian Navy ships and several Royal Australian Air Force squadrons participated in the Confrontation. Altogether about 3500 Australian military personnel took part in the Confrontation operations. Australian losses were 23 killed and eight wounded.[76]

Australian troops serving in Borneo during Confrontation suffered the usual range of tropical diseases—malaria, fungal skin diseases, dysentery and leptospirosis. Troops needing hospital treatment were evacuated by helicopter to a hospital in Kuching, the capital of Sarawak, where a British Army surgical team operated.[77]

Some of the Australians sent to Borneo during Confrontation contracted VD infections.[78] How many cases is uncertain, therefore estimating an infection rate is not possible.

8. Conclusions

Like the occupation of Japan, the Korean War and the Malayan Emergency were a manifestation of a great post-World War II sea change in Australian soldiers' attitudes to sex and STDs. Modern antibiotics released them from the fear of VD and from taking too seriously the lectures, man-to-man chats and urgings to chastity from their chaplains, medical officers and unit commanders.

When the memory of the painful, hazardous, shameful weeks-long VD treatment regimens of the prepenicillin era had receded, for many soldiers sex with VD-infected prostitutes became just another recreation. Like gambling, smoking, drinking and the concerts staged by celebrity entertainers from Australia, it became a way for off-duty soldiers to while away their leisure time. From their own past experience or that of many of their mates, they knew that the 'clap', 'pox', 'soft-sores' (chancroid) and 'gooey stuff' (the discharge from non-gonococcal urethritis) would clear up after a few days in hospital receiving jabs of penicillin. Meanwhile, the 'sexual revolution' of the 1960s blew away the last cobwebs of guilt formerly associated with VD infection.

And so unit VD infection rates leaped to heights inconceivable to previous generations of medical officers. Rates of 446 VD cases per thousand troops in Japan, 386 in Korea and 415 in Malaya! Such figures would have been the stuff of nightmares for Army medical officers in World Wars I and II.

They were, however, the new reality for their successors, the ADF doctors of the later 20th century.

CHAPTER 10

Vietnam, 1962-1975

Like World Wars I and II, the Vietnam War proved to be a 20th century national turning point for Australia. In retrospect, the Vietnam War can be seen as a war that changed Australia forever.

1. Background to the Vietnam War

1969; and the Battle of Binh Ba from 6 to 8 June 1969. Much effort also went into patrols in Phuoc Tuy Province, aimed at maintaining pressure on the communist units and denying them access to local communities.[3] In many engagements they had superior communications, equipment and air support.

Until 1954 Vietnam was a colony within a group of contiguous colonial territories held by France and collectively known as French Indochina. This region in South-East Asia comprised the now independent nations of Cambodia, Laos and Vietnam. The region was continuously afflicted by warfare from the beginning of World War II until 1975, when the USA withdrew its military forces from the region.

During that 30-year period, three separate end-on wars were fought in Vietnam—the Vietnamese nationalists against the Japanese during World War II, then against the French, and finally against the Americans and their allies.

The combatants in these conflicts were the South Vietnamese communists, often called the 'Viet Cong', who fought a guerrilla war against the government of the Republic of [South] Vietnam. The Viet Cong were supported by their North Vietnam communist allies, who in turn were backed by the communist regimes in China and the Soviet Union. On the other side was the Republic of Vietnam, commonly known as South Vietnam, which had major support from the USA and its allies, including Australia.

After 1963 the conflict escalated into a prolonged war as the Allies poured in more troops and North Vietnamese forces entered South Vietnam to support the Viet Cong. The war ended in victory for the Viet Cong-North Vietnamese alliance when Saigon, the capital of South Vietnam, fell to the communist forces on 30 April 1975.[1]

2. Australian involvement in the Vietnam War

The Australian involvement in Vietnam lasted 11 years, from July 1962 until June 1973. About 60,000 Australian military personnel served in Vietnam, over 49,200 of these with the Army.[2]

During their time in Vietnam, Australian troops fought a series of major, sometimes costly battles in which they acquitted themselves well against often superior numbers. These included the Battle of Long Tan on 18 and 19 August 1966; the Battle of Ap My An on 17 and 18 February 1967; the defence of Bien Hoa and Ba Ria during the Tet Offensive of January and February 1968; the Battle of Coral-Balmoral during May and June 1968; the long-running Battle of Hat Dich between December 1968 and February

The war became increasingly unpopular and divisive in Australia. Many Australians took the view that Australia should not be involved because it was essentially a *nationalist* war against the US domination of South Vietnam as well as a *civil* war between communist and anti-communist Vietnamese in South Vietnam. The countervailing view was that, like the Korean War, the war in Vietnam was one in which communist aggressors had mounted a war against an anti-communist majority who had no wish to fall under communist rule. Under those circumstances, Australia should militarily help South Vietnam, an ally, defend itself against a communist takeover.[4]

Apart from those competing perspectives, great controversy in Australia arose also over the deployment to Vietnam of 20-year old conscripts who were still not old enough to vote. Their random selection for service by a ballot based on birthdates was seen as grossly unfair: the majority of Australia's 20-year-olds were not conscripted, but those balloted were, and some of them would be killed.[5] A total of 15,381 conscripted national servicemen were sent to Vietnam between 1965 and 1972. Of these, 202 were killed and 1279 wounded. The conscripts suffered a somewhat higher casualty rate, comprising 39 per cent of the dead but 31 per cent of the 49,211 Australian soldiers who served in Vietnam.[6]

Realising that the tide of public opinion on the war was turning and might even lead to a change in government, the Gorton coalition government (1968 to 1971) began scaling back its commitment to the war in late 1970. Its successor, the McMahon coalition government (1971 to 1972), continued the process which was concluded by the Whitlam Labor government (1972 to 1975). Nearly all the remaining troops were brought back to Australia in early 1973. Only a platoon remained to guard the Australian Embassy in Saigon. That, too, was withdrawn during June 1973.[7]

In the weeks before Saigon fell to communist forces on 30 April 1975, a detachment of eight RAAF Hercules aircraft undertook a series of humanitarian missions. They evacuated civilians displaced by the war, including Vietnamese orphans. Their final airlift, on 25 April, was to return embassy staff to Australia.[8]

3. Medical support of the Australian forces in Vietnam

The first Australian soldiers sent to Vietnam, the Australian Army Training Team, relied on US Army medical support. If they needed hospital treatment, they went to the US 8th Field Hospital at Nha Trang. Any suffering major injuries or illnesses were air-evacuated to the Philippines, where they were admitted into a US military hospital at the Clark Field air base.[9] As the war and Australia's involvement escalated other arrangements, described below, became necessary.

1st Australian Taskforce and the 2nd Field Ambulance

When the Australian government sent more troops to Vietnam to form the 1st Australian Taskforce (1 ATF) in 1965, the number of RAAMC personnel increased to 121. The main medical unit, the 2nd Field Ambulance (2 Fd Amb), was under the command of Lieutenant Colonel W.O. ('Bill') Rodgers.[10] The unit was located at the 1st Australian Logistic Support Group in VungTau but maintained a section at Nui Dat, where the 1 ATF troops would be based. In addition to these facilities, 1 ATF was supported by the RAP attached to the major operational units comprising 1 ATF. Although only two-thirds the size of previous field ambulances, 2 Fd Amb was expected to fulfil the same role, including the ability to move forward to support front-line operations.[11]

Despite its limited size, 2 Fd Amb was obliged to treat large numbers of wounded and sick troops. It had two marquees with 25 beds each at Vung Tau and a forward section with 10 beds for minor sick and injured cases at Nui Dat.[12] Additional support was provided by the US Army's 3rd Field Hospital in Saigon and 36th Evacuation Hospital in Vung Tau, which had a comprehensive range of surgical, laboratory, X-ray and pharmacy facilities.[13]

Australian Force Vietnam and 8th Field Ambulance

In October 1967 the Australian government increased its commitment to the war. A third battalion was added to the Australian Army forces in Vietnam, which was henceforth known as Australian Force Vietnam (AFV). This increased the overall AFV strength to 8000 service personnel.[14]

The 8th Field Ambulance (8 Fd Amb) succeeded 2 Fd Amb in April 1965. The unit commander of 8 Fd Amb was Lieutenant Colonel Ralph Meyer. As previously with 2 Fd Amb, 8 Fd Amb had access to the US 36th Evacuation Hospital at Vung Tau and the 24th Evacuation Hospital at Long Binh. In addition, convalescent cases were sent to the new US 6th Convalescent Hospital at Cam Ranh Bay.[15]

Meyer continued Lieutenant Colonel Rodgers' task of building up the amenities at Vung Tau and Nui Dat. In time these began resembling modern hospital complexes as the tented facilities were replaced by permanent wards plus accommodation, kitchen, stores, and power supply blocks. The planting of lawns and trees and the laying down of sealed roads and concrete paths gave the impression that the Australians were establishing permanent facilities and were in Vietnam for the long term.[16]

1st Australian Field Hospital

The DGMS, Major General Colin Gurner, agreed to expand the AFV medical facilities by establishing a 100-bed field hospital at Vung Tau with a field ambulance element at Nui Dat. These facilities were in place by early 1968. The innovations were timely because they provided the capacity to deal with the casualties from the Viet Cong's Tet Offensive in early 1968.[17]

Figure 10.1: Aerial view of the 1st Australian Field Hospital, Vung Tau, Vietnam, 1970 (AWM P04655.886).

1st Australian Field Hospital (1 AFH) was commanded by Lieutenant Colonel William Watson, who had served as the RMO of 1 RAR in Malaya during 1959 and 1960. The unit took over 8 Fd Amb's 60-bed facility at Vung Tau, which was soon expanded to 100-bed capacity, but 8 Fd Amb continued running the 10-bed unit at Nui Dat. The 1 AFH staff establishment was initially set at 125, comprising 18 officers and 107 other ranks, but was later raised to 160.[18]

By early 1970 the medical support for AFV had become 'extensive and sophisticated ... with [1 AFH] at its heart'.[19] The hospital had developed into a campus of 63 buildings on a 3.2-hectare site. It had a 110-bed capacity with 50 beds each for medical and surgical cases plus 10 for intensive care patients.[20]

At the head of the RAAMC's organisation in Vietnam was the ADMS. This position was successively filled by five RAAMC lieutenant colonels.[21] 1 AFH eventually closed at VungTau on 21 November 1971. Its place was briefly taken by a reduced 8 Fd Amb, which was brought back from Nui Dat after passing its responsibilities there to the Army of the Republic of Vietnam units. The departure of 8 Fd Amb from Vietnam took place on 29 February 1972. By October 1972 only 131 Australian service personnel remained in Vietnam. After 8 Fd Amb departed, the medical needs of the remaining AFV troops became the responsibility of a single medical officer assisted by a medical orderly until they, too, were withdrawn on 18 December.[22]

4. VD statistics in the Australian Army in Vietnam

Unlike the deployments to Japan and Korea, Vietnam was a war in which the medical arrangements were statistically well-documented. The Vietnam War was, moreover, one in which the nine-volume official Australian war history series included a volume on the medical aspects of the war. Published under the general title *The Official History of Australia's Involvement in Southeast-Asian Conflicts 1948-1975*, the series dealt with the Malayan Emergency and Indonesian Confrontation of Malaysia as well as Vietnam.[23]

The medical volume, by Brendan O'Keefe, was published in 1994 under the title *Medicine at War: Medical aspects of Australia's involvement in Southeast Asia 1950-1972*.[24] Part 4 of this book was an 80-page dissertation on the 'Agent Orange' controversy by Professor F.B. Smith of the Australian National University.[25]

O'Keefe's volume was in the tradition of the official Australian military medical histories of Arthur G. Butler and Allan S. Walker, respectively the official medical historians of World War I and World War II. Like Butler (but not Walker), O'Keefe included a comprehensive and detailed set of statistical tables showing the number of cases and the rate of incidence of the various categories of injuries and diseases.[26]

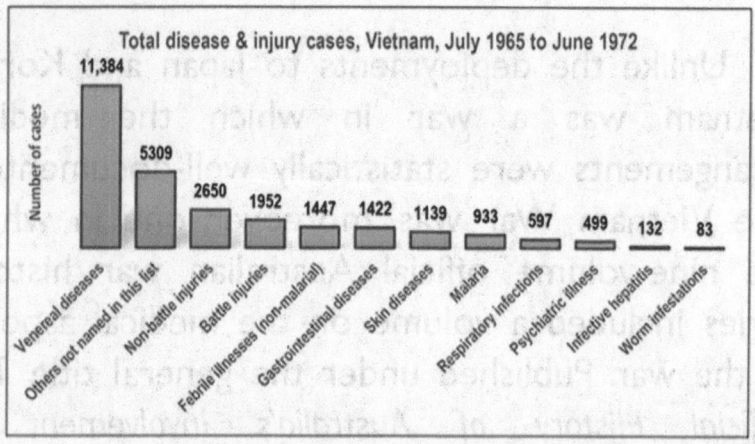

Figure 10.2: Incidence of VD infection compared to other disease and injury cases for Australian troops in Vietnam, 1965-1972 (Brendan O'Keefe, Medicine at War, Tables 6-21, Appendix C).

The chart included here, Figure 10.2, is derived from O'Keefe's statistical tables, and shows the incidence of the major injury and disease groups in the seven years from July 1965 to June 1972.[27] The reason why the date range does not extend across the full 11-year period of the Army's deployment to Vietnam, 1962 to 1973, is that the data for some categories are not available for the period before July 1965 and after June 1972.

As the chart suggests, VD was by far the most common reason for Australian troops being treated in Vietnam either as inpatients or outpatients. Apart from 'other diseases' (which included many of the tropical diseases such as scrub typhus, leptospirosis and viral encephalitis), the next most common category was injuries resulting from either battlefield or 'non-battle' causes. VD exceeded injuries by a factor of 2.5.

The figures in the chart also indicate that the number of VD cases in Vietnam was 12 times those for malaria—11,384 cases of VD compared with 933 for malaria. Yet the Australian Army suffered one of its worst ever epidemics of malaria in Vietnam.[28] If 933 malaria hospitalisations were an 'epidemic', the 11,384 VD cases represented an epidemic too, of major proportion.

O'Keefe's VD statistics are comprehensive enough to permit assessment of the trends in VD infection. The next chart, Figure 10.3, shows the monthly incidence of VD among the Australians in Vietnam from May 1966 until February 1972. As well as the number of monthly cases, the chart indicates the monthly rate of infections, namely, the number of cases per thousand troops.

The trend-line fitted to the chart in Figure 10.3 indicates an overall downward trend for VD infections. The medical officer 'on the ground' in Vietnam might not have seen this trend because both the incidence and rate of VD infections remained historically high.

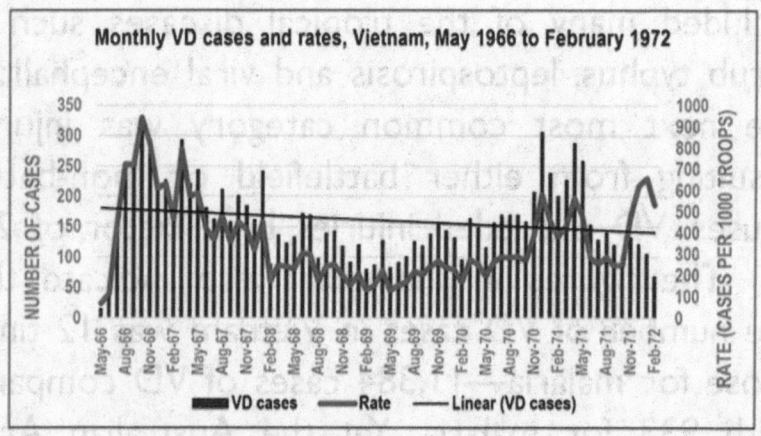

Figure 10.3: Monthly incidence of VD among Australian troops in Vietnam, 1966-1972 (Brendan O'Keefe, Medicine at War, Tables 6-21, Appendix C).

The total number of known cases for VD in Vietnam was 11,384 cases, though because of gaps in some monthly figures the total number of cases represented in Figure 10.3 is 11,215. The average number of VD cases across the 71 months covered in Figure 10.3 was 160 a month.[29]

As for case *rates*, O'Keefe provided monthly and six-monthly rates per thousand troops. He did not, however, give an overall rate for the

11 years the Army had troops in Vietnam. The rate may be readily estimated. Given that 49,211 Australian soldiers were deployed to Vietnam between 1962 and 1973, and that 11,384 VD cases occurred, the overall VD rate was 231 per thousand troops. Those figures indicate that between a quarter and a fifth of the troops sent to Vietnam contracted VD.

A rate of 231 was only half as high as the 446 'scored' by BCOF in Japan, but it was 1.6 times higher than the previous highest rate, 148 in the 1st AIF in Britain 1916 to 1919. Of nine major deployments during the 20th century for which comparable figures exist, Vietnam ranked fourth in terms of VD infection rates, as shown in Figure 10.4.

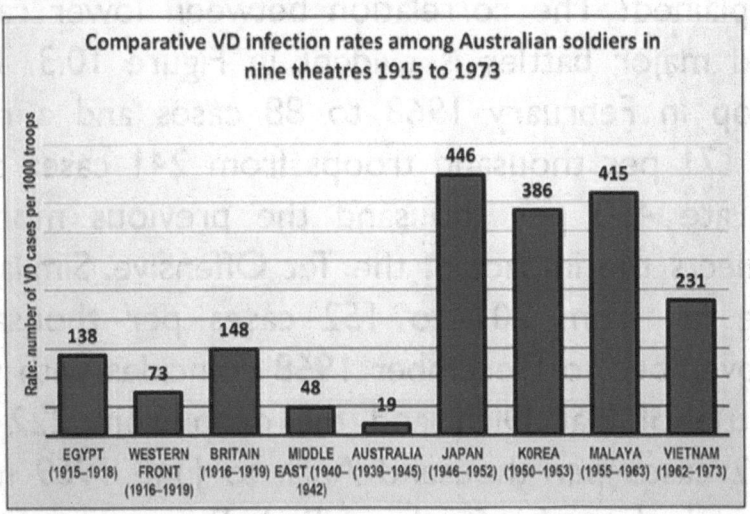

Figure 10.4: VD infection rates among Australian soldiers compared across nine theatres, 1915-1973 (derived from A.G. Butler, Special Problems and Services; A.S. Walker,

Clinical Problems of War, R.N.L. Hopkins, 'Control of VD'; C. Scales, 'Venereal disease, BCOF'; 'Brief History of the Medical Services BCOF'; F.J. Ingham 'Discussion on medical problems in Korea'; Brendan O'Keefe, Medicine at War).

The overall Vietnam rate of 231 is deceptive for it conceals the great variations from month to month revealed in Figure 10.3. As that chart indicates, the highest monthly rate was an astounding 943 cases per thousand troops in October 1966; the lowest was 68 per thousand in May that same year. Apart from October 1966 (324 cases), the highest monthly incidence was 306 cases in December 1970, while the lowest (apart from early 1966) was 88 in February 1968.

How might these huge fluctuations be explained? The correlation between lower rates and major battles is evident in Figure 10.3. The drop in February 1968 to 88 cases and a rate of 171 per thousand troops from 241 cases and a rate 450 per thousand the previous month, reflects the impact of the Tet Offensive. Similarly, the fall from 201 to 152 cases per thousand November to December 1968 coincides with the Battle of Hat Dich, and the drop from 222 to 152 cases per thousand April to June 1969 may be linked to the Battle of Binh Ba.

The number of cases and rates also fluctuated annually, as Table 10.1 indicates.[30]

The peak year was 1967, when the number of cases reached 2407 and the rate was 478 cases per thousand. By contrast, 1969 was a relatively 'low' year for both cases and rate: 1361 cases were recorded, representing a rate of 193 cases per thousand troops.

Table 10.1-**Annual figures for VD cases and rates, Australian Army, Vietnam, 1965-1972**

Year	VD cases	Average strength	Rate per 1000 troops
1965	105	1327	79
1966	1596	3670	435
1967	2407	5034	478
1968	1656	6733	246
1969	1361	7048	193
1970	1987	6928	287
1971	2098	5471	383
1972	174	771	226
Total	11,384		

Source: Brendan O'Keefe, Medicine at War, Tables 6-21, Appendix C.

The 1967 rate, 478, was extraordinarily high. It was the highest longterm rate recorded in the Australian Army during the 20th century, exceeding the rate of 446 per thousand among BCOF in Japan two decades earlier. The overall long-term rate for Vietnam, 231 per thousand, was less than half that, however.

The total number of 11,384 VD cases is an underestimate because it does not include the unknown number of cases that occurred in the period 1962 to 1964, when records were not systematically kept. Nor can it include the cases occurring among soldiers who sought private treatment rather than report their infections to RAAMC units.

Australian Army VD rates compared very unfavourably with those of the French troops, who departed when France quit Vietnam in July 1954. In the nine-year period from the end of World War II until 1954, the number of VD infections among the French and Colonial French troops in Vietnam had totalled a huge 207,436 cases—18 times more than the Australian total across 11 years. The French, however, had maintained a large army of 190,000 in Vietnam—the French Expeditionary Corps—which was 27 times the size of AFV in its peak year, 1969. The overall VD rate of the French force was 14.4 cases per thousand troops, or only a sixteenth that of the Australians.[31]

What does the Australian Army's 11-year overall VD rate of 231 cases per thousand troops signify? The VD cases were the equivalent of 23 per cent of all the Australian soldiers who served in Vietnam. The word 'equivalent' is used advisedly here because of the unknown number of repeat VD infections, meaning that the actual proportion of troops who contracted VD would have been somewhat less than 23 per cent. Using 23 per cent as a rough guide, it could be said that as many as one in five Australian troops who went to Vietnam contracted VD there.

At first sight, that might seem a disturbing proportion, a figure reflecting poorly on the soldiers of AFV, the Army they belonged to, and the nation from which they came. There is another way of looking at the proportions, however, because 77 per cent of the Australians in Vietnam did *not* contract VD. The soldiers within that large majority preferred to spend their leisure time in activities other than booze and sex. Similarly, it may be said that the majority were careful about their health, upheld the traditional moral values of their home society and took care to maintain the Army's reputation as a formation which, under the law, maintained high standards of personal and institutional integrity.

5. Policy and practice in controlling VD among the Australians in Vietnam, 1962-1968

Initially VD was not a problem for the Australians in Vietnam. Few of the Australian Army Training Team Vietnam contracted cases of VD because they spent most of their time in the field with little opportunity for sexual liaisons. It was only after I RAR arrived in Vietnam mid-1965 that the incidence of VD began rising.

American and Australian soldiers often spent their local leave in Vung Tau, which became a resort town with a thriving sex trade. The VD infection rate among I RAR troops soared to heights never before experienced by the Australian Army. The Australian Task Force commanders in Vietnam quickly responded with a series of anti-VD measures. In cooperation with the Americans and the Vung Tau municipal authorities, they introduced provost patrols among the proliferating brothels to try to prevent servicemen from frequenting the bars that were known to be fronts for brothels. A contact tracing system was introduced to identify the women thought to have infected soldiers. Proprietors of the bars and brothels where the women worked were pressured to ensure that the women received medical treatment. The premises of proprietors who failed to comply were declared out of bounds to servicemen.[32]

'These efforts at control were conspicuously unsuccessful,' O'Keefe, the official historian, observed.[33] The VD rate continued soaring, to 447 cases per thousand troops in July 1966, 722 in August and then the astonishing figure of 943 in October. That was the highest incidence of VD recorded in the Australian Army during the 20th century.

Reasons for failure of the anti-VD measures were complex. First, there was a logistical problem. As the bars and brothels of Vung Tau multiplied in response to demand, there were simply too many for the military police to patrol. Second, even if the soldiers had condoms, the prostitutes objected to their use. A soldier wearing a condom took longer to reach orgasm, whereas the prostitute was under pressure from her employer to hasten client through-put in order for her to service more clients and maximise the proprietor's profits. Third, even if the soldier had a condom and remembered to use it, he was often too drunk to fit it correctly.[34]

Figure 10.5: Bar girls in the entrance to the 'Texas Bar', Vung Tau, chatting with American soldiers as a Vietnamese boy claims the attention of one soldier. The sign in the barred window is the Approved Premises' certificate which bar proprietors could display if the women working in their establishments had been issued with identity cards (AWM P00510.021).

The determination of the Vietnamese prostitutes in securing as many customers as possible was truly remarkable. Captain Gavin Hart, an RAAMC medical officer who later specialised in venereology, wrote about this decades later in his autobiography:

> Most soldiers who visited the towns patronised the bars, which were really specialised brothels. There were dozens of these establishments which employed young girls to, firstly encourage customers to patronise their establishment, and then

'entertain' them for a fee. Any westerner walking the streets would be accosted by these girls, usually clutching the man by the penis (the 'Vung Tau handshake') and attempting to lead him into the bar, as a more conventional host would lead someone by the hand ... [Inside the bar] from the outset the girls unfastened a man's trousers and proceeded to perform various sexual acts, demanding various quantities of 'tea'[cash] depending on the act ... This type of activity was not confined to a particular time of the day, nor to a location or type of establishment. Soldiers, on duty, visiting a café on the roadside or in a village, were provided with the same condiments with their refreshments. Some pimps were particularly enterprising and would transport a girl on the back of a scooter to service a section of men (10 soldiers) on the roadside while they were patrolling or undertaking roadworks.[35]

In July 1968, the CO of 3 RAR, Lieutenant Colonel Jeffrey Shelton, responded to the latest set of VD statistics by pointing out to his superiors in Australian Task Force Headquarters why the figures remained at high levels. The problem, he wrote, was that 'basically the men miss female company, and at present the only accessible females are prostitutes'.[36] He also observed that 'the simplest way to prevent VD is to cut the soldiers off from the prostitutes' by keeping them in the field and away from towns. That, however, was not practicable because they needed 'to relax and unwind from months of living in the field and complying with rigid routines'.[37] Shelton argued that because 'it [was] most noticeable how the soldiers improve in efficiency after even a few days' break', they needed time in town—even if that meant some would contract VD.[38]

Despite the failure of the anti-VD measures during 1966 and 1967, the Task Force commanders and their medical officers were obliged to keep persevering in their effort to reduce the incidence of VD. They were mindful that in Australia opposition to the war was mounting, especially to sending National Service conscripts to Vietnam. If the high VD rates continued, this would inevitably become public knowledge in Australia, be politically controversial and add to the ferment of anti-war protest, including vilification of the Army and service personnel.[39]

This realisation prompted the commander of the 8 Fd Amb, Lieutenant Colonel Rodgers, to institute a free clinic service for prostitutes in Vung Tau. The service, conducted cooperatively with the Vietnamese health authorities, provided regular examinations and treatment for prostitutes. Rodgers recognised that the service would have no effect on soldier behaviour, but he hoped it might 'reduce the pool of infection'.[40]

The behaviour of the Australian soldiers remained a continuing concern for the Task Force commanders. During 1967 and 1968 the sustained high VD rates gave rise to additional anti-VD measures. First among these was the introduction of a registration system for 'bar girls', a euphemism for prostitutes. Those registered received a 'clinical card' which showed what treatment they had received and included an identifying photograph. This system lasted only a short period because it was fraught with problems. First, the prostitute population changed constantly. Second, many prostitutes refused registration. Third, to be able to keep working many of the women self-treated with penicillin of dubious quality, which would not fully heal them and which could lead to the emergence of penicillin-resistant strains of VD. Fourth, the Australian military authorities had no control over Allied soldiers, who introduced strains of VD from elsewhere in Asia. Fifth, the military police were too few to patrol the bars and brothels in order to monitor the registration system and ensure that the Australian solders did not frequent bars that had been declared out of bounds.[41]

One scheme that came to nothing was a proposal for the establishment of controlled brothels for Allied servicemen in Vung Tau. The idea was suggested to Lieutenant Colonel Laurence C. Chambers, the CO of the 1st Australian Logistic Support Group, by the local Vietnamese governor. For various reasons their plan went nowhere. The local US commander rejected it outright, fearing public opinion in America. The Australian Army was unlikely to have approved the plan because a similar scheme had already received adverse press publicity in Australia and questions had been raised in parliament. The chaplains, moreover, were becoming restive about the absence of references to morality in the Army's new draft instructions on VD management, and they would certainly have opposed the idea strenuously.[42]

Yet another scheme was a ban on soldiers being allowed to spend the night away from camp. This was accompanied by systematic raids on out-of-bounds premises by the military police.[43]

With 1967 turning into 1968, the medical statistics for the past year demonstrated that 1967 had produced the Army's highest ever long-term VD infection rate—478 cases per thousand troops. This indicated that the equivalent of almost one soldier in two of the Australians in Vietnam, had contracted VD during the year.

Reviewing these figures a generation later, O'Keefe concluded wryly that despite all the Army's anti-VD measures, 'for their part, the Australian servicemen displayed no greater inclination to exercise restraint or take precautions'.[44]

As things turned out, 1968 saw a fall in both the number and rate of VD cases. The number fell from 2407 to 1656 and the rate dropped from 478 to 246 per thousand. This was despite the increase in average strength of AFV by 1700 troops to 6733. The figures declined again the next year, 1969, the annual tally of cases down to 1361 and the annual rate to 193 per thousand, again despite an increase in average AFV strength to a historic high of 7048.

The downward trend in the VD statistics, which is clearly seen in Figure 10.3, reflected the changed operational situation after the Tet Offensive. The troops generally spent more time in the field and less in Vung Tau. At the same time, the new AFV Commander, Major General Arthur L. MacDonald, conducted a vigorous campaign to reduce the incidence of VD. Platoon and company commanders were required to lecture their troops regularly on the dangers of VD. Educational films displayed hideous images of its devastation. Soldiers going on leave were given cards containing 'VD Facts'.[45] These measures had all been tried before in other theatres and other wars, often with little effect. Whether MacDonald's initiatives resulted in anything but a brief and temporary reduction in VD infections is doubtful. After reaching a low point of 79 cases and a rate of 131 per thousand in February 1969, the figures began rising again and remained high for the rest of the war.

6. Policy and practice in VD control, 1969-1973

In 1969 the US Commander in Vung Tau put in place a vigorous action plan to reduce the incidence of VD infections among American troops. Appalled that the local US rate had risen to 300 cases per thousand troops, he secured the cooperation of the city's civil authorities and the other Allied forces, including AFV, in conducting a concerted campaign against the Vung Tau vice trade.[46] The main objectives and strategies of the campaign included these:
- drastic reduction of VD among the city's prostitutes through measures such as (a)

- monthly pelvic examinations, (b) monthly serological tests and (c) fortnightly penicillin injections
- vigorous contact tracing of women believed to have transmitted VD to service personnel
- establishment of a centralised VD medical examination and treatment facility—a VD clinic at the Vietnamese Le Loi Hospital which would be supported by the US 36th Evacuation Hospital
- introduction of identity cards issued to all prostitutes proved to be VD-free and withheld from those found to be VD-infected
- regular inspections of the Vung Tau bars to ensure that the women working there could produce their identity cards
- issuing of a 'Certificate of Approval' to bars in which the women all had identity cards; such certificates to be prominently displayed
- declaring bars that did not have the requisite 'Approved' status to be out of bounds to service personnel.[47]

All these strategies were introduced. They had only limited and temporary success, because the Allies soon discovered that their campaign had a 'darker' side. 'As they tried to carry it through,' O'Keefe points out, 'they found themselves dragged ever deeper into the mire of corruption and vice that existed in Vung Tau.'[48]

One insurmountable obstacle to the success of the campaign was the financial involvement of the Vietnamese police, civic authorities and senior officials in the Vung Tau sex industry. Many people in the Vietnamese community, not just the bar proprietors, had vested interests in prostitution which the US-led campaign threatened. The campaign effectively ended in August 1969 when the mayor of Vung Tau unilaterally cancelled it. One effect of that was an immediate spike in the Australian VD statistics: from September to November 1969 the number of VD cases rose from 118 to 153 a month, while the rate increased from 204 to 237 per thousand.[49]

The campaign resumed after the new CO of the 1st Australian Logistic Support Group, Colonel Maxwell Simkin, and the head of the AFV Provost Unit's Special Investigations Branch, Captain M.G. Ramsay, consulted the mayor. They suggested that unless he reinstituted the program, Vung Tau would be declared out of bounds to Australian soldiers. The mayor quickly succumbed to their threat because the economy of the city largely depended on the Allied military bases nearby. There was a catch, however—the Australian Provosts checking the bars must examine the bars' financial records to ensure that the proprietors and their employees were paying their taxes. Reluctantly, Simkin and Ramsay agreed to this proviso but insisted they would not withhold the coveted 'Approved' status simply because of unpaid taxes.[50]

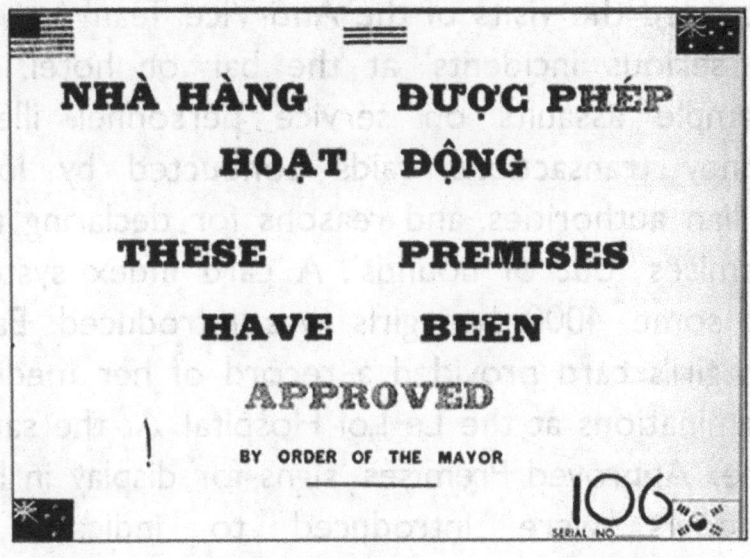

Figure 10.6: The 'Approved Premises' sign for display in bar windows to indicate that a bar was 'in bounds' for service personnel because its female employees had been medically examined and declared 'VD-free' (image courtesy of Max Simkin for use by Brendan O'Keefe, Medicine at War, p.202).

To carry out the necessary surveillance, Colonel Simkin established an 'Anti-Vice Team'. Its responsibility was assisting with the control of VD and Bounds within the City of Vung Tau'. It drew its membership from both the AFV

Provost Unit and the Vietnamese police, supplemented when necessary by US military police.[51]

The task of the Anti-Vice Team was huge. A total of 168 bars and hotels were declared 'in bounds'. A file was maintained on each. It recorded the visits of the Anti-Vice Team as well as 'serious incidents' at the bar or hotel, for example assaults on service personnel, illegal money transactions, raids conducted by local civilian authorities, and reasons for declaring the premises 'out of bounds'. A card index system for some 4000 bar girls was introduced. Each bar girl's card provided a record of her medical examinations at the Le Loi Hospital. At the same time, 'Approved Premises' signs for display in bar windows were introduced to indicate to customers which bars were 'in bounds'.[52]

The revived program made little impact on VD levels among the Australians. Both the incidence of VD and the VD rate continued rising throughout 1970 and 1971. The monthly number of cases reached a four-year high of 306 in December 1970 while the monthly rate rose to 583 per thousand.

Figure 10.7: Australian soldiers in civilian dress approach the 'Mexico' and 'Texas' bars, Vung Tau, 1971 (AWMP00510.022).

The program was 'hampered by Vietnamese dishonesty'.[53] Bar proprietors duplicated the 'Approved' certificates. The certificates had to be made more complex and multicoloured to defeat the forgers. A black-market trade in bar girls' identity cards soon developed. In any case, even a genuine identity card was no guarantee that its bearer was 'clean' because she could well have been infected by her next client after her fortnightly medical examination. Further, the medical examination did not include a test for nongonococcal urethritis, which was common among both the bar girls and their customers. Yet another impediment was that bar managers often sacked employees proved to be

VD-infected. Jobless, the women then took to street prostitution, which was beyond medical and legal control.[54]

O'Keefe observed that 'if the renewed program were to have any impact at all, the Australians would have to find answers quickly to all these problems'. The answers do not seem to have been found.[55]

Vietnamese culture was yet another difficulty. Prostitution in Vietnam was not regarded as 'morally reprehensible' as in many Western nations, Australia included. Most often the prostitutes were from rural peasant communities which sold or hired out their young women to the bar proprietors in the cities. As prostitutes the women could earn $500 a month, double what their fathers gained from a year's labour as farmers. Their earnings helped support their families in their home villages. Prostitution enabled them to fulfil their filial obligations, and to be considered dutiful by doing so. And so the prostitutes of Vung Tau 'had compelling cultural and economic motives to work in their trade'. At the same time, 'economic necessity often demanded that they continue working' regardless of being VD-infected.[56]

Despite the very high rates of infection, VD, unlike malaria, had only a relatively minor impact on AFV manpower. In early 1971 the ADMS,

Lieutenant Colonel Keith Fleming, pointed this out to the new AFV Commander, Major General Donald Dunstan. He argued that VD was 'neither a military nor medical problem in AFV'.[57]

Technically speaking, Fleming was correct. Most VD cases in Vietnam caused only a day or two per episode of lost time. The 11,384 known cases of VD in Vietnam would have amounted to no more than 22,770 lost days, or the equivalent of 62 'man-years'. Considered from that perspective, it seemed a lot but it was only a fraction of the figures from earlier wars. In Vietnam, an average of 5.6 man-years were lost to VD annually; in the UK 1916 to 1919 the comparable figure, 92.5 man-years annually, was higher by a factor of 16.5.

Major General Dunstan was not convinced by relativities like these. The monthly tally of new VD infections told him a different tale. By April 1971 the monthly number of cases had risen to 288 and the rate to 563 cases per thousand of AFV strength. These figures were the fourth highest in the five years since early 1966. Dunstan informed Fleming and his fellow medical colleagues that as RAAMC officers they had a responsibility to advise him how to reduce the incidence of VD.[58]

The CO's views caused the AFV medical officers to reappraise the VD control measures critically during 1971. They were sceptical of the effectiveness of the program of prostitute identity cards, medical examinations and the 'Approved' bars. For all the effort, the results were meagre and had little effect in reducing the overall VD rate. Indeed, the program was having the reverse effect because it lulled soldiers into a false sense of security, encouraging them to neglect precautionary procedures such as using condoms. The medical officers proposed another approach. They recommended that AFV should select a small number of bars for use by Australian soldiers and then impose stringent conditions on the women working in them.[59]

This proposal provoked dissent among other AFV senior officers. Their view was encapsulated in an observation by the CO of the 1st Australian Civil Affairs Unit, Lieutenant Colonel Lawrence Wright. In a long report on anti-VD measures, Wright argued that the doctors' recommendation ignored 'the social, moral and political pressures on the [AFV] Commander'. The RAAMC officers were proposing a scheme that was tantamount to the unacceptable expedient of establishing official Army brothels in Vietnam.[60] The medical officers' proposal was not implemented. Instead, the existing arrangements remained in place until the withdrawal of most of the Australian units from Vietnam during 1972.[61]

The discussion of these issues led to a re-statement of the Army's traditional position on VD in a document titled 'Command and Military Aspects of Venereal Disease'. It began by proclaiming that 'venereal disease has been accepted by Army Commanders over the centuries as a disease which always threatens the efficiency and morale of their troops ... and the greatest single cause of ineffective service'. Despite modern medicine, 'the mental effects, effects on morale and loss of man hours still serve as a constant reminder to commanders of the problems associated with this disease'.[62]

The document argued that the efficiency of an army depended on discipline, which in turn depended largely on the self-discipline of its troops. A series of tendentious statements followed:

- Self-discipline was required in relation to sexual appetite because 'the most effective method of escaping venereal disease is abstention from sexual intercourse'.
- 'An erect penis has no conscience', that is, many soldiers lost their sense of right and wrong when sexual opportunities arose.
- The possibility of transmitting VD to their wives was causing 'tremendous mental

upsets' to many married men who contracted VD, and that 'causes their standard of work to deteriorate and endangers other members of the unit'.
- Each case of VD 'no matter how slight' required at least six trips to the VD clinic, which was 'wasted time to the unit and embarrassing to the individual'.[63]

The document concluded with an affirmation of the 'responsibility of the soldier'. Every soldier, it argued, had a responsibility in relation to VD. The first was to himself, to maintain his own health and welfare. The second was to his family, particularly if he was married. The third was to the Army, as a member of which he was expected to keep himself fit and healthy. Finally, he had a responsibility 'to mankind in general', which obliged him to seek treatment if VD-infected and not to infect others'.[64] This was a step back from the pragmatism that had characterised the Army's approach to VD for the past 30 years. It was redolent of the moralism which had suffused debate over VD during World War I.

Although the proposal by Lieutenant Colonel Fleming and his fellow medical officers for a restricted number of highly controlled bars was rejected, they did get their own way with another innovation. This was the introduction of an American technique for controlling VD—'No Sweat Pills'. These were penicillin capsules that were taken several hours before and after sexual intercourse. Before introducing them, the medical officers had to assess the disadvantages in their use. Among these was the possibility that in giving protection against some STDs, the capsules could obscure syphilis infection. Another was the likelihood that indiscriminate use of the capsules could lead to the development of drug resistance by the VD-causing organisms. Fleming decided in favour of the capsules, pointing out that they were already being widely used in Southeast Asia and were readily available in drugstores. 'If you have a chemoprophylactic agent capable of preventing venereal disease,' he argued, 'you are morally bound to use it.' His recommendation was accepted and the capsules came into use in mid-1971. Rather than containing penicillin, the 'pills' issued were 100-milligram capsules of vibramycin (also called doxycycline), a long-acting form of the antibiotic tetracycline which the medical officers thought would be more effective against gonorrhoea and non-gonococcal urethritis than penicillin. As Figure 10.3 indicates, both the incidence and rate of VD within AFV fell sharply after the capsules were made available.[65]

The finale to the drama of VD among the Australians in Vietnam was played out in the last months of 1971 and early 1972 as the AFV units were being progressively withdrawn and returned home. The monthly rates of infection, though not the actual numbers of cases, shot up again. This reflected the abandonment of the program of medically examining the prostitutes and policing the bars. Meanwhile, the remaining troops had few military duties to distract them from 'having fun', as contemporary idiom put it. Once again, the inverse relationship between the amount of combat and the rate of VD infection was demonstrated.[66]

7. Psychosociology of VD infection among Australian troops in Vietnam

During and after the war, several medical officers who had treated VD in Vietnam wrote about their experiences in the *MJA* but the most important Australian study of VD to emerge from the Vietnam War was the thesis for the degree of Doctor of Medicine (MD) written by an RAAMC medical officer attached to the 1 AFH in Vung Tau, Captain Gavin Hart.[67]

As a result of the seven months he spent working in 1 AFH during 1970, Gavin Hart decided to specialise in venereology. After returning to civilian life he eventually became the chief venereologist in the South Australian public health service. During his service in Vietnam, at 1 AFH in Vung Tau and later at 8 Fd Amb in Nui Dat, he had treated a passing parade of hundreds of patients suffering a great variety of conditions. The range included battlefield injuries, tropical diseases (including scrub typhus, Japanese B encephalitis, amoebiasis, and especially malaria), gastroenteritis, jellyfish stings, snakebite, skin diseases, ear infections, parasitic infestations, and of course VD.[68]

Becoming interested in the epidemiology of VD as a result of treating many VD-infected soldiers, Hart decided to make a special study to identify the social and psychological factors influencing VD infection among soldiers. Encouraged by the physician serving currently at 1 AFH, Major (later Major General Professor) John Pearn, Hart began research on a project entailing the writing of a thesis for the MD degree at the University of Adelaide. Advised by Pearn, Hart chose to research and write on 'The impact of prostitution on Australian troops on active service in a war environment—with particular reference to sociological factors involved in the incidence and control of venereal disease'.[69]

Although Vietnam was not mentioned in the title, the thesis was all about VD among the Australians in Vietnam. Hart considered this theme from different perspectives—geographical, historical, psychological, sociological and clinical. The thesis also inquired into the sex trade in Vietnam, the Army's failure to control VD, the military ramifications of the Army's VD policies, and the wider implications for Australian society of VD among Australians soldiers in Vietnam.[70]

Hart's principal methodological instrument was a multi-choice survey questionnaire containing 98 questions spread across 14 pages. Hart designed this instrument with the help of an RAAMC psychiatrist serving with 1 AFH, Major John Collins. The target population comprised patients attending the VD clinic at 1 AFH. After the draft questionnaire had been distributed for comment to various experts in Australia and Europe, the final version was administered to soldiers visiting the clinic over a three-month period. All soldiers below the rank of sergeant were invited to participate. Most did: 488 accepted and only 27 declined. The reason why sergeants and more senior ranks were not asked to take part was that they were generally hostile to being questioned. Also, they tended to visit the clinic 'after hours' at times inconvenient to clinic staff and unsatisfactory for completing the questionnaire.[71]

The survey was designed to elicit a wide range of information about the individual soldiers who responded to the questionnaire including: the soldier's social class background, family affiliations, marital status, educational attainment, whether he was a regular soldier or conscript, his alcohol consumption habits, previous sexual experience, reasons for *not* engaging in intercourse when the opportunity arose, knowledge about and attitude towards VD, the frequency of his sexual intercourse in Vietnam, whether or not he had used condoms, how often he had suffered previous VD infections, his feelings about his sexual partner(s), the likely attitude of his parents to his sexual experience in Vietnam, the amount of money he paid for sex, whether or not he or his partner initiated intercourse, the venue where he had met the partner, his state of sobriety at the time of intercourse, whether or not he had seen his partner's identity card, his preferred type(s) of sexual habits or activities, his time lost in receiving treatment for VD, his time in hospital, whether or not he would be prepared to marry a Vietnamese woman, and what other diseases he had suffered during service in Vietnam.[72]

To allay the subjects' fears about being questioned at length on such personal matters, they were assured that the responses to the questionnaire were strictly confidential. Participants took about an hour to complete the questionnaire but generally enjoyed the experience, probably because it was a diversion from their routine military duties.[73]

Hart's research revealed much about the psychosociology of VD infection among the Australians in Vietnam. He published his findings in a series of journal articles as well as detailing them in his MD thesis.[74] Among his conclusions were these:

1. VD was more common among younger, single soldiers, those of lower educational attainment, those who had consumed more alcohol, and those who had been charged more often for military offences. Alcohol was a key factor in contracting VD because it helped intensify sexual urges, reduced inhibitions and often rendered soldiers incapable of using condoms.[75]
2. Sociological factors arising from the soldiers' social class background were important determinants because soldiers in the Regular Army were more likely to contract VD than those who were

conscripts (and therefore serving in the Army for only two years). The survey revealed that in that Vietnam era the former group were generally of limited education, from large families, indulged in sex at an earlier age, met with less parental disapproval for doing so, when married were less constrained by their marriage vows, were more reluctant to use masturbation as a sexual outlet, and were more indiscriminate in choosing sexual partners. The professional soldier (member of the Regular Army) was prone to VD because of his characteristic sociological background and he contributed disproportionately to the VD problem both in his stable homeland environment and when he went to war'.[76]

3. Psychological factors were also significant in contracting VD because as a group the VD-infected soldiers were more extroverted, more neurotic, and more intent on proving their manhood by catching a 'dose' of VD. Religious belief played little part in their attitudes towards sex. Antipathy to the Vietnamese was a common factor. At the same time, perhaps ironically, the soldiers who participated in Hart's survey commonly

experienced guilt and remorse for having become VD-infected. They also felt resentful of senior officers who they suspected of contracting VD but who were then able to seek private treatment, thus avoiding the humiliation of being publicly treated in the same manner as low-ranking soldiers such as themselves. This attitude, Hart concluded, was a considerable obstacle in the Army's anti-VD programs.[77]

Hart himself believed that one of his most important findings related to a condition he referred to as 'venereoneurosis'.[78] This was a term he devised to indicate a depressive and acute anxiety state arising from the emotional impact of prostitution on soldiers who had consorted with prostitutes. It was a condition affecting those who had *not* contracted VD as well as those who had. Perhaps ironically, it was more common among the former group than the latter. He later defined the condition in these terms:

> [The prostitutes'] emotional impact [on the soldiers] was both diverse and complex. Emotional sequelae of their physical role were guilt, shame and anxiety due to conflicts concerning marital infidelity or tarnished moral self-images. Venereoneurosis

was the most significant syndrome arising from this involvement and, being the most common single illness in [the Vietnam] campaign, it had a telling impact on both the soldiers themselves and on the medical services.[79]

Other anxiety conditions related to VD were known to psychiatrists. For example, psychiatrists had been aware of syphilophobia, an inordinate fear of contracting syphilis, since 1911. Hart was the first researcher to identify and name venereoneurosis as an emotional illness characterised by strong feelings of fear and worry arising from extramarital sexual contacts in which contracting VD was a risk.[80]

Hart's conclusions would have made good sense to sociologists, psychologists and medical historians, but his project caused outrage among certain senior RAAMC officers when they discovered the nature of his proposed research. His CO, Lieutenant Colonel Naughton, the commander of 1 AFH, approved the project. He was keen for it to be undertaken because he recognised its value for future commanders. He insisted, however, that Hart write to the DGMS in Canberra, Major General Gurner, to obtain his approval. Hart duly drafted a letter to Gurner with assistance from Naughton and Pearn. This was sent on 19 August 1970. The response from the DGMS arrived several weeks later, declaring that:

> From a medical point of view your proposal is interesting and worthwhile, but the press and political aspects are potential dynamite. Venereal disease is a controversial subject at any time ... A year or so ago it was the subject of many questions in Parliament and articles in the paper. Any complaint from a soldier that his private life was being investigated by the Army could have severe press or political repercussions, particularly with increasing pressure by the public and some churches to end our participation in Vietnam. Even were your work approved, it would be impossible to maintain security of your thesis ... Therefore I cannot give my approval of your proposal, and certainly the Army would not do so.[81]

Meanwhile, Gurner also informed Lieutenant Colonel Bill Rodgers, the Saigon-based ADMS of AFV, of Hart's proposed research. Rodgers immediately despatched an angry telegram to Naughton instructing him that neither Hart nor any other medical officer at 1 AFH should undertake surveys of troops' sexual habits. He demanded that any such research should cease forthwith. He also stated that he strongly objected to not having been informed earlier of the proposed project, and to having been bypassed by Hart writing directly to the DGMS.[82]

Naughton relayed the ADMS's instruction to Hart, formally ordering him to cease work on the project. In his autobiography 45 years later, Hart recalled that when his CO informed him of the directive from the ADMS he had said, 'At the official level I am expressly commanding you to cease. Off the record, I know what I would be doing, but I don't want to know anything about it'. Hart inferred that he had received tacit approval to continue, and so he undertook the research.[83] He completed it by the time his service with 1 AFH concluded in December 1970. He wrote up and published the results in a series of eight articles in major medical journals after returning to Australia in April 1971. He later observed that 'there was no adverse outcome, in fact no controversy'.[84] Twenty years after Hart's MD degree had been awarded, his research findings were incorporated in summary form in Brendan O'Keefe's official medical history of the war.[85]

A storm in a teacup? It was rather more serious than that, for it involved serious issues relating to discipline and the RAAMC chain of command as well as the Army's reputation and the management of the Army's public image during an increasingly unpopular war.

From an official Army perspective, Gavin Hart's research did not occur because his project had been terminated early. A potential public scandal over Australian soldiers' high VD rates in Vietnam had seemingly been nipped in the bud. From the Australian medical standpoint, however, Hart's research was the first serious attempt by an Army medical officer to come to grips with the most common disease afflicting troops in operational service. Hart's study was the first to examine the underlying psychosociological factors producing high VD rates among Australian soldiers deployed overseas. As a result, the complex, subtle interplay between the social and behavioural influences propelling soldiers into VD infection was better understood.

CHAPTER 11

Post-Vietnam deployments, 1976-2000, and some conclusions

After the Australian Army's withdrawal from Vietnam in 1973 and the RAAF's assistance in the evacuation from Saigon in 1975, the Commonwealth Government endeavoured to demonstrate that the nation was a 'Good International Citizen' by committing the ADF (established in 1976) to a series of overseas international peacekeeping and humanitarian deployments.[1]

1. Overseas deployments of the Australian Defence Force, 1976-2000

In the post-Vietnam decades, Australia participated in 31 multinational peacekeeping deployments in 22 nations overseas between 1976 and 2000. Australian military personnel were serving abroad in these operations in each of the

25 years during that period except 1981. A total of 18,019 members of the ADF served in these operations.[2]

Some of these deployments were short-term and involved only several specialist ADF personnel. Others were major operations extending over years and involving thousands of personnel.[3] If past experience were any guide, they would have produced a tally of STD infections.

2. The shifting focus of debate on STDs in Australia

By the time the Vietnam War ended, the term STD was supplanting 'venereal disease' in the lexicon of the medical profession. During the early 21st century, STD would itself yield to 'sexually transmitted infection' (STI).

The reason for these semantic changes reflected the constant change in language, driven by the pervasive pressure of what came to be called 'political correctness'. Another influence was medical professionals' wish to reduce the stigma of particular diseases and thus encourage early attendance at treatment clinics.[4]

STDs remained a topic of lively debate in the *MJA* between 1976 and 2000. The journal published at least 70 major articles or editorials and much correspondence about STDs.[5] None of this material related to the ADF's experience.

From the perspective of the 21st century, what is interesting about the *MJA*'s coverage of STDs is the way the focus of attention shifted between topics. Earlier generations of *MJA* readers learned much about subjects such as VD in the armed services, the rise of penicillin-resistant strains of gonorrhoea and periodic outbreaks of syphilis. By the 1980s the focus had shifted to new areas of concern. These included the rising epidemic of STDs among Indigenous communities in northern Australia, STDs among homosexuals, the link between *Chlamydia trachomatis* and non-gonococcal urethritis, the relationship between prostitution and STD infections, and the functioning of the public STD clinics which had meanwhile been rebranded as 'Communicable Diseases Centres' and 'Sexual Health Clinics'.[6]

From 1984, the *MJA* reported extensively on the mounting epidemic of Acquired Immune Deficiency Syndrome, soon universally known by the acronym AIDS. Its causative agent, the human immunodeficiency virus or HIV, also entered the national lexicon. In 1983 the National Health and Medical Research Council of Australia established a working party on AIDS. Its report, titled simply *Acquired Immune Deficiency Syndrome (AIDS)*, was published the next year.[7] After that, AIDS and HIV research in Australia proliferated and was often dealt with in the *MJA*.

3. STDs in the ADF's overseas deployments between 1976 and 2000

Data on the experience of the ADF with STDs post-Vietnam are unavailable. STDs are not mentioned, let alone discussed, in the two published official military histories of the post-Vietnam era.[8]

The dearth of STD data in the post-Vietnam period reflected what one senior ADF medical officer termed 'the confidentiality crisis' generated by the AIDS epidemic.[9] Very few studies on the Army's experience of STDs during the final quarter of the 20th century were conducted. None was reported in the *MJA* or in more specialised publications such as the *Journal of Military and Veterans' Health*.

One relevant study was for a PhD thesis in the School of Medicine at the University of Queensland. The author was Stephen Lambert, whose thesis title was 'A study of *Chlamydia trachomatis*: sexual risk behaviour, infection and prevention in the Australian Defence Force'.[10]

Lambert conducted his research between 2007 and 2013. Although that period is outside the time frame covered by this book, Lambert's findings shed light on the ADF's continuing experience of STDs.

Lambert's project was a survey-based study of a population of 733 ADF personnel who completed an eight-page questionnaire about their sexual behaviour and also provided a urine sample to be tested for the presence of *C. trachomatis*. The participants included both personnel who were on deployment, and others who were serving at military bases in Australia. They were from all three armed services, viz. Navy, Army, and Air Force. They were dispersed across 10 ADF sites in Australia and four deployment sites overseas. The spread was intended to provide a wide cross-section of the ADF population.[11]

Lambert reached these conclusions:

1. Almost a fifth of participants reported having voluntarily visited a health service because of sexual health concerns in the previous 12 months. ADF females were more likely to have done so than males. The participants were three times as likely to have attended an ADF clinic as a civilian health service.

2. ADF sexual health and sexual behaviour were comparable to what prevailed in the wider Australian population; indeed, in some instances the ADF had greater levels of safe sexual practice and lower levels of risk behaviours.

3. The ADF had a lower prevalence of *C. trachomatis* infection than other comparable overseas military populations, as well as a better sexual health and behaviour profile.

4. *C. trachomatis* infection was associated with the subject's number of recent sexual partners. Those who had had two or more sexual partners in the previous 12 months were five times more likely to test positive for chlamydia infection than those who had had one or no partner.

5. As for *C. trachomatis*, so for other STDs: the presence of an STD correlated with the number of sexual partners.

6. The survey population was frequently deployed. More than a quarter, 26 per cent, were on deployment at the time of the survey, and 42 per cent had been deployed in the previous 12 months.

7. In a welcome reversal of 20th-century experience, those who had been deployed

were *less* likely to test positive for *C. trachomatis* infection.
8. ADF sexual health screening was effective because personnel were obliged to undergo various health checks. These included the ADF Comprehensive Preventive Health Examination as well as examinations pre-and post-deployment.[12] (The screenings routinely checked for HIV-AIDS and hepatitis B & C.)

These findings would have been welcome to earlier generations of ADF doctors inured to the expectation that Australian troops sent overseas would soon attain high STD infection rates and would therefore often try to conceal their diseases.

4. Contemporaneous US military experience with STDs

Even though little is known of the nature and extent of STDs in the ADF in the period 1976 to 2000, Australian parallels may be inferred from the literature on STDs in the US Armed Forces. The US military services, being on a much larger scale than the ADF, have the resources to sponsor medical and sociological research that keeps their commanders well informed about trends in the sexual behaviour of their troops.

A comprehensive updating on the situation with STDs was provided in February 2013 in a special edition of the *Medical Surveillance Monthly Report*, a journal of the US Armed Forces Medical Surveillance Centre. This edition included eight research articles dealing with the 'changing landscape' of STDs in the Armed Forces, the continuing problem posed by the two main STDs (gonorrhoea and chlamydia), the incidence of genital warts, and the monitoring of drug-resistant strains of gonorrhoea in particular.[13]

An interesting aspect of the discussion of the first of these issues, the 'changing landscape' of STDs in the Armed Forces, was the attention it gave to STDs among female military personnel. By 2012, almost 214,100 women were serving in the regular US Armed Forces, or 15 per cent of 'active' personnel. The presence of so many women required the military medical services to broaden their traditional focus to include chlamydia and genital warts as well as gonorrhoea and syphilis.[14] The sequelae of chlamydia and genital warts are, arguably, more serious for females than males because women are more vulnerable to complications arising from these STDs, for instance chronic pelvic inflammatory disease, chronic pelvic pain, ectopic pregnancies, infertility, and cancer of the cervix and vulva. With women comprising a growing proportion of uniformed military personnel, military medical personnel could expect to deal with more cases of these particular STDs.[15]

The 'changing landscape' also included the abolition of the 'Don't Ask Don't Tell' policy in the armed services, which was in place from 1993 to 2011. This policy on homosexual, lesbian and bisexual military personnel allowed them to remain in the military services so long as they kept their sexual preferences secret.[16] The dropping of this policy allowed them to 'come out' and be honest and open about their sexuality without penalty. The challenge for the military medical services here was to ensure that clinical specialists and support staff were sensitive to and had the requisite skills to cater to the needs of personnel whose sexual orientation was other than heterosexual. Insofar as STDs were concerned, the new approach also required medical staff to be more attuned to the proliferating research on the worldwide pandemic of HIV-AIDS.[17]

Yet another sign that policy regarding STDs demanded new thinking was the source of STDs. Men serving with the Armed Forces had customarily acquired STDs from prostitutes, but as the proportions of female military personnel rose, the American research showed there was a tendency for people in uniform to acquire

STDs from each other. This shift was particularly obvious in deployments to Afghanistan, Iraq and other Islamic nations which maintained strong sanctions against extramarital sex. Because cultural constraints restricted sexual contacts between the Americans and local populations in those nations, US troops contracted STDs from each other rather than from indigenous partners.

Female soldiers comprised 10 per cent or more of US military personnel serving in Iraq and Afghanistan. Preventing sexual contact between them and their male comrades proved difficult in practice despite severe disciplinary sanctions.[18] One study among US troops in Iraq and Afghanistan found that, over the five-year period 2004 to 2009, gonorrhoea infection rates rose from five cases per 100,000 deployed personnel to 17.6.[19] The source of infection was commonly fellow service personnel. These were minuscule rates by comparison with those in the Australian Army during the 20th century, but the rising trend suggested that the intra-service contraction of STDs might require serious consideration in the future.

5. A century of the Australian Army's attempts to manage STDs

During the century this book has traversed, the Army did all it could reasonably do to control and reduce the incidence of STDs. At one time or another, the Army's commanders, administrators, medical officers and military police tried every known anti-STD strategy. The range included all the following measures:

1. **Semi-criminalising the contraction of STDs**
   - confining VD patients under guard to secure 'lock' hospitals
   - stigmatising VD patients, such as requiring them to use separate dining, ablution and toilet facilities
   - treating VD patients in separate, isolated VD hospitals
   - sending VD patients back to Australia in disgrace
   - ensuring that treatment regimens in the VD hospitals were harsh
   - stopping the pay of VD patients while they were undergoing treatment
   - curtailing leave and other privileges of VD patients

2. **Supervising soldiers' off-duty time to minimise their opportunities for consorting with prostitutes**
   - providing sporting and recreation facilities, often donated and run by the Red Cross or the YMCA
   - declaring red-light districts in towns frequented by soldiers to be out of bounds
   - conducting military police patrols through red-light districts to round up soldiers and send them back to camp
   - frequent bed checks after lights out to ensure that soldiers were in bed and not absent visiting prostitutes
3. **Conducting education and propaganda campaigns on the nature, causes and societal ramifications of VD infection**
   - lectures by chaplains on the moral aspects and consequences of VD infection
   - lectures by medical officers on VD causes and prevention
   - 'man-to-man chats' between unit commanders and their men about the importance of remaining VD-free
   - compulsory written examinations on the types, nature, symptoms, treatment and prevention of VD

- anti-VD posters, pamphlets, information leaflets and articles in Army newspapers
- compulsory viewing of graphic films about the ravages of VD
- inter-unit competition for the 'lowest VD infection rate'

4. **Regular medical examination of soldiers for the symptoms of VD infection**
- initial medical inspection at the time of recruitment
- post-recruitment follow-up medical assessment
- pre-embarkation and post-embarkation examinations
- pre-discharge examination
- so-called 'short-arm' parades, cause of much ribald mirth, conducted as frequently as possible and ideally at short notice

5. **Provision of free, well-publicised prophylactic facilities made available on a 'no questions asked' basis to preserve soldier anonymity**
- 'Blue Light' prophylactic kits containing powerful antiseptic ointments to be rubbed into the penis and surrounding areas immediately before and after coitus
- PACs at all major Army camps and in red-light districts frequented by soldiers

- to provide postcoital irrigation and medicinal dressing of the genitalia
- issuing free condoms
- ready access to 'No Sweat Pills', namely, prophylactic doses of pre-and post-coitus antibiotic medication

6. **Establishment of specialised venereological hospitals or units (ideally staffed by specialist venereologists and trained medical orderlies) to provide the best available treatment regimens**
- Various 'Camp Compounds', 'VD Compounds' and the Langwarrin VD Hospital—Australia, World War I
- No.2 Australian Stationary Hospital—the VD hospital in Egypt, World War I
- No.1 Australian Dermatological Hospital—the Army VD hospital in England, World War I
- British-run 'General (VD) Hospitals'—France, World War I
- Australian Special Hospitals—Middle East and Australia, World War II
- Japan, post-World War II BCOF—no separate hospital for VD patients, who were treated at the 130th Australian General Hospital

- Korean War—no separate hospital for VD patients, who were treated at the 160th Indian Field Ambulance
- Vietnam War—most VD patients went to the 'Special Treatment Clinic' (VD unit) of the 1st Australian Field Hospital

7. **Regulation and punishment of women accused of transmitting VD**
- 'contact tracing' by identifying and locating the women accused of being the source of particular soldiers' infections, then requiring them to receive treatment under pain of prosecution
- persuading civilian police to arrest and charge prostitutes, and then have them prosecuted, convicted, imprisoned and compulsorily treated
- removing from the vicinity of Army camps the 'part-time' and 'amateur' prostitutes who congregated there
- regulating the premises in which prostitutes worked; holding the proprietors responsible for the prostitutes' supervision; and insisting that the prostitutes be medically examined regularly

8. **Authorising particular brothels and prostitutes to service Australian soldiers as a VD control measure in**

Palestine and Syria in 1941-1942, and later in Vietnam
- issuing 'Approved Premises' certificates to brothels declared 'in bounds' for soldiers
- declaring brothels which were not 'Approved' as 'out of bounds' for troops
- enforcing regular medical examinations for prostitutes working in the 'Approved' brothels
- issuing prostitutes in 'Approved' brothels with an identity card or 'permit' showing the date of their last medical examination
- checking of a prostitute's identity card by a soldier before he engaged in intercourse
- making a prostitute liable to arrest and prosecution for failure to produce her identity card on the order of police
- conniving in running a de facto licenced brothel system staffed by licenced prostitutes by issuing prostitutes with permits and granting brothels 'Approved' status

9. **Delayed repatriation of VD-infected soldiers post-deployment to prevent them spreading VD in Australia and consequent political ramifications**
- VD-infected troops were not generally allowed to return to Australia until they

- had either been cured or declared 'non-infectious'
- VD-infected troops at the end of wars were accordingly retained in overseas military hospitals for treatment
- VD-infected troops who were allowed to return home without having been discharged from hospital were immediately sent to specialised VD military hospitals in Australia for continued treatment.

The Army as an institution largely behaved responsibly by adopting the measures outlined above. At the time of their implementation, they were thought best for preventing VD infections. Whatever measures were adopted generally proved ineffective, however. The emphasis accordingly shifted across time—from moralistic, punitive attempts to prevent VD among soldiers (as in World War I) to a pragmatic acceptance that VD would occur and should accordingly be controlled and minimised (as in Vietnam). The best the Army could hope for was to reduce VD infection rates, not eliminate VD from among its troops.

But what might have happened if the Army had not taken the action that it did, allowing the VD infection rates to take their own course? There would certainly have been political consequences as the press, politicians and churches in Australia discovered that the Army was riddled with gonorrhoea, syphilis and other STDs. Inevitably, much VD would have been transmitted into the wider population, afflicting innocent women and unborn children. And as infection rates among the troops soared, the consequences for military operations could have been dire. Could the Army have been defeated twice—once by VD and again by the enemy? These were all possibilities that must have occurred to the Army's commanders.

6. How many Australian soldiers contracted sexually transmitted diseases?

Assigning figures for VD infections per deployment is often problematic. For some deployments no statistics are available; for others estimates must be made. Even where figures have been systematically compiled, inconsistencies exist. Further, often the statistics are understated because some soldiers managed to conceal their symptoms, others escaped detection by self-treating, and yet others were privately treated by civilian doctors. In such cases the number of STD episodes could not be included in the tables compiled by the official medical historians.

Such provisos notwithstanding, the present author estimates that during the 20th century Army medical units treated over 125,000 STD cases among Australian soldiers.[20] The Table 11.1 provides a summary.

Table 11.1 - **Estimated STD cases in the Australian Army during the 20th century**

Deployment	Estimated STD cases (rounded)
Boer War, 1898-1902	Unknown
Boxer Rebellion, 1900-1901	Unknown
World War I, 1914-1918	65,350
World War II, 1939-1945	34,180
Occupation Force in Japan, 1946-1952	7350
Korean War, 1950-1953	4110
Malayan Emergency, 1955-1963	2900
Indonesian Confrontation of Malaysia, 1965-1966	Unknown
Vietnam War, 1962-1973	11,380
Post-Vietnam deployments, 1976-2000	Unknown
Total STD cases, 20th century	125,270

Derived from diverse sources, principally: A.G. Butler, Special Problems and Services (for World War I); A.S. Walker, Clinical Problems of War (for World War II); R.N.L. Hopkins, 'Control of VD', 28 June 1946; C. Scales, 'Venereal disease, BCOF', 19 December 1946, AWM114 267/6/17 Part 1; and 'Brief History of the Medical Services [of] BCOF', 21 July 1947, AWM114 481/11/2 (for Japan); F.J. Ingham 'Discussion on medical problems in Korea: Army health problems', Proceedings of the Royal Society for Medicine, Volume 46, 1953 (for Korea); and Brendan O'Keefe, Medicine at War: Medical aspects of Australia's involvement in Southeast Asia 1950—1972 (for Malayan Emergency and Vietnam).

The total of 125,270 is a minimal figure because it does not include the unknown statistics for four of the 10 sets of deployments. It is a very large sum—the equivalent of six World War 1 infantry divisions.

What might such a huge total signify? Does it reflect badly on the soldiers, on the Army that sent them to fight overseas, on the doctors who safeguarded their health, and on the nation of which they were citizens?

The present author proffers no answers to such questions because he has none. All he can say is that each deployment had its own specificity, which produced its own quantum of STD episodes. Successive chapters have endeavoured to explain why each deployment produced the STD score' that it did. And all that can be said of the grand total—125,270—is that it was of such a scale that STDs were a major problem for the Australian Army during most of the 20th century.

7. Should this book teach anyone anything?

Has any reader learned anything from reading this book, other than that infections from STDs in the Australian Army were on a very large scale? In writing this book the author did not set out to educate, instruct or otherwise intend his readers to learn 'lessons'. His intention was to demonstrate how STDs impacted heavily on the Australian Army in its overseas deployments during the 20th century. Any lessons learnt will be those that readers have themselves inferred from the military medical episodes the book has described.

Looking back, the author realises that he himself has learnt much from writing the book. But exactly what?

First, history is extraordinarily complex. Nothing in history is ever simple or straightforward. The facts of history, the building blocks of any book of history, are never quite as solid as they might seem at first sight. Further investigation shows them to be complicated, subtle, nuanced, connected to and intertwined with other episodes, personalities and background events. They are, moreover, often subject to dispute, to the extent that gaining consensus on what they really are and how they might be interpreted is elusive.

The great 19th century German historian, Leopold von Ranke, enjoined other historians to tell their readers *wie es eigentlich gewesen [war]*—how it really was. He emphasised the importance of 'source-based history'. This book has striven to be as 'source-based' as possible and the author has endeavoured to tell the Army and STDs' story as it really was, which is to say, 'as it appeared to him'. He recognises that other historians using the same sources might tell the story and interpret the 'facts' differently.

Second, soldiers sent overseas to fight wars in which they stand a fair chance of being killed soon are not 'normal' people who behave 'normally'. They are under pressures and subject to stresses that civilians living safely at home never experience and cannot fully appreciate. The steady, responsible young man who would never think of consorting with prostitutes at home in Australia might well do so during overseas military service, especially when egged on by his mates after a few drinks in a bar which is a front for a brothel. Removed from the constraints of his life at home, and facing the prospect of annihilation on the morrow, he might not behave as he normally would at home. He is not necessarily lacking in character, morally deficient, reckless or irresponsible for having succumbed to the temptations of the moment. He is just a young man in a milieu in which he might not have complete control over his own behaviour. In the wider scheme of wartime events, through his STD episode he becomes a victim of war, albeit not as dramatically or irrevocably as those of his comrades killed in action. Similarly, the woman from whom he contracted his STD is also a victim of war, usually impelled into her 'trade' by the vagaries of war and circumstances beyond her control.

Third, STDs had a devastating impact on the ADF (formerly the AMF), particularly in the earlier wars of the 20th century. The cost to the ADF of STDs was huge, whether measured financially, administratively, logistically or in terms of human resources and military efficiency. The cumulative loss in manpower was of the scale of whole army divisions.

After the introduction of penicillin the loss was much less, and the impact of STDs receded in significance. Eventually, as in Vietnam, the effects on manpower were minimal. Before penicillin, STD management involved prolonged hospitalisation, financial penalties and public humiliation for the STD sufferer and perhaps his family as well. Post-penicillin, from Japan and Korea onwards, treatment for STDs was often short and managed on an outpatient basis.

The gross disparities in STD case rates between World Wars I and II on the one hand and Japan, Korea, Malaya and Vietnam on the other can be explained both by the duration and harshness of the STD management systems *and* the availability of penicillin. Without penicillin in World Wars I and II, the treatment extended into months and was generally punitive. The lower comparative infection rates for these earlier conflicts reflected that.

In Japan and afterwards, penicillin and antibiotics reduced treatment times to a couple of days at most; consequently STDs could be regarded as infectious diseases like any others, with no penalties attached. When soldiers had less to fear from STDs, infection rates soared. The difference in the rates pre-and post-penicillin is so great that the figures for both eras cannot really be compared meaningfully.

Fourth, STIs are essentially self-inflicted. An STI 'episode' does not need to happen and can easily be avoided. That it is not is a consequence of the exigencies of the moment. These include the excitement of a sexual encounter in which precautions are overlooked, a lapse in wariness because the coupling was unanticipated, the haste of the act, the dislike of one of the partners for the artificiality of prophylactic devices, the inebriation of one or both of them, or perhaps even the perverse determination of one partner to transmit their disease to someone else. These are each preventable in theory, but they might also be unavoidable in practice because they arise from human frailty and fallibility.

Fifth, each STI episode is its own little tragedy—a case in which STI sufferers realise that they have been foolish, careless or irresponsible, that they have fallen short of the expectations of others and damaged their own sense of self-respect in the process. Beyond those effects are the consequences for relationships with friends and families, which might be irreparably damaged. Factors like these lay behind the emotional condition which Gavin Hart described as 'venereoneurosis', which commonly afflicted soldiers who had consorted with prostitutes in Vietnam, not just the troops who had contracted gonorrhoea as a result. For some soldiers, an unknown percentage, the consequences may be long-term, echoing through the individual STI victim's later life. Failure to remain celibate while serving overseas, it seems, has its own costs.

Sixth, and a matter inevitably and intimately related to the personal impact of consorting with prostitutes, are the sequelae of extramarital dalliances. The soldiers who contracted STDs through consorting with prostitutes were always the husbands, fiancés, sweethearts, sons, brothers, fathers, cousins or friends of Australian women. The womenfolk would have been embarrassed and humiliated to know that the militarily spic-and-span soldiers they had lovingly farewelled would spend months in hospital being treated for diseases that were so taboo they could not be discussed around the family dinner table.

Seventh, readers might conclude that all the measures the Army adopted to control STDs failed. Moral injunctions, appeals to social responsibility, punitive measures, warnings about the dire consequences for families and generations of unborn children, STD education and anti-STD propaganda seem to have had little impact.

Did all these measures fail? Could any of them have been made to succeed? The strictly rational answer to such questions is that from historical experience the best combination of tactics would have been to adopt this formula:

> Military personnel well educated in the causes, prevention, treatment & consequences of sexually transmitted diseases
> + freely available prophylaxis
> + strictly controlled licenced brothels
> + licenced prostitutes checked frequently and treated for STDs
> + a pragmatic, non-judgemental attitude to STDs by military authorities
> + the latest and best in antibiotic medication
> + sexual health clinics which respect patients' confidentiality

+ treatment regimens managed by sympathetic, non-judgemental sexual health specialists
= optimal conditions for holding STDs at minimal levels.

The purely rational approach, however, is rarely entirely satisfactory for it cannot take into account random variables. Moreover, it ignores the reality that the most desirable outcome medically—zero STDs—could not be abstracted from the surrounding matrix of intertwined psychological, sociological, moral and political factors.

Among the random variables impacting on the Australian Army's effort to contain its STD problem was the larrikin nature of the Australian 'Digger' or common soldier. The Digger stereotype has been endlessly debated among historians and by Australian soldiers themselves. The elements of the stereotype vary according to the writer of the moment. One will emphasise the sense of mateship, another the heavy drinking, another the anti-authoritarian egalitarianism, yet another the womanising.

Digger humour made light of VD, as one apocryphal yarn suggests. It involves a young recruit from the latest batch of reinforcements. He goes to the RAP to tell the RMO that a murky discharge is oozing from his penis and so he wonders if his penis might have caught a cold. The RMO tells him to stand in the corner for 15 minutes. If it has not coughed or sneezed in that time then he can be sure it does not have a cold. Instead, he has the clap![21]

The ordinary Australian soldier was a product of his home society and culture. Through writing this book and several others earlier, the present author has learnt that as a class the Diggers were sceptical, irreverent, egalitarian, unpretentious, mocking of pretentiousness in others and loth to accept Army discipline. They gave their respect grudgingly to their officers, and the officers had to work hard to earn and retain it. They placed scant credence on the sermonising of their chaplains, but they admired individual chaplains who shared the rough and tumble of Army life with them. They were suspicious of the nostrums administered by their medical officers. They regarded their free time as their own; if they were intent on using it for recreational sex, they resented the Army telling them where, when, with whom and under what circumstances they could indulge themselves.

As to the error of abstracting desirable medical outcomes from psychological, sociological, moral and political considerations, Army medical practice cannot proceed in a vacuum. It must always take account of these other considerations.

At the same time, for all the shortcomings of the Army's anti-STD education programs during the 20th century, the training of ADF personnel in sexual morality and ethics remains necessary in the 21st century. ADF personnel learn that theirs is a defence force that functions under law as the military branch of a parliamentary democracy. They need also to know that they must maintain the moral standards expected of them by the civilian population whose taxes pay their salaries and by the politicians who determine what deployments the ADF will undertake. This kind of training may not be left to chance. It must be part and parcel of ADF education programs, the desirable moral and ethical values instilled into the personal conduct codes of ADF members.

Finally, eighth, what might readers conclude about the Australian Army from its experience with STDs? The Army was always deeply concerned by its STD problem, to which it responded with due attention to its responsibility to the government and citizens of Australia. The Army is not a law unto itself but is an agency of the Commonwealth of Australia that functions under the law of the Commonwealth. The Army must also maintain a sharp weather eye to public opinion in Australia. Although public opinion is intangible and diffuse, it influences the parliamentarians who are the Army's political masters.

STIs remain controversial in Australian society despite the social and attitudinal changes that occurred during the 20th century. ADF commanders might rationally and realistically regard STIs as an occupational hazard for military personnel serving overseas. But was that all they were? Or were they, like history, more complicated than that?

As the 21st century unfolded, new problems in STI management emerged. Increasing antibiotic resistance in the organisms causing gonorrhoea, syphilis and chlamydia became a concern for medical professionals. Evidence for the evolution of 'superbugs' resistant to all antibiotics accumulated. Further, fears existed that new STIs would be discovered. One such was *Mycoplasma genitalium*, 'MG' for short, an organism causing pelvic inflammation and urethritis in both men and women.[22] Could MG and gonorrhoea superbugs be kept out of Australia? Was the era of easily treated STIs ending? If so, what were the implications of that for the ADF and for its personnel, especially those posted to regions where 'superbugs' might be common?

Whatever the answers to such questions might be, the new century posed new challenges for the ADF health services. Whether these would prove as problematic as STDs had been during the 20th century was uncertain. What was fairly certain was that STIs would continue causing deep concern to the ADF, the government and the national health care system.

Abbreviations

Term	Meaning
AAFVD	Australian Association for Fighting Venereal Diseases
AAMC	Australian Army Medical Corps
AAMWS	Australian Army Medical Women's Service
AANS	Australian Army Nursing Service
ADF	Australian Defence Force, comprising the Royal Australian Navy, Australian Army, and Royal Australian Air Force
ADH	Australian Dermatological Hospital
ADMS	Assistant Director of Medical Services
AFH	Australian Field Hospital
AFV	Australian Force Vietnam
AGH	Australian General Hospital, often prefixed by a serial number to indicate a particular unit
AIDS	Acquired immunodeficiency syndrome, a sexually transmitted infection caused by the retrovirus HIV
AIF	Australian Imperial Force, an army raised for overseas service during World War I and World War II The terms 'First AIF' and 'Second AIF' are often used to distinguish between the two AIF formations
AMD	Army Medical Directorate
AMF	Australian Military Force
AMS	Army Medical Service
ANZAC	Australian and New Zealand Army Corps
APM	Assistant Provost Marshal

ASH	Australian Special Hospital (during World War I), often prefixed by a serial number to indicate a particular unit
ASH	Australian Stationary Hospital (during World War II); often prefixed by a serial number to indicate a particular unit
ATF	Australian Task Force
AWAS	Australian Women's Army Service
AWLA	Australian Women's Land Army
BCOF	British Commonwealth Occupation Force (in Japan)

BEF	British Expeditionary Force
BMA	British Medical Association
CDC	Centers for Disease Control and Prevention (USA)
CO	Commanding Officer
DAPM	Deputy Assistant Provost Marshal
DDMS	Deputy Director of Medical Services
DGMS	Director General of Medical Services
DMS	Director of Medical Services
DMZ	Demilitarised Zone
DNA	Deoxyribonucleic acid, a molecule carrying the genetic instructions used in the growth, development, functioning and reproduction of all known living organisms and many viruses
EEF	Egyptian Expeditionary Force
Fd Amb	Australian Field Ambulance, often prefixed by a serial number to indicate a particular unit
HBV	Hepatitis B virus, causing the viral liver infection Hepatitis B

HIV	Human immunodeficiency virus, a retrovirus that causes AIDS
HPV	Human papillomavirus, a sexually transmitted infection
IFA	Indian Field Ambulance
LGV	Lymphogranuloma venereum, a sexually transmitted bacterial infection
MASH	Mobile Army Surgical Hospital
MG	Military Cross
MG	Mycoplasma genitalium, a bacterium causing a sexually transmitted infection
MJA	Medical Journal of Australia
MO	Medical officer
MRLA	Malayan Races Liberation Army
NSU	Non-specific urethritis, an infection of the urethra not caused by gonorrhoea or chlamydia
NZEF	New Zealand Expeditionary Force
QIC	Officer in charge
PAG	Prophylactic Ablution Centre, a depot at which soldiers could receive early treatment for VD (World Wars I and II)
POW	Prisoner of war
RAA	Recreation Amusement Association

RAAF	Royal Australian Air Force
RAAMC	Royal Australian Army Medical Corps
RAMC	British Royal Army Medical Corps
RAP	Regimental Aid Post
RAR	Royal Australian Regiment
RMO	Regimental medical officer

RSL	Returned and Services League of Australia (formerly the Returned Soldiers' and Sailors' Imperial League of Australia)
STD	Sexually transmitted disease, an infection displaying symptoms that is transmitted through sexual contact
STI	Sexually transmitted infection, increasingly the preferred term instead of STD, as it includes infections with mild or no symptoms
UN	United Nations
US	United States
USA	United States of America
VD	Venereal disease, a term encompassing various sexually transmitted infections but often intended to signify gonorrhoea and syphilis
WPA	Women's Political Association

Glossary

Term	Meaning
Abortive treatment	A treatment regimen designed to cure a patient by chemically killing the microorganisms that are the cause of a disease, especially gonorrhoea and syphilis.
Anterior urethra	The section of the male urethra nearest the end of the penis.
Antibiotic	A substance that is used to prevent and treat bacterial infections.
Antiseptic	A chemical compound used to discourage the growth of disease-causing microorganisms.
Arsphenamine	An arsenic-based drug used in the treatment of syphilis in the era before the introduction of penicillin; sold commercially under the name 'Salvarsan'.
Bacillus (plural bacilli)	Spore-forming bacteria that grow in the presence of oxygen.
Anzacs	Soldiers who fought with the Australia and New Zealand Army Corps (ANZAC) during World War I, and the term 'Anzac' is also used to refer to those who served in the Australian Imperial Force in World War I.
Argyrol	Trade name for a silver-based antiseptic compound often used in treating gonorrhoea.
Bacterium (plural bacteria)	Any member of a large group of unicellular microorganisms, many of which can cause disease.
Bacteriostatic	An antibacterial substance that does not kill bacteria but inhibits their growth and reproduction, allowing the immune system of the host to destroy them.
Balanitis	Inflammation of the glans of the penis.

Blue Light depot	A depot at which soldiers could receive early treatment for VD (World Wars I and II).
Blue Light kit	A small packet containing antiseptic ointments and perhaps condoms, for use by soldiers as a protection against 'unsafe sex' (World War I).
Bubo	A swollen, inflamed lymph node, occurring mainly in the armpit or groin.
Calomel	Trade name for an ointment containing mercurous chloride; at one time often used in treating syphilis.
Calymmatobacterium granulomatis	A disease caused by the bacterium Klebsiella granulomatis, later known as donovanosis and granuloma inguinale.

Candida albicans	The yeast-like organism causing candidiasis infection.
Candidal vaginitis	Inflammation of the vagina caused by candidiasis; a vaginal yeast infection.
Candidiasis	A soft-tissue infection caused by Candida albicans, a yeast-like organism.
Cardiovascular syphilis	Syphilis causing damage to the heart and blood vessels.
Chancre	A lesion on the skin occurring during the primary stage of syphilis infection.
Chancroid	A genital ulcerative disease characterised by necrotising ulcers and possible inguinal lymphadenopathy.
Chlamydia trachomatis	The most common bacterial cause of sexually transmitted infections of the eye (trachoma) and the urogenital system (chlamydia and non-gonococcal urethritis).
Clap	Colloquial term for gonorrhoea.

Coccobacillus (plural coccobacilli)	A type of bacterium with a shape intermediate between coccus (spherical) and bacillus (rod-shaped).
Condom	A thin rubber sheath worn on the penis during sexual intercourse as a contraceptive or as a protection against infection.
Condylomata acuminata	Genital warts.
Congenital Syphilis	Syphilis contracted in utero.
Conjunctivitis	Inflammation of the conjunctiva of the eye; also known as 'pink eye'.
Corynebacterium vaginalis	A bacterium causing vaginitis in women.
Crabs	Colloquial expression for genital or pubic lice.
Diplococcus (plural diplococci)	A spherical bacterium occurring in the form of two joined cells; a pair of cocci.
DNA	Deoxyribonucleic acid, a molecule carrying the genetic instructions used in the growth, development, functioning and reproduction of all known living organisms and many viruses.
Donovanosis	A disease caused by the bacterium Klebsiella granulomatis; also known as granuloma inguinale.
Ectopic pregnancy	A pregnancy where the foetus develops in the fallopian tube rather than the uterus.
Epidemiology	The branch of medicine dealing with the incidence, distribution

Epididymides	Tubes within the male body that store sperm made in the testicles.

Flagellum (plural flagella)	A slender microscopic whip-like appendage which enables many protozoans, bacteria, spermatozoa etc. to propel themselves.
Foetus or fetus	An unborn offspring from nine weeks after conception.
Gardnerella vaginalis	A bacterium causing vaginitis in women.
Genital herpes	A sexually transmitted infection of the genitalia by the herpes simplex virus.
Genital warts	Warts in the genital or anal area caused by the human papillomavirus.
Genome	The complete set of genes or genetic material present in a cell or organism.
GI	General Issue, an expression also widely used to mean a US Army soldier at private rank.
Gonococcal conjunctivitis	Conjuctivitis caused by gonococci.
Gonococcus (plural: gonococci)	A species of bacterium responsible for gonorrhoea.
Granuloma inguinale	A disease caused by the bacterium Klebsiella granulomatis (formerly known as Calymmatobacterium granulomatis). Also known as Donovanosis.
haemolytic	Relating to the destruction of red blood cells.
Haemophilus ducreyi	The bacterium causing chancroid infection.
Hepatitis B (HBV)	A viral liver infection caused by a virus of the genus Orthohepadnavirus.
Herpes	A viral skin infection caused by the herpes simplex virus; characterised by blister-like eruptions on the skin, typically around the mouth and (in its genital form) on the genitalia.

In utero	Within the uterus.
Iodism	Iodine poisoning.
Jack	Colloquial term for gonorrhoea.
Klebsiella granulomatis	The bacterium causing Granuloma inguinale or Donovanosis (formerly known as Calymmatobacterium granulomatis).
Lymphogranuloma venereum	A sexually transmitted infection caused by the bacterium Chlamydia trachomatis.
Meatus, penile	The orifice (opening) at the tip of the penis.
Molluscum contagiosum	A contagious viral infection producing round, domed bumps on
Motile	Capable of motion.
Neisseriagonorrhoeae	The gonococcus (bacterium) causing gonorrhoea.
Neurosyphilis	Syphilis causing damage to the central nervous system.
Non-gonococcal urethritis (NGU)	Inflammation of the urethra, also called chlamydia and nonspecific urethritis; usually caused by the bacterium Chlamydia trachomatis.
Non-specific urethritis (NSU)	Inflammation of the urethra; also called chlamydia and nongonococcal urethritis; usually caused by the bacterium Chlamydia trachomatis.
Papilloma	A benign outwardly projecting skin growth similar to a wart or corn.
Pediculosis	Infestation by lice.
Penicillin	An antibiotic or group of antibacterial drugs produced naturally by certain blue moulds, usually prepared synthetically.
Phthirus pubis	A species of louse commonly and collectively known as pubic lice and crab lice.

Pilus (plural pili)	A hair-like appendage found on the surface of many bacteria.
Posterior urethra	The section of the male urethra nearest the bladder.
Pox	Colloquial term for syphilis.
Pneumococcus (plural pneumococci)	A bacterium which is a major cause of pneumonia. A member of the family Streptococcaceae, it is also called Streptococcus pneumoniae.
Prepuce	The fold of skin covering the head of the penis or clitoris; in males also called the foreskin.
Primary syphilis	The first stage of infection induced by spirochaetes (syphilisproducing bacteria) after invading the human body.
Prostate	A gland within the male genitourinary system surrounding the urethra.
Pubic lice	Parasitic insects of the species Phthirus pubis that infest the human pubic area.
Regimen	In medicine, a prescribed treatment intended to preserve or restore health.
Retrovirus	A virus with the ability to insert a DNA copy of its genome into a host cell in order to replicate itself.
Salpingitis	Inflammation of the fallopian tubes, which may be caused by

Salvarsan	Commercial name of arsphenamine, an arsenic-based compound used in treating syphilis.
Sarcoptes scabiei	The parasitic mite causing scabies; also known as the itch mite.
Scabies	A contagious skin condition producing itchy, red lumps; caused by the blood-sucking mite Sarcoptes scabiei, also known as the itch mite.

Secondary Syphilis	The second stage of infection caused by spirochaetes (syphilisproducing bacteria) after invading the human body.
Sexual health physician	A medical practitioner who specialises in treating sexually transmitted infections.
Sexually transmitted disease	Any one of various diseases or infections transmitted by direct sexual contact.
Sexually transmitted infection	Alternative term for 'sexually transmitted disease'; used more frequently after coming into vogue in the early 21st century.
Sound	In medicine, a medical instrument used to enlarge the urethra in men.
Spirochaete	Spiral-shaped bacteria, including the genus Treponema, which, among others, is the cause of syphilis.
Streptococcus (plural streptococci)	A genus of spherical bacteria that belongs to the family Streptococcaceae.
Sulpha drug or sulfa drug	See 'Sulphonamide'.
Sulphanilamide or Sulfanilamide	One of the sulphonamide group of antibacterial drugs; widely used during World War II.
Sulphonamide or sulfonamide	A group of drugs used in treating bacterial infections. They include sulphanilamide, sulphapyridine and sulphathiazole.
Swab	An absorbent pad or piece of material used in surgery and medicine for cleaning wounds, applying medication, or taking specimens.
Syphilis	The sexually transmitted infection caused by the spirochaete Treponema pallidum.
Tertiary syphilis	The third and final stage of infection caused by spirochaetes (syphilis-producing bacteria) after invading the human body.

Treponema pallidum	The spirochaete (spiral-shaped bacterium) causing syphilis.
Trichomoniasis	A vaginal infection caused by the protozoan parasite, Trichomonas vaginalis.

Vaginitis	Inflammation of the vagina.
Venereal disease	A disease typically contracted by sexual intercourse with a person already infected; a sexually transmitted disease. This was the term commonly used for sexually transmitted diseases/infections until the mid-1970s.
Venereologist	A medical practitioner who specialises in treating sexually transmitted infections.
Venereology	The branch of medicine specialising in the study and treatment of sexually transmitted infections.
Venereoneurosis	An anxiety state and emotional condition arising from having contracted a sexually transmitted disease and/or having consorted with prostitutes.
Virus	A type of microorganism, typically consisting of a nucleic acid molecule in a protein coat too small to be seen by light microscopy, which is able to multiply only within the living cells of a host.

Bibliography

Official records

Australian War Memorial, Canberra

AWM11	Item 1528/1/13, 'Control of Venereal Disease among overseas troops'.
AWM15	Item 14379/7, 'Correspondence on Venereal Diseases'.
AWM15	Item 5131, 'Venereal Disease'.
AWM15	Item 10114, 'Disposal of 27 VD cases from No.3 Depot'.
AWM15	Item 18595, 'Board proceedings on Stores & Equipment at 1st ADH, Bulford'.
AWM21	Item 1502/17, 'Venereal Disease—correspondence regarding conveyors of and suffer [er] s from'.
AWM25	Item 267/26, 'Notes by Major B.T. Zwar (No.2 Australian Stationary Hospital) upon Venereal Disease in Egypt'.
AWM25	Item 267/52, 'Report on the work of the Venereal Section engaged in the treatment of Venereal Diseases amongst Australian and NZ troops in Egypt and Palestine, 1917-1918'.
AWM25	Item 267/53, 'Administrative means for dealing with special cases of venereal disease'.
AWM25	Item 399/6, '1st Australian Dermatological Hospital Report for April 1919'.
AWM25	Item 707/11 file 123, 'Routine Orders, 1st Australian Dermatological Hospital, from 7-9-1918 to 13-5-1919'.

AWM27	Item 376/164, 'Graph showing weekly admissions to hospital for cases of venereal disease in the AIF, Egypt (1918-1919)'.
AWM27	Item 370/12, 'Prevention and Treatment of Venereal Disease (Recommendations of the UK Royal Commission on the Prevention and Treatment of Venereal Diseases, 1917)'.
AWM27	Items 371/97, 376/179, 376/180, 376/181, 376/182, 376/183, all of which relate to No.1 Australian Dermatological Hospital, Bulford, UK.
AWM27	Item 371/98, '1st Australian Dermatological Hospital, A.I.F., Abbassia.
AWM27	Item 376/100, 'Instructions to Medical Officers regarding the prevention of Venereal Disease'.
AWM27	Item 376/101, 'VD Returns, 1st Australian Dermatological Hospital, A.I.F'.
AWM27	Item 376/156, 'Report of Surgeon General R.H.J. Fetherston on war work abroad'.
AWM27	Item 376/173, 'Letter from General Birdwood re Venereal Disease'.
AWM27	Item 376/182, untitled file containing various printed notices about Venereal Disease, including 'Instructions & Precautions', 'Medical Views on Sexual Questions' and 'Warning! Venereal Diseases'.
AWM27	Item 376/184, 'Treatment and prevention of venereal disease'.
AWM27	Item 376/194, 'Committee Concerning Causes of Death and Invalidity in the Commonwealth, Report on Venereal Diseases', May 1916.

AWM38	Item 3DRL 6673/149, Records of Charles E.W. Bean: Papers 1936; relating to Venereal Disease and containing letters from Senator B. Samson and copies of circulars, memoranda and letters by Ettie Rout 1918-19.
AWM38	Item 3DRL 7447/22 Parts 1 and 3, Records of Charles E.W. Bean: Papers 1916-34.
AWM41	Records of A.G. Butler, Historian of Australian Army Medical Services.
AWM52	2nd AIF, unit war diaries, 1939-45.
AWM54	Written records, 1939-45.
AWM103	Item R515/1/1 (Part 1), 'Medical Diseases, General, Venereal Disease'.
AWM114	Item 130/1/45, 'Report on visit to the British Commonwealth Occupation Force Japan by Major General S.R. Burston ... External Co-ordinating Authority for the Medical services'.
AWM114	Item 267/6/17, 'BCOF. Control of Venereal Disease' (Parts 1-12).
AWM114	Item 481/11/2, 'BCOF—History of Medical Services'.
AWM116	Items R515/1/6 and R515/1/7, 'Medical Diseases, General—Venereal Disease'.
AWM292	Records of Assistant Director of Medical Services, Headquarters Australian Force Vietnam.
AWM292	Item 515/1/18 (Med), 'Venereal Disease Prophylaxis'.
AWM292	Med 40/76, Personal letters to DGMS, 27 December 1939 to 12 May 1943.
AWM302	Item R515/5/1, 'Medical Diseases—Venereal Disease'.
AWM313	Item 515/1/2 Part 1, 'Medical Diseases—Venereal Disease'.
AWM322	Item R506/1/2, '110 Signals Squadron—Medical General, VD'.

Australian War Memorial digitalised online biographical databases: 'Embarkation Roll', 'Honour Roll', 'Honours and Awards' and 'Nominal Roll'.

National Archives of Australia

A461	Correspondence files, multiple number series (third system), 1901-1950.
A705	Correspondence files, multiple number (Melbourne) series (Primary numbers 1-323), 1922-1960.
A1194	Orders in Council—Defence Department, 1900-1901.
A1608	Correspondence files, multiple number series with variable alphabetical prefix and general prefix 'SC' (fourth system).
A1 861,7084	Anti-VD posters
A2670	Reference set of War Cabinet agenda with minutes, annual single number series; accumulation dates: 28 August 1939-19 January 1946; control symbol 106/1943.
A5799	Defence Committee agenda, annual single number series; accumulation dates: 1 January 1932-
A5954	The Shedden Collection (Records collected by Sir Frederick Shedden during his career with the Department of Defence and in researching the history of Australian Defence Policy).
B883	Second Australian Imperial Force, personnel dossiers, 1939-1947.
B884	Citizens Military Forces, personnel dossiers, 1939-1947.

B1535	Correspondence files, multiple number series, 1919—1942.
B2455	First Australian Imperial Force, personnel dossiers, 1914—1920.
B5207	Commonwealth Battalions for Service in South Africa, 1902.
CP71/19	Press Cuttings collected by Sir Frederick Stewart.
CP359/2	Correspondence of Colonel R.M.McC. Anderson to the Prime Minister, W.M. Hughes.
MP84/1	Correspondence files, multiple number series, 1894-1953.
MP367/1	General correspondence files, Department of Defence, 1917-1929.
MP367/2	General correspondence files, Department of Defence, 1917—1929.
MP729/6	Secret correspondence files, multiple number series with '401' infix, 1906-1945.
MP729/7	Secret correspondence files, multiple number series with '421' infix, 1939-1945.
MP742/1	General and civil staff correspondence files and Army personnel files, multiple number series.
SP459/1	Correspondence, 1912-1964.

Australian Department of Veterans' Affairs

Australian Department of Veterans' Affairs (DVA), online 'Nominal Rolls' of Veterans of World War I, World War II, Korean War and Vietnam

War, https://www.dva.gov.au/commemorations-memorialsand-war-graves/nominal-rolls.

Standard reference works

Australian Bureau of Statistics, *Year book, Australia* (previously *Official year book of Australia* and *Official year book of the Commonwealth of Australia*), Canberra, annual series from 1928.

Australian Dictionary of Biography, Volumes 7 to 16, Melbourne University Press, Carlton.

Australian War Memorial, *Memorial Encyclopaedia*, https://www.awm.gov.au/.

Concise Medical Dictionary, 3rd edn, Oxford Reference series, Oxford University Press, Oxford, 1987.

Dennis, P., Grey, J., Morris, E., Prior, R., and Bou, J. (eds), *The Oxford Companion to Australian Military History*, 2nd edn, Oxford University Press, Melbourne, 2008.

Department of Veterans' Affairs, *The Korean War: Australian medical services*, https://anzacportal.dva.

gov.au/history/conflicts/korean-war/events/stalemate-war-19521953/australian-medical-services.

Digger History: Unofficial History of the Australian and New Zealand Armed Services, http://www.diggerhistory.htm.

National Library of Australia, *Trove*, https://trove.nla.gov.au.

The Australian Encyclopaedia, 2nd edn, Angus and Robertson, Sydney, 1958.

Wikipedia: The Free Encyclopaedia, httpss://wikipedia.org.

Books

Amery, L.S. (ed), *The Times History of the War in South Africa 1899-1902*, London, Sampson, Low, Marston and Company Ltd, 1900-1909.

Australian Association for Fighting Venereal Diseases, *The Venereal Diseases Problem: A Memorandum Esuedfor the Information of All Responsible Citizens*, self-published (printed by J.C. Stephens Pty Ltd), Melbourne, 1922.

Barrett, J.W., and Deane, P.E., *The Australian Army Medical Corps in Egypt: An illustrated and detailed account of the early organisation and work of the Australian Medical Units in Egypt in 1914—1915*, H.K. Lewis & Co. Ltd., London, 1918.

Bean, C.E.W., *Official History of Australia in the War of 1914-1918, Vol. I, The Story of ANZAC from the outbreak of war to the end of the first phase of the Gallipoli Campaign, May 4, 1915*, Angus & Robertson Ltd, Sydney, 1941.

_____*Official History of Australia in the War of 1914-1918, Vol. II, The Story of ANZAC from 4 May, 1915, to the evacuation of the Gallipoli Peninsula*, Angus & Robertson, Sydney, 1941.

_____*Official History of Australia in the War of 1914-1918, Vol. III, The AIF in France: 1916*, Angus & Robertson Ltd, Sydney, 1941.

Beaumont, Joan, *Broken Nation: Australians in the Great War*, Allen & Unwin, Crows Nest, New South Wales, 2013.

Butler, A.G. (ed), *The Australian Army Medical Services in the War of 1914-1918, Vol. I, The Gallipoli Campaign, The Campaign in Sinai and

Palestine, The Occupation of German New Guinea, Australian War Memorial, Canberra, 1938.

_____*The Australian Army Medical Services in the War of 1914-1918*, Vol. II, *The Western Front*, Australian War Memorial, Canberra, 1940.

_____*The Australian Army Medical Services in the War of 1914—1918*, Vol. III, *Special Problems and Services*, Australian War Memorial, Canberra, 1943.

Collins, Paul J., and Collins, Michael, *Remembered: Collins and Byrne Relatives in the Great War*, Lulu.com, 2017.

Cowdrey, Albert E., *United States Army in the Korean War: The Medics' War*, Center of Military History, United States Army, Washington, D.C., 1987.

Cumpston, J.H.L., *Venereal Disease in Australia*, Commonwealth of Australia Quarantine Service, Government Printer, Melbourne, 1919.

Davies, George, *The Occupation of Japan: The rhetoric and the reality of Anglo-Australasian relations, 1939—1952*, University of Queensland Press, St Lucia, 2001.

Dexter, David, *The New Guinea Offensives*, Vol. VI, Series I, *Australia in the War of 1939-1945*, Australian War Memorial, Canberra, 1961.

Dunbar, Raden, *The Secrets of the ANZACS: The untold story of venereal disease in the Australian Army, 1914-1919*, Scribe Publications, Brunswick (Victoria) and Clerkenwell (London), 2014.

Edwards, Peter G. and Pemberton, Gregory, *Crises and commitments: the politics and diplomacy of Australia's involvement in Southeast Asian conflicts 1948-1965*, Allen & Unwin and the Australian War Memorial, North Sydney, 1992.

Ekins, Ashley K. (with McNeill, Ian G.), *Fighting to the Finish: The Australian Army and the Vietnam War, 1968-1975*, Allen & Unwin, Crows Nest, New South Wales, 2012.

Ellenhorn, Matthew J., and Barceloux, Donald G., *Medical Toxicology: Diagnosis and Treatment of Human Poisoning*, Elsevier, New York, Amsterdam and London, 1988.

Fitzherbert, Margaret, *Liberal Women: Federation-1949*, The Federation Press, Annandale, New South Wales, 2004.

Gerster, Robin, *Travels in Atomic Sunshine: Australia and the Occupation of Japan*, Scribe, Melbourne, 2008.

Grant, Maurice Harold, *History of the War in South Africa 1899—1902 written by direction of His Majesty's Government*, Vol.4, Hurst and Blackett, London, 1910.

Grey, Jeffrey, *The Australian Centenary History of Defence*, Vol. I, *The Australian Army*, Oxford University Press Melbourne, 2001.

Grey, J., and Dennis, P, *Emergency & Confrontation: Australian Military Operations in Malaya and Borneo 1950-1966*, Vol.5 in *The Official History of Australia's Involvement in Southeast-Asian Conflicts 1948-1975*, Allen & Unwin in association with the Australian War Memorial, Sydney, 1996.

Gullett, H.S., *The Australian Imperial Force in Sinai and Palestine, 1914-1918*, Vol. VII in *Official History of Australia in the War of 1914-1918*, 9th edn, Sydney, Angus and Robertson Ltd, 1940.

Gurner, Colin M., *The Royal Australian Army Medical Corps*, Royal Australian Army Medical Corps and Colin M. Gurner, Melbourne, 2003.

Hart, Gavin, *Chancroid, Donovanosis (Granuloma inguinale), Lymphogranuloma Venereum (LGV)*, Venereal Disease Control Division, Bureau of State Services, Center for Disease Control, Public Health Service, US Department of Health, Education and Welfare, Atlanta, Georgia, 1964.

———*Sexually transmitted diseases*, Carolina Biological Supply Company, Burlington, Carolina, 1984.

———*Reducing the impact of sexually transmitted diseases including HIV infection*, Public and Environmental Health Division [of the] South Australian Health Commissioner, Adelaide, 1989.

———*From night clinics to the internet: a history of sexually transmitted diseases in South Australia, 1916—1996*, Royal Adelaide Hospital Department of Human Services, Adelaide, 1999.

His Majesty's Commissioners, *Report of His Majesty's Commissioners appointed to inquire into the military preparations and other matters connected with the War in South Africa*, His Majesty's Stationery Office, London, 1903.

Hooker, Richard [Pseudonym], *MASH*, William Morrow and Company, New York, 1968.

Horner, David M. (ed), *The Commanders: Australian military leadership in the twentieth century*, Allen & Unwin, Sydney, 1984.

Horner, David M., *Crisis of Command: Australian Generalship and the Japanese Threat, 1941-1943*, Australian National University Press, Canberra, 1978.

_____*Australia and the 'New World Order': From peacekeeping to peace enforcement: 1988—1991*, Cambridge University Press, Melbourne, 2011.

Horner, D.M., and Connor, J., *The Good International Citizen: Australian peacekeeping in Asia, Africa and Europe, 1991-1993*, Cambridge University Press, Melbourne, 2014.

Howie-Willis, Ian, *Surgeon and General: A Life of Major-General Rupert Downes, 1885-1945*, Australian Military History Publications, Loftus, New South Wales, 2009.

_____*A Medical Emergency: Major-General 'Ginger' Burston and the Army Medical Service in World War II*, Big Sky Publishing, Sydney, 2012.

_____An Unending War: The Australian Army's struggle against malaria, 1885-2015, BigSky Publishing, Newport, New South Wales, 2016.

Leithhead, Barry, *A Vision for Australia's Health: Dr Cecil Cook at Work*, Australian Scholarly Publishing Pty Ltd, North Melbourne, 2019.

Levine, Philippa, *Prostitution, Race and Politics: Policing Venereal Disease in the British Empire*, Routledge, London, 2003.

LHQ [Land Headquarters], *Standards of Prophylaxis, Treatment and Cure of Venereal Diseases*, LHQ [of Allied Land Forces, South-West Pacific Area], Melbourne, March 1943.

Long, Gavin, *To Benghazi*, Vol. I, Series I, *Australia in the War of 1939-1945*, Australian War Memorial, Canberra, 1952.

_____*Greece, Crete and Syria*, Vol. II, Series I, *Australia in the War of 1939-1945*, Australian War Memorial, Canberra, 1953.

_____*The Final Campaigns*, Vol. VII, Series I, *Australia in the War of 1939-1945*, Australian War Memorial, Canberra, 1963.

Macpherson, W.G., Herringham, W.P., Elliott, T.R., and Balfour, A. (eds), *Medical Services: Diseases of the War*, His Majesty's Stationery Office, London, 1922.

Macpherson, W.G., Horrocks, W.H., and Beveridge, W.W.O. (eds), *Medical Services: Hygiene of the War*, His Majesty's Stationery Office, London, 1923.

Maughan, Barton, *Tobruk and El Alamein*, Vol. III, Series I, *Australia in the War of 1939-1945*, Australian War Memorial, Canberra, 1988.

Maurice, Sir Frederick (ed) *History of the War in South Africa 1899—1902 compiled by direction of His Majesty's Government by Sir Frederick Maurice with a staff of officers*, Hurst and Blackett, London, 1906-1910.

McCarthy, Dudley, *South-West Pacific Area—First Year: Kokoda to Wau*, Vol. V, Series I, *Australia in the War of 1939-1945*, Australian War Memorial, Canberra, 1959.

McNeill, Ian G., *To Long Tan: The Australian Army and the Vietnam War*, Allen & Unwin and the Australian War Memorial, St Leonards, New South Wales, 1993.

McNeill, Ian G., and Ekins, Ashley, *On the Offensive: The Australian Army in the Vietnam War, January 1967-June 1968*, Allen & Unwin and the Australian War Memorial, Crows Nest, New South Wales, 2003.

Mitchell, T.J., and Smith, M.G., *Medical Services: Casualties and Medical Statistics of the Great War*, His Majesty's Stationery Office, London, 1931.

Murray, P.L. (ed), *Official Records of the Australian Military Contingents to the War in South Africa*, Albert J. Mullett, Government Printer, Melbourne, 1911.

Norris, F. Kingsley, *No Memory For Pain: An Autobiography*, William Heinemann Australia Pty Ltd, Melbourne, 1970.

O'Keefe, Brendan G., *Medicine at War: Medical aspects of Australia's involvement in Southeast Asia 1950-1972*, Vol. III in *The Official History of Australia's Involvement in South east-Asian Conflicts 1948-1975*, Allen & Unwin in association with Australian War Memorial, St Leonards, New South Wales, 1994.

O'Neill, Robert, *Australia in the Korean War 1950—53*, Vol. I, *Strategy and Diplomacy*,

Australian War Memorial and the Australian Government Publishing Service, Canberra, 1981.

―――― *Australia in the Korean War 1950-53*, Vol. II, *Combat Operations*, Australian War Memorial and the Australian Government Publishing Service, Canberra, 1985.

Porter, Roy, *The Greatest Benefit to Mankind: A Medical History of Humanity from Antiquity to the Present*, HarperCollins Publishers, London, 1997.

Rees, Peter, *Bearing Witness: The remarkable life of Charles Bean, Australia's greatest war correspondent*, Allen & Unwin, Crow's Nest, New South Wales, 2015.

Rieff, David, *In Praise of Forgetting: Historical Memory and Its Ironies*, Yale University Press, 2016.

Self, Helen J., *Prostitution, Women, and Misuse of the Law: The Fallen Daughters of Eve*, Frank Cass, London, 2003.

Stanley, Peter, *Bad Characters: Sex, Crime, Mutiny, Murder and the Australian Imperial Force*, Pier 9, Sydney and London, 2010.

Steigrad, Joseph, *Prevention of Venereal Disease*, I Australian Mobile Printing Unit, Palestine, December 1942.

Summers, A., Swain, T., Jelly, M., and Verco, C., *Blood, Sweat and Fears IT: Medical practitioners of South Australia on active service after World War II to Vietnam, 1945—1975*, Army Health Services Historical Research Group, Army Museum of South Australia Foundation, 2016.

Tyquin, Michael B., *Little by Little: A Centenary History of the Royal Australian Army Medical Corps*, Australian Military History Publications, Loftus, New South Wales, 2003.

Walker, Allan S., *Clinical Problems of War*, Vol. I, Series 5, *Australia in the War of 1939-1945*, Australian War Memorial, Canberra, 1952,

_____*Middle East and Far East*, Vol. II, Series 5, *Australia in the War of 1939-1945*, Australian War Memorial, Canberra, 1953.

_____*The Island Campaigns*, Vol. III, Series 5, *Australia in the War of 1939—1945*, Australian War Memorial, Canberra, 1957.

_____ Medical Services of the R.A.N. and R.A.A.F., Vol. IV, Series 5, *Australia in the War of 1939-1945*, Australian War Memorial, Canberra, 1961.

Wigmore, Lionel, *The Japanese Thrust*, Volume IV, Series I, *Australia in the War of 1939-1945*, Australian War Memorial, Canberra, 1957.

Wilcox, Craig, *Australia's Boer War: The War in South Africa 1899-1902*, Melbourne, Oxford University Press and the Australian War Memorial, 2002.

Wilson, Graham, *Accommodating the King's Hard Bargain: Military Detention in the Australian Army, 1914-1947*, Big Sky Publishing, Sydney, 2016.

Wilson, Sir William Deane, *Report on the Medical Arrangement on the South African War*, His Majesty's Stationery Office, London, 1904.

Articles, book chapters and encyclopaedia entries

Arthur, Richard, An address delivered to the Officers of the Australian Imperial Force', *Medical Journal of Australia*, 20 May 1916, pp.411-414.

___ 'Some aspects of the venereal problem', *Medical Journal of Australia*, 28 October 1916, pp.361-364.

Avery, A.G., 'On the treatment of gonorrhoea by the general practitioner', *Medical Journal of Australia*, 24 July 1920, pp.71-73.

Barrett, J.W., 'Venereal diseases', *Medical Journal of Australia*, 23 March 1914, pp.1487—1489; 4 April 1914, pp.1503-1505.

___ 'The Venereal Diseases Problem', *Medical Journal of Australia*, 16 June 1928, pp.760-761.

Beard, Donald D., 'Acute epidemic haemorrhagic fever', *Medical Journal of Australia*, 1 March 1952, pp.294-295.

Brown, K.P., 'Discussion on medical problems in Korea: Medicine in Korea', *Proceedings of the Royal Society for Medicine*, Vol.46, 1953, pp.1039-1041.

Cumpston, J.H.L., 'The effect of legislative control on the incidence of ante-natal syphilis', *Medical Journal of Australia*, 20 August 1921, pp.133-136.

Davis, Nevil C., 'Surgical aspects of the Korean War, March 1951 to February 1952', *Medical Journal of Australia*, 13 September 1952, pp.367-373.

Downes, Rupert M., 'The Campaign in Sinai and Palestine', Part II in Butler, A.G., *The Australian Army Medical Services in the War of 1914—1918*, Vol. I, 2nd edn, Australian War Memorial, Melbourne, 1938.

Dylewski, J., and Duong, M., 'The rash of secondary syphilis', *Canadian Medical Association Journal (CMAJ)*, Vol.176 No.1, 2007, pp.33-35.

Editorial Board, 'The Spread of Syphilis', *Medical Journal of Australia*, 27 February 1915, p.196.

Fairley, Christopher K., 'Sexual health—reaching out: Australia should continue to improve its sexual health services, especially access to them, and strive for zero endemic prevalence of sexually transmitted diseases', *Medical Journal of Australia*, 7 April 1997, pp.341-342.

Fairley, Neil Hamilton, 'Studies in Syphilis', *Medical Journal of Australia*, 24 December 1921, pp.588-596.

Fairley, N. Hamilton, and Fowler, Robert, 'The Wassermann Test', *Medical Journal of Australia*, 20 August 1921, p.350.

Fiaschi, Piero EB., 'The prophylaxis of venereal diseases', *Medical Journal of Australia*, 28 January 1922, pp.85-93.

Fowler, Robert, 'Familial Syphilis', *Medical Journal of Australia*, 24 December 1921, pp.599-602.

Frith, John, 'Syphilis—Its Early History and Treatment Until Penicillin, and the Debate on its Origins', *Journal of Military and Veterans Health*, Vol.20, No.4, November 2012, pp.49-57.

Gandevia, Bryan, 'Medical and surgical aspects of the Korean campaign, September to December 1950: Casualties and their evacuation', *Medical Journal of Australia*, 11 August 1951, pp.191-195.

Gibson, N.M., 'Control of Venereal Disease in the Army', *Medical Journal of Australia*, 26 September 1942, pp.290-292.

———— 'The Second Front: Venereal Disease', *Salt*, 2 February 1942, pp.23-26.

_____ 'Gonorrhoea and Syphilis at Work', *Salt*, 9 February 1942, pp.23-26.

_____ 'VD. and the Army', *Salt*, 16 February 1942, pp.23-28.

Harsant, A.G., 'Discussion on medical problems in Korea: Surgery in Korea, *Proceedings of the Royal Society for Medicine*, Vol.46, 1953, pp.1037-1039.

Hart, Gavin, 'Psychological aspects of venereal disease in a war environment', *Social Science & Medicine*, Vol.7, 1973, pp.455-467.

_____ 'Penicillin resistance of gonococci in South Vietnam', *Medical Journal of Australia*, 29 September 1973, pp.638-641.

_____ 'Social aspects of venereal disease: I. Sociological determinants of venereal disease', *British Journal of Venereal Diseases*, Vol.49 No.6, December 1973, pp.542-547.

_____ 'Social aspects of venereal disease: II. Relationship of personality to other sociological determinants of venereal disease', *British Journal of Venereal Diseases*, Vol.49 No.6, December 1973, pp.548-552.

_____ 'Factors influencing venereal infection in a war environment', *British Journal of Venereal Diseases*, Vol.50 No.1, February 1974, pp.68-72.

_____ 'Social and psychological aspects of venereal disease in Papua New Guinea, *British Journal of Venereal Diseases*, Vol.50 No.6, December 1974, pp.453-458.

_____ 'Venereal disease in a war environment: incidence and management', *Medical Journal of Australia*, 28 June 1975, pp.808-810.

_____ 'Sexual behaviour in a war environment', *Journal of Sex Research*, Vol.11 No.3, August 1975, pp.218-226.

Hughes, E.S.R., and Webb, Rowan, 'Medical and surgical aspects of the Korean campaign, September to December 1950: The treatment of open wounds of British Commonwealth battle casualties', *Medical Journal of Australia*, 11 August 1951, pp.195-197.

Ingham, F.J., 'Discussion on medical problems in Korea: Army health problems', *Proceedings of the Royal Society for Medicine*, Vol.46, 1953, pp.1041-1046.

Kater, N.M., 'Epidemic haemorrhagic fever or ryukosei shukketsu netsu', *Medical Journal of Australia*, 15 December 1951, p.824.

_____ 'Helicopter evacuation in Korea, *Medical Journal of Australia*, 13 September 1952, pp.373-374.

_____ 'Some experiences in a Korean prisoner-of-war camp hospital', *Medical Journal of Australia*, 31 March 1953, pp.94-95.

_____ 'Air evacuation of casualties in the Korean War', *Medical Journal of Australia*, 18 July 1953, pp.94-95.

Lind, W.A.T., 'Venereal Disease and the Abnormal Mind', *Medical Journal of Australia*, 15 December 1923, p.643.

Makepeace, Clare, 'Sex and the Somme: Officially sanctioned brothels on the front line', *Daily Mail Australia*, 29 October 2011, also http://www.dailymail.co.uk/news/article-2054914/Sex-Somme-Officially-sanctioned-WWI-brothels-line.html.

McIntyre, Darryl, 'Australian Army Medical Services in Korea in O'Neill, Robert, *Australia in the Korean War 1950—53*, Vol. II, *Combat*

Operations, Australian War Memorial and the Australian Government Publishing Service, Canberra, 1985.

McLeod, Jan, 'The House That Jack Built: DGMS Rupert Downes and Australian Army Preparations for World War II, *Health & History,* Vol.19 No.1, 2017, pp.80-101.

Mindel, A., and Kippax, S., 'A national sexually transmissible infections strategy: the need for an all-embracing approach', *Medical Journal of Australia,* 21 November 2005, pp.502—503.

Morris, Arthur E., 'Army Medical Service: Prophylaxis and treatment of venereal disease', *Medical Journal of Australia,* 13 September 1919, pp.211-217.

Medical Surveillance Monthly Report (MSMR), 'Sexually Transmitted Infections', Vol.20 No.2, February 2013.

Nash, John B., 'A Note from Alexandria, *Medical Journal of Australia,* 27 February 1915, pp.200-201.

National Health and Medical Research Council Working Party on AIDS, 'Acquired immune deficiency syndrome (AIDS)', *Medical Journal of Australia*, 27 October 1984, pp.565-568.

Nysirios, George, 'Should the Australian Defence Force screen for genital *Chlamydia trachomatis* infection?' *ADF Health*, Vol. 7, April 2006, pp.20-21.

'Penicillin and the prevention of syphilis', *Medical Journal of Australia*, 23 July 1949, pp.140-141.

Pisani, E., Purnomo, H., Sutrisna, A., Asy, A., Zaw, M., Tilman, C., Bull, H., and Neilsen, G., 'Basing policy on evidence: low HIV, STIs, and risk behaviour in Dili, East Timor argue for more focused interventions', *Sexually Transmitted Infections*, 82(1), February 2006, pp.88-93.

Potter, W.L., 'The influence of treatment and rest in gonorrhoea, *Medical Journal of Australia*, 13 September 1919, pp.211-217.

Sakamoto, Rumi, 'Pan-pan Girls: Humiliating Liberation in Post-War Japan', *Portal Journal of Multidisciplinary International Studies*, Vol.7 No.2, July 2010, pp.1-15.

Shanks, G. Dennis, 'How World War I changed global attitudes to war and infectious diseases', *The Lancet*, 8 November 2014, pp.1699-1707.

Smith, F.B., 'Agent Orange: the Australian aftermath' in O'Keefe, Brendan G., *Medicine at War: Medical aspects of Australia's involvement in Southeast Asia 1950-1972*, Allen & Unwin in association with the Australian War Memorial, St Leonards, New South Wales, 1994.

Wallace, M.S., 'Prostitution and venereal diseases', *Medical Journal of Australia*, 19 July 1919, p.59.

Willcox, R.R., 'Treatment of gonorrhoea with two grammes of terramycin in divided doses over twenty-four hours', *Medical Journal of Australia*, 21 February 1953, pp.260-261.

Wolff, K., Johnson, R.A., Saavedra, A.P., and Roh, E.K., *Fitzpatrick's Color Atlas and Synopsis of Clinical Dermatology*, 8th edn, McGraw-Hill Education, USA, 2017.

Zwar, B.T., 'The Army Medical Service and the prevention of venereal disease', *Medical Journal of Australia*, 5 July 1919, pp.1-7.

Journals

Australasian Medical Gazette: the Journal of the Australasian Branches of the British Medical Association, Sydney, articles on gonorrhoea, syphilis and related topics, 1881—1914.

Intercolonial Medical Journal of Australasia, Victorian Branch of the British Medical Association, Melbourne, articles on gonorrhoea, syphilis and related topics, 1896—1910.

Journal of Military and Veterans' Health, Australasian Military Medicine Association, Hobart, articles on sexually transmitted infections and related topics, 2007-2018.

Medical Journal of Australia, Australasian Medical Publishing Company, Sydney, articles on gonorrhoea, syphilis, venereal disease, venereology, sexually transmitted diseases and related topics, 1914-2016.

Websites and other digital media

All Saints College Bathurst, *Bean, John Willoughby Butler*, http://www.saints.nsw.edu.au/assets/pdf/anzacproject/anzacs_bean_john.pdf.

Ancestry, *15 fascinating facts from famous death records*, https://blogs.ancestry.com/cm/15-fascinating-facts-from-famous-death-records/.

Appleby, Georgia, *The Digger: the image of the Australian soldier in his own writings*, Ozwords, http://ozwords.org/?p=5105.

Australia @ War, http://www.ozatwar.com/ausarmy.

Australian Army, *Our History: WWI: The Western Front*, https://www.army.gov.au/our-history/history-in-focus/wwi-the-western-front.

Australian Bureau of Statistics, *Sexually transmitted infections*, published 26 June 2012, www.abs.gov.au/AUSSTATS/.

Australian Embassy Tokyo, *Citizenship by Descent*, http://japan.embassy.gov.au/tkyo/citizen_descent.html.

Australian Federation of AIDS Councils, https://www.afao.org.au/about-hiv/hiv-statistics/australia/.

Australian Government, *Australians on the Western Front 1914—1918: The Australian Remembrance

Trail in in France and Belgium, www.wwlwesternfront.gov.au.

Australian War Memorial, 'British Commonwealth Occupation Force 1945-52', *Australians at War*, https://www.awm.gov.au/atwar/bcof/.

_____ *Out in the Cold: Australia's involvement in the Korean War*, https://www.awm.gov.au/visit/exhibitions/korea/ausinkorea/medical.

Bean, C.E.W., 'Australia's Fair Fame', *Adelaide Advertiser*, 22 January 1915, http://trove.nla.gov.au/newspaper/article/5441710, accessed 21 October 2017.

CDC [Centers for Disease Control and Prevention], *Sexually transmitted diseases (STDs)* https://cdc.gov/std/.

Central Intelligence Agency (USA), 'Country comparisons, HIV/AIDS—Adult prevalence rate', *The World Factbook* 2011, https://www.cia.gov/library/publications/the-world-factbook/rankorder/2155rank.html.

City of Melbourne, *Art and Heritage Collection*, http://citycollection.melbourne.vic.gov.au/.

Comacho, Ivan D., *Dermatological Manifestations of Chancroid*, Medscape, http://emedicine.medscape.com/, October 2016.

Damousi, Joy, 'Campaign for Japanese-Australian children to enter Australia, 1957—1968: A History of Post-War Humanitarianism', *Australian Journal of Politics and History*, 17 April 2018, https://doi.org/10.1111/ajph.12461.

Department of Home Affairs: Immigration and Citizenship, *Community Information Summary: Japanese-born*, https://www.dss.gov.au/sites/default/files/documents/02_2014/japan.pdf.

Evershed, Nick, Australian war deaths: a graphic analysis of more than 102,000 records', *The Guardian*, 25 April 2014, https://www.theguardian.com/news/datablog/interactive/2014/apr/25/anzac-statistics-analysis.

Fair Go for Doctors, https://www.fairgofordoctors.org/all-gps-are-rich-right/.

Federation University Australia, https://www.federation.edu.au.

Health communities, *Syphilis and stages of syphilis*, www.healthcommunities.com/syphilis-diagnosissta ges-tratment.shtml.

HistoryNet, *Penicillin: Wonder Drug of World War II*, http://www.historynet.com/penicillin-wonderdr ug-world-war-ii.htm.

Imperial War Museums, https://iwm.org.uk.

Jasek, E., Chow, E.P.F, Ong, J.J., Bradshaw, C.S., Chen, M.Y., Hocking, J.S., Lee, D., Phillips, T., Temple-Smith, M., Fehler, G., and Fairley, C.K., 'Sexually transmitted infections in Melbourne, Australia, from 1918 to 2016: nearly a century of data', *Communicable Diseases Intelligence*, Vol.41 No.3, September 2017, http://www.health.gov.au /internet/main/publishing.nsf/Content/cdi4103-f.

Jones, Ross L., 'The Master Potter and the Rejected Pots: Eugenics Legislation in Victoria, 1918-1939' in Giltrow, Janet, *Academic Reading, Second Edition: Reading and Writing Across the Disciplines*, Broadway Press, Ontario, 2002, http s://books.google.com.au/books.

Kaplan, R.M., *The Prophet of Psychiatry: In Search of Reg Ellery*, R.M. Kaplan, Thirroul, New South Wales, 2014, https://books.google.com.au/books.

Korzeniewski, Krzysztof, 'Sexually transmitted infections among army personnel in the military environment' in Malla, Nancy (ed), *Sexually Transmitted infections: An overview,* 2012, pp.165-182, https://www.intechopen.com.

Lambert, Stephen M., A study of *Chlamydia trachomatis:* sexual risk behaviour, infection and prevention infections in the Australian Defence Force', PhD thesis, School of Medicine, University of Queensland, 2014, https://espace.library.uq.edu.au/view/UQ369477/s33656852_phd_submission.pdf.

McDonough, J.E.R., 'The Treatment of Syphilis in 1915', included as part of an article by Miller, M.G., *Syphilis Treatment During WWI,* www.vlib.us/medical/syphilis.htm.

MedicineNet, *Med Terms Dictionary,* http://www.medicinenet.com/.

Miller, M.G., *Syphilis Treatment During WWI,* Virtual Library, http://www.vlib.us/medical/syphilis.htm.

Museum of Applied Arts & Sciences, https://collection.maas.museum/.

Museums Victoria, *Victorian Collections*, https://victoriancollections.net.au.

National Archives of Australia, https://recordsearch.naa.gov.au/.

'National Health Security (Nation: Disease List) Instrument 2008', *National Health Security Act 2007*, 'Division 2.4-Sexually transmissible infections', https://www.legislation.gov.au/Details/F2016C01001.

National Library of Australia, https://nla.gov.au/.

National Library of New Zealand, https://natlib.govt.nz.

'Norman Maxwell Gibson', *Beyond 1914: the University of Sydney and the Great War*, http://beyond1914.sydney.edu.au/profile/3017/norman-maxwell-gibson.

Parliament of New South Wales, *Lieutenant-Colonel John Brady Nash MD VD (1857-1925)*, https://www.parliament.nsw.gov.au/members/Pages/member-details.aspx?pk=1028.

_____ *Venereal Diseases Act: Act No.46, 1918*, https://legislation.nsw.gov.au/acts/1918-46.pdf.

Peacekeepers, *Australian Defence Force and Police Involvement in Peacekeeping and Peacemaking Operations 1947—Today*, www.peacekeepers.asn.au.

Pedersen, V.C., *A Text-Book of Urology in Men, Women and Children*, Lea & Ferbiger, Philadelphia and New York, 1919, https://books.google.com.au/books.

Public Health Image Library (PHIL), https://www.phil.cdc.gov/.

Reserve Bank of Australia, https://www.rba.gov.au.

Roberts, Michelle, 'Emerging sex disease MG could become the next superbug', *Health*, 11 July 2018, https://www.bbc.com/news/health-44777938.

RSL NSW [Returned Services League of New South Wales], *The Vietnam War*, http://rslnsw.org.au/commemoration/heritage/the-vietnam-war.

SBS [Special Broadcasting Service], *Resources: Immigration Nation—Refugees and Japanese war brides accepted*, www.sbs.com.au/immigrationnation/resources/article/166/reugees-and-japanese-war-bridesaccepted.

State Library of Victoria, *The Rush to Enlist*, http://ergo.slv.vic.gov.au/explore-history/australiawwi/home-wwi/rush-enlist.

The Social Evil Women's Convention, circular about and resolutions of a conference organised by the Women's Political Association, Melbourne, 1916, https://www.marxists.org/history/australia/1916/social-evil.htm.

Thom Blake Historian, https://www.thomblake.com.au/.

United States Holocaust Memorial Museum, *Forced Sterilization,* https://www.ushmm.org/learn/students/learning-materials-and-resources/mentally-and-physicallyhandicapped-victims-of-the-nazi-era/forced-sterilization.

Vircell Microbiologists, *Neisseria gonorrhoeae,* https://en.vircell.com/diseases/40neisseriagonorrhoeae/.

Wellcome Collection, https://wellcomecollection.org/.

Wikimedia, *Wikimedia Commons,* https://commons.wikimedia.org/.

Wikipedia, '3rd Battalion, Royal Australian Regiment'; 'HIV/AIDS in Australia; 'Nazi Eugenics'; 'Timeline of HIV/AIDS', https://wikipedia.org.

Unpublished records

Burston, Samuel Roy, World War II Correspondence: a series of 23 folders of Burston's personal correspondence maintained with various Australian Army Medical Corps colleagues. At the time of writing, this correspondence was held by the Burston family.

Cook, Cecil Evelyn Aufrere, file of documents relating to hygiene in Japan in August-September 1945, from Cecil E.A. Cook's personal papers, held by the Cook family.

Fairley Collection, the papers of Sir Neil Hamilton Fairley, kept in the Basser Library, Australian Academy of Science, Canberra.

Hart, Gavin, 'Behavioural aspects of venereal disease', unpublished manuscript, no date [c.1974] in the possession of the author, Eden Hills, South Australia.

_____ 'The impact of prostitution on Australian troops on active service in a war environment—with particular reference to sociological factors involved in the incidence and control of venereal disease', unpublished thesis for the degree of Doctor of Medicine, University of Adelaide, January 1974, in the possession of the author, Eden Hills, South Australia.

_____ 'From rural Australia to the international scene. An eclectic account of the experiences, interests and philosophies of Gavin Hart', unpublished autobiography, manuscript, no date [c.2016] in the possession of the author, Eden Hills, South Australia.

Howie-Willis, Ian, (1) 'Articles, editorials, notices, reviews and correspondence on Venereal Diseases/Sexually Transmitted Diseases in general Australian medical journals'; (2) general correspondence for Army and STDs' project; (3) notebook of material gathered and interviews conducted for Australian Army and the STIs' project; (4) records of interviews conducted with selected interviewees for Army and STDs' project.

Leithhead, Barry, 'The Life and Times of Dr Cecil Cook', unpublished manuscript, 2013, in the possession of the author, Glenorie, New South Wales.

Pearn, John, personal communication with the author, 2017—2018.

Endnotes

Chapter 1

[1] Terminological usage in the *Medical Journal of Australia (MJA)*, the Australian medical profession's general 'news magazine', will often reflect semantic shifts in medical phrases. Thus, from its foundation in 1914 until the mid-1970s, the *MJA* commonly referred to 'Venereal Disease(s)'. The *MJA* first used the term 'sexually transmitted disease' in an editorial in February 1975. Over the next two years, 'sexually transmitted disease(s)' progressively replaced 'venereal disease(s)', in *MJA* terminology. The *MJA's* first reference to 'sexually transmitted infection(s)' was in a letter-to-the-editor in June 2002. After that, in the *MJA* if not elsewhere this term superseded 'sexually transmitted disease(s)'

[2] Gavin Hart, email to Ian Howie-Willis, 29 November 2016

[3] *Concise Oxford Dictionary.*

[4] Gavin Hart, *Reducing the impact of sexually transmitted diseases including HIV*

	infection, Public and Environmental Health Division of the South Australian Health Commissioner, Adelaide, 1989, pp.5-7
[5]	Vircell Microbiologists, 'Neisseria gonorrhoeae', https://en.vircell.com/diseases/40neisseriagonorrhoeae, accessed 15 May 2017
[6]	Hart, *Reducing the impact of sexually transmitted diseases*, pp.5—7
[7]	Ibid., pp.6—7
[8]	Ibid., p.7
[9]	Ibid
[10]	See, for example, *MJA*, 17 February 1968, pp.275-275, commenting on 'incurable' gonorrhoea among Australian troops in Vietnam.
[11]	Centers for Disease Control and Prevention (CDC), 'Sexually transmitted diseases treatment guidelines: Gonococcal infections', https://www.cdc.gov/std/tg2015/gonorrhea.htm, accessed 16 May 2017.
[12]	A.G. Butler, *The Australian Army Medical Services in the War of 1914-1918*, Vol.3, Special Problems and Services, Australian War Memorial, Melbourne, 1943, p.159
[13]	V.C. Pedersen, *A Text-Book of Urology in Men, Women and Children*, Lea &

Ferbiger, Philadelphia & New York, 1919, pp.75-81
[14] Ibid
[15] George Raffan, 'Suggested reform in the management of the venereal disease problem' in 'Correspondence on Venereal Diseases', AWM15 14379/7.
[16] John Pearn, personal communication, 28 May 2017.
[17] J.H.L. Cumpston, *Venereal Disease in Australia*, Commonwealth of Australia Quarantine Service, Government Printer, Melbourne, 1919.
[18] Ibid., p.11.
[19] Hart, *Reducing the impact of sexually transmitted diseases*, pp.8—10
[20] There are many online lists of famous syphilis sufferers. See for instance '15 fascinating facts from famous death records' on the Ancestry.com website
[21] 'History of Syphilis', *Wikipedia*, https://en.wikipedia.org/wiki/History_of_syphilis, accessed 17 May 2017.
[22] Ian Howie-Willis 'Articles, editorials, notices, reviews and correspondence on Venereal Diseases/Sexually Transmitted Diseases in general

Australian medical journals', unpublished.

[23] John Frith, 'Syphilis—Its Early History and Treatment Until Penicillin, and the Debate on its Origins', *Journal of Military and Veterans' Health*, Vol.20, No.4, 2012, p.56.

[24] Hart, *Reducing the impact of sexually transmitted diseases*, pp.8-10.

[25] Health communities.com, 'Syphilis and stages of syphilis'.

[26] Ibid.; and Hart, *Reducing the impact of sexually transmitted diseases*, p.10.

[27] M.G. Miller, 'Syphilis treatment during WWI', *WWW Virtual Library*, http://www.vlib.us/medical/syphilis.htm, accessed 17 May 2017.

[28] Hart, *Reducing the impact of sexually transmitted diseases* p.10; and 'Syphilis and stages of syphilis', http://www.healthcommunities.com/syphilis-diagnosis-stages-treatment.shtml.

[29] Silverton's account of the treatment of syphilis is set out in his 'Report on the Work of the Venereal Section engaged in the treatment of Venereal Diseases amongst Australian and NZ troops in Egypt and Palestine, 1917-1918', AWM25 267/52. His

account is comparable to that given by J.E.R. McDonough, 'The Treatment of Syphilis in 1915'quoted in Miller, 'Syphilis treatment during WWI'

[30] Frith, 'Syphilis—Its Early History and Treatment Until Penicillin', p.52

[31] Silverton, 'Syphilis', AWM25 267/52

[32] See, for instance, the many dozens of articles about gonorrhoea and syphilis in the *Medical Journal of Australia* in the decades between 1915 and 1960, which indicates a high incidence of infection in the pre-penicillin decades

[33] Derived from figures in the table 'Causes of death', *Year Book Australia*, Australian Bureau of Statistics, Canberra, 1974

[34] Derived from figures in the table 'Notifiable diseases', *Year Book Australia*, 2011

[35] For discussion of the modern epidemiology of sexually transmitted infections see, among other *MJA* articles, Christopher K. Fairley, 'Sexual health—reaching out', 1997, pp.341-342; Arian Mindel and Susan Kippax, 'A national sexually transmissible infections strategy', 2005, pp.502-503.

[36] Gavin Hart, *Chancroid, Donovanosis (Granuloma inguinale), Lymphogranuloma Venereum (LGV)*, US Department of Health, Education and Welfare, Atlanta, 1964, pp.1-11.

[37] Ivan D. Comacho, 'Dermatological Manifestations of Chancroid', *Medscape*, http://emedicine.medscape.com/, published October 2016, accessed 18 May 2017.

[38] Hart, *Chancroid, Donovanosis (Granuloma inguinale), Lymphogranuloma Venereum (LGV)*, pp.1-11.

[39] Ibid., pp.7-9.

[40] CDC, 'Sexually transmitted diseases guidelines: Chancroid', https://www.cdc.gov/std/tg2015/chancroid.htm, accessed 18 May 2017.

[41] Silverton's description is set out in 'Chancroid', AWM25 267/52.

[42] Hart, *Reducing the impact of sexually transmitted diseases*, p.7.

[43] Pearn, personal communication, 28 May 2017.

[44] Ibid.

[45] Ibid.

[46] GDC, 'Sexually transmitted diseases guidelines: Chlamydia', https://www.cdc

	.gov/std/tg2015/chlamydia.htm, accessed 19 May 2017.
[47]	Table 'Notifiable diseases, 1907-2011', *Year Book Australia*, 2012.
[48]	Hart, *Reducing the impact of sexually transmitted diseases*, pp.21—28.
[49]	Table 'Notifiable diseases, 1994-2009', *Year Book Australia*, 2010.
[50]	The graph is based on figures derived from the table 'Notifiable diseases, 1983-2011', *Year Book of Australia*, 2012.
[51]	Various organisations maintain international 'league tables' of national HIV infection rates. The figures cited here are from the US Central Intelligence Agency's online table 'Country comparisons, HIV/AIDS—Adult prevalence rate', quoted in 'The World Factbook' (2011), https://www.cia.gov/library/publications/the-world-factbook/rankorder/2155rank.html, accessed 18 May 2017.
[52]	Hart, *Reducing the impact of sexually transmitted diseases*, p.14.
[53]	Ibid., pp.10-11.
[54]	Hart, *Chancroid, Donovanosis (Granuloma inguinale), Lymphogranuloma Venereum (LGV)*, pp.13-23.
[55]	Ibid.

[56] Hart, *Reducing the impact of sexually transmitted diseases*, p.10.
[57] Ibid., p.8.
[58] Ibid.
[59] Ibid., pp.11-12.
[60] Ibid.
[61] Hart, *Chancroid, Donovanosis (Granuloma inguinale), Lymphogranuloma Venereum (LGV)*, pp.25-33,
[62] Ibid.
[63] Ibid.
[64] Hart, *Reducing the impact of sexually transmitted diseases*, p.12.
[65] Ibid., p.11.
[66] Ibid.
[67] Ibid., p.10.

Chapter 2

[1] *Report of His Majesty's Commissioners appointed to inquire into the military preparations and other matters connected with the War in South Africa*, His Majesty's Stationery Office, London, 1903.
[2] William Deane Wilson, *Report on the Medical Arrangement on the South African War*, His Majesty's Stationery Office, London, 1904.

[3] L.S. Amery, *The Times History of the War in South Africa 1899—1902*, Sampson, Low, Marston and Company Ltd, London, 1900-1909.

[4] Craig Wilcox, *Australia's Boer War: The War in South Africa 1899—1902*, Oxford University Press and the Australian War Memorial, Melbourne, 2002, p.104.

[5] Ibid.

[6] T.J. Mitchell and M.G. Smith, *Medical Services: Casualties and Medical Statistics of the Great War*, His Majesty's Stationery Office, London, 1931, p.273. This book is Volume 1 in the 14-volume British official medical history of World War I.

[7] Australia and the Boer War, 1899-1902', AWM, *Memorial Encyclopaedia*, https://www.awm.gov.au/; 'Second Boer War', *Wikipedia*, https://en.wikipedia.org/wiki/Second_Boer_War, each accessed 26 July 2019.

[8] See *Australasian Medical Gazette*, 1881—1914; *Intercolonial Medical Journal of Australasia*, 1896-1910; and *MJA*, 1914.

[9] Cumpston, *Venereal Disease in Australia*, pp.5-6.

[10] Ibid.

[11] Ibid.

[12] Ibid., p.8.
[13] Ibid
[14] 'Committee Concerning Causes of Death and Invalidity in the Commonwealth, Report on Venereal Diseases', AWM27 376/194.
[15] 'Prevention and Treatment of Venereal Disease', Recommendations of the UK Royal Commission on the Prevention and Treatment of Venereal Diseases, 1917, AWM27 370/12.
[16] Cumpston, *Venereal Disease in Australia*, p.8.
[17] Ibid.
[18] Ibid., pp.9-10.
[19] A.G. Butler, *The Australian Army Medical Services in the War of 1914-1918*, Vol.1, *The Gallipoli Campaign*, Australian War Memorial Melbourne, 1938, p.20.
[20] *MJA*, 28 March 1914, p.1489.
[21] Cumpston, *Venereal Disease in Australia*, p.7.
[22] Butler, *The Australian Army Medical Services*, Vol.1, *The Gallipoli Campaign*, p.25.
[23] Butler, *The Australian Army Medical Services*, Vol.3, *Special Problems and Services*, Table 12, p.882.
[24] Ibid.

[25] Ibid.
[26] Ibid.
[27] Ibid., p.751.
[28] For reports on the activities of these VD isolation hospitals, see 'Administrative means for dealing with special cases of venereal disease', AWM25 267/53.
[29] For a summary of Arthur's career, see his entry in the *Australian Dictionary of Biography (ADB)*, National Centre of Biography, Australian National University, http://adb.anu.edu.au/biography/butler-arthur-graham-5444/text9243, published first in hardcopy 1979, accessed online 9 November 2017.
[30] 'An address delivered to officers of the Australian Imperial Force', *MJA*, 20 May 1916, p.411.
[31] Ibid.
[32] Ibid.
[33] Editorial Board, 'The Spread of Syphilis', *MJA*, 27 February 1915, p.196.
[34] Ibid.
[35] Butler, *The Australian Army Medical Services*, Vol.3, *Special Problems and Services*, Table 16, pp.886-7.
[36] Ibid., p.886.
[37] Ibid., Table 23, p.892.

[38] Ibid., Table 16, pp.886-7.
[39] Butler, *The Australian Army Medical Services*, Vol.1, *The Gallipoli Campaign*, p.25.
[40] W.E. Grigor, 'Special report on VD Cases', 13 February 1916, AWM27 371/98.
[41] C.E.W. Bean, *Official History of Australia in the War of 1914-1918*, Vol. I, *The Story of ANZAC from the outbreak of war to the end of the first phase of the Gallipoli Campaign, May 4, 1915*, Angus & Robertson Ltd, Sydney, 1941, pp.98-99; Peter Dennis et al., *The Oxford Companion to Australian Military History*, Oxford University Press, Melbourne, 2008), p.63.
[42] Bean, *Official History*, Vol. I, *The Story of ANZAC*, pp.115-116.
[43] See for example, Joan Beaumont, *Broken Nation: Australians in the Great War*, Allen & Unwin, Crows Nest, New South Wales, 2013; Jeffrey Grey, *The Australian Centenary History of Defence*, Vol. I, *The Australian Army*, Oxford University Press Melbourne, 2001; and Dennis, *The Oxford Companion to Australian Military History*, pp.194-195.

[44] Bean, *Official History*, Vol. I, *The Story of ANZAC*, p.127.
[45] Ibid.
[46] Ibid.
[47] Ibid., p.128.
[48] Ibid.
[49] Ibid., pp.128-129.
[50] 'Letter from General Birdwood re Venereal Disease', AWM27 376/173.
[51] Bean, *Official History*, Vol. I, *The Story of ANZAC*, p.129.
[52] Butler, *The Australian Army Medical Services*, Vol.1, *The Gallipoli Campaign*, pp.76-8.
[53] Ibid.
[54] Ibid., pp.58, 61.
[55] Ibid., p.61.
[56] Butler, *The Australian Army Medical Services*, Vol.3, *Special Problems and Services*, p.173.
[57] Butler, *The Australian Army Medical Services*, Vol.1, *The Gallipoli Campaign*, p.61.
[58] Ibid.
[59] Ibid.
[60] 'Notes by Major B.T. Zwar upon Veneral Disease in Egypt', AWM25 267/26.

[61]	B.T. Zwar, 'The Army Medical Service and the prevention of venereal disease', *MJA*, 5 July 1919, pp.1-7.
[62]	Ibid.
[63]	Ibid. The chart is based on figures given by Major Zwar.
[64]	Ibid.; and 'Notes by Major B.T. Zwar upon Veneral Disease in Egypt', AWM25 267/26.
[65]	Zwar, 'The Army Medical Service and the prevention of venereal disease'.
[66]	Ibid.
[67]	Ibid.
[68]	G.D. Shanks to I. Howie-Willis, 1 November 2017, Howie-Willis 'general correspondence'.
[69]	John, Pearn, personal communication, 3 November 2017.
[70]	Zwar, 'The Army Medical Service and the prevention of venereal disease'.
[71]	Ibid.
[72]	Ibid.
[73]	Ibid.
[74]	Butler, *The Australian Army Medical Services*, Vol.1, *The Gallipoli Campaign*, pp.76-8.
[75]	Ibid., p.188.

[76] G.D. Shanks to I. Howie-Willis, 1 November 2017, Howie-Willis general correspondence'.

[77] Butler, *The Australian Army Medical Services*, Vol.1, *The Gallipoli Campaign*, pp.102—103.

[78] Ibid., p.188.

[79] Ibid., p.188; J.W. Barrett and P.E. Deane, *The Australian Army Medical Corps in Egypt: An illustrated and detailed account of the early organisation and work of the Australian Medical Units in Egypt in 1914—1915*, H.K. Lewis & Co. Ltd., London, 1918, p.122, give a figure of 1344 between February and September 1915.

[80] For an account of the history of this camp, see Raden Dunbar, *The Secrets of the ANZACS: The untold story of venereal disease in the Australian Army, 1914—1919*, Scribe Publications, Brunswick (Victoria) and Clerkenwell (London), 2014.

[81] Barrett and Deane, *The Australian Army Medical Corps in Egypt*, p.122.

[82] Ibid.

[83] Dunbar, *The Secrets of the ANZACS*, p.184 ff.

[84] Ibid.

[85]	NAA: B2455, 'SSG' [soldier's name]—AIF service record.
[86]	Ibid.
[87]	Ibid.
[88]	Ibid.
[89]	Ibid.
[90]	'In Memoriam' notices for 'ABC', *The Sydney Morning Herald*, 6 November 1916.
[91]	NAA: B2455, 'SSG' [soldier's name]—AIF service record.
[92]	Letter by 'MLS' dated 'Tuesday 8th'[no month given but certainly June 1915], 'Information to Relatives of Men with Venereal Disease', NAA: MP 367/1, 580/1/908.
[93]	OIC Base Records to A.G.' [Adjutant General?], 17 June 1915, 'Information to Relatives of Men with Venereal Disease', NAA: MP 367/1, 580/1/908.
[94]	'In Memoriam' notices for 'ABC', *The Sydney Morning Herald*, 6 November 1916.
[95]	Dunbar, *The Secrets of the ANZACS*, p.184 ff.
[96]	Bean, *Official History*, Vol. I, *The Story of ANZAC*, p.130.

[97]	'Egypt, Australians in' and 'Wazza Riots' quoted in Dennis, *The Oxford Companion to Australian Military History*.
[98]	'Notes by Major B.T. Zwar upon Veneral Disease in Egypt', AWM25 267/26.
[99]	Butler, *The Australian Army Medical Services*, Vol.1, *The Gallipoli Campaign*, pp.188, 485-6.
[100]	Ibid., pp.485-6.
[101]	Ibid.
[102]	Ibid.
[103]	Ibid., p.486.
[104]	Ibid.
[105]	Ibid.
[106]	W.E. Grigor to DMS, AIF [N.R. Howse], 3 February 1916, AWM27 371/97.
[107]	Ibid.
[108]	Ibid.
[109]	Ibid.
[110]	Ibid.
[111]	Ibid.
[112]	Grigor, 'Special report on VD Cases', AWM27 371/98.
[113]	'The Rush to Enlist', *Ergo*, State Library of Victoria, http://ergo.slv.vic.gov.au/explorehistory/australia-wwi/ho

	me-wwi/rush-enlist, accessed 28 June 2018.
[114]	The inflation factor is derived from the Reserve Bank of Australia online inflation calculator on the website, https://www.rba.gov.au/calculator/PreDecimal.html.
[115]	'VD Returns, 1st Australian Dermatological Hospital, A.I.F', AWM27 376/101.
[116]	Ibid.
[117]	Ibid.
[118]	Ibid.
[119]	N.R. Howse to General Birdwood, 19 January 1916, 'Correspondence of Colonel R.M.McC. Anderson to the Prime Minister, W.M. Hughes', NAA: CP359/2, 17.
[120]	Ibid.
[121]	Ibid., 7 March 1916.
[122]	Ibid.
[123]	Ibid.
[124]	The article appeared in both *The Sydney Morning Herald* and *The Advertiser* [Adelaide] on Friday 22 January 1916. Bean had despatched the report on 29 December 1914.
[125]	*The Advertiser*, Friday 22 January 1916, p.6.

[126]	Ibid.
[127]	Ibid.
[128]	For a discussion of Bean's background and upbringing, and his work as a war correspondent, see Peter Rees, *Bearing Witness: The remarkable life of Charles Bean, Australia's greatest war correspondent*, Allen & Unwin, Crow's Nest, New South Wales, 2015.
[129]	*The Advertiser*, Friday 22 January 1916, p.6.
[130]	'Correspondence of Col. R·M.McC. Anderson to the PM, W.M. Hughes', NAA: CP359/2, 17.
[131]	Ibid., 23 February 1916.
[132]	N.N. George to R·M.McC. Anderson, 14 March 1916, NAA: CP359/2, 17.
[133]	Peter Stanley, *Bad Characters: Sex, Crime, Mutiny, Murder and the Australian Imperial Force*, Pier 9, Sydney and London, 2010, p.30.
[134]	Ibid., p.31.
[135]	Ibid.
[136]	Butler, *The Australian Army Medical Services*, Vol.1, *The Gallipoli Campaign*, pp.76-78.

[137]　Butler, *The Australian Army Medical Services*, Vol.3, *Special Problems and Services*, p.886.

[138]　Butler, *The Australian Army Medical Services*, Vol.1, *The Gallipoli Campaign*, Graph 6, following p.466.

[139]　Ibid., pp.76-78.

Chapter 3

[1]　Bean, *Official History*, Vol. 1, *The Story of ANZAC*, p.68.

[2]　Butler, *The Australian Army Medical Services*, Vol.3, *Special Problems and Services*, Table 12, p.882.

[3]　Ibid., and 'Admitted to hospital [for VD]', first [unnumbered] table on p.187.

[4]　Ibid., p.187; Table 14, p.884; Table 19, p.889; and Table 21, p.890. None of the official histories gives a global total figure for the number of troops consigned to the separate theatres in the Middle East and the Western Front, or in the UK. All they give are 'mean average daily strength' by year and theatre.

[5]　Ibid., p.187.

[6]　Australian Army, 'WW1: The Western Front', https://www.army.gov.au/our-hist

ory/history-infocus/wwi-the-western-front, accessed 28 December 2017.

[7] Butler, *The Australian Army Medical Services*, Vol.3, *Special Problems and Services*, Table 58, Appendices.

[8] The desert campaigns are described in H.S. Gullett, *Official History of Australia in the War of 1914-1918*, Vol.7, *The Australian Imperial Force in Sinai and Palestine, 1914-1918*, Angus & Robertson, Sydney, 1940. The medical support of the campaigns is described in Rupert M. Downes, 'The Campaign in Sinai and Palestine', Part II in Butler, *The Australian Army Medical Services*, Vol.1, *The Gallipoli Campaign*.

[9] Downes, 'The Campaign in Sinai and Palestine', pp.552-553.

[10] Gullett, *Official History*, Vol.7, *The Australian Imperial Force in Sinai and Palestine, 1914-1918*, pp.98, 122.

[11] This figure is an estimate derived from statistics set out in Butler, *The Australian Army Medical Services*, Vol.3, *Special Problems and Services*. See note 4 above.

[12] The chart is based on figures in the document 'Graph showing weekly admissions to hospital for cases of

venereal disease in the AIF, Egypt (1918-1919)', AWM27 376/164.

[13] Butler, *The Australian Army Medical Services*, Vol.3, *Special Problems and Services*, p.187.

[14] Downes, 'The Campaign in Sinai and Palestine', p.772.

[15] Butler, *The Australian Army Medical Services*, Vol.1, *The Gallipoli Campaign*, pp.446, 474, 591, 600, 653, 753, 764.

[16] For a summary of Downes's life and career, see his *ADB* entry.

[17] Downes, 'The Campaign in Sinai and Palestine'.

[18] Ibid., p.772.

[19] Ibid.

[20] Ibid.

[21] Ibid., p.773.

[22] Ibid., p.773; Butler, *The Australian Army Medical Services*, Vol.3, *Special Problems and Services*, p.187.

[23] Conversion of 1917 £Australian to 2016 $Australian was done using the Reserve Bank of Australia's on-line 'Pre-Decimal Inflation Calculator'.

[24] Downes, 'The Campaign in Sinai and Palestine', p.774.

[25] Butler, *The Australian Army Medical Services*, Vol.3, *Special Problems and Services*, p.187.
[26] Ibid., p.156.
[27] Ibid., p.154.
[28] Ibid., p.157.
[29] Ibid.
[30] Ibid., p.180.
[31] Ibid., pp.180-181. See also the discussion of the Australian hospitalisation rates in Chapter 4 endnote 87.
[32] Ibid., p.155.
[33] Ibid., p.157.
[34] Ibid.
[35] Ibid., pp.158-160. See also AWM15 item 14379/7; AWM15 item 17826; AWM27 items 376/183 and 376/184; AWM27 item 376/183; All provide details of the course of lectures on VD.
[36] Butler, *The Australian Army Medical Services*, Vol.3, *Special Problems and Services*, p.160.
[37] Ibid.
[38] 'Medical report re lectures given to hospital patients on Venereal Disease by AIF Chaplains in conjunction with Medical Officers', AWM15 item 17826.

[39] For a summary of F.W. Wray's life and career, see his entry in the *ADB*. His awards, CBE and CMG, were formally a 'Commander of the Most Excellent Order of the British Empire' and a 'Companion of the Order of Saint Michael and Saint George'.

[40] Paul J. Collins and Michael Collins, *Remembered: Collins and Byrne Relatives in the Great War*, Lulu.com., 2017, p.138; *The Daily Advertiser* (Wagga Wagga), 'Rev. J.W. Ward', obituary, 30 March 1938, p.4, republished online in 'Trove', https://trove.nla.gov.au/newspaper/, accessed 23 March 2018.

[41] Butler, *The Australian Army Medical Services*, Vol.3, *Special Problems and Services*, p.155.

[42] Ibid.

[43] Ibid., p.158.

[44] George Raffan, 'Instructions to Medical Officers regarding the prevention of Venereal Disease', April 1918, p.3; Appendix 1, p.5, AWM27 376/100.

[45] Butler, *The Australian Army Medical Services*, Vol.3, *Special Problems and Services*, p.158.

[46] Raffan, 'Instructions to Medical Officers', p.3, AWM27 376/100.

[47]	Ibid.
[48]	J.W. Ward, 'Dear General' [presumably the AIF Commander, General Birdwood], AWM27 376/184.
[49]	AIF service file, 'Raffan, George', NAA: B2455.
[50]	Ibid.; Butler, *The Australian Army Medical Services*, Vol.3, *Special Problems and Services*, p.156; Ettie Rout, letters, AWM38 3DRL 6673/149.
[51]	Raffan, 'Instructions to Medical Officers', AWM27 376/100.
[52]	Butler, *The Australian Army Medical Services*, Vol.3, *Special Problems and Services*, p.161.
[53]	Ibid., p.157.
[54]	Raffan, 'Instructions to Medical Officers', p.4, AWM27 376/100.
[55]	Ibid.
[56]	Butler, *The Australian Army Medical Services*, Vol.3, *Special Problems and Services*, p.165.
[57]	'Prevention and Treatment of Venereal Disease', AWM27 370/12.
[58]	Butler, *The Australian Army Medical Services*, Vol.3, *Special Problems and Services*, p.162.
[59]	Ibid., p.163.
[60]	Ibid., p.162, footnote 17.

[61]   Ibid., pp.163-164.
[62]   Ibid., p.164.
[63]   Ibid., p.163.
[64]   Ibid., p.164.
[65]   Ibid., p.162.
[66]   Ibid., p.158.
[67]   Ibid., pp.169-170.
[68]   Ibid.
[69]   Ibid., p.171.
[70]   Ibid., p.172.
[71]   Ibid.
[72]   'Report of Surgeon General R.H.J. Fetherston on war work abroad: Section 14—Venereal Disease', c. June 1918, AWM27 376/156.
[73]   Butler, *The Australian Army Medical Services*, Vol.3, *Special Problems and Services*, p.172.
[74]   Ibid.; Butler derived his information from a large series of archival files now held in the Australian War Memorial. See for example AWM27 371/97, 376/179, 376/180, 376/181, 376/182, 376/183, all of which relate to I ADH.
[75]   Butler, *The Australian Army Medical Services*, Vol.3, *Special Problems and Services*, pp.187-188. Figures derived

	from the third table on p.187 and the second table on p.188.
[76]	Ibid., p.188, last table on that page.
[77]	Ibid., p.170.
[78]	'Report of Surgeon General R.H.J. Fetherston', AWM27 376/156.
[79]	A.G. Butler, *The Australian Army Medical Services in the War of 1914-1918*, Vol.2, *The Western Front*, Australian War Memorial, Melbourne, 1940, p.911.
[80]	Butler, *The Australian Army Medical Services*, Vol.3, *Special Problems and Services*, p.171.
[81]	Ibid.
[82]	Ibid.
[83]	Dixson, Hugh to Minister for Defence, no date but c. June 1917 in file of correspondence of the Surgeon General, Major General R.H.J. Fetherston, NAA: MP367/1, 527/21/101, 'Venereal Disease in AIF Camps in England'.
[84]	Ibid.
[85]	Butler, *The Australian Army Medical Services*, Vol.3, *Special Problems and Services*, p.155.
[86]	Ibid., p.170.
[87]	Ibid.

[88] See, for example, the range of disciplinary charges dealt with at 1 ADH in 'Routine Orders, 1st Australian Dermatological Hospital, from 7-9-1918 to 13-5-1919', AWM25 707/11 file 123.

[89] J.M. Stewart, correspondence to HQ, AIF Depots in UK, Bhurtpore Barracks, Tidworth, 12 May 1919, AWM15 18595. Among others, this file contains a series of about 80 claims for damages to property and equipment.

[90] Butler, *The Australian Army Medical Services*, Vol.3, *Special Problems and Services*, p.170.

[91] '1st Australian Dermatological Hospital Report for April 1919', AWM25 399/6.

[92] J.H. Wilson, 'Venereal Disease', report to B Group HQ, 12 August 1916, AWM15 5131.

[93] Butler, *The Australian Army Medical Services*, Vol.2, *The Western Front*, p.911.

[94] The calculation is: 627 patients annually x 6 weeks' treatment each = 3,762 'treatment weeks' /52 weeks in the year = 72-patient caseload in each week.

[95] Figures estimated from data available at 'Fair Go for Doctors', https://www.

fairgofordoctors.org/all-gps-are-rich-right/, accessed 20 March 2018.
[96] 'Report of Surgeon General R.H.J. Fetherston', AWM27 376/156.

Chapter 4

[1] Butler, *The Australian Army Medical Services*, Vol.3, *Special Problems and Services*, p.153.
[2] Ibid.; and footnote 23, p.170.
[3] Stan Walden, personal communication, 2 January 2018.
[4] Butler, *The Australian Army Medical Services*, Vol.3, *Special Problems and Services*, pp.174-175.
[5] Ibid., pp.154-155.
[6] Ibid., p.177.
[7] Dunbar, *The Secrets of the ANZACS*, p.217.
[8] Butler, *The Australian Army Medical Services*, Vol.3, *Special Problems and Services*, p.178.
[9] Ibid., p.175.
[10] Ibid.
[11] For an outline of R.E. Williams's life and career see his entry in the *ADB*, Volume 12 (1990), from which the

information in this paragraph was drawn.

[12] Butler, *The Australian Army Medical Services*, Vol.3, *Special Problems and Services*, p.176.
[13] Dunbar, *The Secrets of the ANZACS*, pp.78-82.
[14] Ibid., p.208.
[15] Butler, *The Australian Army Medical Services*, Vol.3, *Special Problems and Services*, p.177.
[16] Alan Thomas, 'Conde, Walter Tasman (1888-1974)' in the *ADB*, Volume 8 (1981).
[17] Butler, *The Australian Army Medical Services*, Vol.3, *Special Problems and Services*, p.177
[18] Dunbar, *The Secrets of the ANZACS*, pp.96-97
[19] Ibid., p.83
[20] Butler, *The Australian Army Medical Services*, Vol.3, *Special Problems and Services*, p.177
[21] Ibid., p.171.
[22] Ibid.
[23] Ibid., p.169.
[24] Ibid., p.171.
[25] Ibid.
[26] Ibid.

[27]	Ibid., p.168.
[28]	Ibid., p.172.
[29]	Ibid., pp.167-168.
[30]	Ibid.
[31]	Ibid., p.171.
[32]	Ibid., p.162.
[33]	Clare Makepeace, 'Sex and the Somme: Officially sanctioned brothels on the front line', *Daily Mail Australia*, 29 October 2011, http://www.dailymail.co.uk/news/article-2054914/Sex-Somme-Officially-sanctioned-WWI-brothels-line.html, accessed 28 November 2017.
[34]	Ibid.
[35]	Ibid.
[36]	Butler, *The Australian Army Medical Services*, Vol.3, *Special Problems and Services*, p.169, footnote 21.
[37]	Ibid., p.156.
[38]	Ibid.
[39]	Ibid., p.162.
[40]	Ibid.
[41]	Ibid.
[42]	'Venereal Disease in the Army', *MJA*, 10 August 1918, p.129.
[43]	Ibid.
[44]	Helen J. Self, *Prostitution, Women, and Misuse of the Law: The Fallen Daughters of Eve*, Frank Cass, London, 2003.

[45]	Butler, *The Australian Army Medical Services*, Vol.3, *Special Problems and Services*, p.152.
[46]	Ibid., p.164.
[47]	Ibid.
[48]	Ibid.
[49]	D.M. McWhae to Assistant Provost Marshal, 7 May 1917, AWM15 14379/7.
[50]	APM to D.M. McWhae, 16 May 1917, AWM15 14379/7.
[51]	The exchange of letters is in an Assistant Provost Marshal's file of correspondence on 'Conveyors of and suffer[er]s from VD', AWM21 1502/17.
[52]	ADMS, 3rd Australian Division to Headquarters 'Q', 3rd Australian Division, 18 August 1917; and AA & QMG to APM 3rd Australian Division, 26 August 1917, AWM27 376/184.
[53]	Butler, *The Australian Army Medical Services*, Vol.3, *Special Problems and Services*, p.160.
[54]	Ibid., p.161.
[55]	'Bean, John Willoughby Butler', http://www.saints.nsw.edu.au/assets/pdf/anzacproject/anzacs_bean_john.pdf, biographical file on the website of All Saints College, Bathurst, accessed 28 November 2017.

[56] Beatrice Chase and John Oxenham, *White Knights*, Methuen & Co. Ltd., London, no date, pamphlet in AWM38 3DRL 7447/22 Part 3.
[57] 'Appeal for Scheme "B"', AWM38 3DRL 7447/22 Part 3.
[58] Ibid.
[59] Ibid.
[60] Ibid.
[61] Ibid.
[62] James W. Barrett, letter to the editor, *MJA*, 29 March 1941, pp.401-402.
[63] For a biographical profile of Ettie Rout, see her entry in *The Encyclopaedia of New Zealand*, available online at https://teara.govt.nz/en/biographies/3r31/rout-ettie-annie.
[64] E.A. Rout to Mr Jamieson, (New Zealand representative with the YMCA, London), 7 May 1917, AWM11 1528/1/13.
[65] Ettie Rout entry in *The Encyclopaedia of New Zealand*.
[66] E.A. Rout, 'Prevention of VD in Australia', 30 April 1919, AWM38 3DRL 6673/149.
[67] See for example the reference to RafFan and Rout in Burford Sampson, B 'Notes on circular issued by Miss

Rout to ADMS all Australian Divisions', 31 March 1919, AWM38 3DRL 6673/149.

[68] See for example Butler's comment on Rout in Butler, *The Australian Army Medical Services*, Vol.3, *Special Problems and Services*, p.169, footnote 21.

[69] Rout's views are variously set out in her voluminous correspondence with the AIF's senior medical officers and administrators, politicians and the Anzacs themselves. A sample of this correspondence is contained in AWM38 6673/149.

[70] 'Private Memo from Miss E.A. Rout to Anzac Soldiers', 30 April 1919, AWM38 3DRL 6673/149.

[71] E.A. Rout to Major General Howse, 5 May 1919, AWM38 3DRL 6673/149.

[72] Ettie Rout entry in *The Encyclopaedia of New Zealand..*

[73] Ibid.
[74] Ibid.
[75] Ibid.
[76] E.A. Rout to General Richardson, 15 March 1919, AWM38 3DRL 6673/149.
[77] Ibid.
[78] Burford Sampson to Commandant, Administrative Headquarters, AIF, 21

March 1919; and 'Notes on circular issued by Miss Rout to ADMS all Australian Divisions', 31 March 1919, AWM38 3DRL 6673/149.
[79] Burford Sampson to C.E.W. Bean, 5 August and 17 November 1936, AWM38 3DRL 6673/149.
[80] E.A. Rout to General Richardson, 15 March 1919, AWM38 3DRL 6673/149.
[81] See for example E.A. Rout to W.M. Hughes, 14 March 1919, and W.M. Hughes to E.A. Rout 3 April 1919, AWM38 3DRL 6673/149.
[82] Ettie Rout entry in *The Encyclopaedia of New Zealand*.
[83] Butler, *The Australian Army Medical Services*, Vol.3, *Special Problems and Services*, p.169, footnote 21.
[84] Ibid., Table 57.
[85] Ibid., p.187.
[86] Ibid., pp.886-887. The estimate of 495 cases for 1914 is derived from Butler's approximate proportion of troops being treated for VD at any one time—3.5 per cent. If that proportion is applied to the 14,132 troops in training in Australia September to December 1914, the result is an

estimate of 495 soldiers treated for VD in that time.

[87] The inconsistency of A.G. Butler's figures is evident in a close reading of the statistical tables provided in Butler, *The Australian Army Medical Services*, Vol.3, *Special Problems and Services*. For example, (1) Table 58 indicates a figure of 62,050 VD hospitalisations for the Western Front only 1916-1919. That figure seems too high and is contradicted by other statistics elsewhere in the book. (2) Thus (p.180), Butler states that the overall AIF hospitalisation rate for VD was 158 cases per thousand of total troop strength, that is, 15.8 per cent of the 330,714 Australians who embarked for overseas service or a total of 52,238 cases of hospitalisation. (3) Seven pages later (p.187), he gives the same figure of 52,538 hospitalisations in all theatres 1915-1918, yet (4) lower down that same page (p.187) he includes tables indicating that the total number of cases in Egypt and Palestine was 12,745, while for the UK and the Western Front combined it was 40,880—that is, a total of 53,625 VD

cases in the AIF overseas (not the 52,238 cited further up the page). (5) These sums, however, do not include the VD hospitalisations in Army camps in Australia, of which there were at least 11,230 (see pp.886-887). If the estimate of 495 in the camps in 1914 is added, the result is a total of 11,725 in Australia.

[88] See for example, S. Roy Burston, (ADMS, 6th Australian Division) to the DGMS (Major General Rupert M. Downes), 13 December 1939; and Lieutenant Colonel N.M. Gibson, 'Brief History of VD. in Great War', AWM54 267/16/17 Part 8, Venereal Diseases, Reports 1941-1947'.

Chapter 5

[1] Zwar, 'The Army Medical Service and the prevention of venereal disease'.
[2] Arthur E. Morris, 'Army Medical Service: Prophylaxis and treatment of venereal disease', *MJA*, 5 July 1919, pp.3-5.
[3] W.L. Potter, 'The influence of treatment and rest in gonorrhoea', *MJA*, 13 September 1919, pp.211-217.

[4] Piero F.B. Fiaschi, 'The prophylaxis of venereal diseases', *MJA*, 28 January 1922, pp.85-93.

[5] Neil Hamilton Fairley, 'Studies in Syphilis', *MJA*, 24 December 1921, pp.588-596.

[6] For Arthur's biographical profile see Michael Roe, Arthur, Richard (1865-1932)', *ADB*, Volume 7, 1979.

[7] Ibid.

[8] Richard Arthur, 'An address delivered to the Officers of the Australian Imperial Force', *MJA*, 20 May 1916, pp.411-414.

[9] Richard Arthur, 'Some aspects of the venereal problem', *MJA*, 28 October 1916, pp.361-364.

[10] The figure of 5924 VD hospitalisations is derived from those cited by Major W.E. Grigor in his 'Special report on VD Cases', AWM27 371/98, '1 ADH, AIF, Abbassia'.

[11] A.G. Avery, 'On the treatment of gonorrhoea by the general practitioner', *MJA*, 24 July 1920, pp.71-73.

[12] 'Combating venereal disease', *MJA*, 1 June 1918, p.461.

[13] Ibid.

[14] 'The spread of venereal disease', *MJA*, 17 July 1915, p.65.

[15] The Social Evil Women's Convention, 1916.
[16] For Booth's biographical profile, see: Grant McBurnie, 'Booth, Angela Elizabeth Josephine (1869-1954)', *ADB*, Volume 13, 1993.
[17] Ibid.
[18] Margaret Fizherbert, *Liberal Women: Federation—1949*, Annandale, New South Wales, The Federation Press, 2004, pp.140-146.
[19] McBurnie, *ADB*, Volume 13, 1993.
[20] Ibid.
[21] Ibid.
[22] M.S. Wallace, 'Prostitution and venereal diseases', *MJA*, 19 July 1919, p.59.
[23] Ibid.; McBurnie, 'Booth, Angela Elizabeth Josephine (1869-1954)', *ADB*, Volume 13, 1993.
[24] For Barrett's biographical profile, see: S. Murray-Smith, 'Barrett, Sir James William (1862-1945)', *ADB*, Volume 7, 1979.
[25] James W. Barrett, 'The Venereal Diseases Problem', *MJA*, 16 June 1928, pp.760-761.
[26] 'Venereal Diseases', *MJA*, 1 October 1921, pp.272-273.

[27] Australian Association for Fighting Venereal Diseases, *The Venereal Diseases Problem: A Memorandum Issued for the Information of All Responsible Citizens*, J.C. Stephens Pty Ltd, Melbourne, 1922.
[28] Ibid.
[29] 'Venereal Diseases Conference', *MJA*, 18 February 1922, pp.193-198.
[30] Ibid.; 'Conference on Venereal Diseases', *MJA*, 23 December 1922, p.81.
[31] 'Venereal Disease', *MJA*, 21 January 1922, p.749.
[32] 'Venereal Diseases Conference', *MJA*, 18 February 1922, p.196.
[33] Ibid.
[34] Cumpston, *Venereal Disease in Australia*.
[35] Ibid.
[36] 'Venereal Diseases Conference', *MJA*, 18 February 1922, pp.196-197.
[37] Ibid.
[38] Ibid.
[39] 'The Control of Venereal Diseases', *MJA*, 29 July 1922, p.139.
[40] 'Venereal Disease', *MJA*, 23 December 1922, p.749.
[41] Ibid.
[42] Ibid.

[43] Ibid.
[44] For a summary of such legislation see the 'Contagious Diseases Acts' in *Wikipedia*.
[45] J.H.L. Cumpston, 'The effect of legislative control on the incidence of ante-natal syphilis', *MJA*, 20 August 1921, pp.133-136.
[46] New South Wales Parliament, *Venereal Diseases Act: Act No.46, 1918*.
[47] Ibid.
[48] For the medical profession's campaigning for the adoption of the Venereal Diseases Acts, see J.W. Barrett's articles in the *MJA*: 'Venereal diseases', 23 March 1914, pp.1487-1489 and 4 April 1914, pp.1503-1505; 'The spread of venereal disease', 17 July 1915, pp.65-66; 'Combating venereal disease', 1 June 1918, p.461; 'Venereal legislation in New South Wales', 28 December 1918, pp.538-539; also articles in the *MJA* by J.H.L. Cumpston: 'The effect of legislative control on the incidence of ante-natal syphilis', 20 August 1921, pp.133—136; 'The prophylaxis and treatment of venereal disease', 8 March 1919, pp.195-196; 'The Prophylaxis of venereal disease',

22 March 1919, pp.240-241; 'Control of venereal disease', 6 March 1920, pp.216-217; 'Control of venereal disease', 18 December 1920, p.278; 'The prevention of venereal disease', 18 February 1922, pp.186-187.

[49] For *MJA* editorials on VD, see 'Notification of venereal disease', 29 April 1925, pp.266-269; 'The venereal disease campaign', 3 September 1925, pp.289-290; 'Venereal diseases', 16 January 1926, pp.66—67; 'Venereal diseases in Victoria, 2 June 1928, p.692; 'Legislation and the treatment of venereal disease', 21 June 1930, pp.819—820; 'Venereal disease in New South Wales', 16 May 1936, pp.695-696; 'Syphilis', 9 January 1937, pp.63-64.

[50] On medical practitioners' discussion of VD through the correspondence columns of the *MJA (MJA)*, see for example, 'The treatment of syphilis', 22 September 1917, pp.262-264; 'The Wassermann test', 20 August 1921, pp.350-351; 'The treatment of venereal disease', 7 September 1921, p.231; 'Venereal disease', 1 October 1921, pp.272-273; 'The prophylaxis of

venereal disease', 11 February 1922, pp.169-170; 'Venereal disease', *MJA*, 25 February 1922, p.227; 'The venereal disease problem', 18 March 1922, p.311; 'Venereal diseases', 29 April 1922, p.477; 'The venereal diseases problem', 16 June 1928, pp.760-761; Venereal disease and war', 4 November 1939, p.703; Venereal disease and war', 2 September 1939, p.380; 'Venereal disease and the Army,' 12 October 1940, pp.359-360.

[51] Alex Goldstein, 'The venereal disease problem', *MJA*, 18 March 1922, p.311.

[52] J. Cooper Booth, 'Venereal diseases', *MJA*, 23 May 1925, pp.553-554.

[53] Ibid.

[54] 'Venereal diseases in Victoria, *MJA*, 2 June 1928, p.692.

[55] Barrett, 'The Venereal Diseases Problem', pp.760-761; James W. Barrett, 'Incidence of Venereal Disease in the Army and the civilian population', *MJA*, 25 June 1928, p.254.

[56] 'The Venereal Disease Campaign', *MJA*, 5 September 1925, pp.289-290.

[57] See for example the *Venereal Diseases (Amendment) Act 1963* in New South Wales (Act No.37, 1963) and the

Sexually Transmitted Diseases Act 1956 in the Australian Capital Territory.

[58] See for instance Victoria's *Health (Infectious Diseases) Regulations 2001*.

[59] See 'Division 2.4-Sexually transmissible infections' in 'National Notifiable Disease List', set out in 'National Health Security (Nation: Disease List) Instrument 2008' made under section 11 of the *National Health Security Act 2007*.

[60] Emile Jasek et al., 'Sexually transmitted infections in Melbourne, Australia, from 1918 to 2016: nearly a century of data, *Communicable Diseases Intelligence*, Volume 41, Number 3, September 2017, http://www.health.gov.au/internet/main/publishing.nsf/Content/cdi4103-f, accessed 2 March 2018.

[61] *Official yearbook of Australia* (previously *Official yearbook of the Commonwealth of Australia*), published by the Australian Bureau of Statistics (previously the Commonwealth Bureau of Census and Statistics).

[62] 'Causes of death: Syphilis', *Official yearbook of the Commonwealth of Australia*, 1919 to 1939.

[63] 'Notifiable diseases': 'Syphilis' and 'Gonorrhoea', *Official yearbook of the Commonwealth of Australia*, 1961 to 2010.

[64] Notifiable diseases': 'HIV' and 'Chlamydia, *Official yearbook of the Commonwealth of Australia*, 1988 to 2010 (HIV) and 1991-2010 (Chlamydia).

[65] 'Health of Australians: Morbidity', *The Australian Encyclopaedia* (4th edition, 1983), p.114.

[66] R.M. Kaplan, *The Prophet of Psychiatry: In Search of Reg Ellery*, R.M. Kaplan, Thirroul, New South Wales, 2014.

[67] Ross L. Jones, 'The Master Potter and the Rejected Pots: Eugenics Legislation in Victoria, 1918-1939' quoted in Janet Giltrow, *Academic Reading, Second Edition: Reading and Writing Across the Disciplines*, Broadway Press, Ontario, 2002.

[68] W.A.T. Lind, 'Venereal Disease and the Abnormal Mind', *MJA*, 15 December 1923, p.643.

[69] For Fairley's and Fowler's biographical profiles see Frank Fenner, 'Fairley, Sir Neil Hamilton (1888-1966)' and Colin Smith, 'Fowler, Robert (1888-1965)', *ADB*, Volume 14, 1996.

[70] Fairley, 'Studies in Syphilis'; Robert Fowler, 'Familial Syphilis', *MJA*, 24 December 1921, pp.599-602; N. Hamilton Fairley and Robert Fowler, 'The Wassermann Test', *MJA*, 20 August 1921, p.350.
[71] Cumpston, 'The effect of legislative control on the incidence of ante-natal syphilis'. Cumpston was commenting on Fairley's and Fowler's findings.
[72] Fairley, 'Studies in Syphilis'.
[73] Ibid.
[74] Ibid.
[75] Cumpston, 'The effect of legislative control on the incidence of ante-natal syphilis'.
[76] 'Syphilis', *MJA*, 24 December 1921, p.611.
[77] Ibid.
[78] Ibid., pp.611-612. For Robertson's biographical profile see: E.M. Robertson, 'Robertson, Edward (1870-1969)', ADA, Volume 11, 1988.
[79] Ibid.
[80] The Victorian population figure is from *Official yearbook of the Commonwealth of Australia 1921*.
[81] The VD notification figures and the Australian population estimate are from

Official yearbook of the Commonwealth of Australia 1981.

[82] Jasek et al., 'Sexually transmitted infections in Melbourne, Australia, from 1918 to 2016'.

[83] Ibid.

[84] Allan S. Walker, *Australia in the War of 1939-1945*, Vol.1, *Clinical Problems of War*, Australian War Memorial, Canberra, 1952, p.264.

[85] Ibid.

[86] Ibid.

[87] 'The prophylaxis and treatment of venereal disease', *MJA*, 8 March 1919, pp.195—296.

[88] Ibid.

[89] Ibid.

[90] 'A Public Question', *MJA*, 29 October 1921, pp.380-381.

[91] Wallace, 'Prostitution and venereal diseases', p.59.

[92] Ibid.

[93] Parliament of New South Wales, 'Lieutenant-Colonel John Brady Nash'; see also NAA: B2455, 'Nash, John Brady'; and Nash, John B. (1915).

[94] John B. Nash, 'Venereal Disease', *MJA*, 25 February 1922, p.227.

[95] For J.V. Duhig's biographical profile see: C.A.C. Leggett, 'Duhig, James Vincent (1889—1963)', ADA, Volume 8, 1981.
[96] A.G. Butler and J.V. Duhig, 'Venereal Diseases', *MJA*, 29 April 1922, p.477.
[97] Ibid.
[98] Roy Porter, *The Greatest Benefit to Mankind: A Medical History of Humanity from Antiquity to the Present*, HarperCollins, London, 1997, p.452.
[99] Ibid.
[100] Ibid.
[101] John Frith, 'Syphilis—Its Early History and Treatment Until Penicillin, and the Debate on its Origins', *Journal of Military and Veterans Health*, Volume 20, No.4, November 2012, pp.49-57.
[102] Porter, *The Greatest Benefit to Mankind*, p.453.
[103] Ibid.
[104] Ibid.
[105] Ibid., pp.453-454.
[106] Ibid., p.454.
[107] Ibid.
[108] 'The new outlook on gonorrhoea, *MJA*, 6 July 1940, p.19; 'The use of sulphanilamide in gonorrhoeain the male', *MJA*, 10 August 1940, p.139.

Chapter 6

[1] The statistics in Table 6.1 are derived from those in Walker, *Australia in the War of 1939-1945*, Vol.1, *Clinical Problems of War*, Chapter 22, 'Venereal Diseases'.

[2] AWM, *Memorial Encyclopaedia*, https://www.awm.gov.au/, accessed 16 May 2018; Australian Army during World War I and Australian Army during World War II, *Wikipedia*, https://en.wikipedia.org/wiki/Australian_Army_during_World_War_I and https://en.wikipedia.org/wiki/Australian_Army_during_World_War_II, accessed 16 May 2018.

[3] The statistics set out in Table 6.1 are subject to these qualifications and provisos: The 34,178 VD cases in World War II in Table 6.1 is an estimate. The official medical historian of the war, Dr Allan S. Walker, did not publish a series of statistical tables showing the theatre-by-theatre details of the incidence of all the diseases and medical conditions suffered by Australian soldiers during the war, as Dr A.G. Butler had done in his official medical history of World War I. Instead Walker most often published his figures for VD cases

as 'rates per thousand of average troop strength' not as whole numbers. Because Walker sometimes included the annual average troop strength for some war theatres, it is possible to extrapolate the whole numbers. For instance, the average troop.

strength in the South-West Pacific theatre in 1943 was 74,872 and the VD rate was 1.06 cases per thousand troops. The actual number of cases for that year may accordingly be estimated as ≈ (74,872/1000) × 1.06 ≈ 79 cases.

Elsewhere, notably in the Middle Eastern theatre, Walker provides a global estimate of 11,000 VD cases for the three-year period 1940—1942. Although he gives the rate per thousand troops in all three years, he provides a figure for average troop strength in only one year. A more precise number of cases than his global estimate consequently may not be extrapolated. For the South-East Asian theatre, Walker provides an estimate for only 1941. After that, the figures are unavailable because most of the Australian troops in the theatre had become prisoners of war and no record was then kept of the diseases they suffered. He provides an estimate of 31 VD cases per week for a total of 7000 troops for 48 weeks in 1941—a total of 1488 cases.

Walker's figures for the Australian theatre are only for the period 1942-1945. They do not include the 27-month period from the end of September 1939, when units were being raised and trained in Australia for overseas service. Though contemporary sources indicate that the number of VD cases in Australia during that period was 'negligible', the omission of an estimate by Walker is odd and is not one that Walker attempts to explain. The overall total of 34,178 VD cases is therefore probably an underestimate, but of what magnitude is impossible to calculate.

In view of the considerations discussed in the above points, how accurate are the statistics in Table 6.1? The answer is that they are as accurate as can be under the circumstances. They are derived estimates rather than the actual numbers of cases. That does not mean that the figures are inaccurate, only that they are the closest possible approximations to the number of cases treated by the AMS. They are, moreover, the only figures available.

[4] Dennis et al., Australian Imperial Force (2nd)', *The Oxford Companion to Australian*

Military History, 'Second World War, 1939-1945', AWM, *Memorial Encyclopaedia*, 'Second Australian Imperial Force', *Wikipedia*, https://en.wikipedia.org/wiki/Second_Australian_Imperial_Force, accessed 16 May 2018.

[5] 'Observations on the administration of the Army Medical Service in the first months of the War', AWM54 481/2/40.

[6] Ibid., p.4.

[7] For Street's biographical profile see his entry in the *ADB*, Volume 12.

[8] 'Observations on the administration of the Army Medical Service in the first months of the War', AWM54 481/2/40, p.5.

[9] S.R. Burston to C.H. Disher, 23 January 1940, 'Personal letters to DGMS', 27 December 1937-12 May 1943 AWM292, Med 40/76.

[10] R.M. Downes to Deputy Director of Medical Services, 'VD Prophylaxis', 23 November 1939; DGMS to Secretary for the Army, 'Military Board Agendum No.271/1939: Secretary for the Army: (1) Arrangements for the treatment of VD and (2) 'Establishment of No.3 Special Hospital', 19 January 1940; both communications in 'Dr Walker's

[11]   Records: Venereal Disease', AWM54 267/6/17 Part 8.

[11]   DGMS to Secretary for the Army, 'Military Board Agendum No.271/1939', 19 January 1940, AWM54 267/6/17 Part 8.

[12]   See for example 'Medical Administrative Instruction No.26 by DMS, AIF', 25 December 1940, 'Treatment of Venereal Disease', AWM54 267/6/17 Part 9.

[13]   LHQ [Land Headquarters], *Standards of Prophylaxis, Treatment and Cure of Venereal Diseases*, Melbourne, LHQ [of Allied Land Forces, South-West Pacific Area], 1943; copy in AWM54 267/6/17 Part 8.

[14]   Joseph Steigrad, *Prevention of Venereal Disease*, 1 Australian Mobile Printing Unit, [Palestine], December 1942; copy in AWM54 267/6/17 Part 9.

[15]   G.A. Street, 'Treatment of VD', Military Board Addendum no.271/1939, 'Minute by the Minister', 5 February 1940, AWM54 267/6/17 Part 8.

[16]   'Observations on the administration of the Army Medical Service in the first months of the War', AWM54 481/2/40, p.5.

[17] Jan McLeod, 'The House That Jack Built: DGMS Rupert Downes and Australian Army Preparations for World War II, *Health & History*, Volume 19, 2017, p.80.
[18] Ibid.
[19] The most comprehensive summary of these campaigns is provided in *The Australian Encyclopaedia*, Volume IX, Angus and Robertson, Sydney, 1958, p.400 ff.
[20] Ibid.
[21] A.S. Walker, *Australia in the War of 1939-1945*, Vol.2, *Middle East and Far East*, Australian War Memorial, Canberra, 1953, p.104.
[22] Ibid., p.106.
[23] 'Epidemic' in *Wikipedia*.
[24] Walker, *Australia in the War of 1939-1945*, Vol.1, *Clinical Problems of War*, pp.265, 267.
[25] Ibid., Chapter 4, Figures 4.2 and 4.10.
[26] Ibid., p.265.
[27] Walker, *Australia in the War of 1939-1945*, Vol.2, *Middle East and Far East*, p.88.
[28] Ibid., p.106; 8 ASH war diary, 26 August, 27 October and 4 November 1940, AWM52 11/2/8.

[29] S.R. Burston to C.H. Disher, 'Personal letters to DGMS, 27 December 1937-12 May 1943', 8 March 1940, AWM292, Med 40/76.

[30] Secretary, Military Board to Secretary, Department of Army, 27 February 1941, AWM54 267/6/17 Part 8.

[31] DGMS to Secretary for the Army, 'Military Board Agendum No.271/1939: Secretary for the Army: ... (2) 'Establishment of No.3 Special Hospital', 19 January 1940, AWM54 267/6/17 Part 8.

[32] Walker, *Australia in the War of 1939-1945*, Vol.2, *Middle East and Far East*, pp.91, 117, 119; 'Colour Patches: AMF & 2nd AIF Service Corps, Medical and Hospital Units', *Digger History*, http://www.diggerhistory.info/pages-badges/patches/aasc.htm, accessed 14 May 2018.

[33] Walker, *Australia in the War of 1939-1945*, Vol.2, *Middle East and Far East*, p.106; 'Colour Patches', *Digger History*.

[34] 8 ASH war diary, October 1940 to May 1941, AWM52 11/2/8.

[35] Ibid., March to May 1941.

[36] Ibid., May 1941 to July 1943.

[37] Walker, *Australia in the War of 1939—1945*, Vol.1, *Clinical Problems of War*, Vol.1, p.267; Vol.2, *Middle East and Far East*, p.106.

[38] 8 ASH war diary, 27 May 1941, AWM52 11/2/8; 'Monthly reports, 8th Australian Special Hospital, Gaza Ridge', January and February 1942, AWM54 403/7/22.

[39] 8 ASH war diary, 26 August 1940 and 31 May 1943, AWM52 11/2/8.

[40] Walker, *Australia in the War of 1939-1945*, Vol.1, *Clinical Problems of War*, Vol.1, p.268.

[41] 8 ASH war diary, 17 and 25 December 1940, AWM52 11/2/8.

[42] Walker, *Australia in the War of 1939-1945*, Vol.2, *Middle East and Far East*, p.106.

[43] Ibid., p.460.

[44] J.C. Sproule and R. Lees, 'Report by Colonel J.C. Sproule and Lieutenant Colonel R. Lees ... on a visit made to the Birka Area, Cairo on 4 October 1940', 5 October 1940, AWM54 267/6/17 Part 9.

[45] N.H. Fairley, 'Report on Venereal Disease in the AIF in Palestine with special reference to the Tel Aviv-Jaffa

	area, 17 May 1941, AWM54 26/6/17 Part 9.
[46]	Walker, *Australia in the War of 1939-1945*, Vol.2, *Middle East and Far East*, p.105.
[47]	Walker, *Australia in the War of 1939-1945*, Vol.1, *Clinical Problems of War*, Vol.1, pp.265, 267.
[48]	Ibid., p.268.
[49]	Ibid.
[50]	Ibid.
[51]	N.H. Fairley to DMS, 17 May 1941, AWM54 267/6/17 Part 8.
[52]	'Report on Tour in Palestine, 7th to 13th May 1941, by Colonel N. Hamilton Fairley', 17 May 1941, AWM54 267/6/17 Part 9.
[53]	Ibid.
[54]	N.H. Fairley, 'Report on Venereal Disease in the AIF in Palestine with special reference to the Tel Aviv-Jaffa area, 17 May 1941, AWM54 267/6/17 Part 9.
[55]	Ibid.
[56]	N.H. Fairley, 'The Prevention of Venereal Disease in the [2nd] AIF', 17 May 1941, AWM54 267/6/17 Part 9.
[57]	Ibid.
[58]	Ibid.

[59] Ibid.
[60] Ibid.
[61] 'VD, 7 Aust Div: Extracts from a report of an RMO', undated, author's name not provided; F. Kingsley Norris, 'The problem of VD in 7 Aust Div during fifteen months in the Middle East', Appendix A, undated, AWM54 26/6/17 Part 9.
[62] Ibid.
[63] Ibid.
[64] Walker, *Australia in the War of 1939-1945*, Vol.1, *Clinical Problems of War*, Vol.1, p.266.
[65] Ibid.
[66] Ibid.
[67] Ibid.
[68] Ibid.
[69] Ibid.
[70] Ibid.
[71] Ibid.
[72] Steigrad, *Prevention of Venereal Disease*, AWM54 267/6/17 Part 8.
[73] 'VD in ME'['Venereal Disease in Middle East'], unsigned, undated handwritten notes, AWM54 267/6/17 Part 9.
[74] Ibid.
[75] Gavin Long, *Australia in the War of 1939—1945*, Vol 1, *To Benghazi*,

Australian War Memorial, Canberra, 1952; Gavin Long, *Australia in the War of 1939—1945*, Vol 2, *Greece, Crete and Syria*, Australian War Memorial, Canberra, 1953); Barton Maughan, *Australia in the War of 1939-1945*, Vol.3, *Tobruk and El Alamein*, Australian War Memorial, Canberra, 1966.

[76] Walker, *Australia in the War of 1939-1945*, Vol.1, *Clinical Problems of War*, p.267.

[77] Walker, *Australia in the War of 1939-1945*, Vol.2, *Middle East and Far East*, p.361.

[78] Ibid.

[79] Ibid.

[80] 'VD in ME', AWM54 267/6/17 Part 9.

[81] Ibid.

[82] Ibid.

[83] Walker, *Australia in the War of 1939-1945*, Vol.2, *Middle East and Far East*, p.361.

[84] Ibid., pp.352, 354; 8 ASH war diary, 8 May 1941, AWM52 11/2/8.

[85] E Kingsley Norris, *No Memory For Pain: An Autobiography*, William Heinemann Australia Pty Ltd, Melbourne, Australia, 1970), p.127 ff.

[86] Norris, 'The problem of VD in 7 Australian Division during fifteen months in the Middle East', AWM54 267/6/17 Part 9.
[87] Ibid.
[88] Ibid.
[89] World War II Army service record, 'Loudon, Derby Briton', NAA: B883, NX352.
[90] A copy of Loudon's plan is found in this communication: D.B. Loudon to DDMS, AIF (Middle East), 'Plan for Control of Venereal Disease in AIF (ME)', 14 October 1942, AWM54 267/6/17 Part 9.
[91] Ibid.
[92] Ibid.
[93] Ibid.
[94] Ibid.
[95] Walker, *Australia in the War of 1939-1945*, Vol.1, *Clinical Problems of War*, Vol.1, p.267.

Chapter 7

[1] Walker, *Australia in the War of 1939-1945*, Vol.2, *Middle East and Far East*, p.466.
[2] Ibid.

[3] Ibid.
[4] Ibid., pp.327, 344, 421, 465-467.
[5] Walker, *Australia in the War of 1939-1945*, Vol.1, *Clinical Problems of War*, p.268. Walker estimated that a 'fairly steady' average of 31 VD cases a week occurred in Malaya over the 48-week period February-December 1941, with an upwards fluctuation to 58 cases a week at one point.
[6] Ibid., p.268.
[7] Ibid., p.169.
[8] Because Walker includes both Papua-New Guinea and Borneo cases in his 1945 figure for VD cases in the South-West Pacific Area but only the Borneo total is known, the Papua-New Guinea figure must be estimated. An estimate of 34 cases for Papua and New Guinea 1945 has been made, calculated as follows. In the three years 1942-1944, the 159 Papua-New Guinea VD cases comprised the equivalent of 0.9 per cent of the 17,595 VD cases in Australia during the same three-year period. If that same percentage is applied to the 3755 Australian VD cases in 1945, the result is: 0.9% of 3755 cases = 34

estimated VD cases in Papua-New Guinea in 1945.

[9] Walker, *Australia in the War of 1939-1945*, Vol.1, *Clinical Problems of War*, pp.268-269.

[10] Ibid., p.269.

[11] Dennis Shanks to Ian Howie-Willis, personal communication, 11 April 2016.

[12] Ibid.

[13] Walker, *Australia in the War of 1939—1945*, Vol.1, *Clinical Problems of War*, p 269.

[14] Ibid.

[15] A.S. Walker, *Australia in the War of 1939-1945*, Vol.3. *The Island Campaigns*, Australian War Memorial, Canberra, 1957), p.398.

[16] Walker, *Australia in the War of 1939-1945*, Vol.1, *Clinical Problems of War*, p.269.

[17] Ibid.

[18] The statistics for Army strength and VD rates are from Walker, *Australia in the War of 1939-1945*, Vol.1, *Clinical Problems of War*, p.269. The number of cases of VD has been extrapolated from Walker's figures because Walker did not include the actual case numbers. Thus, for example in 1945,

if the VD case rate among 219,843 troops was 17.08 cases per thousand troops, the number of cases can be derived as follows: thousands of troops x rate = cases, or 219.8 × 17.08 ≈ 3755 VD cases.

[19] Ibid., p.273.
[20] Ibid., p.269.
[21] 'Colour Patches', *Digger History*. The website provides brief data about the Special Hospitals which is not available in A.S. Walker's official medical histories of the war.
[22] Walker, *Australia in the War of 1939-1945*, Vol.1, *Clinical Problems of War*, p.269.
[23] 'Colour Patches', *Digger History*..
[24] Walker, *Australia in the War of 1939-1945*, Vol.1, *Clinical Problems of War*, p.270.
[25] 'National Emergency Measures: National Security (Venereal Diseases and Contraception) Regulations', *MJA*, 17 October 1942, pp.367-368.
[26] Walker, *Australia in the War of 1939-1945*, Vol.1, *Clinical Problems of War*, p.269;N.M. Gibson, 'Control of Venereal Disease in the Army', *MJA*, 26 September 1942, pp.290-292.

[27] World War II Army service record, 'Gibson, Norman Maxwell', NAA: B884, N78718.

[28] World War I and World War II Army service records, 'Gibson, Norman Maxwell', NAA: B2455 and NAA: B884, N78718.

[29] Gibson, 'Control of Venereal Disease in the Army', *MJA*..

[30] N.M. Gibson, group of three articles on VD, *Salt*, February 1942.

[31] Gibson, 'Control of Venereal Disease in the Army', *MJA*.

[32] Ibid.

[33] Ibid.

[34] Ibid.

[35] Ibid.

[36] Notes of meetings and conferences of the Sub-Committee on VD, 'Venereal Diseases. Extracts from notes of conference of DDMS held in Melbourne, 8-10-1940', AWM54 267/6/17 Part 11. This file contains records of diverse meetings and related papers, conducted in the period 1940-1942.

[37] Walker, *Australia in the War of 1939-1945*, Vol.1, *Clinical Problems of War*, p.271.

[38] World War II Army service record, 'Loudon, Derby Briton', NAA: B883, NX352.

[39] LHQ, *Standards of Prophylaxis, Treatment and Cure of Venereal Diseases*, copy in AWM54 267/6/17 Part 8

[40] D.B. Loudon to DGMS, 'Report on Venereal Disease Control in AMF', 16 October 1943, AWM54 267/6/17 Part 8.

[41] Ibid.

[42] 'Report of the Adviser in Venerealogy [sic.], LHQ, Col. Loudon, February 1944', AWM54 267/6/17 Part 8.

[43] Copies of Loudon's, Gibson's and Francis's reports are in the Australian War Memorial's archival collection. See for example AWM54 267/6/17 Parts 8 and 9. Reports in these files include:

D.B. Loudon, 'Venereal Diseases—-Present method of combating as concerns AIF in UK', 26 February 1941;

D.B. Loudon, 'Plan for Control of Venereal Disease in AIF', 14 October 1942;

'Report by Lieut. Col. Francis of 9 September 1943: Suggestions [for managing VD]';

N.W. Francis, 'Report on Venereal disease Control in AMF [Australian Military Forces], 16 October 1943

N.M. Gibson, 'Report of Adviser in Venereology, NSW L of C Area [Line of Communications], 1 January 1944;

'Report of adviser in Venerealogy [sic.], LHQ, Col. Loudon, Feb. 44', undated, February 1944;

N.M. Gibson, 'Army Notes on Prevention of VD in NSW L of C Area, 4 January 1946'

[44] See for example, 'Medical Administrative Instruction No.86 by DMS, AIF: Prophylaxis of Venereal Diseases' in W.P. MacCallum for DGMS, Administrative Instruction No.10: Venereal Disease', 24 September 1942, AWM54 267/6/17 Part 10; 'Treatment of Venereal Disease', AWM54 267/6/17 Part 9.

[45] LHQ, *Standards of Prophylaxis, Treatment and Cure of Venereal Diseases*, AWM54 267/6/17 Part 8.

[46] The newspaper reports are from a wartime file of press clippings. 'Health—cancer, tuberculosis, venereal disease, sex education, birth

rate—Press cuttings', NAA: CP71/14, 19.

[47] See for instance 'Incidence of Venereal Disease' in Advisory War Council Minute, Canberra, 21 March 1944, Nos.215 and 216, 11 and 18 March 1944, NAA: A5954 473/10, 'Incidence of Venereal Disease in Young Women'.

[48] John Curtin to J.M. Fraser, 'Incidence of Venereal Disease in Young Women', 24 March 1944, NAA: A5954, 473/10.

[49] 'Statement by the Acting Prime Minister (Mr Forde): Venereal Disease', 24 May 1944, NAA: A5954, 473/10.

[50] AWM, *Memorial Encyclopaedia*.

[51] Walker, *Australia in the War of 1939-1945*, Vol.1, *Clinical Problems of War*, p.272.

[52] S.R. Burston to Adjutant-General, 20 March 1943, AWM54 267/6/17 Part 8.

[53] Ibid.

[54] Ibid.

[55] Ibid; Walker, *Australia in the War of 1939-1945*, Vol.1, *Clinical Problems of War*, p.272.

[56] 'Colour Patches', *Digger History*, Walker, *Australia in the War of 1939—1945*, Vol.1, *Clinical Problems of War*, p.272. In addition, see the

Australia @ War' website, http://www.ozatwar.com/ausarmy/, for summary details of the foundation and location of the three Army Women's Hospitals.

[57] Walker, *Australia in the War of 1939-1945*, Vol.1, *Clinical Problems of War*, p.271.

[58] World War II Army service record, 'Francis, Neil Whinney', NAA: B883, NX218.

[59] D.B. Loudon to DGMS, 'Enquiry into the Treatment of Syphilis at 126 A.S.H.', 12 December 1944, AWM54 267/6/17 Part 15.

60 LHQ, *Standards of Prophylaxis, Treatment and Cure of Venereal Diseases*, pp.4—5.

[61] Loudon to DGMS, 'Enquiry into the Treatment of Syphilis at 126 A.S.H.', 12 December 1944, AWM54 267/6/17 Part 15.

[62] Ibid.

[63] Ibid.

[64] Matthew J. Ellenhorn and Donald G. Barceloux, *Medical Toxicology: Diagnosis and Treatment of Human Poisoning*, Elsevier, New York, Amsterdam and London, 1988, p.1012 ff.; Professor

John Pearn MD, personal communication, 29 March 2018.
[65] Loudon to DGMS, 'Enquiry into the Treatment of Syphilis at 126 A.S.H.', 12 December 1944, AWM54 267/6/17 Part 15.
[66] Ibid.
[67] Ibid.
[68] Ibid.
[69] Ibid.
[70] Walker, *Australia in the War of 1939—1945*, Vol.1, *Clinical Problems of War*, p.271.
[71] Ibid.
[72] 'Unit War Diary, 126th Australian Special Hospital', February-July 1944, AWM52 11/2/40. The entries for August 1944 are not on the file.
[73] Ibid.
[74] 'War Cabinet Agendum — No.115 / 1941 — Pay of Members of the Military Forces Suffering from Venereal Disease', undated but c. 9 May 1941, NAA: A2670, 115/1941.
[75] 'War Cabinet Minute, Agendum No.432/1945, Supplement No.1, Pay of Members of the Forces Suffering from Venereal Disease', 21 December 1945, NAA: A2670, 115/1941.

[76]	'War Cabinet Agendum—Pay of Members of the Military Forces Suffering from Venereal Disease', 18 March 1941, NAA: A2670, 115/1941.
[77]	Ibid.
[78]	'Pay of Members of Forces Suffering from Venereal Disease', 1 May 1945, NAA: A5799, 106/1945.
[79]	For a brief history of the discovery and introduction of penicillin, see Roy Porter, *The Greatest Benefit to Mankind: A Medical History of Humanity from Antiquity to the Present*, Harper Collins Publishers, London, 1997, pp.454-462.
[80]	Walker, *Australia in the War of 1939-1945*, Vol.3. *The Island Campaigns*, pp.198, 214, 262.
[81]	Ibid., p.262.
[82]	'Penicillin: Wonder Drug of World War II', *HistoryNet*, http://www.historynet.com/penicillinwonder-drug-world-war-ii.htm, accessed 27 March 2018.
[83]	Ibid.
[84]	Ibid.
[85]	Walker, *Australia in the War of 1939-1945*, Vol.1, *Clinical Problems of War*, p.273.
[86]	Ibid.
[87]	Ibid., p.274.

[88]	Ibid.
[89]	Ibid., pp.274-275.
[90]	Walker, *Australia in the War of 1939-1945*, Vol.1, *Clinical Problems of War*, p.275.
[91]	Ibid.
[92]	Ibid. p.275.
[93]	Ibid.
[94]	Ibid.
[95]	Ibid.

Chapter 8

[1]	For a short account of the history of the 34th Australian Infantry Brigade, see the *Wikipedia* entry '34th Brigade (Australia)', https://en.wikipedia.org/wiki/34th_Brigade_(Australia), accessed 7 July 2018.
[2]	Ibid.; 'British Commonwealth Occupation Force', *The Oxford Companion to Australian Military History*, pp.110-112.
[3]	Michael B. Tyquin, *Little by Little: A Centenary History of the Royal Australian Army Medical Corps*, Australian Military History Publications, Loftus, New South Wales, 2003, pp.445-449.
[4]	'British Commonwealth Occupation Force 1945-52', *Australians at war*,

Australian War Memorial, https://www.awm.gov.au/articles/atwar/bcof, accessed 8 July 2018.

[5] Ibid.; 'British Commonwealth Occupation Force', *The Oxford Companion to Australian Military History*; Tyquin, *Little by Little*, pp.445-449.

[6] Ibid.

[7] 'British Commonwealth Occupation Force', *The Australian Encyclopaedia*, Vol.2, pp.130—134; 'British Commonwealth Occupation Force', *The Oxford Companion to Australian Military History*, pp.110-112.

[8] Ibid.

[9] The Stubbe-Burston correspondence is largely contained in Burston's private correspondence, which is held by his granddaughter. See 'Burston, Samuel Roy, World War II Correspondence' in the bibliography.

[10] Ibid.

[11] Ibid.

[12] Tyquin, *Little by Little*, pp.445-449.

[13] Lieutenant Colonel C.E.A. Cook to Deputy DGMS, Advanced Headquarters, Australian Military Forces, no date [but September 1945], 'Cecil E.A. Cook personal papers'.

[14] Ibid.

[15] Ibid.
[16] Ibid.
[17] C. Scales to Medical Officers, BCOF, 30 April 1946, AWM114 267/6/17 Part 7.
[18] For Hopkins's biographical profile, see his entry in the *ADB*, Volume 17.
[19] R.N.L. Hopkins, 'Control of VD', 28 June 1946, AWM114 267/6/17 Part 1.
[20] George Davies, *The Occupation of Japan: The rhetoric and the reality of Anglo-Australasian relations, 1939—1952*, University of Queensland Press, St Lucia, 2001, p.237.
[21] Hopkins, 'Control of VD', 28 June 1946, AWM114 267/6/17 Part 1.
[22] Ibid.
[23] 'Instructions issued by a BCOF Unit to combat venereal disease', 28 June 1946, AWM114 267/6/17 Part 1.
[24] Ibid.
[25] Ibid.
[26] 'VD Questionnaire 1', AWM114 267/6/17 Part 1.
[27] Hopkins, 'Control of VD', 12 September 1946, AWM114 267/6/17 Part 1.
[28] Ibid.
[29] Ibid.

[30]	Ibid.
[31]	Ibid.
[32]	Ibid.
[33]	'VD Control', 4 December 1947, AWM114 267/6/17 Part 7.
[34]	Ibid.
[35]	'M/2/Chaps' to AAS (PS)' re 'VD Control', 5 December 1947, AWM114 267/6 /17 Part 1.
[36]	Ibid.
[37]	Ibid.
[38]	Acting Commander in Chief BCOF, 'Policy in regard to officers who contract venereal disease', 24 February 1984, AWM114 267/6/17 Part 1.
[39]	'VD Control', 4 December 1947, AWM114 267/6/17 Part 7.
[40]	Ibid.
[41]	Administrative Instruction AG 108: Prevention of Venereal Disease—BCOF', 10 February 1948, AWM114 267/6/17 Part 12.
[42]	Ibid.
[43]	J.H. Stubbe to Commander British Commonwealth Base, 30 June 1937, Anti-VD campaign', AWM114 267/6/17 Part 2.
[44]	Ibid.
[45]	Ibid.

[46] Davies, *The Occupation of Japan*, p.238.
[47] Ibid.
[48] Ibid.
[49] Gavin Long, *Australia in the War of 1939—1945*, Vol.7, *The Final Campaigns*, Australian War Memorial, Canberra, 1963, pp.550-551, 577-578.
[50] Walker, *Australia in the War of 1939—1945*, Vol.1, *Clinical Problems of War*, p.275.
[51] Brigadier C. Scales, 'Venereal disease, BCOF', 19 December 1946, AWM114 267/6/17 Part 1.
[52] Ibid.
[53] 'Brief History of the Medical Services [of] BCOF', 21 July 1947, AWM114 481/11/2.
[54] Ibid.
[55] Tyquin, *Little by Little*, p.448.
[56] Davies, *The Occupation of Japan*, p.235.
[57] 'Venereal Diseases—BCOF (Japan)', AWM114 267/6/17 Part 5.
[58] R.N.L Hopkins to Unit Commanders, 34th Infantry Brigade, 21 December 1946, 'VD Control', AWM114 267/6/17 Part 1. 59 'Venereal Diseases—BCOF (Japan)', AWM114 267/6/17 Part 5.
[60] 'VD Control', Minutes of a conference of the Anti-VD Committee, 13 May

	1947, AWM114 267/6/17 Part 2; 'Anti-VD Committee—Minutes of Meeting 6, January 1948', 12 January 1948, AWM114 267/6/17 Part 3.
[61]	'Minutes of Anti-VD conference held at HQ BCOF on the 7 June 1948 at 1400 hrs', AWM114 267/6/17 Part 1.
[62]	Ibid.
[63]	Ibid.
[64]	R.N.L. Hopkins, 'Personnel who have contracted VD: Return to Australia, 17 August 1946, AWM114 267/6/17 Part 1.
[65]	Ibid.
[66]	J. Merry to HQ 34th Australian Infantry Brigade, 24 November 1946, 'Leave in Australia—VD patients', AWM114 267/6/17 Part 1.
[67]	R.N.L. Hopkins to HQ BCOF, 'VD control in Australia', 2 January 1947, AWM114 267/6/17 Part 1.
[68]	Commander-in-Chief, BCOF, 'VD—prevention of spread in Australia, 13 January 1947 and Principal Administrative Officer, 'Venereal disease: Prevention of spread to Australia, 10 October 1946, both in AWM114 267/6/17 Part 1.

[69] Deputy Assistant Adjutant & Quarter Master General, Headquarters, 34th Australian Infantry Brigade, 'Venereal diseases records: documentation [of] personnel returning to Australia, 26 December 1946, AWM114 267/6/17 Part 1.

[70] Unnamed BCOF officer in Japan (probably Sir Ragnar Garrett) to Brigadier C.M.L. Elliott (Army Headquarters, Melbourne), 7 February 1949, AWM114 267/6/17 Part 7.

[71] Colonel Reg Pollard to Sir Ragnar Garrett, 9 March 1945, AWM 114 267/6/17 Part 2. Pollard was the Director of Personnel Administration at Army Headquarters in Melbourne; Garrett was the Army's Chief of General Staff.

[72] Robin Gerster, *Travels in Atomic Sunshine: Australia and the Occupation of Japan*, Scribe, Melbourne, 2008, p.137.

[73] Ibid.

[74] Ibid., p.138.

[75] Davies, *The Occupation of Japan*, p.166.

[76] Gerster, *Travels in Atomic Sunshine*, p.138.

[77] See news-clippings 'VD Problem Must Be Controlled' and 'BCOF Disease Rate "High"', each dated 3 June 1948 and each of which discuss the tabling of the Lloyd-Stanley Report, AWM114 26/16/17 Part 12; Gerster, *Travels in Atomic Sunshine*, pp.137-138.
[78] Ibid.
[79] 'Venereal Disease Prevention Law: Law No.48, 4 April 1927', AWM114 267/6/17 Part 1.
[80] 'The Japanese Venereal Disease Prevention Law' and 'Disposition of cases in the Tokyo area involving violation of ... the VD Prevention Law', 23 June 1949, both in AWM114 267/6/17 Part 4.
[81] Russel C. Snyder, Colonel commanding the Headquarters of Chugoku Military Government Region, 'Measures to reduce venereal disease among Occupation Forces caused by Japanese', 17 April 1948, AWM114 26/16/17 Part 12.
[82] R.N.L. Hopkins, 'Notes for VD Control Officers', 7 October 1946, AWM114 267/6/17 Part 1.
[83] H.W. Allen, Assistant Adjutant General, General Headquarters, Supreme

Commander for the Allied Powers, Memorandum to Imperial Japanese Government re Abolition of licensed prostitution in Japan', 21 January 1946, and 'Instruction [from] Director of the Police Bureau, Home Ministry [re] Abolition of licensed prostitution', AWM114 267/6/17 Part 1.

[84] DDMS, BCOF to Colonel 'A', 'VD control and incidence—military', 26 April 1947, AWM114 267/6/17 Part 1.

[85] H.C.H. Robertson to Supreme Commander Allied Forces, 'Control of Venereal Disease', 6 May 1948, AWM114 267/6/17 Part 1.

[86] Lieutenant Colonel J.S. Thompson (Deputy Provost Marshal, BCOF) to various BCOF recipients, 20 September 1946, 'Control—Venereal Disease', AWM114 267/6/17 Part 1.

[87] 'Treatment of VD at Japanese Hospital, Kure', AWM114 267/6/17 Part 4.

[88] Ibid.

[89] Major D. Harvey Sutton to DDMS BCOF, Alleged treatment of BCOF VD cases by Jap doctors', 28 April 1947, AWM114 267/6/17 Part 12.

[90] Ibid.

[91]	Davies, *The Occupation of Japan*, pp.314—315.
[92]	Ibid.
[93]	Gerster, *Travels in Atomic Sunshine*, p.210.
[94]	Ibid., p.208.
[95]	Ibid., p.209.
[96]	Davies, *The Occupation of Japan*, p.238.
[97]	Gerster, *Travels in Atomic Sunshine*, p.48.
[98]	Davies, *The Occupation of Japan*, p.238.
[99]	Rumi Sakamoto, 'Pan-pan Girls: Humiliating Liberation in Post-War Japan', *Portal Journal of Multidisciplinary International Studies*, Vol.7, No.2, July 2010, pp.1—15.
[100]	Ibid.
[101]	Ibid.
[102]	Ibid.
[103]	See for example Major F.J. Duval, Deputy Assistant Adjutant General, BCOF, 'Campaign against spreaders of VD: Progress report as at 23 April 1948', AWM114 267/6/17 Part 12.
[104]	Ibid.
[105]	Ibid.
[106]	Ibid.
[107]	See for example 'Municipal Ordinances for control of

	prostitution and other related behaviors', 3 June 1951, AWM114 267/6/17 Part 4.
[108]	Ibid.
[109]	F. Nicholas to Assistant Provost Marshal, BCOF, "N.M.', Japanese female convicted by a civil court for carrying on prostitution while infected with VD', 2 June 1949, AWM114 267/6/17 Part 4.
[110]	Ibid.
[111]	Hopkins, 'Notes for VD Control Officers', 7 October 1946, AWM114 267/6/17 Part 1.
[112]	'Duties of personnel comprising the Anti-VD Teams', 28 June 1946, AWM114 267/6/17 Part 1.
[113]	Joy Damousi, 'Campaign for Japanese-Australian children to enter Australia, 1957—1968: A History of Post-War Humanitarianism', *Australian Journal of Politics and History*, 17 April 2018, https://doi.org/10.1111/ajph.12461, accessed 23 May 2018.
[114]	Ibid.
[115]	'Citizenship by Descent', Australian Embassy, Tokyo, http://japan.embassy.gov.au/tkyo/citizen_descent.html, accessed 23 May 2018.

[116] 'Resources: Immigration Nation—Refugees and Japanese war brides accepted', SBS, www.sbs.com.au/immigrationnation/resources/article/166/reugees-and-japanese-war-brides accepted, accessed 23 May 2018; 'Community Information Summary: Japanese-born', Australian Government, Department of Immigration and Citizenship, https://www.dss.gov.au/sites/default/files/documents/02_2014/japan.pdf, accessed 23 May 2018

[117] Snyder, 'Measures to reduce venereal disease among Occupation Forces caused by Japanese'; 17 April 1948, AWM114 267/6/17 Part 12; DDMS, BCOF to Deputy Provost Marshal, 'VD Control', 26 February 1947, AWM114 267/6/17 Part 7

[118] 'Venereal Disease Contact Questionnaire', 28 June 1946, AWM114 267/6/17 Part 7.

[119] 'Petition for the control of public moral', 20 November 1950, AWM114 267/6/17 Part 4.

[120] J.H. Stubbe, 'Venereal disease in Australian Military Force component

	of BCOF', 5 April 1948, AWM114 267/6/17 Part 12.
[121]	Ibid.
[122]	Ibid.
[123]	R.N.L. Hopkins, 'Control of VD', 12 September 1946, AWM114 267/6/17 Part 1.
[124]	Gavin Hart, personal communication, 28 May 2018.
[125]	Ibid.
[126]	G. Dennis Shanks to Ian Howie-Willis, 16 June 2018, email communication in author's correspondence file.
[127]	Ibid.

Chapter 9

[1]	'Korean War', *The Oxford Companion to Australian Military History*.
[2]	'Malayan Emergency', AWM, *Memorial Encyclopaedia*.
[3]	'Korean War, 1950-53', AWM, *Memorial Encyclopaedia*.
[4]	Ibid.
[5]	Ibid.
[6]	Ibid.
[7]	Ibid.

[8] Ibid.; 'Korean War', *Wikipedia*, https://en.wikipedia.org/wiki/Korean_War, accessed 17 May 2018.
[9] 'Korean War, 1950-53', AWM, *Memorial Encyclopaedia*..
[10] 'Korean War', *Wikipedia*; 'Korean Demilitarized Zone', *Wikipedia*, https://en.wikipedia.org/wiki/Korean_Demilitarized_Zone, accessed 2 June 2018.
[11] 'Korean War', *Wikipedia*.
[12] 'Korean War, 1950-53', AWM, *Memorial Encyclopaedia*.
[13] Bryan Gandevia, 'Medical and surgical aspects of the Korean campaign, September to December 1950: Casualties and their evacuation', *MJA*, 11 August 1951, pp.191-195;DVA, 'The Korean War: Australian medical services', *The Anzac Portal*, https://anzacportal.dva.gov.au/history/conflicts/korean-war/events/stalemate-war-19521953/australian-medical-services, accessed 29 May 2018.
[14] Ibid.
[15] Ibid.
[16] N.M. Kater, 'Helicopter evacuation in Korea, *MJA*, 13 September 1952, pp.373-374.

[17]	Ibid.; see also N.M. Kater, 'Some experiences in a Korean prisoner-of-war camp hospital', *MJA*, 31 March 1953, pp.94-95; Kingsley, *No Memory For Pain*, pp.295, 297; 'The Korean War, *The Anzac Portal..*
[18]	Darryl McIntyre, 'Australian Army Medical Services in Korea in Robert O'Neill, *Australia in the Korean War 1950-53*, Vol 2, *Combat Operations*, Australian War Memorial and Australian Government Publishing Service, Canberra, 1985, p.582. See also 'Out in the Cold: Australian involvement in the Korean War, AWM, *Memorial Encyclopaedia*', Nick Evershed, Australian war deaths: a graphic analysis of more than 102,000 records, *The Guardian*, 25 April 2014,; https://www.theguardian.com/news/datablog/interactive/2014/apr/25/anzac-statistics-analysis, accessed 19 May 2018; Australian Army during World War I and Australian Army during World War II, *Wikipedia*, https://en.wikipedia.org/wiki/Australian_Army_during_World_War_I, accessed 17 May 2018, https://en.wikipedia.org/wiki/Australian_Ar

	my_during_World_War_II, accessed 17 May 2018.
[19]	'Out in the Cold', AWM, *Memorial Encyclopaedia*.
[20]	O'Neill, *Australia in the Korean War, Vol 2, Combat Operations*.
[21]	McIntyre, Australian Army Medical Services in Korea'.
[22]	Kingsley, *No Memory For Pain*, p.298.
[23]	Gandevia, 'Medical and surgical aspects of the Korean campaign'.
[24]	McIntyre, Australian Army Medical Services in Korea', p.381.
[25]	Ibid., p.577.
[26]	Norris, *No Memory For Pain*, p.298.
[27]	Ibid.
[28]	McIntyre, Australian Army Medical Services in Korea, p.381.
[29]	Ibid.
[30]	McIntyre, Australian Army Medical Services in Korea, p.582; 'The Korean War', *The Anzac Portal*.
[31]	EJ. Ingham, Army Health Problems' (1953).
[32]	*Ibid.*
[33]	*Ibid.*
[34]	Ingham, EJ., 'Discussion on medical problems in Korea: Army health problems', *Proceedings of the Royal*

	Society for Medicine', Volume 46, 1953, pp.1041—1046.
[35]	Ibid.
[36]	Albert E. Cowdrey, *United States Army in the Korean War: The Medics War*, Center of Military History, United States Army, Washington DC, 1987, p.44.
[37]	Ibid., p.48.
[38]	Ibid. p.49.
[39]	Ibid., p.61.
[40]	Ibid.
[41]	Ibid.
[42]	Ibid., p.149.
[43]	Ibid., p.249.
[44]	Ibid., p.183.
[45]	Ibid.
[46]	Ibid., p.184.
[47]	Ibid.
[48]	Jeffrey Grey and Peter Dennis, *The Official History of Australia's Involvement in Southeast-Asian Conflicts 1948-1975*, Vol.5, *Emergency & Confrontation: Australian Military Operations in Malaya and Borneo 1950-1966*, Allen & Unwin, Sydney, 1996.
[49]	'Malayan Emergency', *The Oxford Companion to Australian Military History*, pp.345-8.

[50] Ibid.
[51] Ibid.
[52] Ibid.
[53] Ibid.; Tyquin, *Little by Little*, p.465.
[54] W.O. Rodgers to Ian Howie-Willis, 6 July 2014, personal correspondence.
[55] Brendan O'Keefe, *The Official History of Australia's Involvement in South east-Asian Conflicts 1948-1975*, Vol.3, *Medicine at War: Medical aspects of Australia's involvement in Southeast Asia 1950-1972*, Part I, 'Malaya and Borneo', Allen & Unwin, St Leonards, New South Wales, 1994.
[56] Ibid., pp.5-6.
[57] Ibid., p.380.
[58] Ibid.
[59] Ibid., pp.376-379.
[60] Ibid., p.12.
[61] Ibid.
[62] Ibid.
[63] Ibid., pp.15-16.
[64] Ibid., p.16.
[65] Ibid.
[66] Ibid.
[67] Ibid.
[68] Ibid.
[69] Ibid.
[70] Ibid., pp.11-12.

[71] Colonel Michael J. Bindley, personal communication, 6 June 2018.
[72] O'Keefe, *The Official History*, Vol.3, *Medicine at War*, pp.12-13.
[73] Grey and Dennis, *The Official History*, Vol.5, *Emergency & Confrontation*. For a short account see 'Indonesian Confrontation', *The Oxford Companion to Australian Military History*, pp.152-155.
[74] AWM, 'Indonesian Confrontation, 1963—66', *Australians at War*, https://www.awm.gov.au/articles/event/indonesian-confrontation, accessed 5 June 2018.
[75] Ibid.
[76] Ibid.
[77] O'Keefe, *The Official History*, Vol.3, *Medicine at War*, pp.32-37.
[78] Ibid.

Chapter 10

[1] The Vietnam War has been comprehensively described in the nine-volume official history, *The Official History of Australia's Involvement in Southeast-Asian Conflicts 1948-1975*. The part played by the Australian Army in the war is detailed in three volumes of this series—Volumes 2, 8 and 9. See Ian

McNeill, *To Long Tan: The Australian Army and the Vietnam War*, Allen & Unwin and the Australian War Memorial, St Leonards, 1993; Ian McNeill and Ashley Ekins, *On the Offensive: The Australian Army in the Vietnam War, January 1967-June 1968*, Allen & Unwin and the Australian War Memorial, Crows Nest, 2003; Ashley Ekins and Ian McNeill, *Fighting to the Finish: The Australian Army and the Vietnam War, 1968—1975*, Allen & Unwin, Crows Nest, 2012.

[2] 'Vietnam War 1962-1975', AWM, *Memorial Encyclopaedia*.

[3] Ibid.; *The Oxford Companion to Australian Military History*, 'Military history of Australia during the Vietnam War', *Wikipedia*, https://en.wikipedia.org/wiki/Military_history_of_Australia_during_the_Vietnam_War, accessed 11 June 2018.

[4] 'Vietnam War', *The Oxford Companion to Australian Military History*, 'Vietnam War', *The Australian Encyclopaedia*, Vol.10.

[5] 'Vietnam War', *The Oxford Companion to Australian Military History*.

[6] RSL NSW, 'The Vietnam War', http://rslnsw.org.au/commemoration/heritage/the-vietnam-war, accessed 12 June 2018;

'Military history of Australia during the Vietnam War', *Wikipedia*.
[7] Ibid.
[8] Ibid.
[9] O'Keefe, *The Official History*, Vol.3, *Medicine at War*, pp.69-70.
[10] Ibid., pp.85-87.
[11] Ibid., pp.85-87.
[12] W.O. Rodgers to Ian Howie-Willis, personal communication, 31 July 2014.
[13] O'Keefe, *The Official History*, Vol.3, *Medicine at War*, pp.89-90.
[14] 'Vietnam War', *The Oxford Companion to Australian Military History*, 'Vietnam War', *The Australian Encyclopaedia*, Vol.10.
[15] O'Keefe, *The Official History*, Vol.3, *Medicine at War*, pp.111-7.
[16] Ibid.
[17] Ibid., pp.119-22.
[18] Ibid., pp.138-9.
[19] Ibid., p.189.
[20] Ibid.
[21] Ibid., p.190. See also the summary Vietnam service records of Lieutenant Colonels J.T. Dunn, W.T. Watson, M.A. Naughton, W.O. Rodgers, R.F. Gregg and K.J.A. Fleming in the on-line 'Nominal Roll of Vietnam Veterans'

database of the Australian Department of Veterans' Affairs, https://www.dva.gov.au/commemorations-memorials-and-war-graves/nominal-rolls.

[22] O'Keefe, *The Official History*, Vol.3, *Medicine at War*, pp.218-220.

[23] Grey and Dennis, *The Official History*, Vol.5, *Emergency & Confrontation*.

[24] O'Keefe, *The Official History*, Vol.3, *Medicine at War*.

[25] F.B. Smith, Agent Orange: the Australian aftermath' in O'Keefe, *The Official History*, Vol.3, *Medicine at War*.

[26] O'Keefe, *The Official History*, Vol.3, *Medicine at War*, Tables 6-21, Appendix C, 'Health and casualty statistics of Australian forces in Southeast Asia, pp.384-399.

[27] Ibid. Figures derived from statistical data.

[28] For a discussion of the malaria epidemic in Vietnam, see Ian Howie-Willis, *An Unending War: The Australian Armys struggle against malaria, 1885-2015*, Big Sky Publishing, Newport, New South Wales, 2016.]

[29] O'Keefe, *The Official History*, Vol.3, *Medicine at War*, Tables 6-21, Appendix C.

[30] Ibid. Figures derived from statistical data.
[31] Figures cited in O'Keefe, *The Official History*, Vol.3, *Medicine at War*, p.67.
[32] Ibid., p.102.
[33] Ibid.
[34] Ibid., p.103.
[35] Gavin Hart, 'From rural Australia to the international scene. An eclectic account of the experiences, interests and philosophies of Gavin Harf, unpublished, pp.87-88.
[36] J.J. Shelton to Headquarters 1st Australian Taskforce, 'VD Statistics June 1968', 11 July 1968, AWM103 R515/1/1 Part 1, 'Medical Diseases, General, Venereal Disease'.
[37] Ibid.
[38] Ibid.
[39] O'Keefe, *The Official History*, Vol.3, *Medicine at War*, p.103.
[40] Ibid.
[41] Ibid., pp.125-126.
[42] Ibid., p.126.
[43] Ibid.
[44] Ibid.
[45] I.G.G Gilmore to All Unit Commanders', 'Venereal Disease', May 1968, AWM313 515/1/2 Part 1. See

	also O'Keefe, *The Official History*, Vol.3, *Medicine at War*, p.147.
[46]	O'Keefe, *The Official History*, Vol.3, *Medicine at War*, p.178.
[47]	Ibid.
[48]	Ibid.
[49]	Ibid., pp.178-179.
[50]	Ibid., p.179.
[51]	M.B. Simkin, 'Venereal Disease Control in Vung Tau', 15 September 1970, AWM116, R515/1/6.
[52]	Ibid.
[53]	O'Keefe, *The Official History*, Vol.3, *Medicine at War*, p.179.
[54]	Ibid., pp.179-180, 201-204.
[55]	Ibid., p.180.
[56]	Ibid., pp.203-204.
[57]	Ibid., pp.224-225.
[58]	Ibid.
[59]	Ibid., p.225.
[60]	Lieutenant Colonel L.A Wright, 'Report on venereal disease control measures and recommendations regarding Australian assistance to VD Clinic', 10 June 1971, AWM116, R515/1/7.
[61]	O'Keefe, *The Official History*, Vol.3, *Medicine at War*, p.226.
[62]	'Command and Military Aspects of Venereal Disease', no date (but 1971),

	AWM322, R506/I/2, T10 Signals Squadron—Medical General, VD.'
[63]	Ibid.
[64]	Ibid.
[65]	H.C. Franklin to Unit Commanders, 'Prevention of Venereal Disease', 7 July 1971, and A study of the use of doxycycline in the prevention of gonorrhoea, AWM302, R515/5/1. See also AWM292 515/1/18 (Med), 'Venereal Disease Prophylaxis', which contains correspondence and reports about the 'no sweat pills' by Lieutenant Colonel K.J.A. Fleming. See also O'Keefe, *The Official History*, Vol.3, *Medicine at War*, pp.226-227.
[66]	O'Keefe, *The Official History*, Vol.3, *Medicine at War*, p.227.
[67]	See for example Hart, Gavin, 'Penicillin resistance of gonococci in South Vietnam', *MJA*, 29 September 1973, pp.638-641 and 23 February 1974, pp.285-286; and Smithurst, B.A., 'Penicillin resistance of gonococci in South Vietnam', *MJA*, 26 January 1974, p.115.
[68]	Hart, 'From rural Australia to the international scene', Chapters 4, 6; see also Anne Summers et al., *Blood, Sweat*

and Fears II: Medical practitioners of South Australia on active service after World War 2 to Vietnam, 1945—1975, Army Health Services Historical Research Group, Army Museum of South Australia Foundation, 2016, pp.82—87.

[69] Summers, Blood, Sweat and Fears II, pp.88-95.

[70] Gavin Hart, 'The impact of prostitution on Australian troops on active service in a war environment—with particular reference to sociological factors involved in the incidence and control of venereal disease', MD thesis, University of Adelaide, 1974, pp. (i)-(viii).

[71] Hart, From rural Australia to the international scene', pp.90—91.

[72] Hart, 'The impact of prostitution on Australian troops', Appendix 21, Appendices pp.33-47.

[73] Hart, 'From rural Australia to the international scene', pp.90-91.

[74] During the period 1973-1975 Hart published articles in Social Science and Medicine (Volume 7, 1973), British Journal of Venereology (Volume 49, 1973

	and Volume 50, 1974) and *MJA* (28 June 1975).
[75]	Hart, 'The impact of prostitution on Australian troops', p.202 ff.
[76]	Ibid.
[77]	This summary of Hart's findings has been paraphrased from O'Keefe's discussion of Hart's research. See O'Keefe, *The Official History*, Vol.3, *Medicine at War*, pp.204-206. It also draws from Hart, 'The impact of prostitution on Australian troops', Section 4, 'Conclusions'; Hart, From rural Australia to the international scene', chapter on Vietnam; Ian Howie-Willis, interviews with Gavin Hart, January 2017.
[78]	For Harfs discussion of venereoneurosis see Hart, 'The impact of prostitution on Australian troops', pp.273-285, 307-308.
[79]	Hart, 'From rural Australia to the international scene', p.104.
[80]	Howie-Willis interviews with Gavin Hart, interview notes, 26 January 2017.
[81]	C.M Gurner to Gavin Hart, no date (but September 1970), quoted in Hart, 'From rural Australia to the international scene', p.92.

[82] W.O. Rodgers to M.A. Naughton, 12 September 1970, quoted in Hart, 'From rural Australia to the international scene', pp.92-93.
[83] Hart, 'From rural Australia to the international scene', p.94.
[84] Ibid., p.92.
[85] O'Keefe, *The Official History*, Vol.3, *Medicine at War*, pp.204-206.

Chapter 11

[1] For accounts of the numerous overseas deployments, see David M. Horner, *Australia and the 'New World Order': From peacekeeping to peace enforcement: 1988-1991*, Cambridge University Press, Melbourne, 2011; David M. Horner and John Connor, *The Good International Citizen: Australian peacekeeping in Asia, Africa and Europe, 1991—1993*, Cambridge University Press, Melbourne, 2014.
[2] Horner, *Australia and the 'New World Order'*, Appendix A: Australian participation in multinational peacekeeping operations', pp.508-513.
[3] Ibid.

[4]   John H. Pearn to Ian Howie-Willis, personal communication, 15 July 2018.
[5]   *MJA*, all 52 half-yearly volumes between 1975 and 2000.
[6]   Ibid., all 18 half-yearly volumes between 1975 and 1983.
[7]   National Health and Medical Research Council, 'Acquired immune deficiency syndrome (AIDS)', *MJA*, 27 October 1984, pp.565-568.
[8]   These official military histories were released under the general series title, *Australian Peacekeeping, Humanitarian and Post-Cold War Operations*. They were David Horner's *Australia and the 'New World Order: From peacekeeping to peace enforcement: 1988—1991*, and David Horner's and John Connor's *The Good International Citizen: Australian Peacekeeping in Asia, Africa and Europe, 1991-1993*.
[9]   G. Dennis Shanks to Ian Howie-Willis, personal communication, 17 July 2018.
[10] Stephen M. Lambert, A study of *Chlamydia trachomatis*: sexual risk behaviour, infection and prevention infections in the Australian Defence Force', PhD thesis, School of Medicine, University of Queensland, 2014, https://espace.library.uq.edu.au/view/UQ:3694

	77/s33656852_phd_submission.pdf, accessed 26 March 2019.
[11]	Ibid.
[12]	Ibid., p. iii.
[13]	'Sexually Transmitted Infections', *Medical Surveillance Monthly Report*, Vol.20(2), February 2013.
[14]	Ibid., p.2.
[15]	Ibid.
[16]	Ibid., p.3.
[17]	Ibid.
[18]	Professor G. Dennis Shanks, personal communication, 24 April 2017.
[19]	Krzysztof Korzeniewski, 'Sexually transmitted infections among army personnel in the military environment' in Nancy Malla, *Sexually Transmitted infections: An overview*, 2012, pp.165—182, https://www.intechopen.com/, accessed 26 March 2019.
[20]	This estimate is based on the figures for total deployment STD episodes given in the foregoing chapters. The diverse sources for the figures are indicated in the note below Table 11.1.
[21]	'T.V.R.' (informant) to Ian Howie-Willis, personal communication, 7 July 2018.
[22]	Michelle Roberts, 'Emerging sex disease MG could become the next superbug'

in 'Health', BBC news online, https://www.bbc.com/news/health-44777938, accessed 25 March 2019.

Back Cover Material

Armies and sexually transmitted diseases have customarily strolled arm-in-arm together throughout history. This is no less true of the Australian Army than of any other. For centuries lumped together as 'Venereal Diseases', or simply 'VD', sexually transmitted diseases accompanied the Army on all its campaigns during the twentieth century. At least 125,000 Australian soldiers contracted VD, most commonly gonorrhoca and syphilis. That number was the equivalent of six World War 1 infantry divisions.

Until the advent of penicillin in the mid-1940s, gonorrhoea and syphilis devastated the Army during its overseas deployments. In this book Ian Howie-Willis tells the perplexing story of how two microscope sexually transmitted organisms, *Ncisseria gonorrhocae* and *treponenea pallidum*, the bacteria causing gonorrhoea and syphilis, wreaked enormous havoc among Australian troops in all beyond. It is an alarming story that has never previously been told in its entirety, and few authors could tell it as frankly, objectively or sympathetically as Ian Howie-Willis.

Index

A

ABC, Private, *118, 125*
abortive treatment, *9, 226*
acquired immune deficiency syndrome (AIDS), *54, 57, 574*
alcohol consumption, *111, 233, 245, 353, 408, 481, 491, 529, 561, 584, 589*
Allied Forces, *479, 519, 578, 642*
Anderson, Robert Murray McCheyne, *149, 150, 154, 157*
anterior urethra, *9, 11*
antibiotics, *4, 7, 26, 40, 48, 54, 318, 578*
antiseptics, *9, 11, 14, 28, 226*
anti-VD education program, *220, 222*
anti-VD legislation, *336*
anti-VD measures, *211, 479, 491, 493, 494, 498, 500, 529, 574, 589, 732*

Anzacs, *97, 99, 114, 127, 277, 309, 314*
Argyrol, *9, 222, 437*
Army camps, *89, 93, 162, 253, 295, 433, 488, 532*
Army-controlled brothels, *476, 486, 488, 491, 503, 587, 732*
Army headquarters in Melbourne, *494, 503, 589, 622*
Army hospitals, *86, 159, 175, 318, 431, 525, 536, 548*
Army Medical Directorate (AMD), *428, 433, 442*
Army Medical Service, *108, 333, 431*
arsphenamine, *28, 408, 460*
Arthur, Richard, *89, 333, 369*
Assistant Director of Medical Services (ADMS), *225, 295, 320, 431, 450, 465, 484, 493*

Assistant Provost Marshal (APM), *295, 299, 630*

Association to Combat the Social Evil, *339*

Australian Army Medical Corps (AAMC), *28, 75, 78, 86, 225, 241, 333, 484*

Australian Army Medical Women's Service (AAMWS), *548*

Australian Army Nursing Service (AANS), *80, 548*

Australian Association for Fighting Venereal Diseases (AAFVD), *339, 345, 357*

Australian Defence Force (ADF), *54*

Australian Dermatological Hospital (ADH), *131, 133, 134, 136, 141, 148, 150, 225, 233, 236, 239, 241, 243, 245, 247, 253, 261, 283, 299, 303, 333*

Australian General Hospital (AGH), *102, 105, 118, 216, 333, 398, 399, 450, 453, 508, 525, 576, 589*

Australian Imperial Force (AIF) with British Expeditionary Force 1916-1919, *281, 283, 285*

in Egypt, *95, 97, 99, 172, 175, 184, 190, 285, 418, 446, 630*

soldiers, *114, 150, 159, 175, 188, 285, 305, 309*

from 1919 to 1939, *331, 333, 336, 339, 345, 348, 350, 353, 355, 357, 360, 364, 366, 369, 370, 373, 376, 378, 381, 384, 387, 390, 393, 394, 398, 399, 404, 408, 410, 412, 415, 418, 421*

from 1939 to 1941, *423, 425, 428, 431, 445, 446, 450, 453, 455, 458, 460, 463, 494, 500, 503*

troops, *113, 114, 129, 165, 175, 208, 216, 233, 236, 239, 281, 285, 320, 328, 398, 446, 510*

Western Front, *192, 197, 200, 203, 208, 211, 233, 236, 247, 253, 254, 255*

World War I, *78, 80, 84, 86, 89, 93, 95, 97, 99, 102,*

118, 125, 127, 154, 157, 159, 162, 165, 167, 169
Australasian Medical Congresses, *75, 369, 381, 418*
Australian Military Force (AMF), *500, 574, 576, 587*
Australian Special Hospital (ASH), *28, 43, 102, 105, 108, 111, 113, 118, 129, 188, 190, 192, 333, 450, 453, 455, 458, 465, 488, 491, 494, 498, 500, 525, 527, 532, 535, 540*
  Mapharsen episode, *558, 561, 564, 567, 569, 571*
Australia, venereal disease in 1919-1939, anti-VD campaigns, *331, 333, 336, 339, 345*
  in Australia 1919-1939, *376, 378, 381, 384, 387, 390, 393, 394*
Australian legislation, *357, 360, 364, 366, 369, 370, 373, 376*
  Dr John H.L. Cumpston's 1919 book, *353*
  First page of the New South Wales Venereal Diseases Act 1918, *360*
  gonorrhoea diagnoses for males and females, *394*
  government VD clinics, *390*
  inter-war, *418, 421*
  John H.L. Cumpston, *348*
  medical opinion, *398, 399, 404, 408*
  Melbourne conference 1922, *345, 348, 350, 353, 355, 357*
  New South Wales Health Department, *370*
  notification rate of four STDs, Australia 2012, *381*
  Salvarsan treatment kit for syphilis, *410*
  sulpha drugs, *408, 410, 412, 415, 418*
  Sulphanilamide ('Sulfanilamide') tablets from 1944-1945, *415*

syphilis diagnoses for males and females in sexual health, *394*
Australia and the Western Front, *261, 264, 266, 268, 271, 274, 277, 280, 281, 283, 285, 290, 292, 295, 299, 301, 303, 305, 308, 309, 312, 314, 318, 320, 321, 325, 328*
AIF within the British Expeditionary Force 1916-1919, *281, 283, 285*
  Church Army, amenities hut, *285*
  Conder, Walter and Johnson, Charles, *277*
  Ettie Rout, *309, 312, 314*
  Langwarrin VD Hospital, *268, 280, 281*
  shunning the VD-infected, *264*
  VD statistics, *318, 320, 321*
  women's role in VD transmission, *290, 292, 295, 299, 301, 303, 305, 308*
Australian and British troops' comparative infection rates, *206*

Australian Army Medical Corps, *28, 118, 131*
Australian Army, venereal disease during World War I, *65, 70, 73, 75, 78, 80, 84, 86, 89, 93, 95, 97, 99, 102, 105, 108, 111, 113, 114, 118, 125, 127, 129, 131, 133, 134, 136, 139, 141, 142, 148, 149, 150, 154, 157, 159, 162, 165, 167, 169*
Abbassia Detention Barracks, *129, 131, 133, 134*
ADH, W.E. Grigor and N.R. Howse, *134, 136, 139, 141, 142, 148*
AIF in Egypt 1914-1915, *95, 97, 99*
  army hospitals, *86, 89*
  Battle of the Wazzir, *127, 129*
  Broadmeadows Army Camp, *86*
  forfeiture of pay, *114, 118*
  before the Gallipoli campaign, *99, 102, 105, 108, 111, 113, 114*

individual returnee's case, *118, 125, 127*
information to Prime Minister, *148, 149, 150, 154, 157*
Langwarrin Venereal Diseases Hospital, *118*
medical politics and STDs, *70, 73, 75, 78*
members of the New Zealand Volunteer Sisterhood, *154*
Mena Camp hospital, Egypt, *102*
overseas service, *80*
prevalence before World War I, *65, 70*
reasons for, *157, 159, 162, 165, 167, 169*
related diseases, *162*
STDs in Australia 1914-1915, *78, 80, 84, 86, 89, 93, 95*
ASH, *33*
January to 1 April 1915, *108*
VD cases in Army camps in Australia 1915-16 and 1916-1917, *89*
Australian Association for Fighting Venereal Diseases, *339*
Australian Defence Force, *54*
Australian Dermatological Hospital, *131, 233, 239, 245, 339*
Australian General Hospital, *102, 118, 216, 450, 508, 589*
Australian medical profession, *21, 70, 75, 333, 408*
Australian Special Hospital, *450, 453, 455, 458, 525, 558*
Australian Stationary Hospital, *28, 102, 190, 192*
Australian War Memorial, *486*
Australian Women's Army Service (AWAS), *548*
Australian Women's Land Army (AWLA), *548*

B

bacillus (plural bacilli), *40*
bacteria, *36, 37, 48, 59, 73, 268, 412, 415*
bacteriostatic, *412*
balanitis, *57*
Barrett, James, *78, 118, 157, 305, 308, 339, 357, 373, 390, 399, 404*
Battle of Romani, *190*
Bean, Charles Edwin Woodrow, *95, 97, 99, 127, 149, 157, 303, 305, 314*
Birdwood, William, *97, 114, 134, 141, 142, 150, 211, 222, 254, 255, 283, 325*
Blackburn, Charles Bickerton, *542*
Blue Light depot, *433, 439, 498, 500*
Blue Light kits, *220, 222, 225, 233, 318, 433, 498, 589, 622*
Bridges, William Throsby, *97, 99*
British Expeditionary Force (BEF), *175, 200, 203, 206, 208, 214, 239, 281, 283, 292*
British Medical Association (BMA), *345, 350, 357, 369, 387, 418*
British Army, *70, 97, 233, 373, 622*
British General Hospital, *283, 285*
British and Australian troops' comparative infection rates, *206*
Broadmeadows Army Camp, *86, 266, 274*
brothels, *150, 154, 157, 285, 312, 589, 622, 642*
   World War II, *469, 476, 481, 484, 486, 491, 493, 494, 503*
Bulford Army Camp, *233, 239*
Burston, Samuel Roy, *431, 433, 450, 460, 463, 465, 469, 481, 535, 536, 548, 551, 589*
Butler, Arthur Graham, *9, 78, 80, 84, 86, 89, 93, 99, 102, 105, 111, 129, 131, 133, 134, 157, 159, 162, 165, 203, 206, 208, 216, 220, 226, 228, 233, 236, 239, 243, 245, 247, 271, 277, 283, 285, 290, 292, 295,*

309, 314, 320, 321, 325, 404, 408, 463

C
Calomel, *31, 43, 220, 222, 226, 437, 439, 442, 469*
Calymmatobacterium granulomatis, *59*
Candida albicans, *57*
candidal vaginitis, *57*
candidiasis, *57*
cardiovascular syphilis, *23*
casualties, *285*
Centers for Disease Control and Prevention (USA) (CDC), *7, 17, 40, 48, 54*
chancre, *23, 37*
chancroid, *37, 40, 43, 70, 73, 197, 241, 268, 277, 376, 390, 393, 630*
chlamydia, *48, 54, 376, 378, 381, 521*
Chlamydia trachomatis, *48, 62, 479*
Chauvel, Harry, *192*
Churchill, Winston, *578*
civilian police, *299, 469*

clap, *285, 589*
see also Gonorrhoea
coccobacillus (plural coccobacilli), *37*
commanding officer (CO), *134, 150, 216, 241, 247, 271, 274, 281, 453, 484, 494, 527, 532, 535, 536, 558, 561, 564*
Commonwealth's National Health Security Act 2007, *376*
Conder, Walter, *271, 274, 277, 281*
condoms, *220, 222, 226, 228, 233, 254, 433, 437, 439, 469, 481, 484, 494, 500, 630*
condylomata acuminata, *59*
congenital syphilis, *17, 21, 387*
conjunctivitis, *48*
Contagious Diseases Acts, *290, 357*
control of VD, *535, 589*
Cordner, Edward Rae, *285*
Corynebacterium vaginalis infection, *59*
crabs, *62*

Cumpston, John H.L., *339, 348, 353*
Curtin, John, *545*

D

deaths, *23, 33, 36, 57, 75, 118, 125, 175, 285, 312, 378, 545, 561, 564, 567, 569, 571, 589*
deoxyribonucleic acid (DNA), *48, 54, 59*
deployments, *108, 175, 325, 500, 510, 584*
Deputy Assistant Provost Marshal (DAPM), *484, 491, 493*
Deputy Director of Medical Services (DDMS), *190, 320, 428, 465, 479, 551, 561, 589, 630*
Director General of Medical Services (DGMS), *118, 266, 428, 431, 442, 494, 535, 536, 540, 548, 558, 732*
Director of Medical Services (DMS), *118, 141, 142, 190, 245, 247, 283, 320, 460, 494, 498*

disciplinary measures, *247, 398, 479, 498, 571*
donovanosis, *59, 376*
Downes, Rupert M., *190, 192, 195, 197, 200, 428, 431, 433, 439, 442, 445, 450, 581*
drugs, *28, 31, 33, 48, 366, 412, 423, 506, 532, 561, 569, 576, 581, 584, 587*

E

ectopic pregnancy, *3*
Egypt AIF in, *175, 182, 184, 188, 190, 192, 195, 197, 200*
   Australian Stationary Hospital, *190, 192*
   gonorrhoea, *197, 200, 226*
   syphilis, *197, 222, 241*
   VD cases, *184, 188, 195*
Egyptian Expeditionary Force (EEF), *148, 175, 182, 190, 195, 197, 200, 253*
epidemic, *89, 157, 159, 233, 254, 255, 445, 446, 450, 460, 486, 503, 506, 584, 587, 630*
epidemiology, *36, 99, 384, 393, 394, 408, 421, 622*
epididymides, *3*

Ewins, Arthur J., *412*

F
Fairley, Neil Hamilton, *333, 384, 387, 390, 450, 460, 463, 465, 469, 569*
Ferguson, Ronald Munro, *280*
Fetherston, Richard H.J., *253, 266, 350*
Fiaschi, Piero, *333*
flagellum (plural flagella), *62*
Fleming, Alexander, *576*
foetus or fetus, *3*
forfeiture of pay, *114, 118, 571, 574, 576*
Fowler, Robert, *384, 387, 390*
Francis, Neil, *453, 488, 491, 540, 558, 561, 564, 567, 569, 571*

G
Gallipoli Campaign, *95, 97, 99, 108, 111, 118, 129, 133, 162, 172, 175, 188, 216, 333*
Gardnerella vaginalis, *59*
genital herpes, *59*
genitalia, *59, 62, 111, 220, 226*
genital warts, *59, 630*

genome, *54*
Gibson, Norman, *527, 529, 532, 535, 540*
gonorrhoea,
  Egypt, *197, 200, 226*
  1914 to 1916, *65, 70, 73, 75, 78, 80, 84, 86, 89, 93, 113, 118*
  1916 to 1919, *305, 314, 318*
  1919 to 1939, *333, 336, 345, 376, 378, 381, 387, 390, 393, 394, 415, 418*
  1939 to 1941, *423, 442, 463, 479*
  1942 to 1945, *521, 532, 555, 576, 578, 581*
  overview, *3, 4, 7, 9, 11, 14, 16, 17, 21, 23, 26, 28, 31, 33, 36, 37, 40, 43, 46, 48, 54, 57, 59, 62*
  United Kingdom, *197, 200, 226*
granuloma inguinale, *59*
Grigor, William Ernest, *134, 136, 139, 141, 150, 157, 247*

H
haemolytic, *412*

Haemophilus ducreyi, *37, 40, 43, 46*
Haig, Douglas, *175*
Hart, Gavin, *3, 4, 26*
hepatitis B virus (HBV), *59, 62*
herpes, *59*
hospitalisations, *70, 93, 118, 162, 175, 188, 197, 203, 208, 318, 320, 325, 521*
Howse, Neville Reginald, *118, 134, 136, 141, 142, 148, 150, 157, 225, 233, 236, 239, 245, 247, 254, 255, 283, 285, 312, 325, 369*
Hughes, William Morris, *149*
human immunodeficiency virus (HIV), *54, 57, 378, 381*
human papilloma virus (HPV), *59*

I
immorality, *195, 228, 404, 589*
infectious diseases, *7, 65, 86, 102, 162, 376, 445, 446, 510*
inflammation, *3, 4, 48, 57, 59*
influenza, *86, 93, 102*
Ingleburn Army Camp, *469*
injections, *11, 26, 31, 33, 43, 150, 460, 532, 558, 561*
injuries, *89, 93, 333*
intercourse, *62, 111, 216, 220, 226, 233, 589*
iodism, *31, 33*

J
Jack, *442, 589*
    see also gonorrhoea,
Josephine of Erquinghem, *299, 301*

K
Klebsiella granulomatis, *59*
Kline test, *558*

L
Langwarrin Army Camp, *266, 271, 277*
Langwarrin VD Hospital, *268*
Lees, Robert, *460, 465*
Lind, William A.T., *381*

Loudon, Derby, *453, 455, 458, 494, 498, 500, 503, 535, 536, 540, 558, 561, 564, 567, 569, 571*
  plan, *494, 498, 500, 503*
lymphogranuloma venereum (LGV), *62*

M

MacArthur, Douglas, *574, 589, 622, 642, 688*
Macpherson, Ian, *228*
malaria, *28, 65, 569, 705*
male genitalia, *3*
Mapharsen, *558, 561, 564, 567, 569, 571, 587*
Massey, William E, *228*
McDonald, Barry, *458*
McLeod, Jan, *442, 445*
McWhae, Douglas Murray, *295, 299*
Meatus, penile, *16, 226, 437*
Medical Journal of Australia (MJA), *7, 89, 93, 331, 333, 336, 339, 369, 370, 373, 381, 384, 398, 399, 415, 418*
medical officer (MO), *9, 16, 21, 134, 190, 233, 247, 277, 308, 431, 437, 484, 558, 589, 705*
Melville Army Camp, *525*
Mena Camp, *95, 97, 99, 102, 108, 111, 118, 129, 148*
Metal syringe, with curved metal urethral catheter, *14*
Middle East, VD epidemic, *460, 463, 465, 469, 476, 479*
Military Cross (MC), *431*
Miller, Geoffrey, *23*
molluscum contagiosum, *62*
Morris, Arthur E., *333*
motile, *62*
Mycoplasma genitalium,

N

Neisseria gonorrhoeae, *7*
New South Wales Prisoners' Detention Act 1908, *73*
New South Wales Venereal Diseases Act 1908, *333, 360*
New Zealand Expeditionary Force (NZEF), *308, 312*

non-gonococcal urethritis (NGU), *48, 630*
non-specific urethritis (NSU) and chlamydia, *48, 54*
  photomicrograph of Chlamydia trachomatis, *48*
  rise of chlamydia infection in Australia from the early 1990s, *48*
Norris, Frank Kingsley, *491, 493, 494*
Northcott, John, *589, 652*
notifiable diseases, *16, 378, 423*

O
O'Brien, Private, *301*
O'Connor, John, *453*
ointment, *43, 220, 433, 437, 498*
officer in charge (OIC), *247*

P
Pacific Islands, VD in Australian troops, *508, 510, 515, 517, 519, 521*
Palestine campaigns, *188, 190*
Papilloma, *59*
pediculosis, *62*
  advent, *408, 423*
  availability, *584, 587*
  based therapies, *43*
  daily dose, *26*
  derivatives, *4*
  impact in STD, *33, 521, 523, 574, 576, 578, 581, 622, 674*
  Mapharsen episode, *571*
  pre-penicillin therapies, *48, 167, 318, 384, 527*
  as wonder drug, *423, 506*
penis, *9, 11, 14, 16, 37, 40, 43, 57, 111, 220, 226, 437, 439*
photomicrograph of Haemophilus ducreyi bacteria, *40*
Phthirus pubis, *62*

pilus (plural pili), *318*
pneumococcus (plural pneumococci), *412*
posterior urethra, *11*
Potter, W.L., *333*
pox, *587*
primary syphilis, *26*
Prophylactic Ablution Centre (PAC), *433, 437, 460, 469, 484, 494, 500, 508, 525, 589*
prophylactic kits, *308, 312, 314*
prophylaxis, *220, 226, 228, 309, 333, 431, 433, 469, 481, 527, 540, 561, 584*
prostate, *3, 11*
prostitutes, *285, 290, 301, 303, 305, 308, 469, 589, 642, 663*
pubic lice, *62, 630*
public education, *73, 345, 408*

Q
quarantine, *105, 348, 350, 353, 542*

R
Raffan, George, *16, 220, 225, 226, 254, 295, 309*

Red Cross, *274, 280, 285, 314, 455, 540*
regimen (treatment), *4, 14, 28, 33, 105, 111, 226, 236, 247, 253, 266, 277, 309, 325, 373, 408, 410, 415, 423, 458, 503, 535, 558, 561, 564, 567, 569, 571, 574, 576, 578, 581, 584, 587, 589, 688*
regimental medical officer (RMO), *16, 303, 433, 437, 469*
retrovirus, *54*
Returned and Services League of Australia (RSL), *118, 264, 339*
Richard, H.J., *253*
Robertson, Edward, *339, 390*
Rout, Ettie Annie, *154, 157, 225, 308, 309, 312, 314, 423*
    New Zealand Volunteer Sisterhood, *285*
Royal Army Medical Corps (RAMC), *233*

S
salpingitis, *3*

Salvarsan, *28, 33, 408, 410, 558*
Sampson, Burford, *314*
scabies, *62, 241, 589, 630*
scandal, *281, 540, 567, 571, 587*
secondary Syphilis, *26*
sex trade, *113, 149, 165, 290, 589, 642*
sexual adventures, *99, 111, 114, 149, 206*
sexual health physician, *26, 36, 40, 48*
sexually Transmitted Diseases (STD), *3, 4, 7, 9, 11, 14, 16, 17, 21, 23, 26, 28, 31, 33, 36, 37, 40, 43, 46, 48, 54, 57, 59, 62, 78, 376, 378, 381, 384, 408, 418, 421*
    see also Gonorrhoea; Syphilis acquired immune deficiency syndrome (AIDS), *54, 57*
    candidiasis, *57*
    chancroid, *37, 40, 43, 46, 48*
    condylomata acuminata, *59*
    Corynebacterium vaginalis infection, *59*
    cutaneous gonococcal lesion, *7*
    donovanosis, *59*
    female genitalia, *4*
    genital herpes, *59*
    human immunodeficiency virus (HIV), *54, 57*
    pediculosis, lice, *62*
scabies, *62, 241, 589, 630*
sexually transmitted infection, *54, 393, 394*
Silverton, Robert J., *28, 46*
South African War, *65, 70*
South-East Asia, VD in Australian troops, *508, 510, 515, 517, 519, 521*
spirochaete, *17, 23, 26, 28, 408, 576*
Steigrad, Joseph, *465, 479*
Stewart, John Mitchell Y., *241, 247*
Street, Geoffrey A., *431*
streptococcus (plural streptococci), *412*

sulfonamidochrysoidine, *412, 415, 418, 463, 521, 532, 581, 584*

sulpha drug, *408, 412, 415, 418, 460, 503, 630*

sulphanilamide, *331, 412, 415, 418, 423*

sulphonamide, *412, 415, 418, 463, 479, 521, 532, 576, 578, 581, 584*

   digitially colourised photomicrograph, *17*

   patient's torso and upper extremities, *26*

syphilis Egypt and United Kingdom, Australian army, *197, 222, 241*

   1914 to 1916, *70, 73, 89, 118, 167*

   1916 to 1919, *268, 277, 285, 290, 301, 305, 314, 318*

   1919 to 1939, *331, 333, 336, 339, 345, 348, 350, 353, 355, 357, 360, 364, 366, 369, 370, 373, 376, 378, 381, 384, 387, 390, 393, 394, 398, 399, 404, 408, 410, 412, 415, 418, 421*

   1939 to 1941, *423, 425, 428, 431, 433, 437, 439, 442, 445, 446, 450, 453, 455, 458, 460, 463, 465, 469, 476, 479, 481, 484, 486, 488, 491, 493, 494*

   1942 to 1945, *532, 558, 576, 578*

   overview, *16, 17, 21, 23, 26, 28, 31, 33, 36, 37, 43*

swab, *46*

T

tertiary syphilis, *21, 23, 26, 73*

Treponema pallidum, *17, 26, 28, 408, 576*

trichomoniasis, *62*

   Australian Dermatological Hospital, *239*

   AIF 1916-1919, *200, 203, 206, 208, 211*

   anti-VD measures, *211, 214, 216, 220*

   Australian Dermatological

Hospital at Bulford 1916-1919, *233, 236, 239, 241, 243, 245, 247, 253*
  gonorrhoea, *197, 200, 226*
  medical anti-VD measures, *220, 222, 225, 226, 228, 233*
  post-Gallipoli deployments, *172, 175*
  syphilis, *197, 222, 241*
  VD cases, *203, 206*
  World War I 'Blue Light' Outfit, *222*

U

United States of America (USA), *373, 415, 469, 688*
urethra, *3, 9, 11, 14, 48, 226, 437, 469*

V

vagina, *3, 57, 59, 62*
vaginitis, *57, 59, 62*
Venereal Disease Act 1918, *369*
venereal disease (VD), see also sexually transmitted diseases (STDs),
  Allan S. Walker's essay on, *581, 584*
  all-out war on, *542, 545, 548*
  anti-VD education program, *220, 222*
  anti-VD legislation, *336*
  anti-VD measures, *211, 214, 216, 220, 479, 491, 493, 494, 498, 500, 529, 574, 589, 732*
  control of, *535, 589*
  Egypt and United Kingdom, *184, 188, 195*
  forfeiture of pay to troops, *571, 574, 576*
  1914 to 1916, *65, 73, 75, 78, 102, 108, 111, 113, 114, 118, 125, 131, 133, 136, 142, 169*
  1916 to 1919, *172, 220, 225, 228, 243*
  1919 to 1939, *339, 345, 348, 350, 353, 355, 357, 360, 364, 366, 369, 370, 373, 376, 378, 381, 384, 387, 390, 393, 394, 398, 399, 404, 408, 410, 412, 415, 418, 421*

1939 to 1941, *423, 425, 428, 431, 433, 479, 481, 484, 486, 488, 491, 493, 494, 498, 500, 503, 506*

1941 to 1945, *498, 500, 503, 506, 508, 527, 529, 532, 535, 536, 540, 542, 545, 558, 574*

Langwarrin VD Hospital, *268, 280, 281*

Middle East, *445, 446, 460, 463, 465, 469, 476, 479*

overview, *16, 17, 48*

penicillin, impact on, *576, 578, 581*

policy on women, *548, 551, 555*

social impact, *486, 488, 491, 493, 494*

in South East Asia, *508, 510, 515, 517, 519, 521*

in United Kingdom, *261, 277, 290, 292, 331*

women's role in transmitting, *290, 292, 295, 299, 301, 303, 305, 308*

Venereal Disease Control Unit, *498, 500*

Venereal Diseases Acts, *339, 350, 355, 360, 369, 370, 373, 376, 384, 387, 408, 410, 418, 423*

venereal infections, *111, 131, 162, 312, 387, 399, 674*

venereologist, *16, 220, 247, 274, 309, 527, 536, 674*

venereology, *89, 247, 255, 258, 331, 339, 353, 418, 453, 460, 494, 503, 527, 536, 540, 589, 674*

adviser, *460, 494, 503, 527, 535, 540, 558*

virus, *54, 59*

W

Walker, Alan Seymour, *398, 425, 446, 455, 458, 463, 469, 476, 479, 484, 508, 510, 515, 517, 519, 521, 523, 535, 540, 548, 571, 576, 578, 581, 584*

Walstab, John, *465*

Ward, John W, *216, 220, 222*

Ward, Joseph, *228*

Wilcox, Craig, *70*

Williams, Robert, *271, 274, 281*

Williams, William Daniel Campbell, *80*
Women's Political Association, *339*
World War I, *65, 70, 84, 86, 255, 258, 261, 266, 320, 321, 331, 373, 376, 415, 418, 425, 428, 433, 460, 463*
World War II (1939-1941),
  2 / 3rd Casualty Clearing Station in Beirut, *491*
  8 Australian Special Hospital (8 ASH), *455, 458, 460*
  anti-VD propaganda poster used in Melbourne early 1940s, *476*
  Australian Special Hospitals, *450, 453, 455, 458, 460*
  Blue Light outfits, *439*
  brothels, *481, 484, 486*
  French Letters (condoms), *439*
  Loudon plan, *494, 498, 500, 503*
  social impact, *486, 488, 491, 493, 494*
  special hospital for VD, *450, 453, 455, 458, 460*
  Syria and Lebanon from July 1941, *479*
  VD cases 1940-1945, *423, 425*
  VD epidemic in the Middle East, *445, 446, 460, 463, 465, 469, 476, 479*
  VD occurrence, *428, 431, 433, 437, 439, 442, 445, 446, 450*
World War I and World War II VD case rates comparison, *425*
World War II 1942-1945,
  AIF troops in South East Asia, *510*
  all-out war on VD, *542, 545, 548*
  anti-VD campaign, *545*
  Ceylon, *508, 510*
  condoms, *532*
  control of VD, *535*
  forfeiture of pay, *571, 574, 576*

girls blind to VD peril, *542*
lectures, *529*
Mapharsen episode, *558, 561, 564, 567, 569, 571*
medical inspections, *529*
Morotai and Borneo, *519, 521*
Papua and New Guinea, *515, 517, 519*
penicillin, impact of, *576, 578, 581*
policy on women service personnel with VD, *548, 551, 555*
prophylactic depots, *532*
short-arm parades, *529*
3rd Australian Women's Hospital, *555*
training, *532*
VD cases, *508, 510, 515, 517, 519, 521, 523, 525, 527*
VD measures, *532*
A.S. Walker's essay on VD in World War II, *581, 584*

Women's Political Association (WPA), *339*
Wray, Frederick W, *214*

Z

Zwar, Bernhard, *105, 108, 111, 113, 114, 157*

www.ingramcontent.com/pod-product-compliance
Lightning Source LLC
Chambersburg PA
CBHW010300010526
44108CB00044B/2701